Running QuickBooks® in Nonprofits

Kathy Ivens

CPA911 Publishing, LLC
Philadelphia PA

Running QuickBooks in Nonprofits

ISBN Number 0-9720669-8-5

Published by CPA911® Publishing, LLC. December 2005

Table of Contents

Acknowledgements

Cover Design: Matthew Ericson

Production: InfoDesign Services (www.infodesigning.com)

Indexing: AfterWords Editorial Services (www.aweditorial.com)

My thanks and gratitude to Shane Hanby and Roger Kimble of Intuit, Inc. for their ongoing expert help, and their generosity in finding time to answer questions and provide advice.

The help and advice of Robert J. Paolini, CPA, one of the founding members of Paolini & Scout, LLC (www.paoliniandscout.com), have been extremely important from the moment I decided to write about adapting QuickBooks for nonprofits. Bob has a great deal of experience in auditing nonprofits (including organizations that use QuickBooks) and his client list includes many nonprofit organizations that use QuickBooks. His explanations and suggestions have been invaluable.

Introduction

This book provides information about using QuickBooks to track financial data in nonprofit organizations. It covers QuickBooks Pro as well as QuickBooks Premier Nonprofit Edition.

This is not a beginner's book in QuickBooks; the topics assume that the reader is already using QuickBooks, although the text is written to accommodate users that are not experienced users (or experts).

Because QuickBooks is so easy to use, and so inexpensive, many nonprofit organizations have adopted it for financial record keeping. However, right out-of-the-box, QuickBooks isn't really designed for the special bookkeeping functions required for nonprofit accounting.

As a result, most nonprofit organizations have to spend extra money to have accounting professionals create reports from their QuickBooks data. The goal of this book is to help you understand how to set up QuickBooks for nonprofit accounting, make it easier to create transactions properly, and reduce the amount of money you spend on accounting fees.

Even QuickBooks Premier Nonprofit edition isn't a solution, because the software wasn't rewritten to accommodate all the needs of nonprofit accounting.

I've worked with, or examined, hundreds of QuickBooks nonprofit installations, and I've seen a wide variety of workarounds (including add-on software) aimed at making QuickBooks work properly. Most of them don't work well, are too complex to be efficient (even for experienced QuickBooks users), and some don't really work at all.

Chapter 1

QuickBooks Limitations for Nonprofits

General limitations

Chart of accounts limitations

Accounting restrictions

Reporting limitations

The way QuickBooks is designed and programmed presents some limitations in the features that are needed by nonprofit organizations. This is true for all editions of QuickBooks, including the QuickBooks Premier Nonprofit Edition, and the QuickBooks Enterprise Solutions Nonprofit Edition. However, there are ways to set up and use QuickBooks that ease the impediments these limits impose. Those workarounds and adaptations are a large part of this book.

If you've been using QuickBooks for a while, you're probably aware of most of the limitations (which are discussed in this chapter). However, I've found that users, and even bookkeepers, aren't aware of the severity of some of these confines, because they haven't been exposed to other, more expensive and more powerful, nonprofit accounting software programs.

If you're new to QuickBooks, it's important to understand the limitations, so you can plan the way you're going to use the software with those restrictions in mind. QuickBooks is a basic, no-frills software application. You're probably using QuickBooks for your nonprofit organization for one (or more) of the following reasons:

- It's inexpensive
- It's easy to use
- Your bookkeeper is familiar with it.
- An accounting professional connected to your organization is comfortable with it, and recommended it

These, and other, reasons for using QuickBooks are all valid, but you must remember that the software isn't designed from the ground up for nonprofit accounting, even though you can adapt it for that purpose. As is true for the application of many "adaptive" technologies, you won't end up with everything you need or want.

As a result, some nonprofits that use QuickBooks spend more money on accounting services than nonprofits using full-featured nonprofit accounting applications. Those accounting tasks are necessary to overcome the limitations in QuickBooks when it's time to file reports with the government, or funding agencies.

However, that extra expense is not necessarily a negative; it's balanced by the advantages QuickBooks offers. QuickBooks costs less to run and maintain than more expensive applications, it's quite easy to find employees (or even volunteers) who are familiar with QuickBooks, and user training is less of an issue.

QuickBooks can be adapted to work reasonably well for small nonprofit organizations that obtain the majority of their funding from unrestricted sources. "Small" is, of course, a relative term, and I don't have a firm definition to offer. However, I don't think I'd try to use QuickBooks for a nonprofit organization with restricted funding that exceeds several million dollars.

Chart of Accounts Limitations

The chart of accounts is limited in QuickBooks, and its principal weakness is the inability to create a divisional chart of accounts, which is the traditional way to track finances for a nonprofit organization. The flat design of the QuickBooks chart of accounts means you can't divide the chart of accounts by location, program, fund types (restricted, temporarily restricted, unrestricted) or any other design factor.

That constrict can be overcome to some extent by using classes, but there's one part of a divisionalized chart of accounts that no adaptive technique can make up for: the inability to automate the way totals are posted to equity accounts.

Understanding a Divisionalized Chart of Accounts

Many accounting software applications offer features that make a divisional chart of accounts possible. There are important advantages in divisionalization for both nonprofit organizations and for-profit businesses.

It's important to understand what a divisional chart of accounts is, and how it works, if you want to use a workaround for this important feature. For QuickBooks users, the workaround is the use of the Class feature. You can configure and use classes productively if you understand how they work to provide some of the features available in a divisionalized accounting system. (Read Chapter 5 to learn how to set up classes.)

A divisionalized chart of accounts has two important ingredients: Numbered accounts, and a numbering system that is designed in sections. For example, you may have a numbering system that follows the format XXXX-YY. The numbers you use for the XXXX section represent accounts. The numbers you use for the YY section represent a division, a department, or a program. For-profit companies usually divide the chart of accounts by division and/or department. Nonprofit organizations are more likely to separate the chart of accounts by program.

For example, you can assign the YY section of the chart of accounts to programs, where 01 is education, 02 is senior citizen services, and 03 is health services. (A for-profit company might use this section of the chart of accounts for departments, such as Research, Sales, and Service).

With such a scheme, you can track revenue and expenses by assigning the appropriate amounts to the YY division. For example, if account number 5000 is Payroll, your chart of accounts has the following three accounts:

- 5000-01
- 5000-02
- 5000-03

On the other hand, you could use the YY section of the chart of accounts to track locations, perhaps making 01 the main building, 02 the senior center, and 03 the day camp.

In a software program with divisionalized accounts, you can even combine two types of "tracking", such as program and location (or division and department in a for-profit company). In that case, you'd have a chart of accounts with the format XXXX-YY-ZZ. For instance the YY section can track the programs, and the ZZ section can track the location. In that case, your Payroll accounts might resemble the following listings:

- 5000-01-01 (payroll for education programs at the main building)
- 5000-01-02 (payroll for education programs at the senior center)
- 5000-02-02 (payroll for senior citizen programs at the senior center)

You can also use three divisions in the divisionalized chart of accounts to track program types along with related subprograms. For example, in the YY section you could assign the program type (e.g. Education or Health Services) and in the ZZ section you can assign the subprogram or specific program type (such as well baby care, or senior citizen health services). In that case, you might have an account 5000-01-02, which is Payroll for health services programs, specifically the well baby care program.

NOTE: *A divisionalized chart of accounts always has a 00 division, representing the overall organization.*

You can create reports on each division of a divisionalized chart of accounts. A for-profit business could create a Profit & Loss Statement for each division. For instance, a company with three branch offices (divisions), each of which has two departments (sales and service) could produce a P & L statement for the sales department of the Chicago division. A nonprofit could produce a statement of revenue and expenses for any program.

When you translate this into classes in your QuickBooks software (covered in Chapter 5), you can accomplish a lot of the same clear transaction tracking by creating all the classes you need (representing the YY sections described here), and use subclasses for more specific tracking (the ZZ sections described here). QuickBooks produces many types of reports that are based on a class, so you can see the income and expenses for any program type, or subtype.

Note that you do not use classes to track specific grants, even for grants that are for specific programs. Grants are Jobs in QuickBooks (the granting agency is a Customer), and you learn how to set up customers and jobs in Chapter 5.

Understanding Automatic Allocation

Another missing ingredient in QuickBooks is the ability to automate the allocation of expenses. Allocation is the transfer of organization-wide (overhead) funds into specific programs. In a divisionalized chart of accounts, automatic allocation lets you set a percentage or dollar figure for each parent (organization-wide) account, and then automatically allocate amounts to that account's divisions. You can perform this task monthly, quarterly, or yearly.

Automatic allocation is important when you have grants or contracts that permit you to use some of the money for certain types of expenses (usually administrative expenses). For example, you may have a grant or contract that permits you to use some of the proceeds for 20% of the education director's salary (because the RFP, and/or the conditions of the grant recognize the fact that about 20% of that person's time will be spent on administration of the grant). Some grants and contracts let you allocate percentages of other types of expenses, such as utilities, or vehicle maintenance.

The lack of automatic allocation in QuickBooks is a side effect of the inability to divisionalize the chart of accounts. In QuickBooks, you have to perform those tasks manually, using journal entries.

Journal entries, of course, don't recognize percentages, so you'll have to calculate the figures in Excel, or with a desktop calculator. I provide easy-to-follow directions for creating journal entries throughout this book. You can find specific coverage of allocation journal entries in Chapter 7.

Accounting Limitations

In many ways, accounting is about totals, and the differences between totals. If you have more revenue than expenses, you have a profit in the for-profit world, and you have a positive net balance in the nonprofit world. (We don't use the word "profit" to describe this situation, because it sounds contradictory to say that a nonprofit has a profit.)

That net figure is the organization's equity (for both profit and non-profit organizations), which is a positive number if revenue exceeds expenses, and a negative number if it's the other way around.

The fact is, accounting principles differ little between for-profit and nonprofit organizations. Transactions are posted in equal and opposite entries (called double-entry bookkeeping), and have an effect on the income statement, balance sheet or both. While the basic principles (as well as the methods employed in entering transactions), are the same, there is a difference in the terminology:

- For-profit organizations track income and expenses in a report named Income Statement, or Profit & Loss Statement.
- Nonprofit organizations track income and expenses in a report named Statement of Activities.
- For-profit organizations track their accumulated net wealth (assets, liabilities and equity) in a report named Balance Sheet.
- Nonprofit organizations track their accumulated net wealth in a report named Statement of Financial Position.

Tracking Net Assets

Beyond the language variations for accounting terms, the real difference between for-profit and nonprofit accounting is in the part of the balance sheet that tracks the accumulated wealth (or loss) of the organization.

- A for-profit organization calls this figure equity, and it represents the net worth of a business.
- A nonprofit organization calls this figure net assets, and it represents the accumulated surpluses and deficits.

Most nonprofits have to track different types of net assets, because they have to track restricted funds separately from nonrestricted funds. You must create the net asset funds you need (called Equity accounts in QuickBooks). The Statement of Financial Position includes the following totals:

- Total assets
- Total liabilities
- Total unrestricted net assets
- Total temporarily restricted net assets
- Total permanently restricted net assets
- Total net assets

QuickBooks only recognizes one equity account for posting net amounts, the Retained Earnings account, which is installed automatically when you create a company file.

You cannot configure QuickBooks to post net earnings to multiple equity accounts (another nifty side-effect of a divisionalized chart of accounts that lets you configure each division to calculate and post net amounts to a net asset account you select).

As a result, you'll have to create the net asset equity accounts you need, and use journal entries to move net asset balances from Retained Earnings to those accounts. Instructions for those tasks are found throughout this book.

Fund Accounting

In nonprofit accounting parlance, a fund is defined as a discrete accounting entity with a self-balancing set of accounts, recording cash and related liabilities, obligations, reserves, and equities. Each fund is segregated for the purpose of tracking specific activities in accordance with any limitations or restrictions attached to the fund.

Until the mid 1990's, fund accounting was de rigueur for nonprofit organizations, because it provided important information to funding sources and donors. Today, pure fund accounting has been replaced by the Statement of Financial Accounting Standards (SFAS) Numbers 116 & 117, which describe the way non-governmental nonprofits should account for contributions, and present financial statements.

The impact of the SFAS financial statement reporting is now on "net asset" classification (as discussed in the previous section), rather than on tracking each fund. In other words, the net asset you track can combine all funds with similar restrictions, and you no longer have to track each fund and its specific net asset.

Most nonprofits don't open separate bank accounts for each restricted grant, to keep the money separated from unrestricted funds. Because they no longer specifically track the funds, many nonprofits find they inadvertently write checks from bank accounts where the unrestricted funds aren't sufficient to cover the checks (although the bank balance is sufficient).

QuickBooks, through its ability to track accounts, including bank accounts, in separate subaccounts, can help you keep an eye on your bank balance, to differentiate restricted funds from unrestricted funds. You can learn how to set up your bank accounts for this purpose in Chapter 3.

Report Limitations

Using the steps, tricks, and workarounds you'll learn in this book, you can expect to be able to track every financial transaction that occurs. You'll be able to find the details of transactions so you can build reports.

Unfortunately, QuickBooks isn't designed to produce all the reports for nonprofit organizations that adhere to the standards of Generally Accepted Accounting Principles (GAAP) or comply with the principles of the Financial Accounting Standards Board (FASB).

However, you can easily export any report to Excel, and then let an accounting professional use Excel to tweak your reports so they're acceptable to government agencies and grant providers. In fact, if you're using QuickBooks it's almost impossible to provide full financial reports and tax returns without using a spreadsheet application.

TIP: The Premier Nonprofit edition has some memorized reports that are quite useful. When I discuss those reports in this book (principally in Chapter 11), I provide instructions for customizing QuickBooks Pro reports to create the memorized reports built into Premier Nonprofit

---

Lack of Customized Periods

You can't configure QuickBooks for a 13th month, the way you can configure other nonprofit accounting software. Nonprofits (and even some for-profit businesses) use the 13th month for end-of-year journal entries covering allocations, depreciation, amortization, and other needed year-end entries.

A 13th period reserved for journal entries makes it easy to determine what the end-of-year transactions were, because they're all in one place (creating an easy to follow audit trail). When you use a 13th period, your

12th period ends on the next-to-last day of your fiscal year, and the 13th period is one day long.

As a workaround, don't enter regular transactions on the last day of your fiscal year (pre-date them by one day). Then, enter all your end-of-year journal entries with the last day of your fiscal year as the transaction date.

Other (Minor) Annoyances

QuickBooks has names for the lists and components of your data file, and you can't change those labels. You'll have to live with the word "customer" for your donors, and the word "job" for the grants and contracts you're tracking on a donor-by-donor basis. This is true even if you use the QuickBooks Premier Nonprofit Edition (where you'd think they'd have taken the time to change the terms).

QuickBooks uses the term "classes" instead of "program" for the component you use to track finances by programs. If you find the terms bothersome, or less than elegant, you can export all your reports to Excel, change the wording, and print your reports from Excel.

Chapter 2

Getting Started

Gathering financial information

Creating a company data file

Updating from previous QuickBooks versions

A lthough most of this chapter covers topics important to users who are just starting to use QuickBooks, you should probably read the information even if you're already using QuickBooks. Within the concepts I discuss here, you may find some answers to things that have been troubling you.

Gathering Financial Information

If you try to get through the setup procedures without having all the information you need at hand, you'll have a frustrating, slow experience. Additionally, any task you don't finish doesn't go away; you'll just have to catch up later.

Therefore, before you open QuickBooks and start setting up your data file, I'll spend some time describing what you'll need. It may take you a while to assemble all of this data, and you may have to call your accountant for some of it.

Deciding on the Start Date

The *start date* is a very important concept when you're setting up accounting software. The term actually has two definitions:

- The date that QuickBooks begins tracking transactions in order to produce reports. That date is the first day of your fiscal year (frequently earlier than the date on which you begin using QuickBooks).
- The date that marks the beginning of your use of QuickBooks for entering transactions. This is your "go live" date, and starting with this date, every individual financial transaction that takes place must be entered in QuickBooks.

Those definitions seem identical, but they're not. There's a subtle difference, and within that difference is the amount of work you have in front of you as you set up QuickBooks.

Transaction Tracking Start Date

The date that QuickBooks begins tracking transactions in order to produce reports is the earliest date for which financial information is available in your QuickBooks company file. That date is the first day of your fiscal year.

Many of the reports you need show financial balances on a "year to date" basis. At the end of your fiscal year, of course, you must produce reports that show the numbers (and the changes in numbers) from the first day of the fiscal year to the last day of the fiscal year.

You must enter historical transaction information into QuickBooks to provide accurate balances for your accounts. You don't have to enter every individual transaction that's taken place this year; instead, you can combine transactions and enter the total that represents all similar transactions.

For example, if you've started using QuickBooks on the first day of the third month of your fiscal year, you can enter one transaction for all your telephone bills up to that date, another single transaction to represent the rent payments prior to that date, and so on.

By the same token, if you've received multiple checks from any individual donors, you can enter one receipt for each donor to enter the total. However, if you've issued invoices to donors, you may want to enter the individual invoices so you can discuss the details of each invoice if the donor questions any amounts. (If you have detailed records to refer to, you can enter one invoice for the total; what's important is to be able to resolve questions and disputes.)

Your decision about the level of detail to enter when you're recording historical transactions is influenced by the "go live date". See the next section, "Go Live Start Date" for more information, and suggestions.

It's important to realize that you don't have to enter your historical transactions before you can start using QuickBooks. You can enter those historical transactions at any time, as long as you're careful to date each transaction properly.

CAUTION: *QuickBooks uses the current date on most transaction windows, so you'll have to remember to change the date to match the earlier date of the historical transaction you're entering.*

Go Live Start Date

The date that marks the beginning of your use of QuickBooks for entering transactions is literally the date on which you begin entering new transactions in QuickBooks. You can enter totals for transactions between the date that QuickBooks begins tracking transactions (the first day of your fiscal year) up to this date, but from this date on you must enter every transaction in QuickBooks. The date you select as your "go live" date has an enormous impact on how much work it's going to be to get your historical data for this fiscal year into QuickBooks.

If your "go live" date is early in your fiscal year, the best way to set up QuickBooks is to enter every individual transaction that took place so far this year. It sounds like a lot of work, but it really isn't. In fact, it's a great way to train everyone in using QuickBooks.

Data entry for existing transactions doesn't require a lot of thinking, because you already know everything you need to know—the account to which the transaction is posted, the vendor or donor, and so on. This is a good way to get familiar with the QuickBooks transaction windows.

If it's later in the fiscal year, enter transactions that contain monthly or quarterly running totals to bring your account totals up to your "go-live" date.

If it's very late in the fiscal year, you may want to postpone going live with QuickBooks until your new fiscal year starts. In that case, your start up tasks are to enter your opening balances for asset, liability, and equity accounts, along with any open customer or vendor balances.

TIP: *Your "go live" date must be the first day of a period; the year, the quarter, or the month.*

Balance Sheet Account Balances

You have to know the balances, as of the QuickBooks starting date, of all your asset, liability, and equity accounts. This is why it's best to make your start date the first day of your fiscal year. You can use a Trial Balance from your accountant, or your manual bookkeeping records to get the numbers.

Bank Account Balances

You have to tell QuickBooks what the balance is for each bank account you use. Don't glance at the checkbook stubs—that's not the balance you need. The balance you need is the reconciled balance. In addition, it has to be a reconciled balance as of the starting date you're using in QuickBooks.

If you haven't balanced your checkbooks against the bank statements for a while, do it now. In addition to the reconciled balance, you need to know the dates and amounts of the transactions that haven't yet cleared.

If you're lucky, your bank statements (and therefore your bank reconciliation) are on a true month basis, which means they cover the period from the first of a month to the last day of a month. If your bank statements represent any other period, such as the 15th of the previous month to the 14th of this month, it's more difficult to calculate the reconciled balance for your "go live" date (which is the beginning of a period).

You should enter a reconciled balance as of the last day of the previous month (using the transaction dates on the printed statement), but if that's difficult, ask your accountant to advise on a procedure. Then, call your bank and see if you can switch your statement to a true month basis.

Some accounts that are listed as bank accounts in your chart of accounts aren't really bank accounts, but you must know the account balances for these accounts. For example, you may be tracking petty cash, or a cash register till.

Other Asset Balances

Besides your bank accounts, you have to know the balances (as of the QuickBooks starting date), of the following asset account types:

- Fixed Assets (e.g. property, equipment, leasehold improvements)
- Other Current Assets (e.g. prepaid expenses)

Notice that Accounts Receivable is not included on my list. If you're tracking A/R and the account has a balance, you don't enter the starting balance, you create it by entering transactions, which is the only way to track receivables by donor.

You don't have to enter each individual transaction (although, you can if you want to). The same thing is true of your inventory asset account (if you track inventory for products you sell). You must track inventory by entering the receipt of goods, letting the system automatically add the quantities and values to your inventory asset.

If you've been depreciating any of your fixed assets, the opening balance for the fixed asset is the current net value (after accumulated depreciation) as of the QuickBooks start date. It's best to enter the original value of the fixed assets, and then enter the depreciation figure to date. However, if your accountant has the historical records, ask whether it's acceptable to enter only the current net value.

Liabilities Balances

You need the balances, as of the QuickBooks start date, for the following liability account types:

- Debt (notes, short term debt, long term debt)
- Deferred income
- Accrued expenses—not including those connected to payroll
- Current liabilities—not including accounts payable or payroll liabilities

Payroll related liabilities, and current A/P are not entered as a starting balance. Instead, the starting balances are created by entering the appropriate transactions, either in bulk (monthly or quarterly totals), or as individual transactions.

For payroll records, you must track totals by the month and by the quarter (because that's how you report those totals the federal, state, and local government agencies). And, of course, your QuickBooks files must have the correct totals for each employee at the end of the year, to track W-2 totals. You can't issue two W-2 forms (one from your QuickBooks transactions, and another from your pre-QuickBooks transactions).

Net Assets Balances

You need the balances, as of the QuickBooks start date, for the following net asset accounts:

- Unrestricted net assets
- Temporarily restricted net assets
- Permanently restricted net assets

You'll be adjusting these accounts via journal entries to produce reports, because QuickBooks does not automatically use them (see Chapter 1 for details). QuickBooks only posts net equity to the Retained Earnings account, and you have to use journal entries to allocate that posting to the equity accounts you track as a nonprofit organization.

Program Information

You need a detailed listing of your programs, and their classifications. This will help you create the QuickBooks classes you use to track income and expenses by program.

Be sure you have detailed information about specific restrictions connected to each grant or contract. In addition, note any clauses in the grant or contract that permit you to allocate overhead to the program funded by the grant or contract.

Creating a Company File

The first step is to create your company data file, which starts as a set of basic configuration options, and grows to include your customizations and your transaction data. You have two methods for creating this file:

- Use the QuickBooks EasyStep Interview, which is a wizard that walks you through the set up and configuration of the company file.
- Manually set up your company file.

The first time you use QuickBooks, after you see a message about managing software updates, the Welcome to QuickBooks window offers you the following choices:

- Overview tutorial
- Explore QuickBooks
- Create a new company file
- Open an existing company file

Since this discussion is about creating a QuickBooks data file, I'll go over the steps you need to take to create a company file. Selecting the choice Create A New Company File starts the QuickBooks EasyStep Interview, which looks like Figure 2-1 if you're using QuickBooks 2006 or later.

If you're using a version of QuickBooks earlier than 2006, the window looks different, and lacks a Skip Interview option. After you create a name for your company file you can click the button labeled Leave to continue the file setup process manually.

EasyStep Interview

I usually recommend against using the EasyStep Interview, and for nonprofit organizations, I strongly urge that you not use this wizard. You'll spend a lot of time entering information that is more easily entered manually. For that reason, I'm not going to cover the steps involved in setting up your company file with the EasyStep Interview.

- In versions of QuickBooks prior to 2006, click the button labeled Skip Interview, which appears in the fourth wizard window.
- Starting with QuickBooks 2006, a Skip Interview button appears on the opening window. Use it!

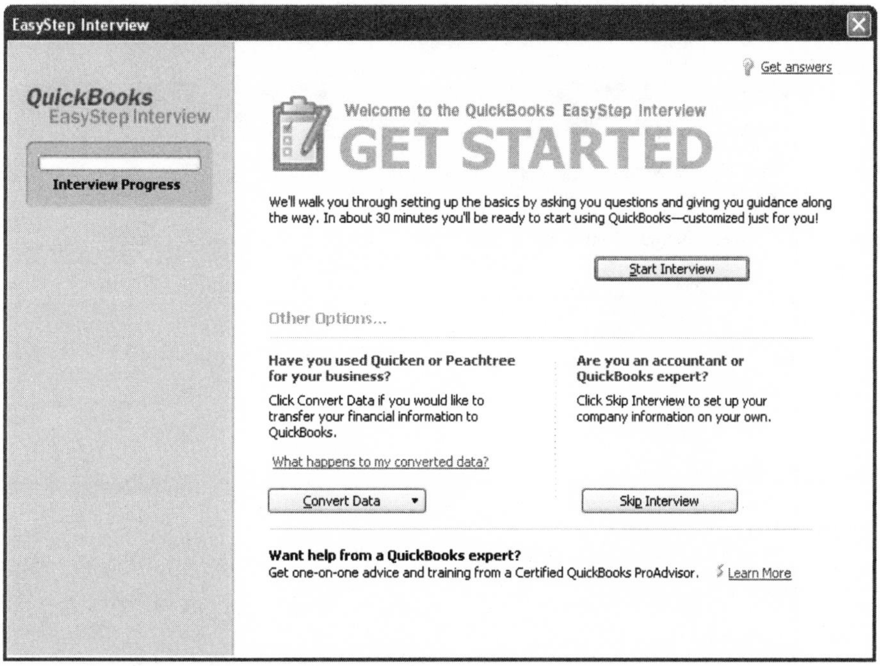

Figure 2-1: The first chore is to create a company file.

While the QuickBooks 2006 EasyStep interview is shorter than previous versions, you can't leave when you feel you've entered enough information to proceed manually. If you exit the wizard before completing all the windows, QuickBooks displays a message telling you that you can finish the interview the next time you open the company file.

Then QuickBooks abruptly closes the file, leaving you to stare at the No Company Open window. The next time you open the company, the EasyStep Interview picks up where you left off—and it will keep doing that until you finish the entire interview.

Creating the Company File Manually

If you click the Skip Interview button on the fourth wizard window of the EasyStep Interview (or the Leave button in earlier versions of QuickBooks), the Creating New Company dialog opens, and you can enter the basic information quickly (see Figure 2-2).

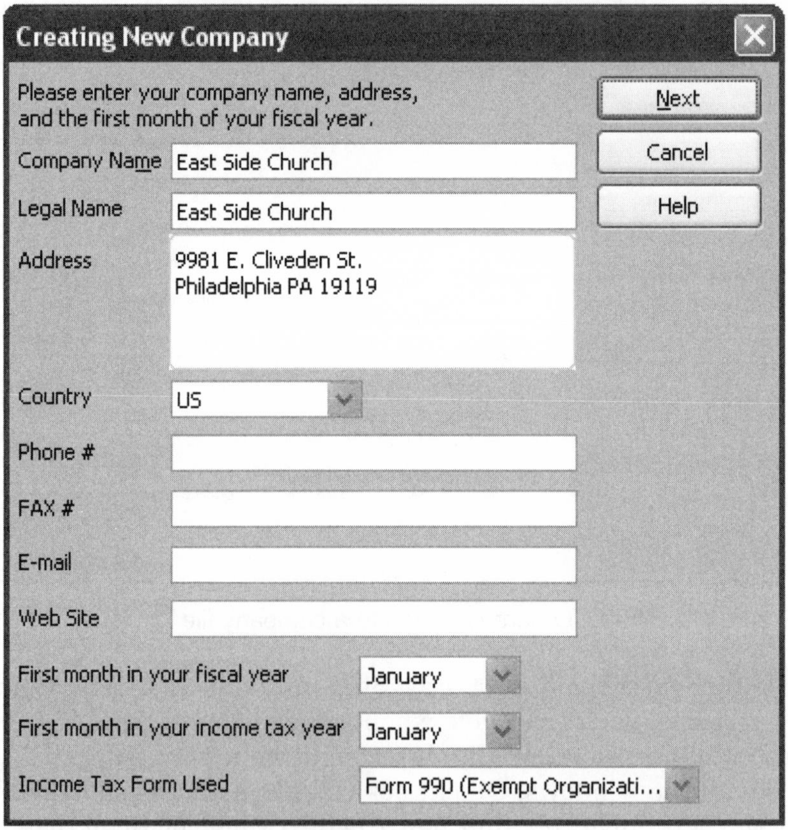

Figure 2-2: You can enter company information directly into the
Creating New Company dialog.

The only required information is the organization's name. However, it's a good idea to fill out the address and telephone information so it appears on transaction forms you print. Click Next, and select the type of business using these guidelines:

- If you're using QuickBooks Premier Nonprofit edition, choose Nonprofit Organization. QuickBooks installs the UCOA for nonprofits.
- If you're using QuickBooks Pro, choose No Type (see Figure 2-3). Then read Chapter 3 to learn how to import the UCOA, or create your own chart of accounts with your accountant's help.

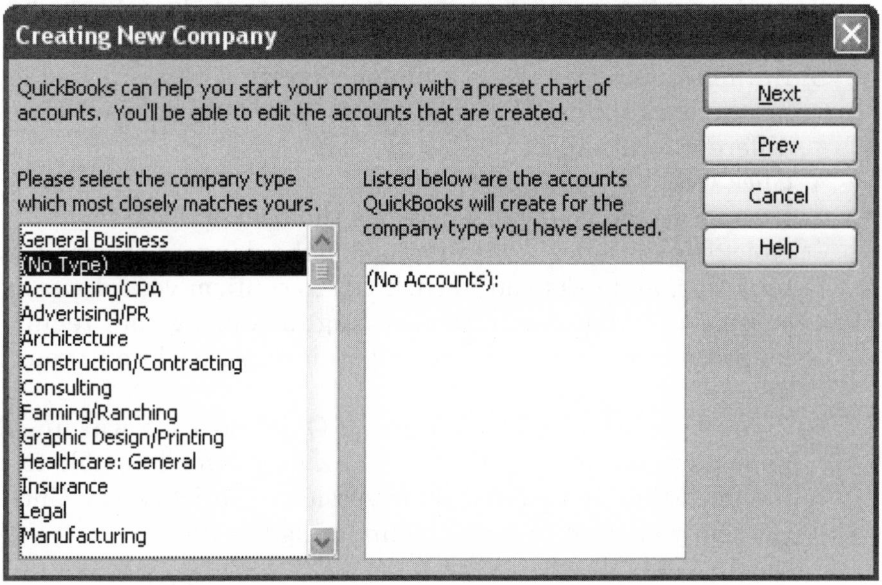

Figure 2-3: In QuickBooks Pro, the nonprofit chart of accounts isn't well designed, so don't select nonprofit as your business type.

Click Next to save the data file in QuickBooks.

Updating an Existing Company File

If you updated to your current version of QuickBooks from a previous version of QuickBooks, the first time you launch QuickBooks the software attempts to open the company file that was open when you last closed QuickBooks. Of course, the last time you closed QuickBooks, you weren't using this newer version of QuickBooks.

Instead of loading your company file in the software window, QuickBooks opens the Update File To New Version dialog. Take the following steps to update your company file:

1. Confirm the conversion by typing **Yes** and clicking OK. (Even though the dialog shows all capital letters, you can use lowercase letters.)
2. In the next message dialog, which says that QuickBooks has to back up the existing file before updating it, click OK.
3. In the QuickBooks Backup dialog, specify a filename and location for the backup file. Use the Browse button if you want to select a different location.
4. Click OK.
5. If you selected your hard drive as the backup location, QuickBooks issues a warning about the dangers of hard drive back ups, and asks you to click OK to confirm your decision. Of course, you'd backed up the existing file during your regular backup procedure, so it's okay to save this extra backup to your hard drive.
6. If you have a multi-user version of QuickBooks, a warning dialog appears to remind you that network users won't be able to use the file until they've updated their version of QuickBooks. Click Yes to confirm you want to continue updating the file.

Restoring and Updating a Backup File

You can also restore and update a backup file. Even if no company file is open, the File menu is activated (as is the Help menu). Choose File → Restore to open the Restore Company Backup dialog. Locate the backup file (look for *CompanyName*.QBB), and select it.

When the fields at the top of the dialog are filled in with the data identifying the backup file, QuickBooks automatically fills in the bottom of the dialog with data identifying the restored file. The name of the company file remains the same, but the extension changes from .QBB (a backup file) to .QBW (a company file). The default location is the folder that holds your QuickBooks software.

If you prefer to keep company data files in their own subfolder, click the Browse button at the bottom of the dialog to open the Restore To dialog.

- If the subfolder exists, double-click its icon and then click Save. You return to the Restore Company Backup dialog.
- If the subfolder doesn't exist, click the New Folder icon on the Restore To dialog, and enter a name for the folder (e.g. Company Files). Press Enter to save the new subfolder. Then double-click its icon to open the folder, and click Save. You return to the Restore Company Backup dialog.

Click Restore. QuickBooks restores the backup (which takes a few seconds or a few minutes, depending on the size of your company file), and then begins the update process to convert the file to your new version of QuickBooks.

The rest of this book provides the instructions and information you need to set up and run your nonprofit organization in QuickBooks.

Chapter 3

Chart of Accounts

Designing a chart of accounts

Creating accounts

Using subaccounts

Manipulating accounts

Unified Chart of Accounts for nonprofit
organizations

Entering opening balances

Before you can enter transactions in QuickBooks, you have to have a chart of accounts. If you already have a chart of accounts, you can use the information in this chapter to tweak it and customize it to make it more efficient for nonprofit bookkeeping.

In this chapter, I discuss the issues you need to understand to design and use accounts properly. For example, QuickBooks doesn't provide equity accounts suitable for nonprofits, so you have to create your own.

Also in this chapter is a discussion of the Unified Chart of Accounts (UCOA) for nonprofit organizations, which has become a standard for nonprofit accounting, although it's common for small nonprofit organizations to use their own, shorter and simpler, chart of accounts.

Designing the Chart of Accounts

If you're designing your own chart of accounts, be sure to do so carefully, because you have to live with the results every time you use QuickBooks. Also, discuss the design with your accountant, and with other people who perform bookkeeping chores for nonprofit organizations. They'll be able to help you design a scheme that works for the transactions you have to enter, and the reports you need.

You have several decisions to make about the general scheme you'll use for your chart of accounts. You need to decide whether you'll use numbered accounts, and if so, how many digits to use for each account.

You should also design a scheme for using subaccounts. Subaccounts make it possible to post transactions in a way that makes it easier to identify the components you're tracking (programs, funds, and other special nonprofit considerations).

In addition, you must create a protocol for account naming, and make sure everyone in your organization who works in the QuickBooks data file understands the protocol, and applies it.

Using Account Numbers

By default, QuickBooks does not assign numbers to accounts, and you should switch your QuickBooks configuration options to correct that oversight. A chart of accounts with numbers is easier to design, and easier to work with. Numbered accounts also have account names, of course, but the accounts are arranged by number, not by name. You'll appreciate how important account numbers are when you create and customize reports.

NOTE: *If you select the UCOA while you're setting up QuickBooks Premier Nonprofit Edition, account numbers are automatically enabled.*

Configuring QuickBooks to Use Numbered Accounts

In order to use numbered accounts, you have to change one of the QuickBooks settings. Use the following steps to switch to a number format for your chart of accounts:

1. Choose Edit → Preferences from the menu bar to open the Preferences dialog.
2. Click the Accounting icon in the left pane.
3. Click the Company Preferences tab in the right pane.
4. Select the Use Account Numbers check box (see Figure 3-1).

When you select the option to use account numbers, the option Show Lowest Subaccount Only becomes accessible (it's grayed out if you haven't enabled account numbers). This option tells QuickBooks to display only the subaccount on transaction windows, instead of both the parent account and the subaccount, making it easier to see precisely which account is receiving the posting. (Subaccounts are discussed later in this chapter, in the section "Using Subaccounts".)

After you make this configuration change, QuickBooks automatically assigns numbers to any existing accounts in the chart of accounts it installed (if you installed a chart of accounts during setup). You can change those automatically generated numbers to match the numbering scheme you want to use (see the section "Editing Accounts" later in this chapter). In addition, when you create a new account an Account Number field is available in the New Account dialog.

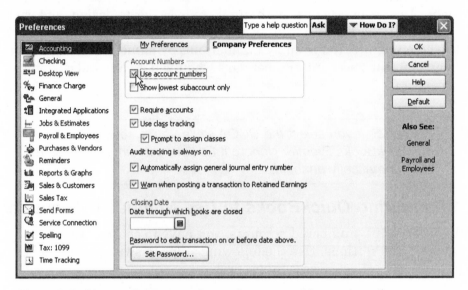

Figure 3-1: Change the accounting options to enable numbers for your chart of accounts.

When you select the option Show Lowest Subaccount Only, QuickBooks might display an error message telling you that you cannot enable the option until all your accounts have numbers assigned.

QuickBooks does not automatically assign a number to accounts you added to the chart of accounts manually; only the accounts QuickBooks created during setup are automatically numbered when you click OK in this Preference dialog. After you've assigned numbers to the accounts you added manually you can return to this Preferences dialog and enable the Show Lowest Subaccount Only option.

Designing the Numbering Scheme

As you create new accounts, you must use the numbers intelligently, assigning ranges of numbers to account types. You should check with your accountant before finalizing the way you use the numbers, but here's an example of a common approach that uses four numbers.

- 1000-1999 Assets
- 2000-2999 Liabilities
- 3000-3999 Net Assets
- 4000-6999 Income
- 7000-9999 Expenses

NOTE: *You can have as many as seven numbers (plus the account name) for each account.*

If all or most of your experience with accounting software has been in commercial (for-profit) companies, you'll notice a difference in the way number ranges are assigned. Commercial enterprises usually have a shorter range for income accounts, such as 4000-4999, and a larger range for expense accounts (5000-9999). Tracking revenue for nonprofits is more complicated, and usually the income section requires a larger range of numbers.

You can use sub ranges for specific expense types. For example, you could use 7000-7499 for expenses relating to fund raising, 7500-7999 for general operating expenses, 8000-8999 for program-related expenses, and so on.

NOTE: *If you sell products and track inventory you can reserve a section of the chart of accounts for cost of goods accounts. Usually, COG accounts are at the end of the Income accounts number range.*

Give careful thought to the way you break down asset accounts. For example, here's a typical assignment of numbers:

- 1000 through 1099 for bank accounts.
- 1100 through 1199 for accounts receivable.
- 1200 through 1599 for other current assets.
- 1600 through 1799 for fixed assets.

- 1800 through 1999 for other assets.

Follow the same pattern for liabilities, starting with current liabilities and moving to long term.

TIP: Keep all the payroll liabilities together, using contiguous numbers.

Usually, you should add accounts by increasing the previous account number by ten, so that if your first bank account is 1000, the next bank account is 1010, and so on. This gives you room to continue to add more accounts that belong in the same general area.

If you don't think you can enter all your accounts and still leave room for additional accounts, use more numbers, perhaps five or six. When you use subaccounts (and you should), you need more digits in your account scheme to make sure you have enough numbers available to create all the subaccounts.

Understanding QuickBooks Account Sorting

You have to create a numbering scheme that conforms to the QuickBooks account types, because QuickBooks sorts your chart of accounts by account type. If you have contiguous numbers that vary by type, you won't be able to view your chart of accounts in numerical order. QuickBooks sorts the chart of account in the following manner:

Assets

- Bank
- Accounts Receivable
- Other Current Asset
- Fixed Asset
- Other Asset

Liabilities

- Accounts Payable
- Credit Card

- Other Current Liability
- Long-Term Liability

Equity

Equity accounts are sorted by number.

Income

Income accounts are sorted by number.

Cost Of Goods Sold

COG accounts are sorted by number.

Expense

Expense accounts are sorted by number.

Other Income

Other Income accounts are sorted by number.

Other Expense

Other Expense accounts are sorted by number.

Non-Posting Accounts

Non-posting accounts are created automatically by QuickBooks when you enable features that use those account types, such as Estimates, Purchase Orders, and Sales Orders. (Sales orders are only available in Premier editions.)

By default, when QuickBooks creates non-posting accounts, it assigns a single digit number to each account. You can edit the account to match the number of digits you're using.

Designing Account Name Protocols

You need to devise protocols for naming accounts, whether you plan to use numbered accounts, or only account names. When you're posting transactions to the general ledger, the only way to know which account should be used for posting is to have easy-to-understand account names.

Your protocol must be clear so that when everyone follows the rules, the account naming convention is consistent. Why is this important? Because when I visit clients who haven't invented and enforced protocols, I find accounts with similar names, such as Tele Exp, Tele Expense, and Telephone.

I almost always find that every one of those accounts has amounts posted. That's because users "guess" at account names and point and click on whatever they see that seems remotely related. If they don't find the account the way they would have entered the name, they invent a new account (using a name that seems logical to them). Avoid all of those errors by establishing protocols about creating account names, and then make sure everyone searches the account list before applying a transaction.

Here are a few suggested protocols—you can amend them to fit your own situation, or invent different protocols that you're more comfortable with. The important thing is to make sure you have absolute consistency.

- Avoid apostrophes and other punctuation characters.
- Set the number of characters for abbreviations. For example, if you permit four characters, telephone is abbreviated "tele"; a three-character rule produces "tel"; utilities is abbreviated "util" or "uti".
- Decide whether to use the ampersand (&) or a hyphen. For example, is it "repairs & maintenance" or "repairs-maintenance"? Do you want spaces before and after the ampersand or hyphen?

Creating Accounts

After you've done your homework, made your decisions, invented your protocols, and checked with your accountant, adding accounts is a piece of cake. Start by opening the Chart of Accounts List. QuickBooks provides a variety of ways to open the Chart of Accounts List window:

- Press Ctrl-A
- Click the Chart of Accounts icon on the Home page (QuickBooks 2006 and later)
- Click the Accnt icon on the Icon bar (QuickBooks 2005 and earlier)

- Choose Lists → Chart of Accounts from the menu bar

Press Ctrl-N to open a New Account dialog, and select an account type from the Type drop-down list. This dialog changes its appearance depending on the account type, because different types of accounts require different information. Figure 3-2 shows the New Account dialog for an expense account.

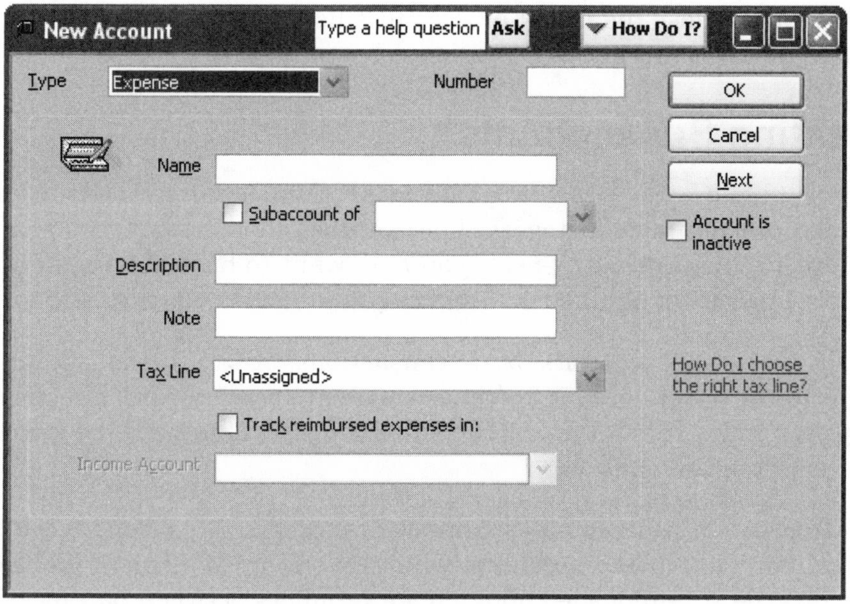

Figure 3-2: The only required entries for a new account are a number (assuming you've enabled account numbers) and a name.

If you've configured QuickBooks for account numbers, there's a field for the account number. The Description field is optional, as is the Note field (which only appears on some account types).

If you don't want anyone to post transactions to the account at the moment, you can select the Account is Inactive option, which means the account won't be available for posting amounts during transaction entry. See the section "Hiding Accounts by Making Them Inactive", later in this chapter.

Some account types (for example, accounts connected to banks) have a field for an opening balance. Don't use it. The best way to put the account balances into the system is to enter an opening trial balance as a journal entry (see the section "Entering Opening Balances" later in this chapter), and to create transactions (for customer and vendor balances).

As you finish entering each account, click Next to move to another blank New Account dialog. When you're finished entering accounts, click OK and then close the Chart of Accounts list by clicking the X in the upper right corner.

Creating Subaccounts

Subaccounts provide a way to post transactions more precisely, because you can pinpoint a subcategory. For example, if you create an expense account for insurance expenses, you may want to have subaccounts for vehicle insurance, liability insurance, equipment insurance, and so on.

If you use subaccounts, post transactions only to the subaccounts, never to the parent account. When you create reports, QuickBooks displays the individual totals for the subaccounts, along with the grand total for the parent account.

To create a subaccount, you must first create the parent account. If you're using numbered accounts, when you set up your main (parent) accounts, be sure to leave enough open numbers between parent accounts to fit in all the subaccounts you'll need. If necessary, use more than four digits in your numbering scheme to make sure you have a logical hierarchy for your account structure. For example, suppose you have the following parent accounts:

- 8010 Insurance
- 8050 Utilities

You can then create the following subaccounts:

- 8011 Vehicles
- 8012 Liability
- 8013 Equipment
- 8051 Heat

- 8052 Electric

You can have multiple levels of subaccounts. Using the same 8010 Insurance account as an example, you could have the following insurance accounts:

- 8011 Vehicles (subaccount of 8010)
- 8012 Cars (subaccount of 8011)
- 8013 School Vans (subaccount of 8011)

Of course, to make this work you have to widen the numerical interval between Vehicles and Liability, or use more than four numbers in your account numbering scheme.

When you view the Chart of Accounts list, subaccounts appear under their parent accounts, and they're indented. When you view a subaccount in a drop-down list within a transaction window, it appears in the format:

- ParentAccount:Subaccount
- ParentAccount:Subaccount:Subaccount.

For example, using the structure I just created, the drop-down list in the Account field of transaction windows shows the following text: 8010 Insurance:8011 Vehicles.

Because many of the fields in transaction windows are small, you may not be able to see the subaccount names without scrolling through the field. This can be annoying, and it's much easier to work if only the subaccount to which you post transactions is displayed.

That's the point of enabling the preference Show Lowest Subaccount Only, discussed earlier in this chapter. When you enable that option, you see only the last part of the subaccount in the transaction window (using the example I cited, you'd see only "8011 Vehicles"). This makes it easier to find the account you need.

QuickBooks offers two methods for making an account a subaccount:

- Use the New Account dialog.
- Drag an account listing to an indented position.

Creating Subaccounts in the New Account Dialog

To use the New Account dialog for creating subaccounts, create the parent account, and then take the following steps:

1. Open the Chart of Accounts list.
2. Press Ctrl-N to create a new account.
3. Select the appropriate account type.
4. Click the Subaccount check box to place a check mark in it.
5. In the drop-down box next to the check box, select the parent account. (This gives you access to the parent account number if you're using numbered accounts—which makes it easier to assign the appropriate number to this subaccount.)
6. If you're using numbered accounts, enter the appropriate number.
7. Enter the subaccount name (just the portion of the name you're using for the subaccount). For instance, if the parent account is Insurance, name the subaccount Vehicle.
8. Click OK.

Creating Subaccounts by Dragging Account Listings

You can omit the extra steps of selecting the Subaccount check box and selecting the parent account. Instead, create all your parent accounts and subaccounts by entering only the account type, account number, and account name. (Make sure you assign account numbers with subaccounts in mind.)

Open the Chart of Accounts List window and position your mouse pointer on the diamond symbol to the left of the account you want to turn into a subaccount. Your pointer turns into a four-way arrow.

Drag the diamond symbol to the right to indent it. QuickBooks automatically configures the account as a subaccount of the unindented listing immediately above this account. Repeat the action for the remaining listings under the parent account.

After you've created a subaccount, if you drag an account listing below that subaccount further to the right, creating another level of indentation, QuickBooks makes that account a subaccount of the subaccount above it.

Creating Bank Accounts for Fund Accounting

In nonprofit accounting parlance, a fund is defined as a discrete accounting entity with a self-balancing set of accounts, recording cash and related liabilities, obligations, reserves, and equities. Each fund is segregated for the purpose of tracking specific activities in accordance with any limitations or restrictions attached to the fund.

Until the mid 1990's, fund accounting was de rigueur for nonprofit organizations, because it provided important information to funding sources and donors. Today, pure fund accounting has been replaced by the Statement of Financial Accounting Standards (SFAS) Numbers 116 & 117, which describe the way non-governmental nonprofits should account for contributions, and present financial statements.

The impact of the SFAS financial statement reporting is now on "net asset" classification, rather than on tracking each fund. The net asset categories are: Unrestricted, Temporarily Restricted, and Permanently Restricted. In other words, the net asset can combine all funds with similar restrictions, and you no longer have to track each fund and its specific net assets.

QuickBooks and Fund Accounting

QuickBooks does not support the "net asset" paradigm, because it doesn't let you configure your system to post net amounts to specific net asset accounts. As a result, you or your accountant must use journal entries to transfer amounts to the appropriate net asset equity accounts.

Some nonprofit organizations continue to use fund accounting, even though they no longer have to produce year-end reports on a fund-by-fund basis. These organizations find that tracking their financial activities internally is easier if they stick to the fund accounting method. Some accountants believe that fund accounting is the optimum record-keeping approach for nonprofits.

QuickBooks does not inherently support fund accounting features, because you cannot divisionalize the chart of accounts. Fund accounting software is designed to create fund divisions out-of-the-box, and many traditional (for-profit) accounting software applications can easily be configured for fund divisions.

Fund Accounting Workaround for QuickBooks

If your organization wants to track financial transactions by fund in QuickBooks, there's a workaround that's rather easy to set up.

Create two subaccounts under each bank account that receives or disburses program funds. Name one subaccount Restricted, and name the other subaccount Unrestricted. Then deposit and disburse funds using the appropriate subaccount.

If you entered an opening balance for the bank account during account set up, or you entered an opening balance via an opening trial balance (see the section "Entering Opening Balances" later in this chapter), transfer all the funds out of the parent account into the appropriate subaccounts. Here's how to do this:

1. Choose Banking → Transfer Funds to open the Transfer Funds Between Accounts dialog.
2. In the Transfer Funds From field, select the parent bank account from the drop-down list.
3. In the Transfer Funds To field, select the restricted subaccount from the drop-down list.
4. In the Transfer Amount$ field, enter the amount of funds in the parent account that are restricted, to transfer that amount to the restricted subaccount.
5. Click Save & New to open a new Transfer Funds Between Accounts dialog.
6. In the Transfer Funds From field, select the parent bank account from the drop-down list. (Notice that the balance that's displayed

for the account hasn't changed even though you transferred money to the restricted account.)

7. In the Transfer Funds To field, select the unrestricted subaccount from the drop-down list.

8. In the Transfer Amount$ field, enter the amount of funds in the parent account that are unrestricted, to transfer that amount to the restricted subaccount.

9. Click Save & Close.

When you open the Chart of Accounts window, you'll see that the parent bank account displays the total deposited in the bank, and the two subaccounts display amounts that add up to the amount displayed for the parent account.

As you create transactions for receiving income or disbursing funds, post each transaction to the appropriate subaccount instead of the parent account. (See Chapter 6 to learn how to handle income, Chapter 7 to learn how to manage disbursements, and Chapter 8 to learn about moving money between bank accounts.)

Manipulating Accounts

You can edit, delete, and merge accounts, which means you can constantly fine-tune your chart of accounts to make sure your reports are detailed and easy to understand. In addition, you can make accounts inactive, so they continue to exist, but nobody can post transactions to them.

Editing Accounts

If you need to make changes to an account's configuration, open the chart of accounts window, click the account's listing to select it, and press Ctrl-E. The Edit Account dialog appears, which looks just like the account dialog you filled out when you created the account.

You can edit any field in the account, including (with some exceptions) the account type. If you want to change the account type, the following restrictions apply:

• You cannot change A/R or A/P accounts to other account types

- You cannot change other account types to be A/R or A/P accounts
- You cannot change the account type of accounts that QuickBooks creates automatically (such as Undeposited Funds).
- You cannot change the account type of an account that has subaccounts. You must first make the subaccounts parent accounts (it's easiest to drag them to the left in the window), change the account type of each account, and then create the subaccounts again (drag them to the right).

Deleting Accounts

To delete an account, select its listing in the Chart of Accounts window, and press Ctrl-D. QuickBooks displays a confirmation message, asking if you're sure you want to delete the account. Click OK to delete the account (or click Cancel if you've changed your mind).

Some accounts cannot be deleted, and after you click OK, QuickBooks displays an error message telling you why you cannot complete the action. Any of the following conditions prevent you from deleting an account:

- The account is linked to an item
- The account has been used in a transaction
- The account has subaccounts

If the problem is subaccounts, you must first delete all the subaccounts. If any of the subaccounts fall into the restrictions list, make them parent accounts in order to delete the original parent account.

If you're trying to delete an account because you don't want anyone to post to it, but QuickBooks won't delete the account, you can hide the account by making it inactive (covered next).

An account that was created automatically by QuickBooks can be deleted (as long as it doesn't fall under the restrictions), but a warning message appears to tell you that if you perform actions in QuickBooks to warrant the use of the account, the system will automatically create the account again. For example, if QuickBooks created an account for purchase orders, you can delete it if you haven't yet created a purchase order, and you don't think you will be creating purchase orders. If you ever create a purchase order, QuickBooks once again adds the account to your chart of accounts.

Hiding Accounts by Making Them Inactive

If you don't want anyone to post to an account but you don't want to delete the account (or QuickBooks won't let you delete the account), you can make the account inactive.

Right-click the account's listing and choose Make Inactive from the shortcut menu. If the account is a parent account, its subaccounts are automatically made inactive, too.

Inactive accounts don't appear in the account drop-down list when you're filling out a transaction window, and therefore can't be selected for posting. Of course, they also don't appear in the Chart of Accounts List window by default, which can be confusing. For example, you may have money market bank accounts that you don't want anyone to use during transaction postings. However, if you don't see the account in the Chart of Accounts List window, you won't know its current balance. In fact, you might forget it exists.

To view all your accounts, including inactive accounts, in the Chart of Accounts List window, select the option Include Inactive (at the bottom of the window). A new column appears on the left side of the window, headed by a large black X. Inactive accounts are easily identified by the display of a large black X in this column, as seen in Figure 3-3.

TIP: If the Include Inactive option is grayed out, there are no inactive accounts.

To make an inactive account active, click the X to remove it (it's a toggle). If the account is a parent account, QuickBooks asks if you want to make all its subaccounts active.

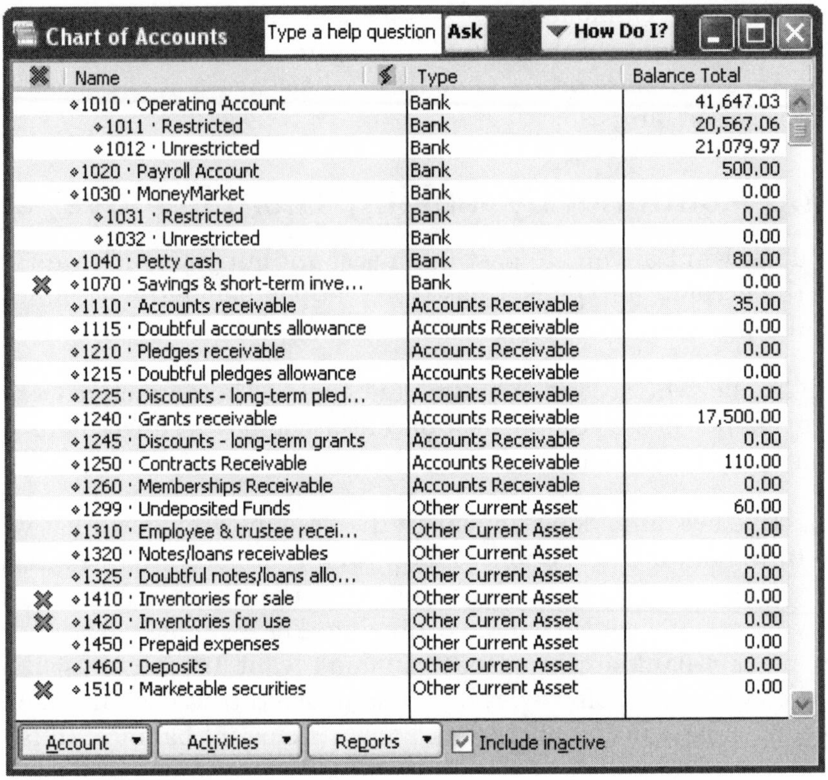

Figure 3-3: Inactive accounts are clearly discernable.

Using Hidden (Inactive) Accounts

In organizations that have multiple users entering transactions in QuickBooks, the bookkeeper or a director often wants to prevent other users from posting transactions to certain accounts (such as equity accounts). Sometimes users select those accounts by mistake, by clicking on the wrong listing. Occasionally, users select an account that seems logical, but is totally inappropriate. To avoid problems, the account is made inactive, and doesn't appear in drop down lists.

But, suppose the bookkeeper, director, or other knowledgeable user wants to be able to post amounts to those accounts? Don't worry, you can use a hidden (inactive) account at any time. You don't even have to activate the account, and then mark it inactive again after you've finished using it.

When you're entering a transaction, don't use the drop-down list (because of course, the account won't appear). Instead, enter the account name or number manually. QuickBooks displays a message asking you if you want to use the account just once, or reactivate the account. Click the option to use the account just once. You can use the account "just once" as many times as you want to.

Merging Accounts

Sometimes you have two accounts that should be one. For instance, you may be splitting postings inappropriately, and your accountant suggests that one account would be better. An example is an account named Telephone-Education Programs, and another account named Telephone-Health Programs. The distinctions between telephone expenses for these programs shouldn't be made with the chart of accounts; they're made by tracking programs with the Class feature.

Sometimes you may find that you have two accounts that cover the same category; the second account should never have been created. Users have posted transactions to both of the accounts. For example, you may have two accounts for Telephone Expenses, one named Telephone, and the other named Tel.

In these cases, the solution is to merge accounts. Accounts must meet the following criteria in order to merge them:

- The accounts must be of the same type
- The accounts must be at the same level (parent or subaccount)

If the accounts aren't at the same level, move one of the accounts to the same level as the other account. After you merge the accounts, you can move the newly merged account to a different level.

Take the following steps to merge two accounts:

1. Open the Chart of Accounts List window.

2. Select (highlight) the account that has the name you *do not* want to use.
3. Press Ctrl-E to open the Edit Account dialog.
4. Change the account name and number to match the account you want to keep.
5. Click OK.

QuickBooks displays a message telling you that the account number you've entered already exists for another account, and asking if you want to merge the accounts. Click Yes to confirm that you want to merge the two accounts.

Unified Chart of Accounts for Nonprofits

Nonprofits have to file a great many detailed reports about their financial activities. Federal and state governments have filing requirements, and grant-givers frequently require financial information. Except for the Form 990 model on the federal level, there's no particular across-the-board standard you can take for granted (although most states will accept the Federal Form 990).

The Unified Chart of Accounts (UCOA) is an attempt to standardize the way nonprofits keep financial records, and report them. The UCOA is based on Form 990, but it's useful and efficient even for nonprofit organizations that don't file Form 990. Developed by the California Association of Nonprofits, and the National Center for Charitable Statistics (NCCS), UCOA provides a way to unite all of your reporting needs into one set of accounting records. By using UCOA as a model for your own chart of accounts, you'll find it easier to produce reports for all who demand them.

If you're just starting to use QuickBooks you should use the UCOA. You can easily customize the chart of accounts to your own needs (or your own taste) by adding or removing accounts. You can also rename accounts that don't use the terminology you prefer.

If you're already working in QuickBooks and have a chart of accounts, you should examine the UCOA and use it to tweak, enhance, and otherwise improve your chart of accounts.

Using the UCOA in Premier Nonprofit Edition

In QuickBooks Premier Nonprofit edition, if you select the nonprofit chart of accounts during the EasyStep interview, or during a manual setup of a company file, you've selected the UCOA.

If you're using QuickBooks Premier Nonprofit 2005 or earlier, the chart of accounts isn't really ready for use, because all the accounts are inactive. See the section "Modifying the UCOA".

Some users don't select the nonprofit chart of accounts during QuickBooks setup, because they have a chart of accounts from their accountant.

NOTE: If you're upgrading from one version of QuickBooks to a later version or from QuickBooks Pro to QuickBooks Premier Nonprofit Edition, you don't perform a company setup, so you don't have the opportunity to select a chart of accounts.

Using the UCOA in QuickBooks Pro

QuickBooks Pro does not offer a copy of the UCOA. If you're creating a new company file, and you choose Nonprofit as your industry type, the chart of accounts that's loaded isn't very well thought out for nonprofit organizations.

If you selected that chart of accounts, you can download the UCOA and open it in Excel to examine it and use it to tweak your existing chart of accounts. Or, you can import it (which doesn't work quite as easily in QuickBooks Pro as it does in Premier editions—see "Importing the UCOA into QuickBooks").

Downloading the UCOA for QuickBooks Pro

If you're not using QuickBooks Premier Nonprofit edition, you can download the UCOA from several Internet Web sites. You can use the file as a model for modifying your current chart of accounts, or import the file into QuickBooks.

One popular site is the National Center for Charitable Statistics, at http://nccs.urban.org/ucoa/nccs-ucoa2.htm. This Web page also has links to several files related to the UCOA.

You can also download the UCOA from http://www.cpa911publishing.com. Click the Downloads navigation button on the left side of the web page, and use the link to the UCOA. Do **not** open the file from your browser; instead save the file to your hard drive. Note the folder in which you save the file so you can locate it when you're ready to import it. This file is ready for importing, and the accounts are all active.

Importing the UCOA

To import the UCOA, use one of the following actions:

- In QuickBooks 2006 and later versions, choose File → Utilities → Import → Import IIF Files.
- In QuickBooks 2005 and earlier versions, choose File Import → IIF Files.

In the Import dialog, navigate to the folder that holds the IIF file you want to import and double-click its listing. After a few seconds, QuickBooks displays a message telling you the data has been imported.

Importing into QuickBooks Pro

In QuickBooks Pro, before you import your chart of accounts, you must make sure the import procedure will work. This involves the following tasks:

- Enable account numbers in the Accounting section of the Preferences dialog (see the instructions in the section "Configuring QuickBooks to Use Numbered Accounts", earlier in this chapter).

- Be sure your current chart of accounts doesn't have an account number that is duplicated in the chart of accounts you're importing.

The second item can be a bit tricky, but it's important. In QuickBooks Pro, imports fail the first time they encounter a record in the currently installed file that is a duplicate of a record in the import file. When you're using numbered accounts, the check for duplication is made against account numbers.

NOTE: *In QuickBooks Premier editions, the import feature is more sophisticated and doesn't shut down when a similar or identical account exists. If the import encounters a duplicate account number, it checks the name. If the name is the same, nothing happens. If the name is different, the account is imported. You can end up with duplicate account numbers, but you can edit, delete, or merge the accounts.*

For example, if you have an account named 1010 Checking Account, and the import file has an account named 1010 Bank Account, the import will fail because of the duplicate account number.

To rid your current chart of accounts of numbers that are duplicated in the UCOA you want to import, edit each existing account to add another number (a zero is best) to the end of the account number. Turning all the account numbers into five-digit numbers ensures the import's success, because the UCOA chart of account uses four-digit numbers.

Modifying the UCOA

The UCOA needs some modifications before you can use it to create transactions and reports in QuickBooks. You have to change generic account names to names that are related to your organization (see the section "Changing UCOA Account Names), and you should also delete accounts you don't plan to use

If you're using a version of QuickBooks Premier Nonprofit Edition prior to 2006, all the accounts are configured as Inactive. (Starting with the 2006 version of the Premier Nonprofit Edition, QuickBooks activated all the accounts in the built-in UCOA.) When you open the Chart of Accounts window, if the option Include Inactive isn't selected, you won't see your chart of accounts. Instead, you'll see only a few accounts that QuickBooks automatically defined during setup.

When you select the option Include Inactive, all the accounts in the UCOA have a large X in the left column, indicating the accounts are inactive, and therefore hidden. Hidden accounts don't appear in the drop-down list of accounts when you create transactions in QuickBooks, so you won't be able to get any work done until you change the status of your accounts to Active.

You must go through the list to activate the accounts you want to use. To activate an account, click the X in the left column, and your action automatically removes the X (it's a toggle). Here are the guidelines:

- A subaccount can't be activated until the parent account is activated. If you click the X of a subaccount, nothing happens.
- When you activate a parent account, QuickBooks asks if you want to activate all the subaccounts. Click Yes to save yourself the extra mouse clicks.

TIP: *If you downloaded the UCOA from www.cpa911publishing.com, all the accounts are active.*

Replace the generic account names with names that are specific to your organization, and add accounts and subaccounts as needed. You should also remove accounts you won't use. See the section "Deleting Accounts", earlier in this chapter.

TIP: Don't worry if your existing accounts have transactions, because you can merge each account with the appropriate UCOA account after the import procedure.

Changing UCOA Account Names

The UCOA is populated with accounts that have generic names. You should change the account names to make them more specific to your organization, which makes them easier to use.

For example, the UCOA has a bank account named Cash in Bank - Operating. If your operating checking account is with Ninth National Federal Bank of East Overcoat Iowa, change the account name to Ninth Fed. To change an account name, select the account's listing in the Chart of Accounts window and press Ctrl-E to put the account in "edit mode". Then enter the new name.

Some name changes aren't efficient. For example, I worked with a user who changed the account named Earned revenues:Federal contracts/fees to Earned Revenues:Federal Contract #9998887. This name change occurred after the organization received a federal contract to run a program, and she wanted the account to reflect the specific program.

No, no, no, no. Programs aren't tracked in the chart of accounts; they're tracked with classes. And, funding sources are tracked by customer (in QuickBooks, a donor is a customer).

An account is a "bucket" that holds transaction amounts for a certain type of transaction, regardless of the program or the donor. The programs are tracked with the Class List; the donors are tracked with the Customer:Job List.

Entering Opening Balances

Don't ever enter opening account balances in the company file setup interview, nor when you add accounts to your chart of accounts. Instead, enter your opening balances all at once in a journal entry. An opening balance, sometimes called an *opening trial balance*, consists of balance sheet accounts (assets, liabilities, and equity). Work with your accountant to create your opening trial balance.

In the for-profit arena, the balancing entry for an opening trial balance is posted to an equity account (such as Retained Earnings). For a nonprofit organization, the equity amounts must be distributed among the appropriate net asset accounts. (See the section "Equity Accounts" later in this chapter.)

Unlike more robust accounting software applications, QuickBooks doesn't really have a function called the "opening balance". However, every account register is sorted by date, so using the first day of your fiscal year creates an opening balance automatically. Remember that the offset equity has to be posted properly to multiple equity accounts. It's best to confer with your accountant to develop the opening balance.

Opening Balances for A/R and A/P

There are a couple of QuickBooks idiosyncrasies you run into when working with journal entries. For JEs involving balance sheet accounts (assets, liabilities, and equity), a journal entry can contain only the A/P account or the A/R account; you cannot use both of those accounts in the same journal entry (and the odds are good that both accounts have balances in your opening balance). You'll get an error message that says, "You cannot use more than one A/R or A/P account in the same transaction" (which is not a clear explanation). This restriction does not have its roots in accounting standards, it's just a rule that QuickBooks built into the software arbitrarily.

Unfortunately, QuickBooks doesn't issue the error message until you've entered all the data and then try to save the journal entry (talk about frustrating and annoying!).

Another problem is that QuickBooks insists you attach a single customer or vendor name to the entry if you're making a journal entry that involves either the A/R or the A/P account. That's rarely the situation for open A/R or A/P balances.

As a result, don't enter opening balances for A/R and A/P in a journal entry. Putting A/R and A/P balances into a journal entry isn't a good idea anyway. The entry is only a total, which means you lose the details. Enter existing open (unpaid) invoices and open (unpaid) vendor bills as discrete transactions, using their actual dates (which pre-date your QuickBooks start date).

Fixed Assets Opening Balances

If you've been depreciating any of your fixed assets, the opening balance for the fixed asset is the current net value (the original cost, less the accumulated depreciation) as of the QuickBooks start date.

It's worth taking a bit of extra time to enter depreciation in a way that shows the history of the depreciation (so you can easily ascertain the original cost of the asset). To accomplish this, create accounts and subaccounts for each type of fixed asset you're tracking.

For example, if you're tracking vehicles, create a Fixed Asset parent account named Vehicle Assets. Then create the following subaccounts:

- Vehicle (e.g. Van, if you want to track each vehicle individually), or Vehicles, if you want to track multiple vehicles in one account.
- Vehicle AccumDeprec

For the opening balance, enter the original cost of the vehicle in the Vehicle subaccount, and the current depreciation in the Vehicle AccumDeprec subaccount. Notice that you don't post any amounts to the parent account, but the parent account will show the net amount when you print balance sheet reports.

If you want to track individual vehicles, create a subaccount for each. If you wish, you can create a separate depreciation subaccount for each individual vehicle, or post depreciation for all vehicles to the same subaccount (ask your accountant's advice).

Take the same approach for other fixed asset accounts that require depreciation (such as equipment, buildings, leasehold improvements, and so on).

For information on entering depreciation in the future (now that the opening balances are recorded), see Chapter 11, which explains the tasks that have to be performed at the end of your fiscal year.

Table 3-1 displays the entries for a sample (and admittedly very oversimplified) opening balance journal entry.

Account	Debit	Credit
Bank	10000.00	
CDs	15000.00	
Fixed Asset	4000.00	
Accum Deprec-Fixed Asset		3000.00
Bank Loan		2000.00
Unearned/Deferred Revenue		15000.00
Unrestricted Net Asset		5000.00
Temporarily Restricted Net Asset		2000.00
Permanently Restricted Net Asset		2000.00

Table 3-1: Sample Opening Trial Balance

Equity Accounts

QuickBooks provides two equity accounts automatically: Retained Earnings, and Opening Bal Equity. These equity accounts don't work properly for nonprofits.

You must create the equity accounts you need to track your net assets properly. A nonprofit organization requires multiple equity accounts (called *net asset* accounts), to wit:

- Permanently Restricted Net Assets
- Temporarily Restricted Net Assets
- Unrestricted Net Assets

The Retained Earnings account that QuickBooks automatically creates is really the account for Unrestricted Net Assets. You can rename the Retained Earnings account, using the name Unrestricted Net Assets, or something similar. The UCOA names this account "Unrestrict (retained earnings)".

Many organizations add subaccounts to these equity accounts, in order to track details. As you post transactions to the subaccounts, you can link the transactions to programs or donors. The subtotals in the subaccounts are displayed as the total for the parent account in your reports.

For example, you might want a structure similar to the following set of equity accounts:

- The Permanently Restricted Net Assets parent account could have subaccounts for specific permanent endowments or permanently restricted gifts. As restriction conditions are met, the funds are moved.
- The Temporarily Restricted Net Assets parent account could have subaccounts named Restricted By Type and Restricted by Time. As restriction conditions are met, the funds are moved.
- The Unrestricted Net Assets parent account could have a subaccount for Transfers. This account receives postings as you use transaction forms to bring funds in and out. Using transactions (invoices, sales receipts, vendor bills, direct disbursements, or journal entries) lets you assign classes and customers to the postings.

If you're using the Unified Chart of Accounts these equity account types are already available. If you're creating your own chart of accounts, or updating an existing chart of accounts, you must add the equity accounts required for nonprofits.

QuickBooks Retained Earnings Account

QuickBooks uses the Retained Earnings account to post the calculated net profit (or loss) automatically at the end of your fiscal year. When you view the chart of accounts, the Retained Earnings account is the only balance sheet account that doesn't display the current balance.

In versions of QuickBooks previous to QuickBooks 2005, if you try to open the register, the following message is displayed: "This account is a special automatically created account. It does not have a register."

However, in all versions of QuickBooks, you can always post transactions to the Retained Earnings account, even if you can't open it. If fact, like many other business owners, I perform a journal entry at the end of each year to move the balance in the Retained Earnings account into the Previous Earnings account (an account I created so that the Retained Earnings account balance starts with the current year's net earnings).

Starting with QuickBooks 2005, you can open the register of the Retained Earnings account. When you double-click the account's listing, an Account Quick Report opens, displaying all postings to the account. You can easily distinguish QuickBooks' automatic postings of profit (or loss) from transaction postings. Automatic postings have the following characteristics:

- The Type column displays the text Closing Entry.
- The Date column displays the last day of your fiscal year.
- You cannot drill down into the transaction (hovering your mouse over the listing does not change your mouse pointer to a "zoom" (a Z enclosed in a magnifying glass).

Transaction postings have the following characteristics:

- The Type column displays the transaction type (e.g. General Journal, or Invoice).
- You can drill down to see the original transaction. Hover your mouse over the listing, and when your mouse pointer changes to a zoom pointer, double-click to view the original transaction window.

QuickBooks Opening Bal Equity Account

If you fill in any balance amounts during the setup interview, or if you fill in opening balances when you create accounts, customers, vendors, or inventory items, QuickBooks uses an account named Opening Bal Equity as the offset account.

There's a certain logic to this approach, because the amounts posted to the Opening Bal Equity account represent balances that already existed on your QuickBooks start date, and are therefore opening balances.

However, this logic has a serious flaw: the QuickBooks start date is not necessarily the first day of your fiscal year. Almost always, the amount automatically posted to the Open Bal Equity account includes current fiscal year amounts.

Even worse for nonprofits, after determining which amounts should not be considered previous year balances, those amounts have to be divided into the appropriate net asset accounts.

NOTE: *There's never a reason for a balance to exist in the Opening Bal Equity account even in a for-profit business. Accountants routinely use journal entries to move balances out of this account into the appropriate equity account.*

Before you enter any transactions in QuickBooks, check to see whether the Opening Bal Equity account has a balance. If so, create a journal entry to transfer the appropriate amounts to the other net asset accounts, so that the Opening Bal Equity ends up with a zero balance.

After you clear out the balance in the Opening Bal Equity account, you must keep an eye on it. Any of the following actions puts funds back into the account:

- Entering an opening balance when creating a new account (for those account types that have an Opening Balance field).
- Entering an opening balance when creating a new customer.
- Entering an opening balance when creating a new vendor.
- Entering an opening balance when creating a new inventory item.
- Letting QuickBooks make an adjustment when bank reconciliation doesn't balance.

It's easy to avoid the first four items on this list, but there's no way to avoid an adjustment when a bank reconciliation fails to balance. Most failed bank reconciliations are eventually resolved. Usually, the error is discovered, and an adjusting journal entry removes the amount from the Opening Bal Equity account. Sometimes, an equal and opposite error occurs the following month, and the QuickBooks automatic adjustment sets everything back the way to zero. (When this occurs, it usually means the user missed an item during the first reconciliation and failed to clear it, and sees the item the next time the bank account is reconciled).

Chapter 4

Configuring Preferences

Enabling the features you need

Configuring the way QuickBooks works

QuickBooks has a Preferences dialog in which you set accounting, transaction, and overall configuration options. These options determine the display of transaction windows, the way transactions post, and what you see when QuickBooks opens.

To open the Preferences dialog, choose Edit → Preferences. The dialog's display has three panes:

- The left pane contains icons for the categories.
- The center pane contains the My Preferences and Company Preferences tabs, which change content depending on the selection in the left column.
- The right pane contains command buttons.

In this chapter, I'll cover some (but not all) of the categories in the Preferences dialog, omitting those that aren't directly connected to common QuickBooks installations, and presenting only a quick overview for those settings that are self-explanatory.

Each category in the Preferences dialog has two tabs: My Preferences and Company Preferences. Not all of the categories offer options in the My Preferences tab.

The My Preferences tab offers options that are applied when you work in QuickBooks, in the currently selected company file. If you've created individual users, QuickBooks remembers the settings for each login name (the login name you use to enter QuickBooks, not the logon name you may be using to log on to Windows).

The Company Preferences tab offers options for the currently opened company (QuickBooks remembers the preferences you set for each company and reloads them when you open that company file). If you're using logins and have set up user permissions, you must have administrator permissions to set My Company preferences.

Accounting Preferences

In QuickBooks Premier editions, the My Preferences tab contains the option Autofill Memo In General Journal Entry. This nifty feature automatically enters the text you put in the Memo field of the first line of JE into every line of the JE.

Most people only enter memo text in the first line, so when you open an account register for any account that appears in the JE (except the account in the first line), the reason for the JE is a mystery. You have to open the original transaction to find out why a JE was created.

In QuickBooks Pro, the My Preferences tab for this category has no options, so head for the Company Preferences tab, which is seen in Figure 4-1.

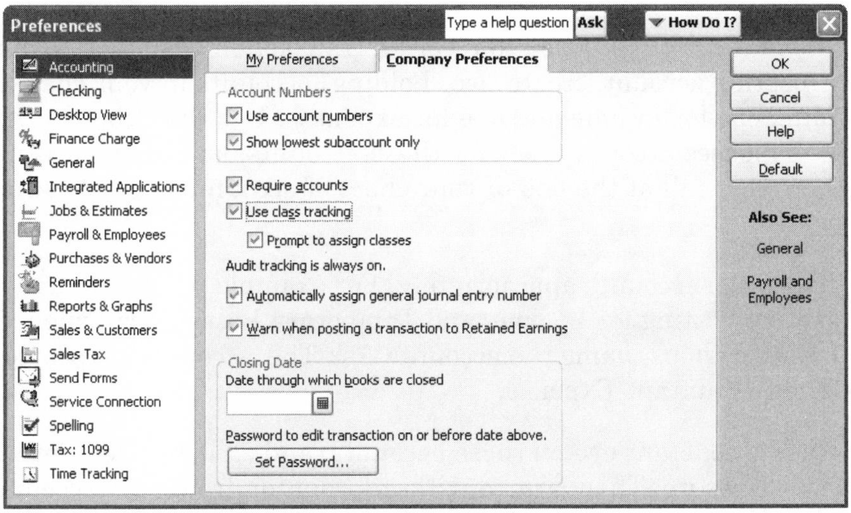

Figure 4-1: The Company Preferences dialog has a variety of important configuration options.

Use Account Numbers

As discussed in Chapter 3, assigning numbers to the accounts in your chart of accounts is a good idea. The Use Account Numbers option enables this feature. When enabled, the New Account and Edit Account dialogs include a field for an account number, and all reports include the account number in addition to the account name.

Show Lowest Subaccount Only

Also discussed in Chapter 3, this tells QuickBooks to display only the subaccount number and name in drop-down lists in transaction windows.

Require Accounts

This option, when enabled, means you cannot record a transaction unless you have assigned the transaction to an account. If you disable the option, QuickBooks will create an account called "Uncategorized" and post the transaction amount to it. (Actually, QuickBooks creates two accounts, one for uncategorized income and the other for uncategorized expenses). Do not disable this option; posting to an uncategorized list is no way to keep books.

If you occasionally need to record a transaction when you're unsure of the posting account, create two "holding" accounts in your chart of accounts, one for income and one for expenses. Use the Other Income and Other Expenses account types for these accounts, and assign account numbers that fall at the end of your chart of accounts (e.g. 9998 and 9999).

Name the accounts appropriately. For example, you could name them Temporary Posting for Income, and Temporary Posting for Expense. Or, even more obvious, name the accounts Ask The Accountant-Income and Ask The Accountant-Expense.

Keep a constant eye on these accounts, and call your accountant as a balance shows up. Then, armed with information from your accountant, edit the original transaction to post it to the appropriate account, or create a journal entry to move the balance (depending on your accountant's preferences—some accountants dislike journal entries, other accountants dislike editing original transactions).

Use Class Tracking

Enabling this option turns on class tracking, without which you cannot manage QuickBooks for a nonprofit organization. Chapter 5 covers setting up and using classes to track programs.

Prompt To Assign Classes

Enabling this option means a reminder appears whenever you fail to fill in the Class field in a transaction window. However, QuickBooks will let you continue to save the transaction without class assignments. A non-profit organization, because it relies on classes to produce accurate reports and track finances, must train users in the importance of assigning classes.

Audit Tracking

This option, which is always on in QuickBooks 2006 and later, can be enabled or disabled in QuickBooks versions previous to 2006. The audit trail keeps a log of all transactions that are changed or removed. To see the audit log, choose Reports → Accountant & Taxes → Audit Trail.

When your file grows large, and if you're running QuickBooks on a network with multiple simultaneous users, the audit trail can make QuickBooks respond a bit slower. However, an audit trail can be an important tool for resolving problems. Remember, unlike most accounting software, QuickBooks permits users to delete transactions, and that security hole could make embezzling easier. The audit trail lets you know when a transaction has been deleted.

Automatically Assign General Journal Entry Number

This option tells QuickBooks to assign a number to a general journal entry automatically. The first time you create a general journal entry, you must fill in a number (or accept the default number, "1"), and thereafter QuickBooks assigns the next available number.

Warn When Posting a Transaction to Retained Earnings

Enabling this option means that when anyone tries to post an amount to the Retained Earnings account, QuickBooks displays a warning message. The message explains that the Retained Earnings account is designed to track profits, and the amounts that are posted to the account automatically are generated, not manually posted through a transaction.

The warning message doesn't prevent the user from continuing with the transaction, and posting to the Retained Earnings account. However, if this is a user who doesn't understand the account (or inadvertently chose the account from a drop-down list), the warning message might prevent the user from going on (which is almost always a good thing).

For for-profit businesses, I always advise that the warning option remain enabled. Business users can spend years running their companies in QuickBooks without ever encountering a need to post anything to the Retained Earnings account.

However, it's different for nonprofit organizations. Users who are knowledgeable about accounting, and/or the organization's own accountant, may use the Retained Earnings account frequently. It's common to create journal entries to move money from the Retained Earnings account into the other net asset accounts that nonprofits use.

If you retain this option (and I think you should), it means that even your accountant will see this message. Clicking OK to clear the message and continue the transaction isn't onerous. In fact, your accountant may be relieved to see the message because it provides some assurance that users haven't been using the account inappropriately.

> **NOTE**: See Chapter 3 for more information about the Retained Earnings account.

Closing Date

This section of the dialog lets you set a closing date for your books, and assign a password to protect transactions that fall on or before the closing date. See Chapter 12 to learn how to close your books at the end of the fiscal year.

Checking Preferences

Click the Checking category in the left pane of the Preferences dialog to configure your preferences for check writing. There are options on both the My Preferences and the Company Preferences tabs.

My Preferences for the Checking Category

The My Preferences tab, seen in Figure 4-2, lets you preselect the bank account you want to use for specific transaction types. This is useful if you have multiple bank accounts, and you transfer funds among them in order to use a specific bank account for a specific purpose.

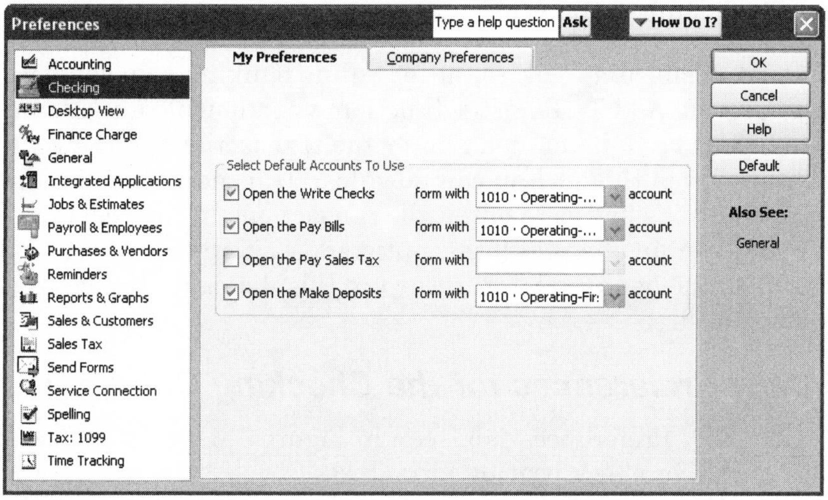

Figure 4-2: Assign transaction types to a default bank account.

For example, you may deposit revenue to an interest bearing account, and then transfer the necessary funds to your operating account when it's time to pay your bills. Even though you can always select a bank account when you're working in a transaction window, pre-selecting the appropriate account eliminates the possibility of error. You've probably noticed that a payroll account isn't listed in this dialog—payroll account information is configured in the Company Preferences tab (discussed next).

Click the check box next to a transaction type to activate its account field. Then click the arrow to display the chart of accounts in a dropdown list, and select the appropriate bank account for that field.

If you have multiple bank accounts and you don't set default options in this dialog, the first time you open a transaction window you must select an account. Thereafter, QuickBooks will use the last-used account for each transaction type.

If you change the account in a future transaction, QuickBooks uses that account automatically for the ensuing transactions of the same type. Setting the default account here means that when you change the account for a single transaction, the next time that transaction type is created, the default account is back.

If you've enabled a bank count for online banking, you can select the option to use the Add To Register function when downloading transactions from your bank if you don't enter the transactions in the register. (Incidentally, even though you can download transactions you didn't bother to enter, it's better to enter all transactions in the register). If you haven't set up online banking, this option doesn't appear in the dialog. (If you set up online banking later, return to this dialog and select the preferences you desire.)

Company Preferences for the Checking Category

In the Company Preferences tab, seen in Figure 4-3, you can choose the default options for check writing procedures.

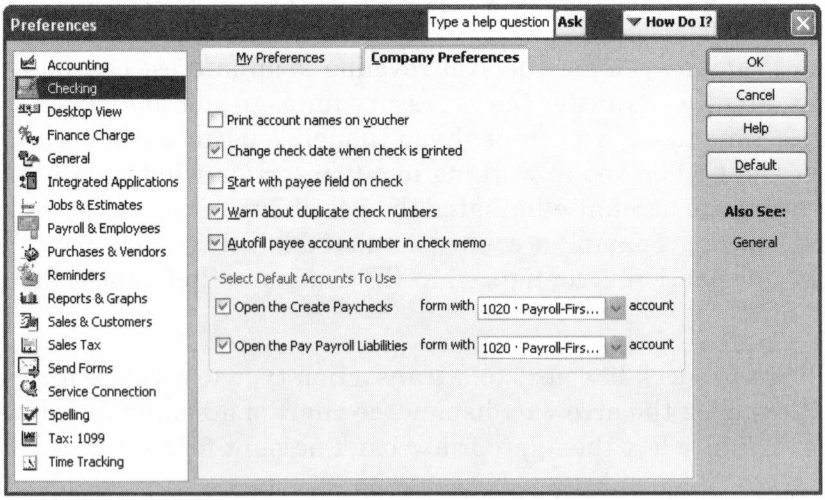

Figure 4-3: Set the default options for check writing.

Print Account Names on Voucher

This option tells QuickBooks to add account information to the voucher (check stub). By default, if you use check forms with vouchers, QuickBooks prints the payee, date, memo, and amount on the voucher. If you enable this option, the following information is added to the voucher:

- For A/P checks, the name of each account to which you posted amounts to create this check, along with the amount posted to each account. This option is useful if you're using check forms that have vouchers, and you tear off and save the vouchers (I don't imagine the vendors to whom you send the checks care about your internal account postings).
- For payroll checks, the name of each payroll item included in the check, along with the amount assigned to each item.
- For checks used to purchase inventory items, the name of each inventory item included in the payment made by this check.

Change Check Date When Check is Printed

This option determines the date that appears on checks you print. This feature is useful if you don't print checks the same day you create them, and you always want the check date that's printed on the check to be the actual date on which you printed the check.

For example, you may run the Pay Bills process, or create direct disbursement checks, every Monday, but you wait until later in the week to print and mail the checks. If this option is disabled, all the checks you print display Monday's date.

Start With Payee Field in Check

This option applies to transaction windows connected to payables. If you enable the option, when you open the transaction window your cursor is automatically placed as follows:

- For the Write Checks window, your cursor is in the Payee field instead of the Bank Account field at the top of the window. The Bank Account field is automatically populated with the default bank account for writing checks (if you selected one in the My

Preferences window), or the bank account you used the last time you worked in the Write Checks window.

- For the Enter Bills window, your cursor is in the Vendor field instead of the Accounts Payable field at the top of the window. However, the Accounts Payable field doesn't appear in the window unless you have multiple A/P accounts in your chart of accounts. If you don't have multiple A/P accounts, the default cursor placement becomes the Vendor field anyway.

- For the Enter Credit Card Charges window, your cursor is in the Purchased From field instead of the Credit Card field at the top of the window. This is only meaningful if you set up your credit cards as liability accounts and enter credit card charges as you incur them, instead of paying the credit card bill as a regular vendor account. (If you opt to track your credit cards as liabilities, you must perform credit card account reconciliation.)

Warn About Duplicate Check Numbers

This option, enabled by default, makes sure you don't use the same check number twice (unless you're silly enough to ignore the warning, because QuickBooks only warns, and won't actually prevent you from using a check number twice). Disabling this option can cause extreme stress when you're trying to reconcile your bank account, go over your finances with your accountant, or deal with a disputed bill payment.

Autofill Payee Account Number in Check Memo

This option, enabled by default, is another useful feature. Most vendors maintain an account number for their customers, and your account number can be automatically printed in the check's Memo line on the lower-left section of the check. For this to work you must fill in your account number in the Vendor record (on the Additional Information tab).

Select Default Accounts

Use this section to set the default accounts for payroll checks, if you do payroll in-house. Select the account to use for payroll checks, and the account to use for remitting payroll liabilities.

Online Banking

You can enable payee aliasing (the option only appears on the dialog if you've enabled online banking). Payee aliasing lets you match payee names you enter when you use online bill paying to the existing vendor names in your QuickBooks company file.

Many people don't use the exact spelling of the vendor name when working online, and QuickBooks can't match the transactions when you download your online transactions. The ability to establish an alias means you can tell QuickBooks "I use Joe's Hardware when paying the bill online, but my vendor record is named Hardware-Joe". When a transaction using an alias is downloaded, QuickBooks searches the aliases in your vendor records, and automatically links the alias to the vendor name.

Desktop View Preferences

In versions of QuickBooks prior to 2006, only the My Preferences tab has options in this dialog.

My Preferences for Desktop View

The My Preferences tab, seen in Figure 4-4, offers choices about the way the QuickBooks window looks and behaves. The available options are not just aesthetic, some of them have a direct effect on the way you work in QuickBooks, and the amount of time it takes to open and close QuickBooks.

In the View section, you can choose between displaying one QuickBooks window at a time, or multiple windows. Choosing One Window limits QuickBooks to showing one window at a time, even if you have multiple windows open. The windows are stacked atop each other, and only the top window is visible.

You can switch among the windows by selecting a window's listing in the Open Window List. If you don't display the Open Window List, use the Window menu on the QuickBooks menu bar to select the window you want to work in.

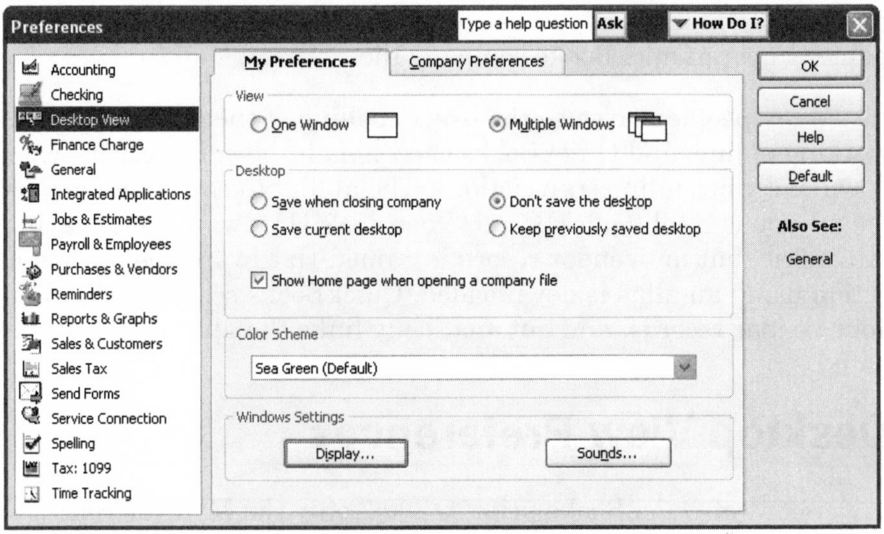

Figure 4-4: Customize the QuickBooks software window.

Choosing Multiple Windows activates the arrangement commands on the Windows menu item. These commands allow you arrange open windows in a way you find convenient. You can overlap the windows so the titles are visible, or arrange multiple windows side by side so you can get to the window you need with a single click. Another advantage to choosing Multiple Windows is that you can resize a window, which is another way to see, and quickly move between, multiple windows.

In the Desktop section, specify what QuickBooks should do when you exit the software.

Save When Closing Company

Selecting this option means that the state of the desktop is remembered when you close the company file, or close QuickBooks with the current company file loaded. The windows that were open when you closed the file reappear when you open the file, so you can pick up where you left off.

Save Current Desktop

Use this option to lock the state of the desktop as it is at this moment. The same desktop configuration appears every time you open QuickBooks. Select this option after you've opened or closed the QuickBooks windows you want to see when you start the software.

If you choose this option, an additional choice named Keep Previously Saved Desktop appears on the window the next time you open the Desktop View category of the Preferences dialog. You can select that option, and if you re-align the desktop and make it the new "locked" desktop, you can restore the desktop to the previous settings if you change your mind.

Don't Save The Desktop

This option tells QuickBooks to ignore the state of the desktop when you close a company, or the software. When you open QuickBooks, or open a new company, the desktop has no open windows.

TIP: QuickBooks takes quite a bit of time to open after you select it from your Programs menu or a desktop icon. In addition, when you exit QuickBooks, it takes a long time for the program window to close. If you hate to wait, you can improve the speed by selecting the option Don't Save The Desktop and by deselecting the option to display the Navigator or Home page.

In QuickBooks versions prior to 2006, this dialog has a Navigators section, and the option to display a navigator whenever you open a company file is selected by default. This means the navigator window appears when you start QuickBooks, because QuickBooks opens the last used company file when it opens. If you don't want to use the navigator, deselect the option. If you want to open a navigator when you open a company file, select the navigator you want from the drop-down list.

Starting with QuickBooks 2006, the Home page (along with Customer, Vendor, Employee, and Report Centers) replaces the

Navigators. You can specify whether you want to open the Home page whenever you open this company file.

Color Scheme and Windows Settings

In the Color Scheme section, you can select a scheme from the drop-down list. The Windows Settings section contains buttons that lead you to Windows dialogs for setting Display and Sounds options. Clicking either button opens the associated applet in your Windows Control Panel. Be careful about making changes because your changes affect your computer and all your software, not just QuickBooks.

Company Preferences for Desktop View

Starting with QuickBooks 2006, the Company Preferences tab offers choices about the icons you want to place on the Home page (see Figure 4-5).

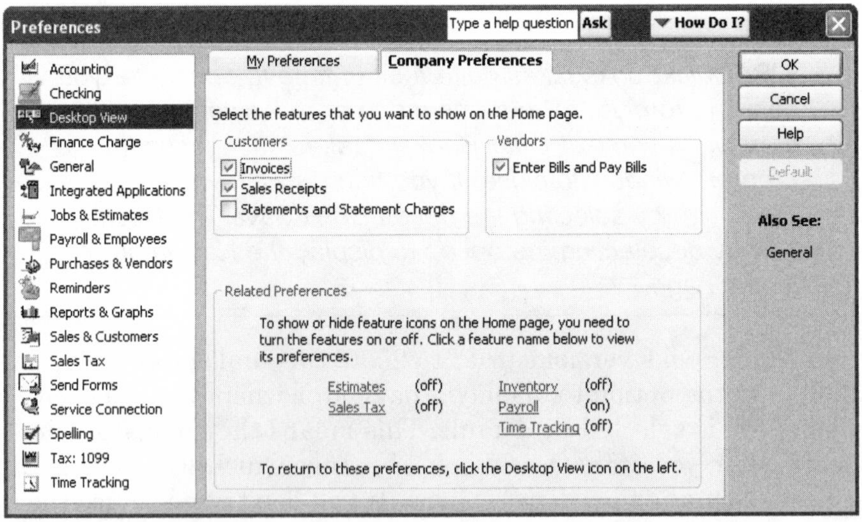

Figure 4-5: Configure the Home page for instant access to all the QuickBooks functions you use.

The dialog displays the current status of features; in order to have an icon on the Home page, a feature must be enabled. Clicking a feature's link takes you to the Preferences dialog for that feature, where you can enable the feature and set the its configuration options.

General Preferences

The General category has options on both tabs, although the selections in the My Preferences tab have a greater effect on your comfort and efficiency as you work in QuickBooks.

My Preferences for the General Category

The options in the My Preferences tab of the General category (see Figure 4-6) are designed to let you control the way QuickBooks behaves while you're working. If your QuickBooks system is set up to have users login, the options you select here have no effect on any other QuickBooks user, so you're free to tweak the settings to your own advantage.

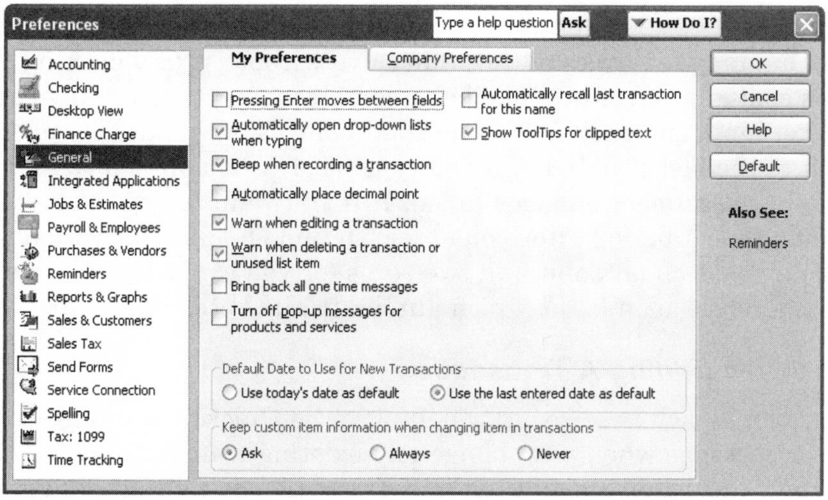

Figure 4-6: Select the options that reflect the way you want to work in QuickBooks.

Pressing Enter Moves Between Fields

This option exists for people who always forget that the Tab key is the normal key for moving from field to field in any Windows software application. When these people press Enter instead of Tab, the record they're working on is saved, even though they haven't finished filling out all the fields.

If you fall in this category, QuickBooks gives you a break from the need to force yourself to get used to the way Windows works. If you select this option, when you press the Enter key, your cursor moves to the next field in the window you're using. To save your work, click the appropriate button (usually labeled Save or OK).

Beep When Recording A Transaction

For some transactions types, QuickBooks provides sound effects to announce the fact that you've saved the transaction. Besides a beep, you might hear the chime of a bell (well, it's more like a "ding"), or a ka-ching (the sound of an old fashioned cash register). If you don't want to hear sound effects as you work in QuickBooks, you can deselect the option.

Automatically Place Decimal Point

This is a handy feature, and I couldn't live without it (my desktop calculator is configured for the same behavior). It means that when you enter characters in a currency field, a decimal point is automatically placed to the left of the last two digits. If you type 5421, when you move to the next field the number changes to 54.21. If you want to type in even dollar amounts, type a period after you enter 54, and QuickBooks will automatically add the decimal point and two zeros (or you can take the time to enter the zeros, as in 5400, which automatically becomes 54.00).

Warn When Editing A Transaction

This option, which is selected by default, tells QuickBooks to flash a warning message when you change any existing transaction and try to close the transaction window without explicitly saving the changes. This means you have a chance to abandon the edits. If you deselect the option, the edited transaction is saved automatically, unless it is linked to, and affects, other transactions (in which case, a warning message appears to apprise you of this complication).

It's not a good idea to disable this option, because there are times when you make changes to a transaction, and you don't want to save the changes. The most common occurrence is when you want to print a packing slip for an invoice. After you save the invoice, you can bring it back into the Create Invoices window and select a packing slip template. That template lacks many of the fields that are important for an invoice, such as the price of the goods and services you sold. After you print the packing slip, and close the window, you can click No when QuickBooks asks if you want to save the change you made to the invoice.

Warn When Deleting A Transaction Or Unused List Item

When selected, this option produces a warning when you delete a transaction or an item that has not been used in a transaction—it's a standard message asking you to confirm a delete action. (QuickBooks doesn't permit you to delete an item that has been used in a transaction.)

Bring Back All One-Time Messages

One-time messages are those dialogs that include a Don't Show This Message Again option. If you've selected the Don't Show option, select this check box to see those messages again (and you'll probably once again select the Don't Show This Message Again option).

Turn Off Popup Messages For Products And Services

This option is only available in QuickBooks 2006 and later. Selecting it stops QuickBooks from displaying messages that ask you if you're interested in buying additional services from QuickBooks.

Automatically Recall Last Transaction For This Name

This option means that QuickBooks will present the last transaction for any name (for instance, a vendor) with all the fields filled with the data from that last transaction. Most of the time, you merely have to change the amount. All the other information (such as the posting accounts, and the text in a memo field), can often be retained for the current transaction

This feature is useful for transactions that are repeated occasionally, or irregularly. (Repeating transactions that are scheduled regularly are best managed with memorized transactions.). One problem that occurs with this option is that users don't remember to check the text in the memo field, which often contains the invoice number from the vendor.

The current transaction is usually linked to a different invoice number, so if you enable this option you need to get into the habit of checking all fields to make sure they're appropriately filled out.

Show ToolTips For Clipped Text

This option (enabled by default) means that if there is more text in a field than you can see, hovering your mouse over the field causes the entire block of text to display. Very handy!

Default Date To Use For New Transactions

Use this option to tell QuickBooks whether you want the Date field to show the current date or the date of the last transaction you entered when you open a transaction window.

If you frequently enter transactions for the same date over a period of several days (for example, you start preparing invoices on the 27th of the month, but the invoice date is the last day of the month), select the option to use the last entered date so you can just keep going. When that job is finished, and you're back to entering individual transactions, you can return to this window and change the setting.

Of course, next month, when you begin the repetitive work, return to this window, and reset the option. It's actually faster to set the option as you need it than to remember to change the date for each transaction you're creating.

Keep Custom Item Information When Changing Item In Transactions

This option, available only in QuickBooks 2006 and later, is a bit complicated to explain (and I can't believe it was added as the result of widespread user demand).

If you enter an item in a transaction, and then type your own customized text in the Description column, and then say "Oops, that's not the item I meant to select", and then you select a different item in the Item column, QuickBooks will keep the customized text you typed in the Description column instead of entering the default description text for the new item you selected.

Got it? If this happens to you all the time, select Always, if it happens to you sometimes, select Ask, and if you don't think you're likely to face this scenario, select Never.

Company Preferences for the General Category

The Company Preferences tab in the General section has the following three configuration options:

- Time Format, which lets you choose the format you want to use when you enter data related to time. Your choices are Decimal (for example, 11.5 hours) or the Minutes, which uses the standard HH:MM format (e.g., 11:30).
- Always Show Years As 4 Digits, which you can select if you prefer to display the year with four digits (01/01/2005 instead of 01/01/05).
- Never Update Name Information When Saving Transactions. By default, QuickBooks asks if you want to update the original information for a name when you change it during a transaction entry.

It's usually a good idea to select that last option, which is disabled by default. The best example of this scenario is when an organization doesn't want to add names for certain types of transactions that occur frequently, and don't need to be tracked in detail.

You may collect donations for which you don't want to create a record for the donor, because you don't want to end up with hundreds or thousands of these donor names in your QuickBooks file. Perhaps you're tracking those names outside of QuickBooks, or you don't need a permanent record of the names because you're not planning to track the donor's activities. When you receive a donation, you use a generic customer name (such as Donor) in the Sales Receipt transaction window.

However, sometimes a donor wants a printed receipt, and wants a name and address on the receipt. In the Sales Receipt window, you fill in the real donor's name and address, and print the receipt. When you close the window, you don't want QuickBooks to offer to change the information on the generic customer named Donor by adding the name and address you typed into the transaction window.

Incidentally, the name and address information for the transaction isn't lost; it's retained in the original transaction window. If you want to find a the name and address of a particular donor, open a Sales Receipt window and use the Previous button to move backwards to find the transaction. Alternatively, open the register of the appropriate Income account and double-click the transaction line to open the original transaction window.

Jobs & Estimates

The Company Information tab of this category lets you set the terminology you want to use for tracking jobs (grants and contracts). As you can see in Figure 4-7, the preconfigured terms are generic, and might do. However, many nonprofits prefer to change the status text to more specific terminology.

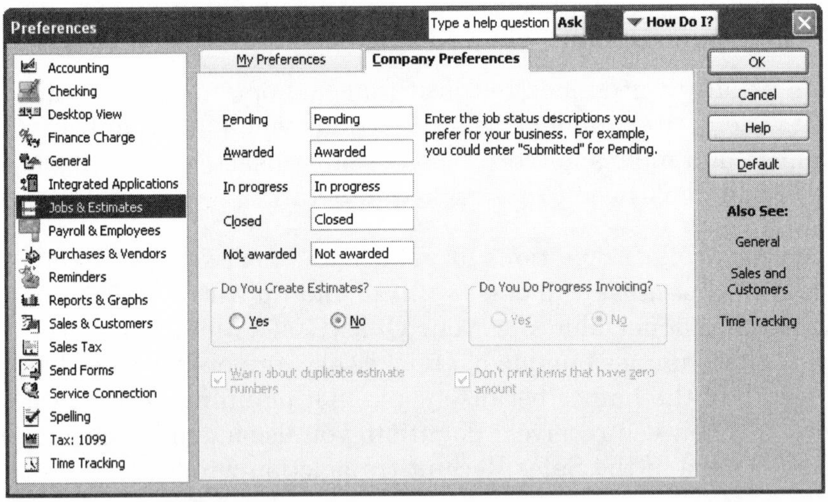

Figure 4-7: Change the text that describes the status of the jobs you're tracking.

Some nonprofits change the Pending text to "RFP" (to indicate an RFP has been submitted), or use the term "Submitted". The term "Completed" might work better for nonprofits than the default text "Closed".

Sales & Customers

Some of the options in this category cover features that aren't used much (or at all) by nonprofit organizations. The functions that are pertinent, however, are quite powerful, and I'll discuss those in this section. All of the options are in the Company Preferences tab, seen in Figure 4-8.

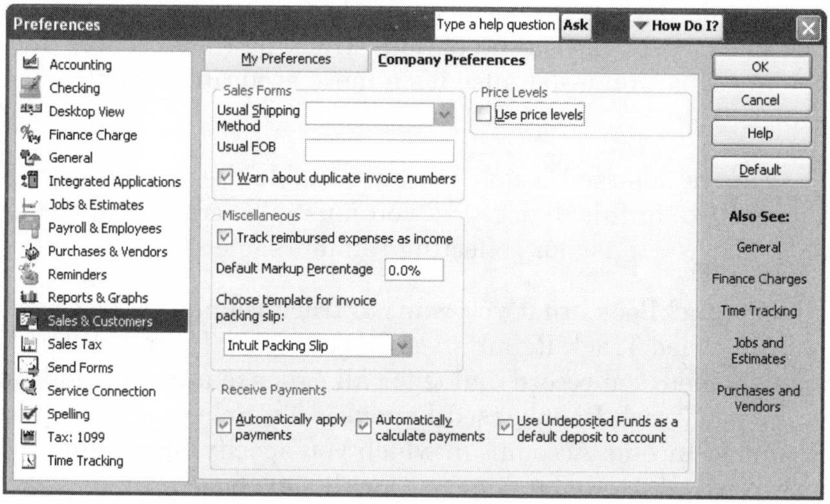

Figure 4-8: For nonprofits, these configuration settings work well.

Track Reimbursed Expenses as Income

A reimbursable expense is one for which you and the customer (donor agency) agree that you can invoice the customer to recover certain costs. There are two common types of reimbursable expenses:

- General expenses, such as long-distance telephone charges, parking and tolls, and other incidental expenses. The portion of the expense that applies to the agreement with the customer is invoiced to the customer.
- Specific goods or services that are purchased specifically to fulfill the terms of the agreement with the customer.

When you have a reimbursable expense, you can handle the accounting in either of the following ways:

- Pay the bill, invoice the customer, and post the reimbursement amount to the expense account you used when you paid the bill. This washes (cancels) the original expense, and your operating statement shows only the net amounts for the expense accounts.
- Pay the bill and post the reimbursement to an income account that's created specifically for that purpose. This method lets you track totals for both the expense and the reimbursements.

You should discuss these choices with your accountant, but many organizations prefer the second option—tracking the expenses and reimbursements separately—because it's a more accurate view of your income and expenses.

To track reimbursed costs, you must enable the reimbursement tracking feature in this dialog, and you must also create the income accounts that you'll use for collecting reimbursements.

To tell QuickBooks that you want to track reimbursable costs, select the option labeled Track Reimbursed Expenses As Income. When the option is enabled, the record dialog for all expense accounts adds another option, named Track Reimbursed Expenses To. Selecting this option adds a field named Income Account, in which you specify the income account to which you'll post reimbursements for this expense.

Whenever you post a vendor expense to this account, and also indicate that the expense is reimbursable, the amount you charge the customer for reimbursement is automatically posted to the income account that's linked to this expense account.

You may have multiple expense accounts that qualify for reimbursable expenses, such as portions of telephone bills, travel expenses, subcontractor expenses, and so on. The easiest way to manage all of this would be to configure those expense accounts to track reimbursements and post the income to an income account you create for that purpose. After all, it's only important to know how much of your total income was a result of reimbursements.

Sadly, QuickBooks doesn't approach this with a great deal of logic. Instead, you must create a separate income account for each expense account that's configured for reimbursements. As a result, if you have multiple expense accounts for which you may receive reimbursement (a highly likely scenario), you must also create multiple income accounts for accepting reimbursed expenses.

Most of the time, you only care about the total income received as reimbursement, so the best way to set up the income accounts you'll need is to use subaccounts. Create a parent account named Reimbursed Expenses, and then create subaccounts for each type of expense (Reimbursed Telephone, Reimbursed Travel, and so on). Your reports will show the total amount of income you received for reimbursed expenses, and you can ignore the individual account totals unless you have some reason to audit them.

NOTE: The Preferences dialog includes a field in which you can tell QuickBooks how much to mark up any expense you're going to invoice as a reimbursable expense. This is not a common practice in a nonprofit organization.

Chapter 7 has directions for recording an expense as reimbursable when you pay a vendor bill, and Chapter 6 shows you how to create an invoice to recover reimbursable expenses.

Receiving Payments from Customers

The Receive Payments section of the Sales & Customers Preferences dialog has options that let you determine the way you manage income. (If you're using an older version of QuickBooks, the Receive Payments options don't exist.)

Automatically Apply Payments

This option tells QuickBooks to apply payments to invoices automatically, using the following rules:

- If the payment matches the amount of an invoice, it is automatically applied to that invoice.
- If the payment doesn't match the amount of any invoice, it is automatically applied to the oldest invoice.

This option is enabled by default, and if you use balance forward accounts receivable, it saves you some steps. This is also a handy feature if your customers almost always pay off the oldest invoice.

If you disable this option, you must manually select the invoice(s) against which you're applying payments.

TIP: You can always "unapply" an automatically applied payment if the customer's check was for a different, or later, invoice.)

Automatically Calculate Payments

If you tell QuickBooks to calculate customer payments automatically, you can skip entering the amount of the payment in the Amount field at the top of the Receive Payments window. Head directly for the list of invoices in the Receive Payments window, and as you select each invoice for payment, QuickBooks calculates the total and places it in the Amount field. If your customers' checks always match the amount of an open invoice, this saves you some data entry.

If the option is disabled, when you select an invoice listing without entering the amount of the payment first, QuickBooks issues an error message.

This option is enabled by default, and the first time you select an invoice before entering the payment amount in the Amount field, QuickBooks displays a message explaining the option, and asking if you'd like to disable it.

Use Undeposited Funds as a Default "Deposit To" Account

Selecting this preference causes QuickBooks to set Undeposited Funds as the default account for depositing payments. When this preference is enabled, the Deposit To field disappears from the Receive Payments and Sales Receipt transaction windows. The money you're receiving in those windows is automatically deposited to the Undeposited Funds account, and you use the Make Deposits feature to post bank deposits.

When this preference is off, QuickBooks displays the Deposit To field on the Receive Payments and Enter Sales Receipt windows. You must choose a destination account from the drop-down list. (The Undeposited Funds account is available in that list.)

Using Undeposited Funds, and moving the money to your bank account register after you actually go to the bank, makes bank reconciliation easier. If you receive three checks in one day, and post each receipt to your bank account, your bank statement won't show the three individual checks. Instead, the bank statement shows the total you deposited on that day. Using the Make Deposits feature to post all the checks you took to the bank to your bank account register reflects reality, matches the information on the statement, and makes bank reconciliation easier.

Sales Tax

Although nonprofits are generally tax-exempt when they purchase goods and services, many nonprofit organizations sell goods and services for which they must collect and remit sales tax. Check with your accountant to see if any of your retail (or quasi-retail) activities require you to apply sales tax. If you do, read this section to learn how to manage sales tax in QuickBooks. (Don't forget to get a sales tax license from your state.)

Enabling the Sales Tax Feature

Start by setting the basic options for sales tax in the dialog shown in Figure 4-9. You must set up sales tax codes to link to your customers, so you know whether a customer is liable for sales tax. You must also set up sales tax items, so you can set a rate (a percentage), and you must link the sales tax item to a taxing authority (usually your state tax department).

Enable the sales tax feature by selecting the Yes option under the label Do You Charge Sales Tax? Then, in the Owe Sales Tax section, specify whether you remit sales taxes when you invoice your customers, or when you receive payments from your customers. The information that arrived with your sales tax license should clearly state which option is applicable in your state.

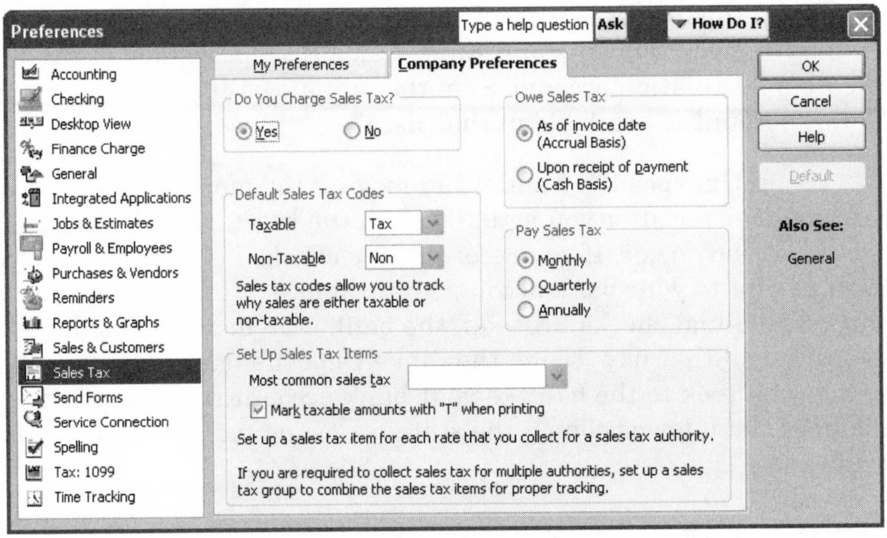

Figure 4-9: Check your sales tax license for the information you
need to configure sales tax remittances.

In the Pay Sales Tax section, indicate the frequency of your
remittance to the taxing authority. You don't get to choose—the
notice that arrived with your sales tax reporting forms (commonly a
coupon book) indicates the schedule you must use. Many states base
the frequency on the amount of tax you collect, usually looking at
your returns for a specific period—perhaps one specific quarter (the
term they examine is usually referred to as the *lookback* period). If
your sales tax liability changes dramatically during the lookback
period, you may receive notice from the state that your remittance
interval has changed. (They'll probably send you new forms.) If that
occurs, don't forget to return to the Preferences window to change the
interval.

More and more states are moving to online payments for remitting
sales tax. If your state has adopted this policy, it notified you of your
remittance interval, and provided the web site address for reporting your
tax liability. In that case, you don't receive a coupon book.

Most states that use online reporting and payment offer two methods
for remitting your sales tax collections:

- An electronic withdrawal from your bank, in which case you must fill out the bank information (routing code and account number).
- A credit card payment, in which case you must sign up with an approved vendor for collecting the sales tax via credit card and remitting the amount to the state. (This method usually involves fees from the approved credit card vendor).

Understanding Tax Codes and Tax Items

QuickBooks has two discrete entities for configuring sales tax: Sales Tax Codes and Sales Tax Items. Many QuickBooks users get them confused, so I'll attempt to clarify everything, and I'll start by defining each entity:

- A sales tax code indicates tax liability, which means the entity to which it's linked (a customer or an item) is deemed taxable or nontaxable, depending on the code. Tax codes contain no information about the tax rate or the taxing authority; they just offer a Yes or No answer to the question "taxable?"
- A sales tax item contains information about the tax rate and the taxing authority to which you remit taxes and reports. Like all items, the sales tax item appears on sales forms. The amount of tax due is calculated when you add the sales tax item to the taxable line items (products and services) on an invoice or sales receipt.

Working with Sales Tax Codes

Linking a sales tax code to customers and items lets you (and QuickBooks) know whether sales tax should be calculated for that item for this customer. A customer's sales tax liability is like a light switch; it's either on or off. However, if a customer is liable for sales tax, it doesn't mean that every item you sell the customer is taxable, because some items aren't taxable—like customers, items have a tax liability switch that operates as an on/off switch. For sales tax to kick in, both the item and the customer must have their tax liability status set to "taxable".

I can't give you a list of taxable/nontaxable categories, because each state sets its own rules. For example, in Pennsylvania, food and some other necessities of life aren't taxable, but some types of consulting services are. Other states don't tax services at all, reserving the sales tax for products. Some states seem to tax everything—California comes to mind.

QuickBooks prepopulates the Sales Tax Preferences dialog with the following two sales tax codes:

- Tax, which means liable for sales tax
- Non, which means not liable for sales tax

For many of us, that's enough; we don't need any additional tax codes for customers or for items. We can move on to creating sales tax items so tax rates can be calculated on sales forms. However, for some organizations, those two tax codes aren't enough. Some taxing authorities care about the "why"—most often they want to know why a customer isn't liable for sales tax.

If your state sales tax report form wants to know why a customer is taxable, it's probably really asking about the tax rate for that customer, not for the "yes/no" designation of tax liability. Many states are setting up multiple sales tax rates, basing the rate on location (county, city, town, or zip code). Identifying a customer as "taxable because he's in the Flummox County of our state" means the tax charged on sales to that customer are the tax rates assigned to Flummox County. (Tax rates are configured in sales tax items, not sales tax codes. See the section "Working with Sales Tax Items".)

Most taxing authorities are only interested in the "why not" question. Is a customer nontaxable because it's out of state and the rules say you don't have to collect taxes for out-of-state sales? Is the customer nontaxable because it's a nonprofit organization, or a government agency? Is the customer nontaxable because it's a wholesale business and collects sales tax from its own customers? If your state requires this information, you must create tax codes to match the reporting needs required by your state.

Creating Sales Tax Codes

If you want to create codes to track customer sales tax status in a manner more detailed than "taxable" and "nontaxable," follow these steps to add a new sales tax code:

1. Choose Lists → Sales Tax Code List.
2. Press Ctrl-N to open the New Sales Tax Code window.
3. Enter the name of the new code, using up to three characters.
4. Enter a description to make it easier to interpret the code.
5. Select Taxable if you're entering a code to track taxable sales.
6. Select Non-taxable if you're entering a code to track nontaxable sales.
7. Click Next to set up another tax code.
8. Click OK when you've finished adding tax codes.

This procedure works nicely for specifying different types of nontaxable customers. For example, you could create tax codes similar to the following for nontaxable categories:

- NPO for nonprofit organizations
- GOV for government agencies
- WSL for wholesale businesses
- OOS for out-of-state customers (if you aren't required to collect taxes from out-of-state customers)

For taxable customers, the permutations and combinations are much broader, of course. If you're required to collect and remit sales tax for some additional states, just create codes for customers in those states, using the postal abbreviations for each state.

The problem is that QuickBooks' tax code setup doesn't work well for categorizing taxable customers if you do business in a state with complicated multiple tax rates. Those states issue codes for each location and its linked rate, and the codes are almost always more than three characters—but three characters is all QuickBooks permits for a sales tax code.

The workaround for this lies in the ability to assign a sales tax item to a customer, as long as the customer's configuration indicates "taxable" (using the built-in Tax code, or any other taxable-yes-based code you created). Sales tax items are discussed next.

Working with Sales Tax Items

A sales tax item is a collection of data about a sales tax, including the rate and the agency to which the sales tax is remitted. QuickBooks uses sales tax items to calculate the amount on the Tax field in sales forms, and to prepare reports for tax authorities.

Creating the Most Common Sales Tax Item

The Sales Tax Preferences dialog has a field named Most Common Sales Tax, and you must enter a sales tax item (not a sales tax code) in that field. This is the tax item that's automatically assigned to customers you create.

This step is required in order to save the information in the Sales Tax Preferences dialog, but you haven't yet created any sales tax items, because you can't create sales tax items until you've enabled the sales tax preference. If you do business in a state that has a single sales tax, the sales tax item you create here works fine. If you do business in a state that requires you to report multiple rates, you may need to assign customers and items a sales tax group item, not a single sales tax item.

However, you can't create a group item in this dialog, so you can invent any sales tax item you wish in this dialog (it's a placeholder). After you've enabled sales tax collection, you can create your sales tax items and groups. Then, you can return to this dialog and change the most common sales tax item to the one that really is the most common sales tax item.

Click the arrow next to the Most Common Sales Tax field, and choose <Add New> from the drop-down list to open the New Item dialog. Follow these steps to create the new sales tax item:

1. Select Sales Tax Item as the item type.
2. In the Tax Name field, enter a name for the item.
3. Enter a description to describe this sales tax on your transaction forms.
4. Enter the tax rate. QuickBooks knows the rate is a percentage, so it automatically adds the percent sign to the numbers you type (for instance, enter 6.5 if the rate is 6.5%).
5. Select the tax agency (the vendor) to which you pay the tax from the drop-down list, or create the vendor by choosing <Add New> (see Chapter 2 for information on adding vendors).
6. Click OK.

In the future, when you need to enter additional sales tax items or groups, open the Item list and press Ctrl-N to open the New Item dialog.

When you create new sales tax items, you can use the Tax Name field to enter those complicated, pesky tax rate codes if you're in a state that has codes you couldn't use because of the three-character limitation of the tax code in QuickBooks. In fact, even if you'd created tax codes for multiple tax venues and attached them to customers, you'd still have to create these tax items in order to calculate rates and assign the tax authorities.

When you've finished configuring sales tax, click OK to close the Sales Tax dialog. QuickBooks displays a message offering you the opportunity to assign a tax status to existing customers and existing non-inventory and inventory parts (see Figure 4-10). This tax status query is about a tax code, the Yes or No taxable status, not about applying a tax item to customers and items.

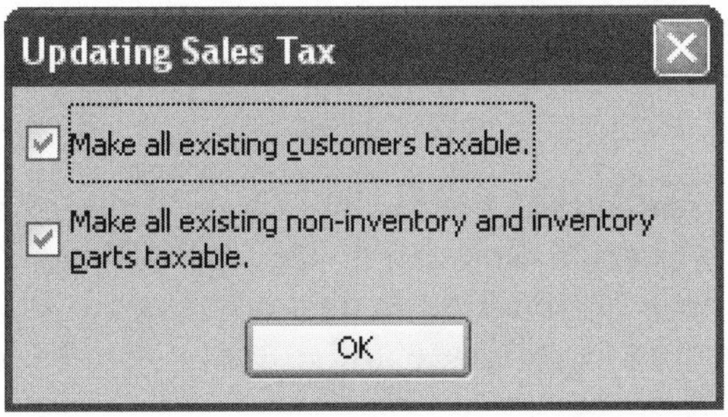

Figure 4-10: Automatically apply a tax status to existing entities in your company file.

Select or deselect the options as needed. QuickBooks marks all existing customers and inventory/non-inventory items taxable or nontaxable, depending on your selection.

Unfortunately, if you have existing service items, they aren't marked taxable, and if they are taxable, you'll have to edit your service items to change their tax status (editing items is discussed in Chapter 5).

The default you set doesn't just apply to existing customers and items. As you add new customers and items, they are automatically marked with a tax code of taxable or nontaxable, matching the selection you made in this dialog.

Unfortunately, the automatic application of the tax status to newly created items isn't limited to inventory and non-inventory parts; it includes new Service items and Other Charges items you create. If your services are not taxable, you'll have to make sure you change the tax status of each service item you create in the future.

This is the same function that did *not* mark service items taxable when you were offered the opportunity to mark customers and inventory/non-inventory parts taxable. Now, new service items you create are automatically marked as taxable.

Linking Customers to Sales Tax Items

All customer records contain both a sales tax code and a sales tax item. When you create a new customer, assuming you opted to make customers taxable, the sales tax item you specified in the Most Common Sales Tax Item in the Sales Tax Preferences dialog is automatically applied.

If you're in one of those states that have adopted multiple tax rates depending on the customer's location, you can go through all your customer records and change the Tax Item field (on the Additional Info tab) to the sales tax item you created for the rate and authority that the customer falls under.

If that sounds incredibly boring, you can wait until the next time you create a sales transaction for each customer. When you open a sales transaction form and enter a customer name, the customer's sales tax item appears in the Tax field, right under the line items. (The customer tax code appears below the sales form, at the bottom of the form's window.) If you change the sales tax item on the sales form, when you save the transaction QuickBooks offers to change the customer record to match the change in the sales tax item. Very handy!

Sales Tax Groups

In some states, the tax imposed is really two taxes, and the taxing authority collects a single check from you, but insists on a breakdown in the reports you send. For example, in Pennsylvania, the state sales tax is 6%, but businesses in Philadelphia and Allegheny Counties must charge an extra 1%. The customer pays 7% tax on taxable items, and a check for 7% of taxable sales is remitted to the state's revenue department. However, the report that accompanies the check must break down the remittance into the individual taxes (the subtotals for the 6% tax and the 1% tax, and the total for both taxes).

In other states that have different rates for certain cities or counties, the customer pays a single tax, but the business that collects the tax remits two reports and two checks: the portion of the tax that represents the basic state sales tax is remitted to the state, and the locally added tax is remitted to the local taxing authority.

Your challenge is to display and calculate a single tax for the customer on your invoices and sales receipts, and yet be able to report multiple taxes to the taxing authorities. Sales tax groups meet this challenge.

A sales tax group is a single tax entity that appears on a sales transaction, but behind the scenes, it's really multiple sales tax items. QuickBooks creates the tax amount on the transaction by calculating each of the multiple entries in the group and displaying the total (the customer is being charged the "combo" rate). When you prepare sales tax reports and checks, QuickBooks breaks out the individual totals.

A sales tax group is an item, and you create it the way you create a sales tax item (in the Items list), but the sales tax items that are included in the group must be created first. For example, in Pennsylvania, businesses in Philadelphia County create the following items:

• A Sales Tax item named PABasic (or something similar), configured for 6%, and specifying the vendor code for the Pennsylvania Department of Revenue as the tax agency.

- A Sales Tax item named Phila (or something similar), configured for 1%, and specifying the vendor code for the Pennsylvania Department of Revenue as the tax agency.
- A Sales Tax Group item named PA Tax (or something similar), which consists of both of the previously created items (see Figure 4-11).

If your sales tax reporting rules are to send the basic state sales tax to the state, and remit the local sales tax to a local taxing authority, use the same system described here, but specify the appropriate vendor codes for the tax agencies connected to each tax item in the tax group. QuickBooks will respond correctly when you run reports and create the checks.

Tax 1099

If you hire subcontractors or freelance professionals for whom you must issue 1099's at the end of the year, this dialog is the place to set up your 1099 tracking (see Figure 4-12). After you configure your 1099 options, you must remember to specify the 1099 check box in each applicable vendor record. See Chapter 5 for information on setting up vendors.

You must assign an account to each 1099 category you use. You can assign multiple accounts to a single 1099 category, but you cannot assign any account to more than one 1099 category. For example, if you have an expense account "subcontractors", and an expense account "outside consultants", both of the accounts can be linked to the 1099 category Nonemployee Compensation. However, once you link those accounts to that category, you cannot use those same accounts in any other 1099 category.

To assign a single account to a category, click the category to select it. Click the text in the account column (it says "none") and then click the arrow to select an account for this category.

To assign multiple accounts to a category, instead of selecting an account after you click the arrow, choose the Selected Accounts option (at the top of the list). In the Select Account dialog, select Manual and scroll through the list, clicking each account you want to include. Selecting an account puts a check mark next to its listing.

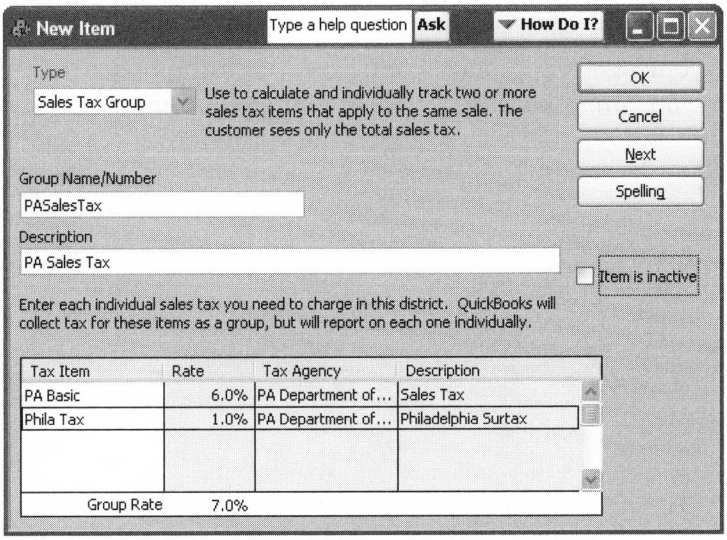

Figure 4-11: A Sales Tax Group is a combination of multiple sales tax items.

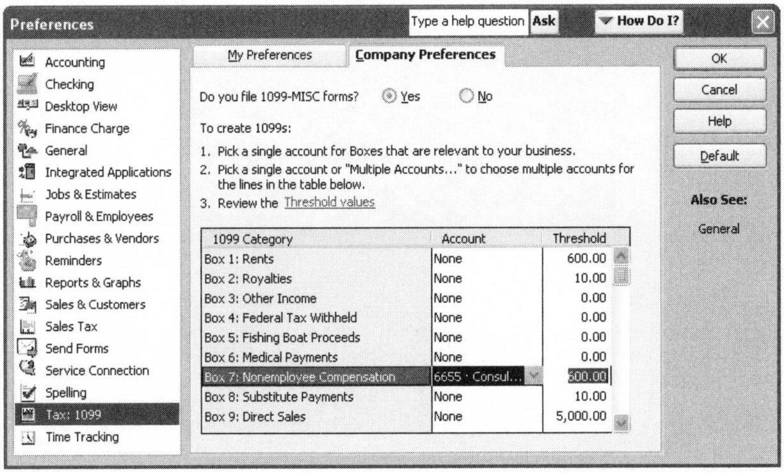

Figure 4-12: Configure the accounts that can be linked to vendors who receive a Form 1099.

If you don't want to scroll through the list, and you know which accounts you want to include, select Automatic. Then enter an account and click Apply, and repeat until you've entered all the accounts. Click OK to assign the accounts to the 1099 category.

Now that your preferences are configured, and the features you need are turned on, you can start using your QuickBooks company file.

Chapter 5

Configuring Classes and Lists

Using classes to track programs

Setting up your lists

Creating custom fields

Lists are mini-files within your QuickBooks company data file, and they contain listings of the data you use when you create a transaction. For example, your customers (donors) and vendors are lists. (Database developers usually refer to these files-within-the-main-file as *tables*.)

Classes are really just another list, but I'm treating them separately because they're so important for nonprofit accounting with QuickBooks. For nonprofit organizations, classes provide the only way to track and report on programs. You cannot track this information with the chart of accounts, because QuickBooks doesn't support a divisional account structure. (Chapter 1 has a full discussion of that topic.)

Classes

Nonprofit organizations can't use QuickBooks without using classes to track transactions. Without classes, getting the reports you need for funding agencies, government agencies, and your board of directors is extremely difficult. You either have to spend many hours (or days) entering transactions into a spreadsheet program, or spend a lot of money to have your accountant perform tasks (in a spreadsheet program) that wouldn't be necessary if you'd used classes.

NOTE: *To use classes you must enable the class feature. As explained in Chapter 4, you accomplish this in the Preferences dialog, in the Accounting category. Don't forget to turn on the option to prompt users to assign classes if they try to save a transaction without filling out the class field.*

Planning the Class List

By law (for nonprofits that file tax forms), and according to accounting standards, you must track the total amount of expenses for each of the following three categories:

- Program services
- Management (administration)

- Fundraising

These are also the expense breakdowns that most funding agencies want to see when they consider your organization for grants. In fact, these are usually the breakdowns your board of directors wants to see.

Therefore, it makes sense to use these categories as classes (because you can create specific reports of income and expenses on a class-by-class basis in QuickBooks).

You can also create any additional classes and subclasses you need. For example, many nonprofit organizations create a class for special events, and for capital improvement projects.

You also need a class to track restricted income, and some nonprofits add a class for temporarily restricted income (check with your accountant). When you receive a grant with restrictions (it's safe to say that most grants have restrictions), you link the income to the restricted income class. Then you reclassify the money as you use it, according to the terms of the restrictions.

You should also create a class named Other, because you need to accommodate those times when the person doing data entry doesn't know which class is appropriate.

You could instruct users to skip the class field in those cases, and use the QuickBooks report on unclassified transactions to edit the transactions later. However, in the interest of good training and consistent data entry, it's better to create a class named Other. Periodically, create a report on transactions that posted to the Other class, and edit the transactions to link them to the appropriate class.

It's important to understand what classes are **not**:

- Classes are not a way to track the source of revenue, because the donor is a Customer (and you can track customers when you enter transactions).
- Classes are not a way to track specific grants or contracts, because they are jobs (and you can track jobs when you enter transactions).

The bottom line is: Use whatever design you're comfortable with. Your design is valid as long as you can get the reports you need. Make sure your accountant participates in the decision.

TIP: Generally, you assign fund classes (restricted, temporarily restricted, etc.) when you're creating transactions involving revenue. You use the program classes when you're creating transactions involving expenses.

Subclasses

Subclasses let you post transactions to specific subcategories of classes. Many nonprofit organizations use subclasses for their programs class, which makes it easier to meet reporting requirements imposed by funding agencies or their boards of directors.

For instance, one of my clients has an extensive range of youth services programs, including computer education, tutoring programs, and the teams they field in the local youth sports leagues. They created a Youth Services class, and have a subclass for each service program.

Subclasses work similarly to subaccounts in your chart of accounts (covered in Chapter 3). If you set up a subclass, you must post transactions only to the subclass, never to the parent class.

However, unlike the chart of accounts, classes have no option to force the display of only the subclass when you're working in a transaction window. As a result, if you're using subclasses you must keep the name of the parent class short, to make it easier to see the entire class name when you're working from a drop-down list.

NOTE: You can also have subclasses of subclasses if you need a tri-level hierarchy to produce reports.

Class Name Protocols

Before you create the classes you need, give some thought to the naming protocol you want to use for classes. Class names should be consistent, precise, and easy to understand; otherwise, you risk errors when you assign transaction amounts to a class.

You have to decide whether your class names can include spaces and symbols (such as & and —). You should make it a rule to shun apostrophes. I think you'll find it easier to work with class names that have no spaces, dashes, or other symbols.

As an example, consider the class names that are used by a nonprofit organization that has two programs: one for computer education, and one for health education for senior citizens. In the drop down list that appears in the Class field of a transaction window, the classes appear in the following order (alphabetically):

- Admin
- ComputerTraining
- Health
- FundRaising
- Other
- RestrictedFunds

You can use numbers at the beginning of class names, which lets you control the way the class list displays. Numbered class names let you display the class list with all similar types of classes appearing contiguously, which is a more efficient approach than a list that's displayed alphabetically. Using numbers as part of the names, the same class list appears as follows:

- 100ComputerTraing
- 200Health
- 700Admin
- 800FundRaising
- 900RestrictedFunds
- 999Other

Notice that the program classes appear together, and are at the top of the list, which is usually more convenient during data entry. The gaps in the number range can be filled in as additional programs (and their attendant classes) are added.

Creating a Class

To create a class, choose Lists → Class List from the QuickBooks menu bar to open the Class List window. Press Ctrl-N to open a blank New Class dialog (see Figure 5-1).

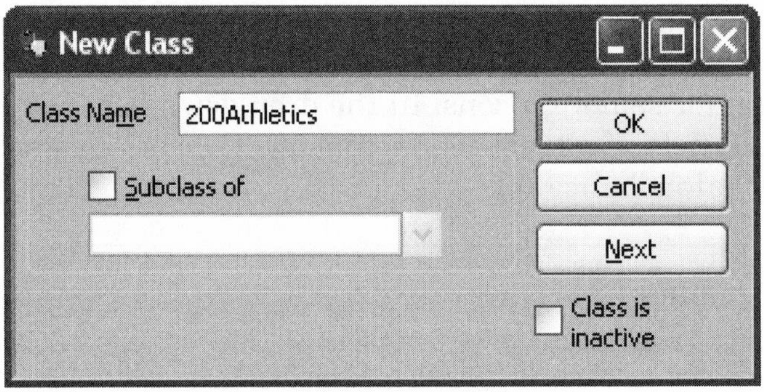

Figure 5-1: It's very easy to create a class.

Enter the name of the class, and click Next to add another class, or click OK if you are finished adding classes.

Creating a Subclass

You create a subclass using the same steps required to create a class. Choose Lists → Class List from the QuickBooks menu bar, and then use either of the techniques discussed in the following sections to create the subclass.

Create a Subclass in the New Class Dialog

If you want to specify the parent class at the time you create the subclass, first create all the parent classes you need. Then add subclasses with the following steps:

1. Enter the subclass name.
2. Click the check box next to the option Subclass Of to install a check mark.
3. Click the arrow next to the field at the bottom of the dialog, and choose the appropriate parent class from the drop-down list.

Turn a Class into a Subclass

Many people find it easier to create all the class names as quickly as possible, and then create subclasses after-the-fact. This technique saves a few mouse clicks. However, it only works if you're using numbers at the beginning of your class names, because the classes have to be sorted in "ready-to-create-subclasses" order.

Enter a class name and click Next to enter the next class name (skipping the steps that create a subclass). Continue until all class names are entered, and then click OK. The Class List window displays all the classes you've created, and they're all regular (parent) classes.

For each entry you want to turn into a subclass, position your pointer on the asterisk to the left of the class listing until your pointer turns into a four-headed arrow. Drag the list to the right to indent it. The listing turns into a subclass of the non-indented class above.

Manipulating Classes

You can change, remove, and merge classes in the Class List window, which you open by choosing Lists → Class List.

Editing a Class

To edit a class, double-click the class listing you want to modify. You can enter a new name, turn a parent class into a subclass, turn a subclass into a parent class, or mark the class Inactive.

Deleting a Class

To delete a class, select its listing in the Class List window and press Ctrl-D. If the class has a subclass, or has been used in transactions, QuickBooks won't let you delete it.

If the problem is subclasses, delete the subclasses and then you can delete the class. If the problem is that the class is linked to transactions, you can't delete it, but you can hide it (covered next).

Hiding a Class (Inactive Class)

You can hide a class by making it inactive. An inactive (hidden) class doesn't appear in drop-down lists, so it isn't easily available for posting in transaction windows.

To configure a class as inactive, right-click its listing in the Class List window, and choose Make Inactive. To see all your classes, including inactive classes, in the Class List window, select the option labeled Include Inactive. Inactive classes are displayed with a large black X in the left column.

Using a Hidden (Inactive) Class

In organizations that have multiple users entering transactions in QuickBooks, the bookkeeper or a director often wants to prevent other users from posting transactions to certain classes (such as the Restricted Funds class). Sometimes users select those classes by mistake, by clicking on the wrong listing in a drop-down list. To avoid problems, you can make the "sensitive" classes inactive, so they don't appear in drop down lists.

However the bookkeeper, director, or other knowledgeable user has to be able to link appropriate transactions to those classes. You can use a hidden (inactive) class at any time, without having to change its configuration to Active.

When you're entering a transaction, don't use the drop-down list (because of course, the class won't appear). Instead, enter the class name or number manually. QuickBooks displays a message asking you if you want to use the class just once, or reactivate the class. Click the option to use the class just once. You can use the class "just once" as many times as you want to.

Merging Classes

It's not unusual to start out with a class list you think will be effective and then, as you use QuickBooks and generate reports, decide that your class list isn't quite as efficient as you'd originally thought.

In some cases, you may find you want one class where you'd created two, because the details in the classes can be tracked more efficiently through customer or job reports. However, you don't want to lose the class information that was attached to transactions (and reports) by the class you decide you no longer need. The solution is to merge the records of two classes into one class.

To merge two classes, start by double-clicking the listing for the class you want to get rid of. The class record opens in Edit mode. Change the name to match the name of the existing class you want to keep. QuickBooks displays a message telling you that the name is in use, and asking if you want to merge the classes. Clicking Yes tells QuickBooks to go through all transactions that contain the now-removed class and replace the Class field with the class you're keeping.

Splitting Classes

Sometimes the problem is the opposite of the scenario described for merging classes. You may find that a single class is too broad, and you need to create reports that are more specific.

If this happens, you can either create subclasses for the class that's too broad, or create one or more classes to cover the detailed tracking you need. For example, you may have created a class named Sports for the athletic programs you provide. Later, you realize that because of grants, contracts, or other reporting needs, you should have had classes for your youth teams and also for your senior citizen Olympic teams.

You can create subclasses for Sports, or you could create a class named YouthSports and another class named SeniorSports.

Changing Classes in Transactions

After you split classes, you need to re-post existing transactions to make sure they appear on class reports. To accomplish this, follow these steps:

1. Open the Class list and select (highlight) the original class.
2. Press Ctrl-Q to open a Quick Report on the class. Make sure the Dates field displays This Fiscal Year-To-Date.
3. Double-click each transaction listing to open the original transaction window, and change the class (see Figure 5-2). Changing the class doesn't change the finances or the postings, so you're not doing harm to your bookkeeping totals.
4. Close the transaction window and answer Yes when QuickBooks asks if you want to save your changes.

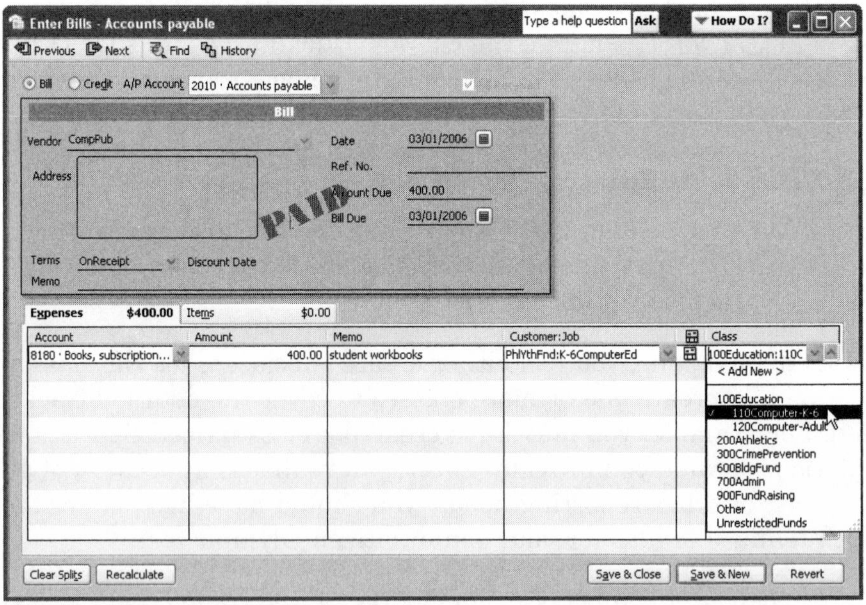

Figure 5-2: Change transactions to link them to the right class.

While this seems to be a lot of work, it's less work than you'll face if you have to perform these tasks at the end of the fiscal year when you're trying to create the reports you need for donors and for your board.

Changing Classes with a Journal Entry

Sometimes, the new class or subclass doesn't have to be changed one transaction at a time. If a particular expense or income account was used in the original class, but is exclusively used for the new class, you can assign the new class to the totals that originally posted to the account.

For example, if you had an equipment rental expense that was only used for a certain activity, and you created a new class for that activity, change the class linked to the expense with a journal entry as follows:

1. Choose Company → Make General Journal Entries to open the Make General Journal Entries transaction window.
2. Enter the appropriate account in the Account column.
3. For an expense account, enter the amount you're re-assigning in the Credit Column (reversing the expense), and enter the original class in the Class column.
4. For an income account, enter the amount you're re-assigning in the Debit Column (reversing the revenue), and enter the original class in the Class column.
5. Move to the next line, and enter the same account in the Account column. QuickBooks automatically enters the original amount in the appropriate column (if the amount was in the Debit column in the first line, the same amount is automatically placed in the Credit column). This reverses your original reversal, so everything is back the way it was.
6. Enter the new class in the Class column, and click Save & Close (or click Save & New if you have another journal entry to enter).

Creating Lists

Populating your QuickBooks lists is one of those basic chores you have to get through, even though it's probably not the most creative (or most fun) task.

If you enter all the data you need in your lists before you start creating transactions, your day-to-day work in QuickBooks is easier. Most of the fields in the QuickBooks transaction windows require a selection from a list. If the selection you need isn't there, you can create it while you're creating the transaction (which is called *on the fly* data entry). However, that interrupts the process of creating a transaction, which makes you less productive.

In the following sections, I'll go over the basics for creating some of the lists you need to work in QuickBooks (the most important, and most-used lists). Detailed information on all lists is available in *QuickBooks: The Official Guide*. (If you're using QuickBooks Premier Nonprofit edition, a copy of the book is in the software package.)

QuickBooks List Limitations

QuickBooks limits the number of entries you can have in a names list. The names lists are the following:

- Employees
- Customers
- Vendors
- Other Names

Actually, there are two limitations for names lists in QuickBooks: one for the combined total of entries in all names lists, and another for any individual names list:

- The combined total of names for all the names lists cannot exceed 14,500.
- No individual names list can exceed 10,000 names.

Once you have reached 14,500 names in your combined lists, you can no longer create any new names in any names list. Once you have reached 10,000 names in a single list, you cannot create any new entries for that list.

When QuickBooks locks a names list it's a permanent decision. Deleting names doesn't free up space for new names. It's too late.

This means you have to know approximately how many individuals may be donors, or members, so you can decide whether you can create entries for individual donors and members within your QuickBooks company file. If you choose not to enter individual donors and members, you can track those names outside of QuickBooks (a spreadsheet is a good way to track the information you need).

You can, of course, opt to track members, but not individual donors (or the other way around). You'll still enter the financial information in QuickBooks, using a batch process (total amount of membership fees received this day, or total amount of individual donations received this day). Chapter 6 has information on entering cash receipts that aren't connected to a customer that exists in your company file.

You must create list entries for any customers for whom you track transactions (grant and contract providers). However, I'm sure you don't have enough grant and contract providers to worry about exceeding the customer list limitations in QuickBooks.

You also should create list entries for any customers to whom you send an invoice, which usually means a Pledge Form for collecting pledges (covered in Chapter 6). However, it's possible to track names of people who pledge donations outside of QuickBooks. Then, mail the pledge forms (invoices) by printing a generic QuickBooks Invoice, or by creating a pledge form as a word processing document. Then, just record the transaction amounts in QuickBooks.

QuickBooks also has limitations on all its other components, described in Table 5-1.

TIP: *To see your current list sizes, press F2 to open the Product Information window.*

Component	Maximum
Transactions	2,000,000,000
Chart Of Accounts	10,000
Items (Excluding Payroll Items)	14,500
Job Types List	10,000
Vendor Types List	10,000
Customer Types List	10,000
Purchase Orders	10,000
Payroll Items List	10,000
Classes List	10,000
Terms List (Combined A/R And A/P)	10,000
Payment Methods List	10,000
Shipping Methods List	10,000
Customer Messages List	10,000
Memorized Reports List	14,500
Memorized Transactions	14,500
To Do Notes	10,000

Table 5-1: QuickBooks size limitations.

Customer & Jobs List

Starting with QuickBooks 2006, the list of customers and jobs changed its name, and the way you access it. The list is called Customers & Jobs, and you can get to it only in the Customer Center. The Lists menu no longer has the Customer:Jobs List entry you see if you're running a version of QuickBooks prior to 2006. Regardless of the version of QuickBooks, pressing Ctrl-J opens the list.

> **NOTE**: Even though the name of the Customers & Job list changed in QuickBooks 2006, in transaction windows the drop-down field for selecting a customer or job is still called Customer:Job

A Customer is a donor, and a donor is any entity (individual or organization) that sends you money. You have to use the standard QuickBooks terminology *Customer* for your donors, even if you're running QuickBooks Premier Nonprofit edition. (Unfortunately, Intuit Inc. didn't bother to change the terminology for its more expensive nonprofit software product.)

To make this discussion match your QuickBooks software windows, I often use the word *customer* in the following discussions, but we can all agree that I really mean *donor*.

QuickBooks calls this list the Customer & Job List because job tracking is built into QuickBooks, and jobs are always attached to a customer. For a nonprofit organization, a job is a grant or a contract. Each grant/contract that requires reporting must be entered as a discrete job.

Customers that don't require reports don't need jobs. This definition fits most donors that provide unrestricted funds. For example, you may receive general donations from individual donors, from people who pay fees for membership, or from people who pay fees to participate in activities.

If you have a substantial number of members and individual donors, don't enter them as individual customers in QuickBooks, because that tactic fills your QuickBooks file. Even if you don't reach the file size limits, the larger your file is, the slower QuickBooks runs. After all, you don't have to provide detailed reports that include these names to government or funding agencies.

Instead, create customers named Donor and Member (or something similar), and post all unrestricted funds to those customers. You can track the total amount of funds for unrestricted donations by posting the transaction to the appropriate accounts (membership fees, individual donations, and so on) and, of course, posting the funds to classes (programs).

Customer Name Protocols

You have to be as careful and precise about designing your customer list as you are when you design your chart of accounts and your classes.

When you create a customer in QuickBooks, the first field in the New Customer dialog is Customer Name. Think of that customer name as a code rather than a real name, or a full name. This code is a reference that's linked to all the information you enter in the customer record (company name, primary contact name, address, and so on). The code doesn't appear on printed transactions (such as invoices or sales receipts); the company name you enter appears instead. You must invent a protocol for this customer code so you enter every customer in the same manner.

Notice the Customer Name field in Figure 5-3. The customer code entry has no apostrophe or space, even though the customer name contains both. Avoiding punctuation and spaces in codes is a good protocol.

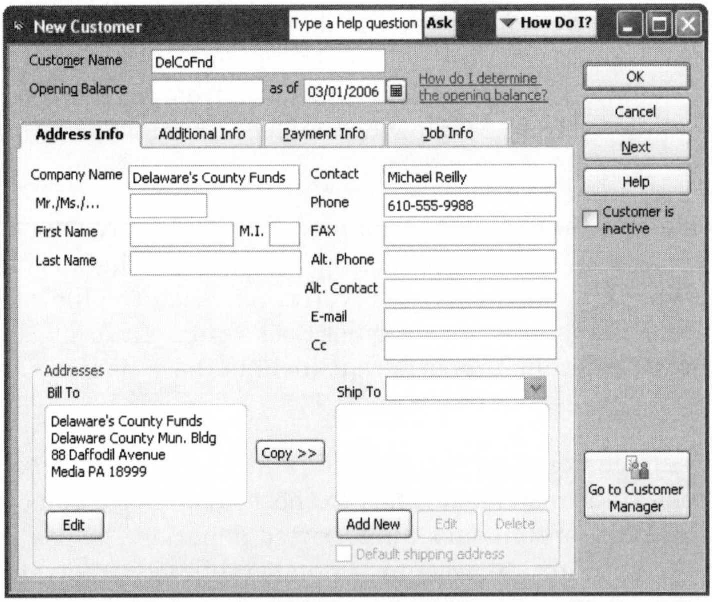

Figure 5-3: Develop a consistent protocol for entering data in the Customer Name field.

Job Name Protocols

For a nonprofit organization, a job is a contract that's connected to a customer. In other words, all your grants are jobs. If a single funding agency provides multiple grants, you have to create a job for each grant. If a funding agency only provides one grant, create a job for that grant (in case you get another grant from the same agency in the future).

If a funding agency issues multiple grants, but requires only a single report, you should still create a separate job for each grant so you can track the details internally. Then, you can create reports that include all the job details to present a unified, combined, report to the agency.

Creating Customers

Entering customers into QuickBooks takes minimum effort. Start by opening the Customers & Jobs list window by pressing Ctrl-J. Press Ctrl-N to open a blank customer card dialog. Enter the data for this customer using the guidelines in the following paragraphs.

Customer Names

Enter the customer code in the Customer Name field. Each customer code must be unique. If you have customers with similar names, you need to work out a system for creating unique names.

For example, if your organization is in the town of Smith, you may have a number of funding sources with "Smith" in their names (Smith Foundation, Smith County Youth Services, Smith Chamber of Commerce, and so on). Use a customer code such as SmithFnd, SmithCYS, SmithCC, etc.

Customer Opening Balance

Skip the Opening Balance field. Even if this customer owes money (you have a grant but you haven't received all or some of the money), don't use that field to enter an opening balance. Instead, after you've finished setting up your lists, enter an invoice to create a discrete record for the transaction, even if the date pre-dates your QuickBooks starting date. This makes it easier to track activities in detail.

Customer Address Information

In the Name and Address section of the Address Info tab, enter the company name, optionally enter a contact, and enter the billing address. When you enter the company name, that information is automatically transferred to the address field, so all you have to do is add the street address.

Enter a shipping address if you ship products (not common for non-profits). If the shipping address is different from the billing address, type it in the Ship To address box. Otherwise, click Copy to duplicate the billing address in the Ship To address box.

Customer Additional Info Tab

The data you enter in the Additional Info tab ranges from essential to convenient. You don't have to use every field, and in this discussion I'll go over the fields commonly used by nonprofit organizations.

Most of the fields are also QuickBooks lists, and if you haven't already entered items in those lists, you can do so as you fill out the fields in the Customer card. Each field that is a list has an entry named <Add New>, which opens the appropriate new blank entry window when clicked. I'll discuss the lists involved in the Customer record as they come up in the following discussion.

Customer Type

Customer Type is an optional criterion you can create to sort customers by categories you invent, and then produce reports on customer types or reports that subtotal by customer type.

You could create customer types for foundations, corporations, local government agencies, state government agencies, federal government agencies, your members, people to whom you render services for a fee, and so on. Then, you can easily create reports on a "by-type" basis.

It's easier to use the Customer Type field if you create your customer types ahead of time, as explained in the section "Customer & Vendor Profile Lists" later in this chapter (instead of using the <Add New> function to invent the types as you're filling out customer records).

Customer Terms

Terms, of course, means payment terms, which you only need if you send invoices. Most nonprofit organizations don't send invoices (although they create them for internal tracking of funds due in the future from donors).

However, if you provide services and send invoices for those services instead of collecting cash at the time the services are rendered, you may want to set up terms. (See the section "Customer & Vendor Profile Lists" later in this chapter to learn how to set up the Terms List.)

Some nonprofits use invoices to remind members when their current membership expires. Chapter 15 has information on tracking and invoicing membership fees.

Once you set up terms, and apply terms to invoices, you can take advantage of the Accounts Receivable reports available in QuickBooks, and track the amount of money due by periods, such as 30 Days Late, 60 Days Late, and so on. In addition, you can send statements to donors indicating their "lateness".

Sales Rep

Rep means sales representative, and is commonly used to track commissions on invoices, which isn't an issue for nonprofits. However, if you have people in your organization who are designated the "official" contact for any customer, you can use this list to track that information.

Creating Reps is covered in the section "Customer & Vendor Profile Lists" later in this chapter

Preferred Send Method

The Preferred Send Method is the default method for sending invoices, sales receipts, estimates, or any other transaction document to this customer. The drop-down list in this field has the following three entries: E-Mail, Mail, and None.

- E-mail uses the QuickBooks Billing Solutions services to send the transaction to your customer. The e-mail service is free, but you must register with the QuickBooks Billing Solutions services to use them.
- Mail also uses the QuickBooks Billing Solutions services, but this feature is not free. You send the invoice to QuickBooks, and the invoice is reproduced on a page with a tear-off form at the bottom, and sent to your customer, along with a return envelope that's

addressed to you. Your customer encloses the tear-off form with the payment.

- None means the customer has no special handling for invoices. You print the invoice, put it in an envelope, and mail it.

Although this field has a drop-down list, it's not a real "list" in QuickBooks. You can't open the list, and you can't add to, or modify, the list contents. Information about using the E-mail and Mail services is available in Chapter 6.

Sales Tax Information

Use this field for customer sales tax liability information if you sell products for which you must charge and remit sales tax. You must enable and configure Sales Tax in the Preferences dialog. Chapter 4 has detailed information about setting up the sales tax feature.

Price Level

The Price Level list is a collection of pricing schemes, usually designed to give volume customers special discounts. It's unusual for a nonprofit organization to use this feature, but if you have some reason to use a price level, read the section "Price Level List", later in this chapter.

Custom Fields

This feature gives you an opportunity to invent fields for sorting and arranging your QuickBooks lists. This is a very powerful feature, and is covered in the section "Adding Custom Fields to Lists", later in this chapter.

Payment Info Tab

The Payment Info tab holds information about the customer's payment methods. All the fields are self-explanatory.

Job Info Tab

The Job Info tab is designed to be used for customers to whom you will never link more than one job and therefore you can omit the step of creating a discrete job.

However, even though you can store job information in this tab, it's better to be consistent by creating a discrete job for every customer that provides a grant or a contract.

Creating a Job

Jobs are attached to customers; they can't stand alone. To create a job, press Ctrl-J to open the Customer:Job List and select (highlight) the customer for whom you're creating a job. Right-click the customer listing and choose Add Job to open the New Job window, seen in Figure 5-4.

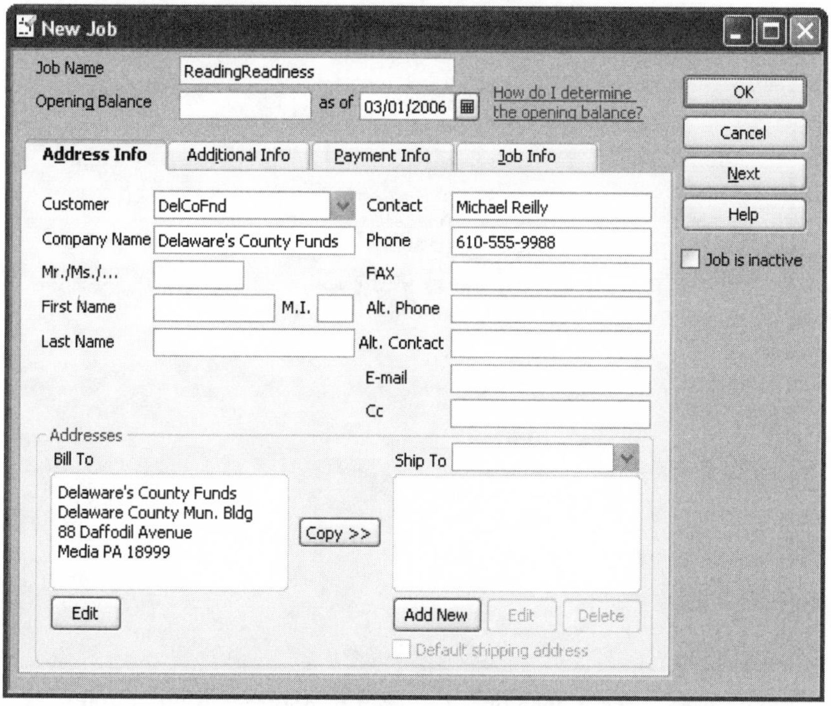

Figure 5-4: Just enter the job name; everything else that's important is already filled in from the customer record.

Create a name for the job (you can use up to 41 characters). If this job has a different customer contact, or even a different address, make the appropriate changes. QuickBooks maintains this information only for this job, and won't change the data in the main customer record.

The Additional Info tab and the Payment Info tab are related to the customer rather than the job, so you can skip them.

Job Info Tab

The Job Info tab is optional, but I've found it useful to track the progress of applications for grants and contracts. As you can see in Figure 5-5, the fields on this tab provide quite a bit of information about the job.

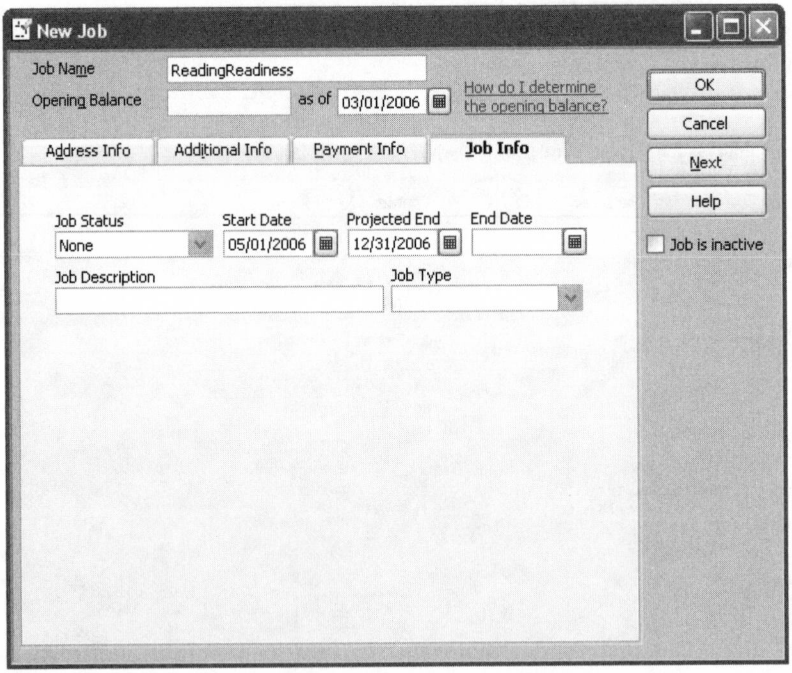

Figure 5-5: Track details about a grant or contract in the Job Info tab.

Use the following steps to fill in the Job Info tab:

1. Choose a job status from the drop-down list (see the next section "Changing the Job Status Terminology").
2. Optionally, enter a description of this job.

3. Select or create a Job Type if you want to categorize jobs for reports (e.g. one-time grants, two-year programs, and so on). See the section "Job Type", later in this chapter, for more information.
4. Enter a start date.
5. Enter the expected completion date.

TIP: *When the job is completed, you can note the real end date in the End Date field if it differs from the expected completion date.*

When you finish entering all the data, choose Next to create another job for the same customer. Otherwise, click OK to close the New Job window and return to the Customer:Job List window. The jobs you created appear in the Customer:Job window—job listings are indented under the customer listing.

Changing the Job Status Terminology

The job status drop-down list offers a list of choices, and you can change the text of each status level to suit your own taste with these steps:

1. Choose Edit → Preferences to open the Preferences dialog.
2. Click the Jobs & Estimates icon in the left pane (see Figure 5-6).

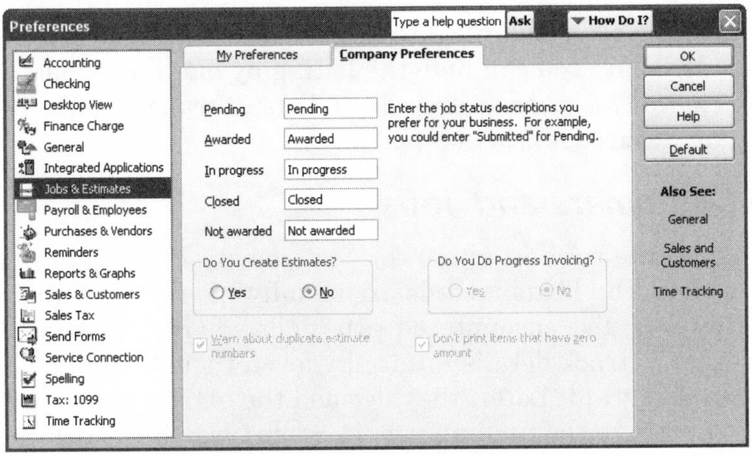

Figure 5-6: Change the job description text to match your own jargon.

3. Click the Company Preferences tab to see the current descriptive text for each job status level.
4. Change the text of any status level.
5. Click OK.

Editing Customer and Job Records

You can make changes to the information in a customer record quite easily. Open the Customer:Job List and double-click the listing for the customer record or job you want to change.

When you open the customer record dialog, you can change information, or enter data you didn't have when you first created the customer entry.

You shouldn't change the contents of the Customer Name field unless you've reinvented the protocol you're using for that entry. Many high-end (translate that as "expensive and powerful") accounting software applications lock this field and never permit changes. QuickBooks lets you change it, so you have to impose rules.

Deleting Customers and Jobs

To delete a customer or a job, open the Customer:Job List and select (highlight) the customer or job of interest. Press Ctrl-D to delete the job.

If the customer or job is linked to any transactions, QuickBooks won't let you delete it. You can hide the listing by making it inactive, which means it won't appear in drop-down lists in transaction windows (preventing any future transaction postings).

Merging Customers and Jobs

If you have duplicate records, either for a customer or for a job, you can merge the records. Duplicate records are usually the result of an inadvertent error. However, I've encountered situations where nonprofits created two jobs in order to track details internally, even though both jobs were covered in a single grant. Later, they decided the extra work involved in creating the reports to the funding agency wasn't worth the details they were collecting.

When you merge customers or jobs, QuickBooks updates all references in transactions. References to the customer or job that disappears are changed to the customer or job that is maintained after the merge.

Merging Customers

To merge two customers, open the Customer:Job List window, and double-click the listing for the customer you don't want to keep. Change the text in the Customer Name field to match the name of the customer you want to retain.

When you click OK, QuickBooks displays a message telling you the name is in use, and asking if you want to merge the records. Click Yes.

Merging Jobs

You can only merge jobs that are linked to the same customer. To merge two jobs, use the same technique described in the previous paragraphs for merging customers.

Creating Customer and Job Notes

When you're editing a customer or job record, a button named Notes appears on the dialog (the button doesn't exist when you create a customer or job). Clicking the Notes button opens a Notepad window that's dedicated to this customer or job (see Figure 5-7).

These notes can be extremely useful, and you can use them for all sorts of information and reminders about the customer. Here are the guidelines for using the notepad:

- Click the Date Stamp button to automatically enter the current date, and then enter your text.
- You can enter additional text at any time (which makes using the Date Stamp is a good idea).
- If the note is about a future action, click New To Do to enter a reminder about this note in your QuickBooks Reminder list.
- Click Print to print a copy of your note.

Use the notepad as a follow-up tickler file for customers, so you don't miss submission deadlines for proposals, reports, or other important milestone events. The notepad is also a good place to keep a contact list for various parts of the contract.

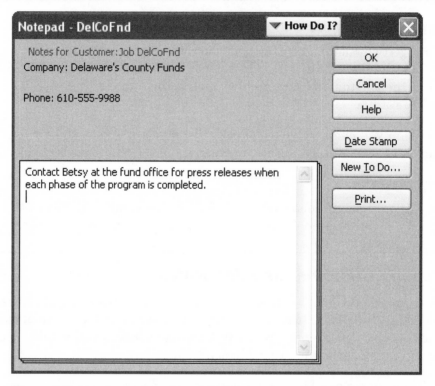

Figure 5-7: Use the notepad to store information about a customer or job.

In QuickBooks 2005 and earlier, when you view the Customer:Job List, an icon appears in the Notes column for each customer that has a note in its record. Click the icon to open the notepad. In QuickBooks 2006 and later, when you select a customer or job, the first few lines of the note appear in the right pane, along with an Edit Notes button that you click to open the note.

Vendor List

You can't pay vendors unless they exist in the system, and it's easier to enter your vendors before you start entering transactions. It's annoying to start entering a transaction and then have to stop and go through the process of creating the vendor and entering all the important information.

To open the Vendor List, click the Vend icon on the icon bar, or choose Lists → Vendor List from the menu bar. When the Vendor List window opens, press Ctrl-N to open a New Vendor card (see Figure 5-8) and fill out the fields.

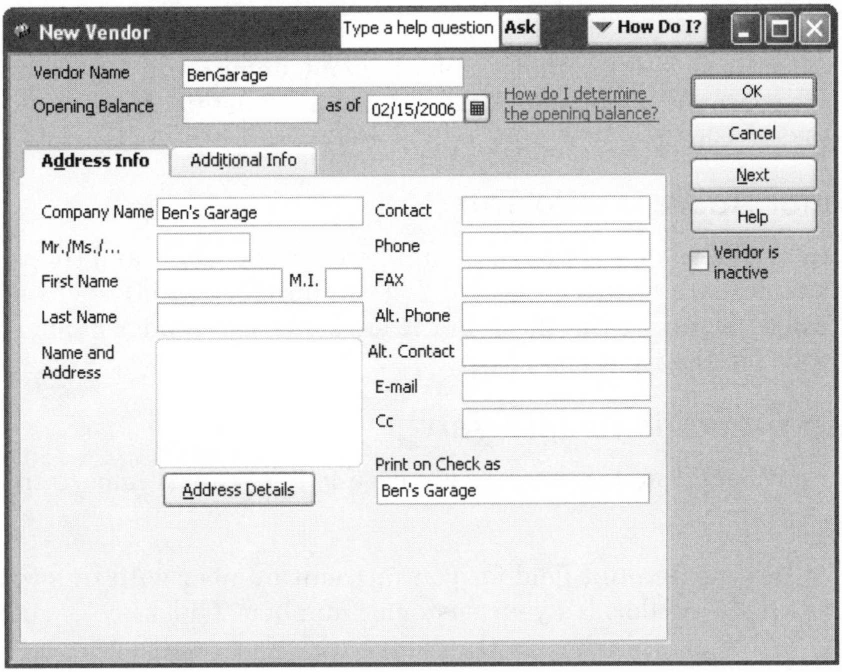

Figure 5-8: Vendor records are less complicated than customer records.

As with customers, you should have a set of protocols about entering the information in the Vendor Name field. The text in this field doesn't appear on checks or purchase orders; it's used to sort and select vendors when you need a list or a report. Think of it as a code.

You can use the Company Name field or the Print On Check As field to indicate the payee name that appears on printed checks. (If you fill in the Company Name field, the text is automatically copied to the Print On Check As field.) This is handy if you send separate checks to the same company for separate services.

For instance, if you receive multiple bills from the telephone company (for multiple telephone lines), and you have to send separate checks, create the vendor by using the telephone number for the vendor name (code), and then use the name of the telephone company (e.g. Verizon), for the Company Name and Print On Check As fields. The check payee is filled out from the Print On Check As field.

Skip the Opening Balance field. Instead, enter a bill (or multiple bills) to represent an open balance, so you have details about the transaction(s). See Chapter 7 for information about entering vendor bills.

Vendor Address Info Tab

Use the Address field if you're planning to print checks, and the vendor doesn't enclose a return envelope. You can purchase window envelopes, and when you insert the check in the envelope, the vendor name and address is in the right spot.

Vendor Additional Info Tab

The Additional Info tab, seen in Figure 5-9, has several important categories:

- Use the Account field for your account number with this vendor (to the vendor, it's your customer number). QuickBooks automatically puts this data in the memo field of printed checks.
- Use the Type field if you want to sort vendors by type.
- In the Terms field, select the terms that match those for this vendor, or create a new term.
- Use the Credit Limit field if this vendor has imposed a credit limit.
- Use the Tax ID field to enter the social security number or EIN number if this vendor receives Form 1099. Also, select the check box for Vendor Eligible For 1099.

Choose Next to open another blank vendor card, and enter the next vendor. When you're finished entering vendors, click OK.

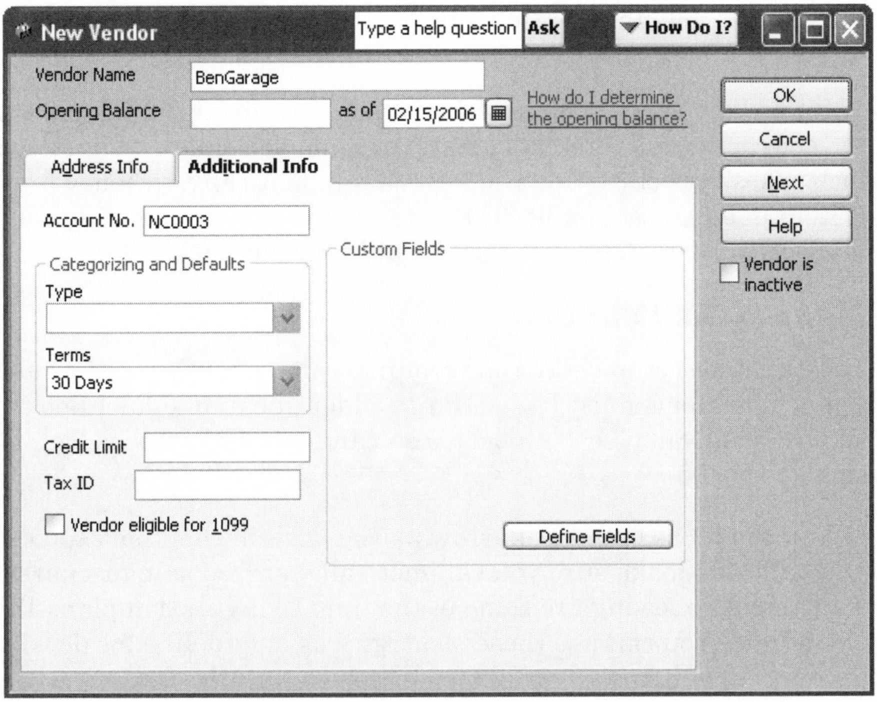

Figure 5-9: Add information to the Vendor record to make it easier to
produce detailed reports.

TIP: When you view or edit a vendor card you previously cre-
ated, a Notes feature is available, just like the one described
in the previous section on customer notes.

Manipulating Vendor Records

You can edit, delete, and merge vendor records using the same steps
described in the preceding sections for performing those actions on customers.

Item List

Items are the "reasons" money arrives. In a for-profit company, an item
is a product or service that the company sells. The items are used in

transaction windows, and they provide a way to track details about the revenue that's received.

Items let you enter data without worrying about the behind-the-scenes accounting. When you create an item, you link it to an account, which takes care of posting the income automatically. Whenever you use the item in a transaction, it posts an entry to that account, as well to the offset account (accounts receivable, bank account, etc).

Planning the Item List

This is another setup chore that requires some planning and protocols. Each of your items must have a unique identification (QuickBooks calls that the Item Name Or Number). You can have subitems as well as items.

You can be as broad or narrow as you wish in the items you create (as long as you make sure you can meet all your reporting requirements). For example, following are some of the item configuration plans I've encountered: You can use these strategies as a guideline for developing your own set of items.

One-level Item Plan

This plan is best for nonprofit associations that have uncomplicated revenue streams and reporting requirements. Items are linked to their associated income accounts.

- Grant
- Service Contract
- Donation
- Membership Dues
- Earmarked Projects (such as building fund campaigns)
- Services/products you provide to the public

Two-level Item Plan

You can use subitems as a way to produce reports that have more detail. For example, Table 5-2 shows a typical, rather simple, two level item design.

Item	Subitems
Grant	Government Corporate Foundation Other Nonprofit
Service Contract	Government Corporate Foundation Other Nonprofit
Donation	Regular Memorial Other
Membership Dues	Individual Corporate Sustaining Gold Club
Earmarked Projects	New roof on gym New parking lot

Table 5-2: Subitems make it easy to track details in your bookkeeping records.

---

*NOTE: When you're filling out transaction windows subitems appear in the drop-down list in the format: **Item:Subitem**.*

Understanding Item Types

QuickBooks provides a variety of types of items, and each item type has a unique item record dialog (because each type requires different configuration options). Following is an overview of the item types:

- **Service.** Used for services, which can be any non-tangible item, such as professional services, hourly consulting services, and so on. Most nonprofits use service items for grants, contracts, and fees.
- **Inventory part.** Used for tangible goods you purchase and resell, and track as inventory. It's unusual for nonprofits to have inventory that is tracked, and inventory tracking is a complicated accounting chore.

- **Noninventory part**. Used for tangible goods you buy and resell, but don't track the way inventory is usually tracked.
- **Other charge**. Used for miscellaneous labor, material, or other charges you include in invoices and cash sales, such as delivery charges, setup fees, and service charges.
- **Group**. Used to put together individual items that are often sold together. The invoice or cash sales receipt shows one item, which you've created in the Group Item list by listing the individual items that make up the group.
- **Subtotal**. Used to total all items above the line on which it's entered, up to the last subtotal (or the first line item, if no previous subtotal exists). This is useful if you want to apply a discount to the items above the subtotal line instead of applying the discount to all the items in the transaction (see the Discount item).
- **Discount**. Used to subtract a percentage or fixed amount from a total or subtotal.
- **Payment**. Used to record a partial (or full) prepayment you received at the time of the sale. The amount you enter reduces the amount owed on the invoice. Set up this item without a default amount, and fill in the amount when you record the invoice for which you accepted a deposit.
- **Sales tax item**. Used to calculate a single sales tax at a specific rate that you pay to a single tax agency. See Chapter 4 to learn how to set up sales tax items.
- **Sales tax group**. Used to calculate, and individually track, two or more sales tax items that apply to the same sale. The customer sees only the total sales tax, but QuickBooks maintains separate totals so you can report your sales tax accurately. Useful if your city or county imposes sales tax over and above the basic state sales tax, or if you must report different sales taxes to different tax agencies. See Chapter 4 to learn how to set up sales tax groups.

In addition, QuickBooks Premier and Enterprise editions have an item type of Inventory Assembly, used to create an inventory item out of existing inventory parts. It would be unusual for a nonprofit to be involved in this type of manufacturing, so I'm not covering this rather complicated issue. If you use a Premier/Enterprise Nonprofit edition, and you require this feature, read Running QuickBooks Premier Editions (CPA911 Publishing), which is available at your favorite bookstore or online bookseller.

Creating Items

To create an item, open the Item List window by clicking the Item icon on the Icon Bar, or by choosing Lists → Item List from the menu bar. Then press Ctrl-N to open a New Item dialog.

When the New Item dialog opens, it displays a list of item types, and you must select the correct type for the item you're creating. For nonprofit organizations, most (if not all) of the items you create are of the type Service, and the New Item dial looks like Figure 5-10. (The fields in the New Item dialog vary according to the type of item you're creating.)

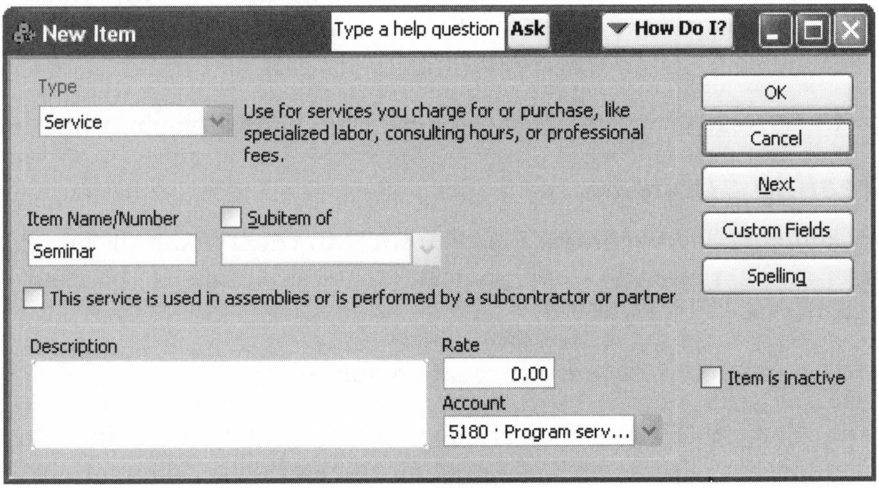

Figure 5-10: Service items have only a few fields.

Enter a unique identification code in the Item Name/Number field. When you are filling out transaction windows, this is the name you see in the drop-down list.

Optionally enter a description, which appears on printed sales transaction forms (invoices, and sales receipts).

In the Rate field, enter the price for this item, if it's always the same. If it varies (the common scenario for most items), leave the rate at zero.

TIP: When you're creating a parent item for which you'll add subitems, always enter the rate as zero.

Select the income account to which you post revenue for this item. If you're using the UCOA, you'll probably find a subaccount that matches the item you're entering, because the chart of accounts has plenty of subaccounts for specific types of income.

If you created your own chart of accounts, and you have a single account for a particular type of income (for example, Donations), use that account. Then you can create reports on items to determine which specific types of donations you received (assuming you created multiple donation items to cover all the possibilities).

Click Next to create another item, or click OK if you're finished.

Creating Subitems

Use subitems for any items that you want to track in detail. For example, under an item named Grant, you can create subitems for different types of grants (see Figure 5-11).

Use the following steps to create a subitem:

1. Enter the Item Name/Number of the subitem (don't include the parent item as part of the name; QuickBooks takes care of that).
2. Select the check box Subitem Of, and choose the parent item from the drop-down list.
3. Optionally, enter a description.
4. Don't enter a rate unless the item has a specific rate (usually applies only to products or services you sell).
5. Enter the posting account.

Click Next to create another subitem, or click OK if you're finished.

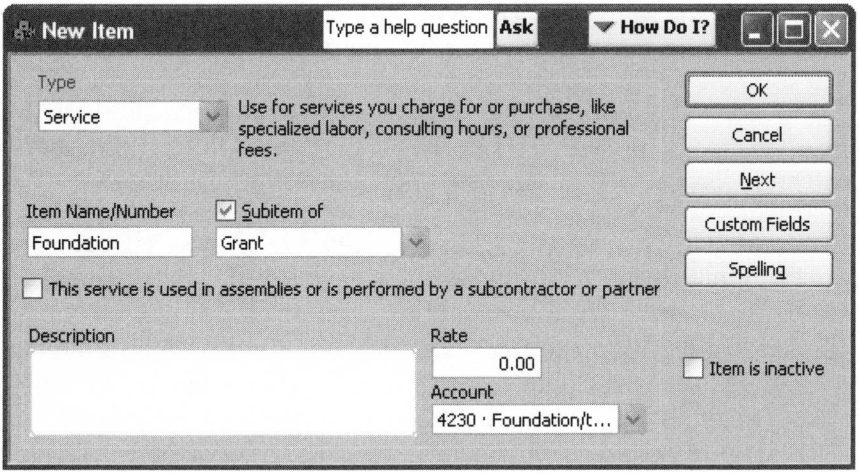

Figure 5-11: Subitems let you track revenue in a more granular fashion.

Price Level List

The Price Level list is a way to fine-tune your pricing schemes. You can use price levels to provide special pricing to certain customers.

NOTE: *The Price Levels list only appears on the Lists menu if you enabled Price Levels in the Sales & Customers section of your Preferences dialog.*

QuickBooks offers two types of price levels:

- Fixed percentage price levels, available in all editions of QuickBooks.
- Per item price levels, available only in QuickBooks Premier and Enterprise editions.

Creating Fixed Percentage Price Levels

Fixed percentage price levels can be applied to a customer, a job, or an individual sales transaction. The price levels are applied against the standard price of items (as recorded in each item's record). For example, you may want to create a price level that gives paid members of your organization a discount on retail items you sell to the public.

To create a fixed percentage-based price level, open the Price Level list by choosing Lists → Price Level List from the QuickBooks menu bar. When the Price Level List window opens, follow these steps:

1. Press Ctrl-N to open the New Price Level dialog. (If you're using a Premier edition of QuickBooks, select Fixed % from the drop down list to create a fixed percentage price level)
2. Enter a name in the Price Level Name field. Use a name that reflects the algorithm you're using for this price level, such as 10Off, or 10Disc (for a ten percent reduction).
3. Specify whether the price level is a decrease or increase against an item price.
4. Enter the percentage of increase or decrease. (You don't have to enter the percent sign—QuickBooks will automatically add it.)
5. Click OK.

Rounding Up Prices

When you use a percentage-based price level, the resulting price is frequently not an even amount. Rounding lets you change an uneven amount to a whole number. The rounding feature changed with QuickBooks 2006.

In versions of QuickBooks prior to 2006, you can only round up to the next dollar. To accomplish this, choose Edit → Preferences and select the Sales & Customers category. In the Company Preferences tab (which is where you enabled price levels), select the option Round All Sales Prices Up To The Next Whole Dollar For Fixed % Price Levels.

This means if you apply a price level configured for a ten percent reduction to an item that's priced at $11.00, making the resulting price $9.90, QuickBooks rounds the price up to $10.00. However, depending on the standard price of the item, and the percentage you apply, you could have amounts such as $80.10 rounding up to $81.00 (in effect, taking away much of the discount).

Starting with QuickBooks 2006, the rounding feature is built into the process of creating a price level, and uses the common algorithms for rounding. The New Price Level dialog has a field labeled Round Up To Nearest, with a drop-down list of rounding algorithms (see Figure 5-12). In addition, the User Defined choice lets you create a rounding scheme of your own.

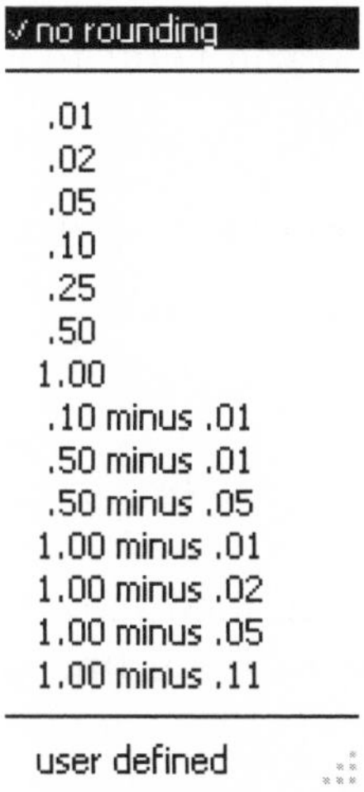

```
√ no rounding

  .01
  .02
  .05
  .10
  .25
  .50
  1.00
   .10 minus .01
   .50 minus .01
   .50 minus .05
  1.00 minus .01
  1.00 minus .02
  1.00 minus .05
  1.00 minus .11

  user defined
```

Figure 5-12: You can create a rounding scheme for each price level
you create.

Applying the Fixed Percentage Price Level

You can link price levels to customers and jobs, or apply price levels while you're creating sales forms (invoices, sales orders, sales receipts, and credit memos). The method you use produces different results, as follows:

- If you link a price level to customers or jobs, the price level is automatically applied to all items whenever you use that customer or job on a sales form.
- If you apply the price level while you're creating a sales form, the price level is applied against the standard price for the item. If the item is already discounted because of a price level applied to the

customer, that original discounted price is ignored in favor of the price level you're applying to the sales form.

Linking a Fixed Percentage Price Level to Customers and Jobs

To link a price level to a customer or a job, you need to edit the customer or job record to reflect the link. Open the Customer:Job list by choosing Lists → Customer:Job List, then take the following actions:

1. Double-click the listing for the customer or job you want to link to a price level, to open the Edit Customer dialog.
2. Move to the Additional Info tab.
3. Click the arrow in the Price Level field to display a drop-down list of all the price levels you've created.
4. Select the appropriate price level.
5. Click OK.

Repeat this for all the customers and jobs you want to link to a price level. If you link a price level to a customer, it applies to all jobs for that customer. The price level you link to the customer is applied to the price of any item in any sales form created for the customer. If you link a price level to a specific job, only sales forms related to that job reflect the price level.

Applying a Fixed Percentage Price Level in a Sales Form

You can change the price of an item on a sales form by applying a price level as you create the sales form. This gives you quite a bit of flexibility for passing along discounts (or price hikes) to any customer. Use the following steps to apply a price level to a sales form:

1. Fill out the sales form in the usual way.
2. Click the arrow in the Rate column to display your price levels (see Figure 5-13).
3. Select a price level to apply to the item.

This can get complicated, because the price level you're selecting is applied to the recorded price of the item, which may not be the price displayed on the sales form. If you linked a price level to the customer, the price that appears on the sales form reflects the price level. Applying another price level at this point may be butting into a rate that has already had a price level applied. The price level you select while you're working in the sales form wins—any amount calculated by a customer-linked price level is overwritten.

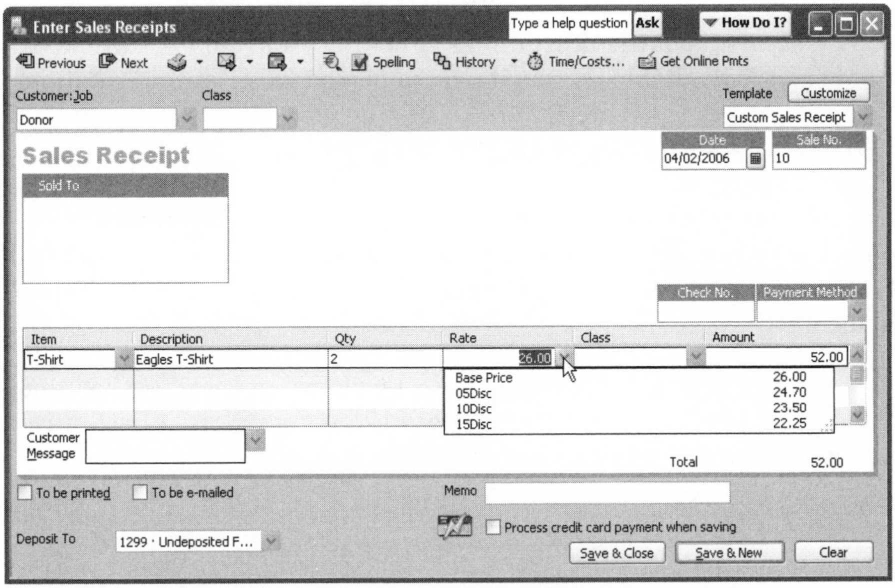

Figure 5-13: The drop-down list shows each price level, and its resulting price.

For example, the customer or job for this sales form may be linked to a price level that caused the item's price to be reduced automatically by ten percent. If you select a five percent price level decrease from the drop-down list in the sales form, the customer pays more. While this gives you some flexibility in determining prices for a customer, you need to be careful about undoing a promised discount.

Creating Per Item Price Levels

Available only in Premier and Enterprise editions of QuickBooks, per item price levels let you set different prices for each item you sell, and then apply the appropriate price level when you're creating a sales form. This paradigm gives you a great deal of flexibility when you sell goods and services to customers.

Most nonprofits that use QuickBooks don't purchase the more expensive Premier/Enterprise editions, but even those nonprofits that use those editions rarely need per item price levels. This feature is designed for manufacturing, wholesale, and retail businesses. As a result, I'm not going to cover this feature in this book. If you wish to use the feature, you can learn about it in Running QuickBooks Premier Editions (CPA911 Publishing), available in your favorite bookstore or online retailer.

Customer & Vendor Profile Lists

QuickBooks provides a group of lists that let you keep information that qualifies customer and vendor records. Most of the lists are fields in the customer and vendor cards, such as Customer Type, Vendor Type, Terms, and so on.

You can select the lists you need by choosing Lists → Customer & Vendor Profile Lists, and then selecting the appropriate list. Press Ctrl-N to open a new record and enter the data.

Sales Rep

In the for-profit world, a sales rep is usually the person assigned to a customer, who collects commissions on sales to that customer. That sales rep can be an employee, or a free-lance representative. Many nonprofits use this list to connect a representative to a donor (although it's not usual to pay the sales rep a commission).

You can use the sales rep field to enter the names of the people who are the primary contacts for donors. Sometimes the primary contact is an administrative person, whose job it is to report back to the donor (usually, this means the donor is a foundation or a government office).

You can also use the sales rep field to enter the name of the primary contact for donations. In many nonprofit organizations, the sales rep is a board member, especially for large donors.

You can produce reports that are sorted by sales rep, which means you can provide each sales rep with a list of his or her customers/donors. You can also produce reports that let you see which sales reps have generated the largest total donations.

Before you can create a sales rep, the name must already exist in your system, in the Employee, Vendor, or Other Name list.

TIP: *If you want to use a board member as a sales rep, enter the board member's name in the Other Names list.*

In transaction windows, and on reports, the sales rep data appears as initials, instead of displaying the full name. Therefore, when you create a sales rep, you must select an existing name, and then create the sales rep initials that are connected to that name. The initials must be unique, so if you have an employee named Amy Abacus, and a board member named Abner Autocrat, you'll have to invent initials for each because they cannot both be in your QuickBooks system as sales reps named AA.

Creating Sales Reps

To create a sales rep, follow these steps:

1. Choose Lists → Customer & Vendor Profile Lists → Sales Rep List, to open the Sales Rep List window.
2. Press Ctrl-N to open the New Sales Rep dialog (see Figure 5-14).
3. Click the arrow on the right side of the Sales Rep Name field, and select the name you want to use for this sales rep from the drop-down list.
4. Choose the initials for this sales rep. QuickBooks automatically enters the first letter of the existing name, or first letters of each word if the name has two words. You can change those initials to avoid duplicates. You can use up to five characters for the sales rep initials.
   Click Next to create another sales rep, or click OK to save this sales rep and close the New Sales Rep dialog.

QuickBooks automatically fills in the Sales Rep Type field, to match the list from which you selected this sales rep (Employee, Vendor, or Other Name). The field is not accessible, so you cannot change the data.

Clicking the Edit Name button on the New Sales Rep dialog opens the record for this name, so you can make changes to any data in that record. (It's not common to have to make changes to a record just because you're creating a sales rep.)

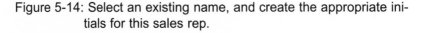

Figure 5-14: Select an existing name, and create the appropriate initials for this sales rep.

Assigning Sales Reps

You can link a sales rep to a new customer, or to an existing customer, by adding the sales rep initials to the Rep field in the customer record. The rep field is on the Additional Info tab of the customer record.

As with most QuickBooks drop-down lists, when you click the arrow next to the Rep field in the customer record, the top listing is <Add New>. You can use that selection to add a new sales rep to your system.

> **NOTE**: The Rep field only exists in the Additional Info field for a customer record; it does not exist in a Job record. You cannot have a different rep for a customer's job(s). Transactions for a job are linked to the sales rep for the job's customer.

You can add the Rep field to a sales transaction window (Invoice, Sales Receipt, Pledge, and so on). If you enter (or change) a sales rep in that transaction window, QuickBooks asks if you want to have that information appear next time. That means QuickBooks will add the sales rep initials to the Rep field in the Additional Info tab of the customer record, making the assignment permanent. (To learn how to customize the transaction window so a Rep field appears, see Chapter 6.)

Customer Type

Customer Types let you categorize your customers in a way that's useful for special reports. For example, you may use customer types of Grantor, Student, Government, Foundation, Member, and so on.

One useful application of customer types is to categorize recipients of mailings, usually for fundraising. You can create customer types that match the content and purpose of mail, or even telephone calls. Then, just run a report sorted by type, or use the QuickBooks mail merge feature and select the recipients by customer type.

See Chapter 15 to learn about using sorted lists and mail merge for contacting customers and vendors for fundraising.

Creating Customer Types

To create a customer type, follow these steps:

1. Choose Lists → Customer & Vendor Profile Lists → Customer Type List, to open the Customer Type List window.
2. Press Ctrl-N to open the New Customer Type dialog (see Figure 5-15).
3. Enter the name of the new customer type (you can use up to 31 characters).
   Click Next to enter a new customer type, or click OK to close the New Customer Type dialog.

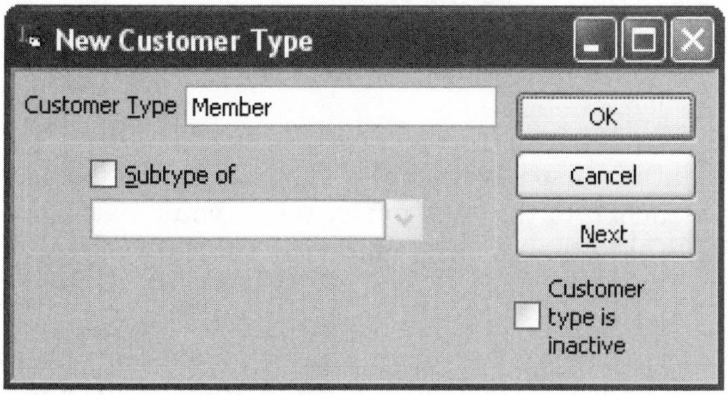

Figure 5-15: Create customer types to track customers by category.

Creating Customer Subtypes

You might find it useful to create subtypes of customers, to divide similar customer types. You can use the subtypes to produce reports or mail merge documents for targeted audiences.

For example, you may want to separate the customer type Member by subtypes such as Individual, Family, Corporate, Senior Citizen, Student, etc.

To create a customer subtype, first create the customer type as described in the previous section. Then, take the following steps:

1. Enter the subtype name in the Customer Type field of the New Customer Type dialog.
2. Select the option labeled Subtype Of, which activates the field below the option.
3. Click the arrow to the right of the field and select the parent (original) customer type.
4. Click Next to create another subtype for this parent customer type, or click OK to close the New Customer Type dialog.

Assigning Customer Types and Subtypes

You can assign a customer type or subtype to a new customer by selecting the appropriate type or subtype in the Type field on the Additional Info tab.

To add a customer type to existing customers, open the customer record by double-clicking its listing in the Customer:Job List window. Move to the Additional Info tab, and select the type or subtype from the drop-down list in the Type field.

Customer type data is also saved in the Type field of the Additional Info tab of any job attached to that customer. When you create a new job, the Type field is filled in automatically, matching the data in the customer record.

However, when you assign a customer type to an existing customer that has existing jobs, QuickBooks does not automatically fill in the customer type data on those existing jobs. This is a bug that I've reported to QuickBooks for years, but as of the time I write this, it's still not fixed. If you ever want to sort jobs by customer type, you have to enter the data for existing jobs manually (on the Additional Info tab of the job record).

NOTE: *In addition to the customer type assigned to the job, QuickBooks offers a Job Type to help you categorize jobs. For more information on Job Types, see the section "Job Type", later in this chapter.*

Vendor Type

If you occasionally need reports that would be more useful if you could report your expenditures by broad categories (instead of the narrow categories afforded by accounts), use Vendor Types to describe your vendors.

For example, you may want to use categories such as Grantees (if you give grants or donations), or Subcontractors for vendors who run programs for your organization. You could also design your Vendor Type List to be an efficient way to sort your vendor list for mail merge correspondence.

Creating Vendor Types

To create a vendor type, follow these steps:

1. Choose Lists → Customer & Vendor Profile Lists → Vendor Type List, to open the Vendor Type List window.
2. Press Ctrl-N to open the New Vendor Type dialog (see Figure 5-16).
3. Enter the name of the new vendor type (you can use up to 31 characters).
   Click Next to enter a new vendor type, or click OK to close the New Vendor Type dialog.

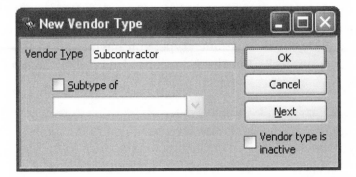

Figure 5-16: Vendor types let you sort reports about vendors efficiently.

Creating Vendor Subtypes

You might find it useful to create subtypes for vendors, to divide similar types of vendors. You can use the subtypes to produce reports or mail merge documents for targeted audiences.

For example, you may want to separate the vendor type Subcontractor by subtypes, such as individuals who need a 1099 Form at the end of the year, organizations, etc.

To create a vendor subtype, first create the vendor type as described in the previous section. Then, take the following steps:

1. Enter the subtype name in the Vendor Type field of the New Vendor Type dialog.
2. Select the option labeled Subtype Of, which activates the field below the option.
3. Click the arrow to the right of the field and select the parent (original) vendor type.
4. Click Next to create another subtype for this parent vendor type, or click OK to close the New Vendor Type dialog.

Assigning Vendor Types and Subtypes

When you create a vendor, you can assign a vendor type by selecting a vendor type or subtype from the Type field's drop-down list. The type field is on the Additional Info tab of the vendor record.

To assign a vendor type or subtype to an existing vendor, open the Vendor List window, and double-click the appropriate listing. Move to the Additional Info tab, and select a type or subtype from the drop-down list in the Type field.

Job Type

If you'd find it efficient to create reports that are specific to types of jobs (grants, contracts, and other funding sources that require reports), create job type entries to track the information you require. To create a job type, follow these steps:

1. Choose Lists → Customer & Vendor Profile Lists → Job Type List, to open the Job Type List window.
2. Press Ctrl-N to open the New Job Type dialog.
3. Enter the name of the new job type (you can use up to 31 characters).
4. Click Next to enter a new job type, or click OK to close the New Job Type dialog.

NOTE: You can use job types without using customer types.

Creating Job Subtypes

You might find it useful to create subtypes for jobs, to differentiate among similar types of jobs. You can use the subtypes to produce detailed reports.

To create a job subtype, first create the job type as described in the previous section. Then, take the following steps:

1. Enter the subtype name in the Job Type field of the New Job Type dialog.
2. Select the option labeled Subtype Of, which activates the field below the option.
3. Click the arrow to the right of the field and select the parent (original) job type.
4. Click Next to create another subtype for this parent job type, or click OK to close the New Job Type dialog.

Assigning Job Types and Subtypes

When you create a job, you can assign a job type by selecting a job type or subtype from the Type field's drop-down list. The type field is on the Job Info tab of the job record.

To assign a job type or subtype to an existing job, open the Customer:Job List window, and double-click the appropriate job listing. Move to the Job Info tab, and select a type or subtype from the drop-down list in the Type field.

Terms

The Terms List holds terms for both customers and vendors. QuickBooks may have prepopulated the list with terms, and you can create additional terms to match the terms you need for both your customers and your vendors.

To create a new entry for your Terms List, choose Lists → Customer & Vendor Profile Lists → Terms List, to open the Terms List window. Press Ctrl-N to open the New Terms dialog, and then select the type of terms you want to create. QuickBooks supports two types of terms:

- Standard terms, which have a due date following a certain amount of time after the invoice date.
- Date driven terms, which are due on a particular day of the month, regardless of the invoice date.

Create a name for the new terms, using a name that makes it easy to understand the terms when you see it on a drop-down list in a transaction window.

For example, if you create standard terms of 30 days, name the entry 30Days. If you create date driven terms where the payment is due on the 15th of the month, name the entry 15thMonth, or something similar.

Creating Standard Terms

To create terms that are standard (measured in days), select Standard, and fill out the dialog to match the terms.

Net Due is the number of days you allow for payment after the invoice date. To give customers a discount for early payment, enter the discount percentage and the number of days after the invoice date that the discount is in effect. For example, if you allow 30 days for payment but want to encourage customers to pay early, enter a discount percentage that is in effect for 10 days after the invoice date.

NOTE: Terms that provide discounts for early payment are commonly used by manufacturers and distributors of products (usually when selling to wholesale customers). It would be unusual for a nonprofit organization to have such terms for customers, or to receive such terms from vendors.

Creating Date Driven Terms

To create terms that indicate the invoice is due on a certain date, select the Date Driven option. Enter the day of the month the invoice payment is due. Then enter the number of days before the due date that invoices are considered to be payable on the following month (for example, it's not fair to insist that invoices be paid on the 10th of the month if you mail them to customers on the 8th of the month).

To give customers a discount for early payment, enter the discount percentage and the day of the month at which the discount period ends. For example, if the standard due date is the 15th of the month, you may want to extend a discount to any customer who pays by the 8th of the month.

Customer Message

Customer messages are printed at the bottom of sales transactions forms (invoices and sales receipts). You probably see customer messages on the bills you receive, such as "Thank you for your business", or "Thank you for paying on time".

To create a new customer message, choose Lists → Customer & Vendor Profile Lists → Customer Message List, to open the Customer Message List window. Then press Ctrl-N to open the New Customer

Message dialog. Enter the text for the message. You can use up to 101 characters (including spaces).

To enter a customer message when you create a sales transaction, select the appropriate message from the drop-down list in the Customer Message field.

Payment Method

This list provides information about the forms of payment from customers. Tracking the payment method provides details about transactions in case you're having a conversation with a customer about invoices and payments.

For example, if an individual donor needs detailed information (perhaps for her accountant or for the IRS), it's nice to be able to confirm that you received a donation by a specific credit card on a certain date.

In addition, specifying the payment method lets you group deposits by the appropriate categories. When you get your statement, your bank probably separates credit card receipts, or direct electronic deposits, from deposits made up of cash and checks. Depositing funds by payment method total makes it easier to reconcile the bank account. (Detailed information about separating bank deposits by type is in Chapter 6.)

The Payment Method choices in QuickBooks are two-part entries, combining a specific payment method, and the type of payment for each method.

QuickBooks prepopulates the Payment Method list with two methods (cash and check), and a number of payment types (see Figure 5-17). You can add additional payment methods as required. For example, you might want to add payment methods for certified checks, traveler's checks, and so on. If you receive funds by electronic transfer, add a payment method entry for that event, and link it to the type Other.

To add, remove, or modify payment methods, choose Lists → Customer & Vendor Profile Lists → Payment Method List.

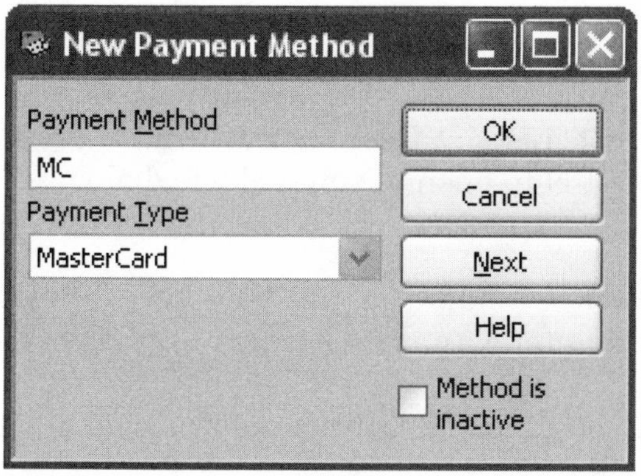

Figure 5-17: You can create a payment method, and link it to a payment type.

To add entries, press Ctrl-N to open the New Payment Method window. Name the payment method entry, and select a payment type from the drop-down list.

To modify entries, double-click the listing of interest, and change the payment method or the type.

Ship Via

Use this list to create entries that describe the way you ship goods on your sales transactions (in the field named Via), which many customers appreciate. QuickBooks prepopulates the list with a variety of shipment methods, but you may need to add more.

To add a shipping method, choose Lists → Customer & Vendor Profile Lists → Ship Via List. Press Ctrl-N to add a new Ship Via entry to the list. All you need to do is enter the name, for example OurTruck, or Bozo's Delivery Service.

Vehicle List

The Vehicle List lets you set up vehicles for mileage tracking. You can use the mileage information to bill customers for mileage expenses, if the terms of a grant or contract permits it.

However, even if you don't bill customers for mileage, the Vehicle list is a way to track information about the vehicles your organization uses.

To add a vehicle to your list, Lists → Customer & Vendor Profile Lists → Vehicle List. Press Ctrl-N to open a New Vehicle dialog, which has two fields:

- Vehicle, in which you enter a name or code for a specific vehicle. For example, you could enter Van, BlueFord, or any other recognizable name.
- Description, in which you enter descriptive information about the vehicle.

The best use of the Description field is to track information such as the VIN, the license plate number, the expiration date for the plate, the insurance policy number, or other similar information. You can enter up to 256 characters in the field.

Information about tracking vehicle mileage in QuickBooks (and invoicing for reimbursement when permitted) is in Chapter 7.

Adding Custom Fields to Lists

You can invent additional fields, called *custom fields*, for the Names lists (except the Other Names list), and the Item list. Names lists are those lists that contain names: Customers & Jobs, Vendor, and Employee.

Custom fields are useful if there's information you want to track, but QuickBooks doesn't provide a field that fits. For example, I maintain the books for a membership-based organization, and I track member activity in QuickBooks (the membership is of a manageable size so I'm not worried about running out of room in my lists). Dues are based on the calendar year, and some members pay for several years at a time.

To track each member's expiration date, I created a field named YEAR in the Customer list. I customized the Invoice and Sales Receipt transaction templates so they include my custom field.

Each time I send an invoice, or fill out a cash receipts transaction (when I receive a membership check without an invoice), I update the

YEAR field for the customer. I can create a report filtered by the current year, and send the members who appear on the report a reminder about next year's dues. (Information about customizing transaction templates is in Chapter 6.)

Adding Custom Fields to Names Lists

To add a custom field to a names list, open the Customer:Job or Vendor list and follow these steps:

1. Double-click any name on the list to open the record in Edit mode.
2. Move to the Additional Info tab.
3. Click the Define Fields button.
4. In the Define Fields dialog, name the field(s) and indicate the list(s) for which you want to use the new field (see Figure 5-18).
5. Click OK.

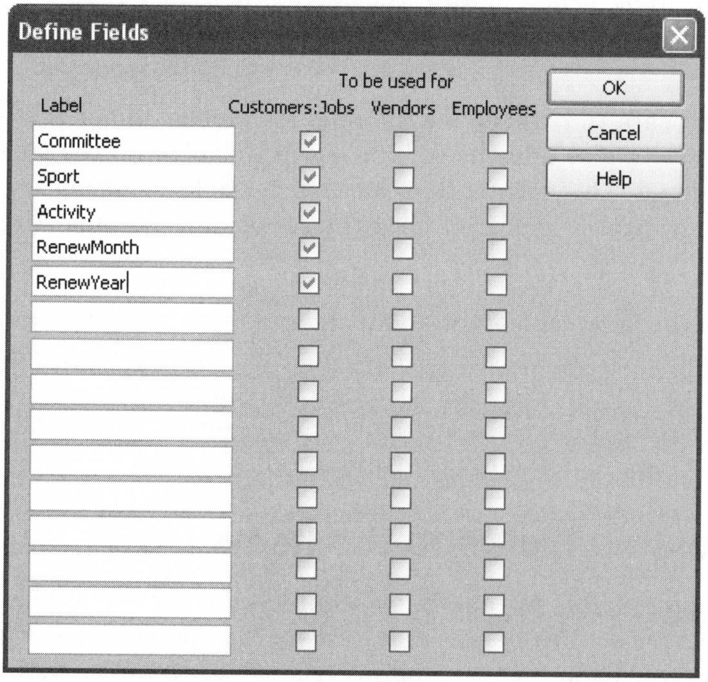

Figure 5-18: This type of data is valuable for reporting on specific information or activities.

QuickBooks displays a message to tell you that you can add these fields to your transaction templates if you customize the templates. Click OK to make the message disappear (and select the option to stop showing you the message). You can learn how to customize templates in Chapter 6.

Entering Custom Data in Names Lists

When you create a custom field, the Additional Info tab on every record in the list contains the new field. To fill in the custom fields for each name that should contain detail for customized fields, follow these steps:

1. Open the appropriate list and select the name you want to use for the custom field.
2. Press Ctrl-E to open the Edit Name dialog, and move to the Additional Info tab.
3. Enter the appropriate data in the custom field (see Figure 5-19).
4. Click OK.

You can add data to the customized field for any customer that's appropriate. You can also add the field to a specific job, and the customer record isn't changed. This means that customized fields relating to grants can have different data in each job (grant) of the same customer (funding agency).

You have to be very consistent about the data you enter for custom fields, or else you can't select the data for reports. There's no drop-down list, so you must enter the data identically. For example, in a custom field that requires the name of a month, you can't enter Apr in one customer or vendor record, and enter April in another record.

Adding Custom Fields to the Items List

You can add custom fields to your items in much the same manner as you do for names. Start by opening the Items list, and double-click the listing for any item. Then take the following steps to create a custom field:

1. Click the Custom Fields button. If this is your first custom field, a message appears telling you that there are no custom fields yet defined. Click OK.
2. In the Custom Fields for [*Item Name*] dialog, click Define Fields.
3. In the Define Custom Fields for Items dialog, enter the new field's name in the Label text box.
4. Click the Use box to use the field. (You can deselect the box later if you don't want to use the field any more.)
5. Click OK.

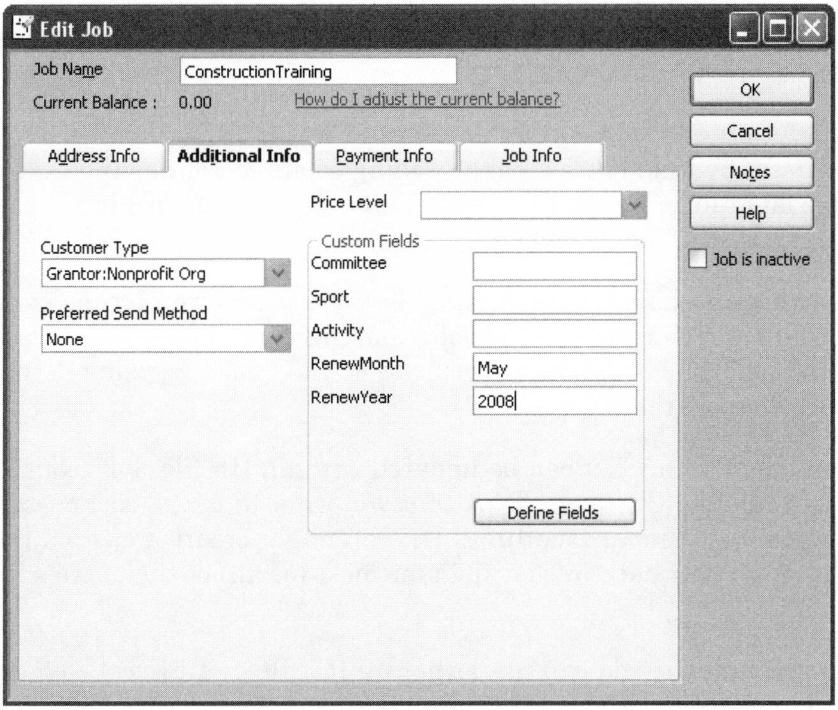

Figure 5-19: Tracking the renewal date gives this organization a heads-up for preparing the next grant application.

QuickBooks displays a message to tell you that you can use these fields on templates (forms such as Invoices and Purchase Orders). Click OK and select the option to stop displaying this message in the future.

Entering Custom Data for Items

To enter data for the custom fields in an item, open each item from the Items list and click the Custom Fields button on the Edit Item window. Then enter data in the appropriate field.

Importing Profile List and Custom Field Data

Tweaking and updating list information with the use of Customer & Vendor Profile entries, as well as custom fields, is a common practice as users become more familiar with QuickBooks. The additional data helps you produce the detailed reports required by funding agencies, board members, and the accountant.

Performing these tasks on a customer-by-customer, vendor-by-vendor, or item-by-item basis means opening each record, moving to the appropriate tab, entering the data, closing the record, opening the next record, and... on and on and on.

Not only is this time consuming, but users are often inconsistent about data entry in the custom field, making it hard to track the needed information. The fastest, most accurate method for upgrading data in lists is to import the information.

Any field in any list can be updated with an IIF file. For example, you may create a Customer Type that you want to use to sort customers in reports, or to prepare mailings. Or, you might create a custom field and have to enter data in that field for most (or all) of the entries in a list.

For some lists, you can use either an IIF file or an Excel XLS file. Only the following lists can accept XLS imports:

- Customer
- Vendor
- Items
- Chart of accounts

However, not all fields are available for import when you use an XLS import file. For example, you cannot import data for custom fields, which is a severe limitation. As a result, I just use IIF files for these tasks.

Creating Import Files to Update Existing Lists

Start by exporting the appropriate list from the company file:

- In QuickBooks 2006 and later, choose File → Utilities → Export → Lists to IIF Files.
- In QuickBooks 2005 and earlier, choose File → Export → Lists to IIF Files.

Don't export multiple lists, even if you want to update more than one list; instead, update the lists one at a time. Save the file with a filename that indicates its contacts, such as custlist.iif, or items.iif.

Open the resulting IIF file in Excel and look for the first row of "real" data, which has the list name preceded by an exclamation point. Select all the rows above that row and choose Edit → Delete to remove those rows from the worksheet. Figure 5-20 displays a customer list where all the rows above !CUST have been selected for deletion.

The data in the deleted rows isn't needed for importing information, and removing it makes it easier to work with columns (because the column names for the rows you're deleting are not the same column names you'll work with as you add data).

To add data, you must be able to see the NAME column. Freeze the column that holds the names so that as you scroll through the columns the NAME field stays visible. Use the following steps to freeze the column:

1. Click the column heading of the column to the right of the NAME column to select it.
2. Choose Window → Freeze Panes.

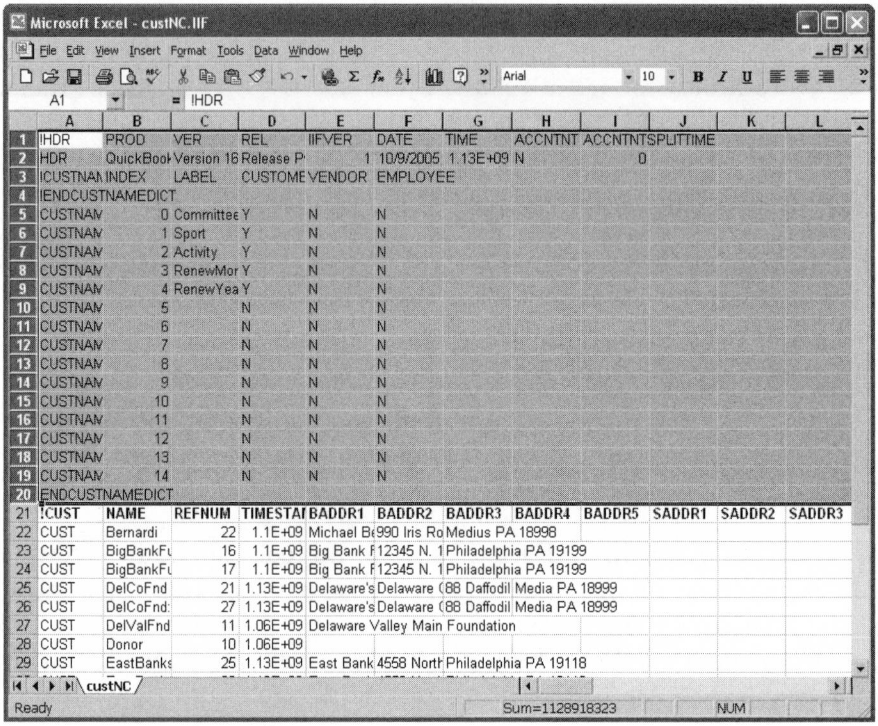

Figure 5-20: Find the first row of real data, and eliminate every row above it.

Adding Profile List Data

When you're adding data to a customer, vendor, or employee record, the data you enter in any column must match the data already in the QuickBooks profile list. For example, if you're adding Customer Type data to your customers, the data must match the Customer Type entries you created in the Customer Type list.

If you created a Customer Type named Corp Grantor, you must enter the text exactly; you can't enter CorpGrantor and omit the space.

If you created subtypes, you must not only enter the text exactly as it appears in the profile list, you must remember to put a colon between the type and subtype text. You cannot have a space before or after the colon.

To make sure you enter data correctly, open the profile list you're using to update all your names and press Ctrl-P to print the list. Then, with the entries in the Customer Type, Price Level, or whatever list in front of you, you'll be able to enter the text correctly.

When you're working in Excel, you can take advantage of the Windows clipboard and the Excel data entry tools to enter data.

1. After you enter data in the first row (record) for which you're entering or modifying text, select the cell and press Ctrl-C (or right-click in the cell and choose Copy) to copy the text to the clipboard.
2. Find the next row that needs the same data, and press Ctrl-V to paste the text (or right-click in the cell and choose Paste).
3. Move to the next row that needs the same data and press Ctrl-V to paste the text there. Continue to paste until you've pasted this text into all the records that should have it. (Once you have text in the Windows clipboard, you can continue to paste it endlessly, as long as you don't stop pasting to perform another task.)
4. Enter the next data text into the appropriate row, and follow the same pattern to paste that text into every row that's appropriate.

If you have a section of contiguous rows that require the same data (e.g. all the jobs listed below a customer), enter the data in the first row, and then select that cell. Position your mouse in the lower right corner of the cell, and when your pointer turns into vertical and horizontal intersecting lines, drag down to fill all the cells with the same data.

Adding Custom Field Data

The Custom Field columns do not have the name of the custom fields you created. The columns are labeled CUSTFLD1, CUSTFLD2, and so on. Open the custom field list in QuickBooks to see the names of the custom fields you created. The top custom field is CUSTFLD1, the next is CUSTFLD2, etc. Write down the names of the custom fields in the right order, so you know the type of data you have to enter as you update the list. To see the list, take one of the following actions:

• In the Items list, open any item, and click the Custom Fields button to see the custom fields.

- In a Names list, open any entry in the list and move to the Additional Info tab to see the custom fields.

When you enter data into custom fields, you must be consistent, or else it will be difficult to create reports on the contents of the fields. For example, if you have a custom field that calls for a date, such as a month, you need to instruct all users whether to enter the data as 6, June, or Jun.

Saving the Import File

I always use the Save As command in Excel to save the file with a different filename. This retains the original exported data (in case I have to repair a mistake I made). I usually add a dash and a number to the original filename (such as custlist-1, if the original exported file was named custlist).

Save the file as a Text (Tab Delimited) file. Excel issues warnings about text files not holding on to formatting, etc. Just ignore the warnings. Then close Excel.

Importing Updated Data into QuickBooks

Before you import data in batches with an import file, back up the company file. If anything goes amiss, you can restore the backup and continue to work in the file. If the import process failed, examine your import file to find any errors, and try again (backing up the file again first, if you've worked in the file).

To import the file, choose File → Utilities → Import → IIF files (in QuickBooks 2006 and later) or File → Import → IIF files (in QuickBooks 2005 and earlier)

Select the file you saved and click Open. QuickBooks automatically imports the data. Open the list you tweaked and make sure everything is as you expected.

Once you have your classes, lists, and customized fields configured, you can begin entering transactions with all the details you need to track your revenue and expenses properly.

Chapter 6

Managing Revenue

Understanding types of revenue

Setting up Accounts Receivable

Creating invoices

Tracking pledges

Invoicing for reimbursable expenses

Giving credits to customers

Receiving payments

Making bank deposits

Customizing templates

Tracking receivables

Nonprofits derive income from a variety of sources. The reports you're required to submit to donor agencies, the government, and your board of directors must have detailed information about the sources and types of income. To make those reports possible, you must be very careful about the way you enter data in the transaction windows that track revenue.

Understanding Types of Revenue

Both nonprofits and businesses have two types of revenue: Money that is promised (such as grants or pledges for nonprofits, and goods sold via invoices for businesses), and money that was received without a previous promise (such as donations or fees for services for nonprofits, and retail sales for businesses). You must track revenue by type, so you always know the amounts you expect to receive in the future, and the amounts you've already received and deposited into your bank account.

Revenue that is due (promised) but not yet received is called a *receivable*, and is tracked by posting transactions to an account built specifically for that purpose, called *accounts receivable*.

In addition to these two common classifications for revenue, nonprofits have another classification to consider—whether the revenue is restricted or unrestricted. This classification refers to the terms under which the money is received, and those terms regulate the way the money can be spent. Restricted funds are generally connected to grants.

We use the terms *accrual basis* and *cash basis* to differentiate between reports that include revenue receivables or only report revenues paid. Generally, nonprofits are required (by government agencies and accounting standards) to track their accounting information on an accrual basis.

QuickBooks offers you a choice between accrual and cash bases whenever you create a financial report. Your accountant may want to see both types of reports. You can learn how to create reports in Chapter 11.

You can read about basic bookkeeping, including the way accrued revenue is tracked, in Appendix A.

Accrual-based Accounting

Money that is promised (and not yet received) includes several categories, such as grants you've been awarded, contracts you've been awarded, or pledges that individual donors have submitted.

You track these promised, but unrealized, funds in QuickBooks because the expectation of money in the future is an asset, and an important part of your organization's financial condition.

Additionally, tracking these receivables means you can take whatever steps are necessary to collect the funds when the promised delivery date arrives. Depending on the source of the funds, you may have to send an invoice, make a telephone call, or fill out a form, in order to receive the funds.

When you enter a transaction for money that isn't yet in hand, that's called *accrual accounting*. Accrual accounting means that income and expenses are recognized on the date they arise, instead of the date on which cash actually changes hands.

For example, if you receive a grant notice on February 1st that you've been awarded $10,000, and the funds will arrive on April 1st (when you actually start the program for which the grant is awarded), you enter the $10,000 in QuickBooks as a receivable (meaning money you will receive in the future). When you create reports on the financial condition of your organization, those receivables are included because they're an important part of your financial position.

On the expense side, accrual accounting recognizes an expense the day you're notified of its existence, rather than the day on which you pay the expense. This means you enter the bill in QuickBooks the day it arrives, accruing the expense. When you pay the bill, the accrued amount is reclassified as cash spent. Chapter 7 is all about managing expenses.

Cash-based Accounting

The other type of accounting, called *cash-based accounting*, recognizes income (and expenses) on the date that cash is actually exchanged.

For example, when you receive a donation, which may arrive as a check in the mail, cash handed over during a fundraising event, or a fee paid for services you provide, that's a cash transaction. No matching receivable (a record of expected income in the form of an invoice) was previously entered in QuickBooks. You just deposit the money in your bank, both figuratively (in QuickBooks), and actually.

In the for-profit world, cash accounting is used by companies that don't send invoices to customers (retailers fit this description), and only enter expenses when they write the checks.

Companies that use cash accounting put their vendor bills in an envelope or folder, and don't tell their accounting software about those pending bills. They enter the checks in the software when they write them (or they print the checks through the software, which automatically enters the transaction).

If you don't track expenses that are due in the future (by entering a vendor bill into QuickBooks when it arrives), it can be difficult to judge your financial status. Money that's owed is part of the real financial picture.

Restricted Revenue

Nonprofits are required to report restricted, temporarily restricted, and unrestricted net assets separately. A net asset is the difference between revenue and expenses (called *net profit* in the for-profit world).

In order to meet this requirement, you must classify your revenue when you enter it in QuickBooks. You can do this by assigning the appropriate class when you enter the revenue in a transaction window. See Chapter 5 to learn about setting up classes, and if you have restricted revenue, be sure you create classes for restricted, temporarily restricted, and unrestricted revenue. (Appendix A has information and explanations about restricted revenue.)

Accounts Receivable (A/R)

For nonprofits, tracking income source and income type is far more complex than it is in the for-profit business world. You must track receivables by creating transactions in QuickBooks in a way that lets you create reports with the detailed information required for nonprofit accounting.

Accounts receivable transactions are posted to an accounts receivable account, which is a type of account in your chart of accounts. The common way to post a transaction as a receivable is to create an invoice (see the section "Invoices", later in this chapter).

Creating Multiple A/R Accounts

Nonprofits should track receivables by category, because government reports and standard accounting procedures for nonprofits require a breakdown by type of receivable.

Even if your nonprofit organization doesn't file a report with the IRS, your board wants to know the breakdown of receivables. If you report to the board that your current receivables total $25,000, I can almost guarantee that some board member will ask, "How of much of that is from grants, how much is from membership fees due, and how much is from donor pledges that aren't paid yet?" If you haven't been tracking every transaction in QuickBooks with categories, you have a lot of work in front of you to answer that question.

If you're using the UCOA, you have multiple A/R accounts, so you can track receivables by type. Depending on the type of income you generate, you may need to add more A/R accounts to your chart of accounts (and remove those you don't need). If you're not using the UCOA, be sure to add the A/R accounts you need to your chart of accounts.

Following are some of the A/R accounts I've entered in nonprofit client files. These may not mirror your needs, but they should stimulate your thinking as you plan the A/R section of your chart of accounts.

- Accounts Receivable: Used for invoices for services or goods you sell.
- Grants Receivable: Used for invoices entered to track expected grants.
- Contracts Receivable: Used for invoices entered to track expected service contracts.
- Tuition Fees Receivable: Used for invoices for tuition (if you are a school, or if you offer classes as part of your services).
- Pledges Receivable: Used for invoices for pledges you've received from individual donors.
- Dues Receivable: Used for invoices for membership dues.

Tracking Long Term Receivables

Accounting rules that govern the way nonprofits report their financial conditions are contained in a document called *Statement of Financial Accounting Standard* (SFAS). Those rules are recognized by the government, funding agencies, and, in a de facto fashion, by every board member of a nonprofit organization.

The SFAS has set rules for tracking receivables (usually grants) that cover a period longer than a year. These are called *long term promises to give*, and they must be reported separately instead of being co-mingled with financial data on shorter term grants. In addition, these long term fund commitments may have to be reported with information about discounts or growth that determine the real value of that money in the future. The need to report differences over the long term varies, depending on the source of the funds, the type of nonprofit organization, and the way in which the long term money is managed (invested, parked in the bank, etc.).

Check with your accountant to make sure you're managing and reporting long term commitments properly. If the funds have to be separated for reports, you'll have to create additional accounts (and, probably, classes), to create those reports.

Using A/R Accounts in Invoice Transactions

If you have multiple A/R accounts, all invoice transaction windows have a field named Account at the top of the window. You have to remember to enter the appropriate A/R account for the invoice you're creating. (See the next section, "Invoices", to learn how to create and post invoices.)

Entering the A/R account does more than post the transaction to the right account—it affects the invoice numbering system. Invoice numbers are automatically incremented, using the last invoice number in the A/R account being used for the invoice transaction. This means each of your invoice types has its own, discrete, numbering system, which is quite handy.

Invoices

An invoice is a notice that someone owes you money. In the for-profit business world, an invoice is created when a customer purchases goods or services on credit. The invoice is sent to the customer with the understanding that the customer will send payment.

Just as important, or perhaps more important, the invoice is recorded in QuickBooks so the business owner knows that money has been earned, and is expected.

In the nonprofit world, an invoice is created when an agreement is reached that money will be received in the future. The agreement itself can take the form of an award letter for a grant, or a service contract.

While businesses always mail the invoices to customers, nonprofits often create the invoice merely to record the transaction internally, and don't mail the invoice to the funding agency. The funding agency knows how much is due, and when it is due, because those details are in the RFP or the contract.

When invoices are recorded, your financial reports reflect their postings. The total amount of outstanding invoices is your Accounts Receivable total on your balance sheet (Accounts Receivable is an asset—see Appendix A for more explanations of bookkeeping terminology).

In addition, perhaps your organization renders services that recipients pay for (e.g., the use of a gym, a knitting class, etc.). You may agree to send an invoice instead of collecting money at the time the service is performed. In that case, you need to create and send an invoice, and connect its total to the type of service that you rendered.

If you have membership fees, or tuitions, and you send renewal notices, you can make those notices invoices instead of letters. In that case, you've created yet another category of receivables, which you can track (and report on). Check with your accountant about using accounts receivable techniques for membership and tuition renewals.

Most nonprofits also deal with pledges—donations, usually from individuals rather than agencies that are promised for the future. This is another scenario in which you'd create and send an invoice, and be able to create a report that shows how many pledges are still outstanding.

As you can see, managing your receivables (expected funds) in a systematic way lets you produce reports that are very exact. In addition, over time you can see patterns about the percentage of receivables that are actually collected (usually you don't have to track the patterns for grants and contracts, just for other types of receivables). Armed with the information you garner from these reports, you can design strategies for fund raising that are more successful.

Creating an Invoice

To create an invoice, press Ctrl-I to open the Create Invoices window, which is a blank invoice form.

> **NOTE**: QuickBooks provides other ways to open the Create Invoices window, including icons on the Home page (for QuickBooks 2006 and later), icons on the Icon bar (QuickBooks 2005 and earlier), and a command on the Customers menu.

There are several invoice templates built into QuickBooks, and you should select the one that's appropriate. Look at all the templates before settling on the one you want to use. To do that, click the arrow next to the Template field and select another invoice template.

- The Professional and Service templates are almost identical. There's a difference in the order of the columns, and the Service template has a field for a purchase order number.
- The Product template has fields and columns related to item numbers, quantity, and price-per-item, because it's designed for selling products.
- In QuickBooks Premier Nonprofit edition, the Standard Pledge template is available. It's a simple form, and has fewer fields than the other invoice templates.

See the section "Tracking Pledges" for information on using this template in QuickBooks Premier Nonprofit Edition. See the section "Creating a Pledge Form" to learn how to create this template in QuickBooks Pro.

Regardless of the template you use, an invoice has the following three sections:

- **Header**. This is the top portion of the invoice, and it contains basic information related to the customer, irrespective of the specific revenue source.
- **Line items**. This is the middle section, where the revenue items are listed.
- **Footer**. This is the bottom section, and it contains the totals, sales tax information, and optional messages to customers.

Entering Invoice Header Data

The Header starts with the customer or the job. Click the arrow to the right of the Customer:Job field to see a list of all your customers. If you've attached jobs to any customers, those jobs are listed under the customer name. Select the customer or job for this invoice.

TIP: *If the customer isn't in the system, choose <Add New> to open a New Customer window and enter all the data required for setting up a customer. Read Chapter 5 for information on adding new customers.*

Use the Class field in the header section to assign a class, if the entire invoice can be posted to that class. If the individual items on your invoice are linked to separate classes, use the Class column on each of the line items.

You should have more than one Accounts Receivable account, which means an Account field appears on the invoice form. Enter the Accounts Receivable account to which you're posting this invoice.

The Date field displays the current date. If you want to change the date of the invoice, type in a new date or click the calendar icon to select a date.

The Invoice # field works by automatically incrementing the number as you create invoices. The first time you enter an invoice, fill in the invoice number you want to use as a starting point. (Each A/R account maintains its own invoice numbering system.)

The Bill To address is taken from the customer record. If you're using the Product invoice template, the header also has a Ship To field. You can change either address for this invoice, and if you do, QuickBooks offers to make the new address the default for the customer. Click Yes or No, depending on the circumstances.

The Terms field is filled in automatically with the terms you entered for this customer when you created the customer. You can change the terms for this invoice if you wish. If terms don't automatically appear, it means you didn't enter that information in the customer record. If you enter it now, when you finish the invoice, QuickBooks offers to make the entry the new default for this customer by adding it to the customer card. If you don't use terms, you can remove the field from your invoice template (see the section "Customizing Templates", later in this chapter).

If you're using the Product or Service template, the header has a field for Purchase Order No. For product sales, you may have a purchase order from this customer, and if so, enter it here. If you're not selling a product, you may want to use this field to reference a contract number (or some other similar reference). You can change the title of the field if you wish; see the section "Customizing Templates" later in this chapter to learn how.

Entering Line Item Data

Now you can begin to enter the items for this invoice. Depending on the invoice template you're using, the order in which the columns appear differs. If there are columns you don't need (e.g. Quantity or Rate), you can just skip them. You can also permanently remove unnecessary columns from the template (see the section "Customizing Templates" later in this chapter).

The Item column displays an arrow when you click anywhere in the column—click the arrow to see your item list. Select the item you need. The description and price are filled in automatically if you entered that information in the item record; otherwise, you must enter the data.

If your items have prices attached, and you've used the Qty column, QuickBooks does the math, and the Amount column displays the total of the quantity times the price. If you don't use the Qty column, manually enter the amount in the Amount column. If the item and the customer are both liable for tax, the Tax column displays a "T."

Repeat this process to add all the items that should be on this invoice. You can add as many items as you need; QuickBooks automatically adds additional pages to your invoice when needed.

Entering Footer Data

The footer has the total of all the line items, and QuickBooks takes care of entering that figure. The footer also has a field named Customer Message, which you can use to print a short message at the bottom of the printed invoice. Customer messages are stored in a QuickBooks List (see

Chapter 5 for information about creating the messages in the list), and you can select an existing message (in the Customer Message list), or enter choose <Add New> from the drop-down list and create a new message.

You can enter text in the Memo field at the bottom of the invoice. A memo doesn't appear on the printed invoice, it appears only on the screen (you'll also see it if you re-open this invoice to view or edit it), and on reports.

However, it's important to know that memo text *does* appear on statements, next to the listing for this invoice. Therefore, if you send statements, be careful about the text you use—don't enter anything you wouldn't want the recipient of a statement to see.

Printing Invoices

If the field labeled To Be Printed has a check mark, QuickBooks saves the invoice in a print queue, and you can print your invoices in a batch by choosing File → Print Forms → Invoices from the menu bar.

If you don't want to print and send the invoice (because you're recording the transaction for internal use), deselect the To Be Printed option on the invoice form. It's common to create invoices for grants and contracts just to have an internal record that the money is expected.

However, if the invoice is for a pledge, member dues, or for services/products you've sold, you should print and mail the invoice (you can also e-mail it or use the QuickBooks invoice mailing service, covered next).

If you want to print a single invoice as soon as you create it, use the Print button at the top of the Create Invoices window. This way, you can print some invoices, and omit printing for others.

Printer Setup and Configuration for Invoices

Your printers are already set up in Windows (or should be), so QuickBooks, like all Windows software, has access to them. Now you have to tell QuickBooks about the printer you'll be using to print invoice, and configure that printer for the way you want to print invoices:

Choose File → Printer Setup from the menu bar, to open the Printer Setup dialog. Select Invoice from the Form Name drop-down list.

In the Printer Setup dialog for Invoices (see Figure 6-1), click the arrow next to the Printer Name box to choose a printer if you have multiple printers available. This printer becomes the default printer for Invoice forms. If you have multiple printers connected to your computer, or over a network, you can assign different printers to different forms, which is a nifty time-saver.

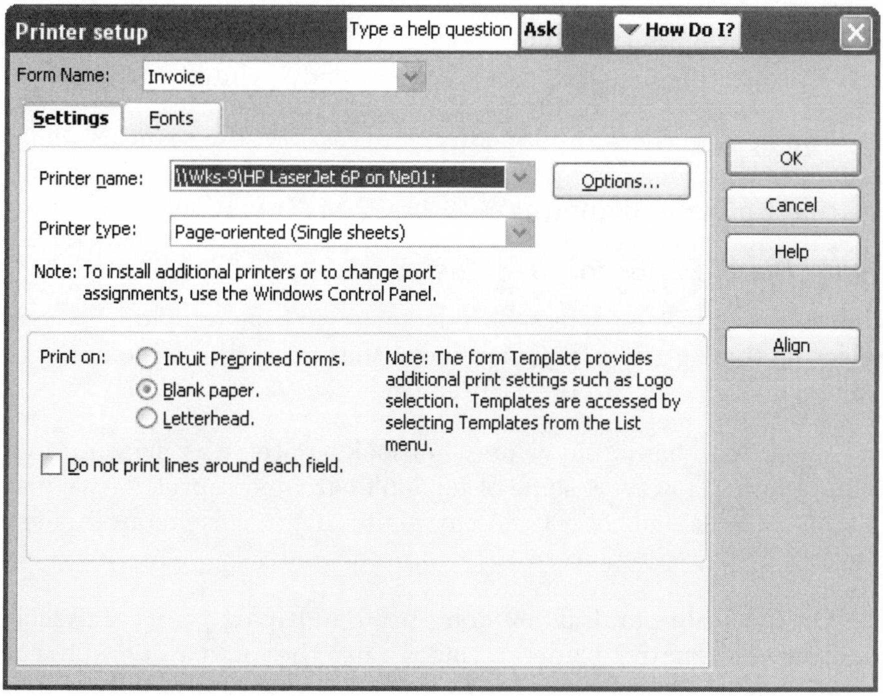

Figure 6-1: Select the options you need to print invoices.

In the bottom of the dialog, select the type of form you're planning to use for invoices, which are explained next.

Choosing the Type of Paper for Invoices

The QuickBooks Invoice printer configuration includes selecting the type of paper you use when you print invoices. The available options are explained in the following sections.

Using Preprinted Invoice Forms

These are printed invoice forms you purchase from Intuit or from another printed form company. Most bookkeeping form suppliers know about QuickBooks settings, and forms you purchase from them work just as well as forms you purchase from Intuit.

These forms preprint your organization's information (name, address, etc.), the field names, and the row and column dividers. Selecting this option tells QuickBooks that only the data needs to be sent to the printer because these fields are already printed.

You need to check, and modify, if necessary, the printing alignment, to make sure everything prints in the right place. (See the section "Setting Up Form Alignment".)

Using Blank Paper for Invoices

This selection is the easiest, because you don't have to adjust alignment. Selecting this option tells QuickBooks that everything, including field names, must be sent to the printer.

Printing to blank paper may not look as pretty as printing to a pre-printed form. However, some of us don't care about pretty—we just want to ship invoices and collect the payments. If you care about image this may not be a great choice.

On the other hand, if you don't need multipart printing (which requires a dot matrix printer), you can use the fonts and graphic capabilities of your laser or inkjet printer to design a professional-looking invoice that prints to blank paper. To accomplish this, you can change the fonts and font sizes in your invoice (explained in the section "Customizing Templates", later in this chapter).

Using Letterhead for Invoices

Choose this option if you want to print your invoices on paper that has your organization's name and address (and perhaps a logo) preprinted. Selecting this option tells QuickBooks not to print the company information at the top of the page when it prints the invoice.

TIP: For blank paper, and letterhead, it's a good idea to print lines around each field to make sure the information is printed in a way that's easy to read. To accomplish that, make sure the option titled Do Not Print Lines Around Each Field is deselected.

Setting Up Form Alignment for Invoices

You have to test the QuickBooks output against the paper in your printer to make sure everything prints in the right place. To accomplish this, click the Align button in the Printer Setup dialog and select the invoice template you're using (e.g., Service, Product, etc.), then click OK. The dialog you see to set up alignment differs, depending on the type of printer and the specific template you've selected.

Aligning Dot Matrix Printers

If you're using a continuous feed printer (a dot matrix printer that uses paper with sprocket holes), you'll see a dialog that lets you perform both coarse and fine adjustments. This is necessary because you must set the placement of the top of the page, which you cannot do with a page printer (laser, inkjet):

Start by clicking the Coarse button. A dialog appears telling you that a sample form is about to be printed and warning you not to make any physical adjustments to your printer after the sample has printed. QuickBooks provides another dialog where you can make any necessary adjustments. Make sure the appropriate preprinted form, letterhead, or blank paper is loaded in the printer, and click OK.

The sample form prints to your dot matrix printer and QuickBooks displays a dialog asking you to enter pointer line position. You can see the pointer line at the top of the printed sample. In the dialog, enter the line it's on (the printout numbers the lines), and click OK. Continue to follow the instructions as QuickBooks takes you through any adjustments that might be needed. (I can't give specific instructions because I can't see what your sample output looks like.)

If you want to tweak the alignment a bit further, choose Fine. (See the information on using the Fine Alignment dialog in the section "Aligning Laser and Inkjet Printers" that follows this section.) Otherwise, choose OK.

When the form is printing correctly, QuickBooks displays a message telling you to note the position of the form now that it's printing correctly. That means you should note exactly where the top of the page is in relation to the print head and the bar that leans against the paper.

TIP: The best way to note the position of the forms in your dot matrix printer is to get a marker and draw an arrow with the word "invoice" or the letter "I" at the spot on the printer where the top of the form should be. I have mine marked on the piece of plastic that sits above the roller.

Aligning Laser and Inkjet Printers

If you're using a page printer, you'll see only the Fine Alignment dialog. Click Print Sample to send output to your printer. Then, with the printed page in your hand, make adjustments to the alignment in the dialog. Use the arrows next to the Vertical and Horizontal boxes to move the positions at which printing occurs.

Click OK, and then click OK in the Printer Setup dialog. Your settings are saved, and you don't have to go through this again for printing invoices.

E-mailing Invoices

QuickBooks provides a way to e-mail invoices and credit memos to customers. (From here on, I'll refer to invoices in the discussion, but all the same instructions apply to credit memos and other transaction forms.) To use this feature you must sign up for QuickBooks Billing Solutions, covered later in this section (the e-mail feature is free).

To e-mail an invoice, make sure the completed invoice is in the Create Invoices window. (If you saved the invoice previously, open the Create Invoices window and use the Previous button to move backwards through saved invoices.) Then follow these steps:

1. Click the arrow to the right of the Send icon on the Create Invoices window toolbar, and select E-mail.
2. In the Send Invoice dialog (see Figure 6-2), select E-mail, and make sure the e-mail addresses in the To and From fields are correct. If you didn't enter e-mail address data for your company, or for the customer, enter the e-mail addresses now.
3. If you wish, make changes to the text of the message; the invoice itself is an attachment. See the section "Changing the Default Message Text".
5. Click Send to e-mail the invoice immediately, or click Send Later to save the invoice and mail it (with other invoices) in a batch.

TIP: If you manually enter an e-mail address, QuickBooks notifies you that the address doesn't match the current stored data for the customer, and offers to update the customer record. This often means the current stored data is missing (you didn't fill in the e-mail address field), and if that's the case, accept the offer.

Sending an E-mail Immediately

If you click Send, QuickBooks opens a browser window and takes you to the QuickBooks Business Services section. Your regular e-mail software doesn't open; this is all done by QuickBooks, through the Internet. Follow the prompts to complete the process. When your e-mail is sent, QuickBooks issues a success message.

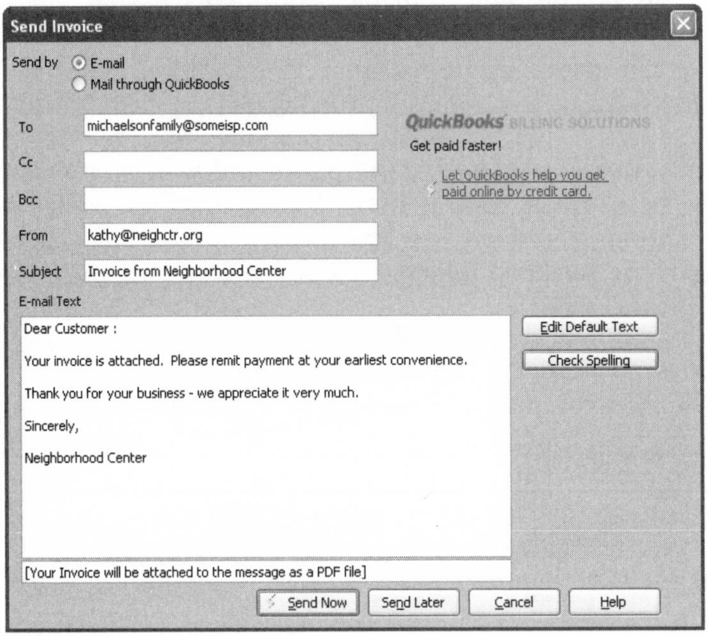

Figure 6-2: Send an invoice as an e-mail attachment.

Sending E-mail in Batches

If you click Send Later, QuickBooks saves the message, along with any others you save, until you're ready to send all of them. To send the batch of messages, choose File → Send Forms to open the Select Forms To Send dialog, and follow these guidelines:

- By default, all e-mails are selected. You can deselect an e-mail message by clicking the check mark in the leftmost column of its listing. Click again to put the check mark back.
- You can delete any item by selecting it and clicking Remove. You're not deleting the invoice; you're deleting the e-mail. You can return to the invoice and send it anytime.
- To edit the message text of any e-mail, select its listing and click Edit E-mail. Make your changes and click OK.

- Click Send Now to e-mail all the selected items.

When the customer receives your e-mail invoice, the invoice is a PDF attachment, which requires Acrobat Reader. In addition to the message text you sent, the e-mail message body contains information about opening the attached invoice, with a link to the web site where Acrobat Reader is available for download. If your customer doesn't have Acrobat Reader installed, clicking the link sends your customer to the Adobe website, where the software can be downloaded at no cost.

Changing the Default Message Text

The default message text isn't really suitable for nonprofits. You can change the text every time you e-mail a transaction document, but it's more efficient to change the default text.

Choose Edit → Preferences and move to the Send Forms category of the Preferences dialog. In the Company Preferences tab, change the e-mail message text to suit your needs (see Figure 6-3). In fact, you can create specific text for each type of form you e-mail. Select the appropriate form from the drop-down list, and enter message text that's fitting for that form.

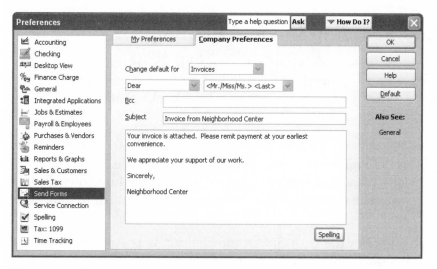

Figure 6-3: Customize the message text for each form you send by e-mail.

QuickBooks Billing Solutions

To use e-mail services, you must sign up for QuickBooks Billing Solutions, but there's no fee for the e-mail service itself. The first time you e-mail a form, QuickBooks opens the browser and travels to the QuickBooks Billing Solutions site, where you can register for the service. You can sign up ahead of time by selecting Billing Solution Options from the drop-down list on the Send icon.

Other services are available for a fee, including printing services, and online customer payments. The printing services take the invoice (or other form) you've created, and print the invoice on paper that has a tear-off section at the bottom. Your customer can return the tear-off (pre-printed with the appropriate information) with the check.

Online customer payments are available if you sign up for a Merchant Card account through QuickBooks. Your customers can click a link in an e-mailed invoice to pay online. The customer's browser opens to travel to a secure site that accepts the credit card information. The payment is sent to your QuickBooks Merchant Card account, and you're notified that it was received.

Understanding Invoice Postings

It's important to understand what QuickBooks is doing behind the scenes, because everything you do has an impact on your financial reports. When you save an invoice, QuickBooks posts amounts to your general ledger as follows:

- The Accounts Receivable Account you selected on the invoice form is debited for the total amount of the invoice.
- The Income account linked to the item on the invoice is credited with the amount of the item. If you have multiple items on the invoice, each item's linked account is credited.

In addition, the transaction information is posted to the customer, job and class involved in the transaction.

Tracking Pledges

Many donations start out as pledges, and nonprofit associations have a number of creative methods for obtaining pledges from friends of the organization. You may have a pledge form that you hand out, a sign-up sheet that's passed around at an event, or even a website that contains a form to make a pledge.

Whatever you do to get pledges, when a pledge is promised you should record it in QuickBooks to make sure your financial reports are complete (a pledge, like an invoice, is part of your accounts receivable assets).

Creating a Pledge

QuickBooks Premier Nonprofit edition provides a template for a pledge, seen in Figure 6-4. The template, named Intuit Standard Pledge, is in the drop-down list of templates in the Create Invoices window. (You can also open the form by choosing Nonprofit → Enter Pledges from the menu bar.)

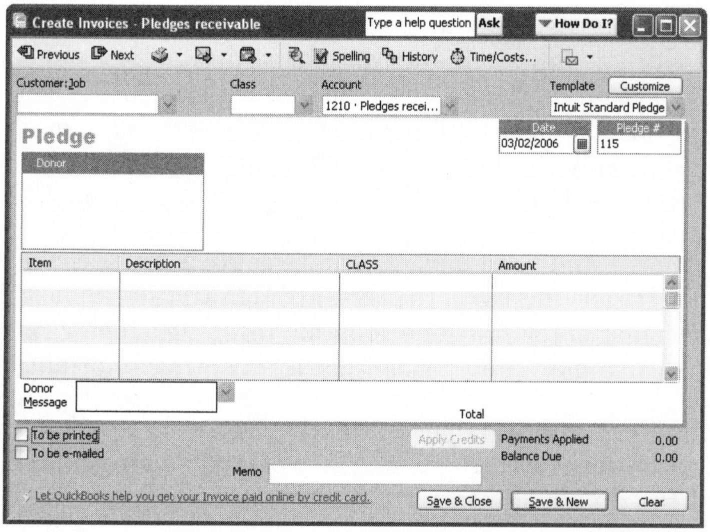

Figure 6-4: A Pledge is an accounts receivable transaction.

If you're using QuickBooks Pro, you can create a template for pledges quite easily. See the section "Creating a Pledge Form", later in this chapter.

Filling out the Pledge template is almost exactly the same as filling out a standard invoice. However, if you're using the UCOA, select the Pledges Receivable A/R account in the Account field at the top of the form. If you're not using the UCOA, you should add a Pledges Receivable account to your system. (The title bar of the Pledge window contains the name of the A/R account you've assigned to the transaction.)

The Pledge template is quite straightforward, and less "busy" than the standard invoice templates. This makes the Pledge template useful for all invoicing for many nonprofit organizations. The only problem is that the word "Pledge" appears at the top of the printed invoice, and if you're mailing invoices, this could be confusing to recipients. It's easy to create an invoice template that is based on the Pledge template, but has the title "Invoice". See the section "Customizing Templates", later in this chapter.

Using Pledges Efficiently

Unlike high-end (expensive) accounting software, QuickBooks isn't designed to provide an unlimited amount of data in its files. As QuickBooks files get large, the software operates more slowly. Therefore, if you're not planning to print and mail the pledge, you may not want to enter a pledge for each individual person who signs a pledge card. (See Chapter 15 for information about file limitations in QuickBooks.)

If you don't print and send pledge forms, create a generic customer named Pledge or Donor and track pledges through that customer. To create the customer, just enter the generic name in the Customer Name field in the New Customer dialog. Don't enter any other information.

You can track the actual names in another software application, such as a spreadsheet or database program. The work you do in QuickBooks is designed to get the financial totals into the system (you probably have no reporting requirements that insist on listing every individual who pledges money).

If you want to print and send pledge forms (as reminders), you still don't have to create a customer to get a name and address entered on the form. Instead, open the form you use (Invoice or Pledge), and follow these steps:

1. Select the generic customer.
2. In the Bill To section of the form, enter the donor's name and address.
3. Fill out the form.
4. Click the Print icon on the form window to print the pledge form.
5. Click Save & New to create another entry, or click Save & Close if you're finished.
6. When QuickBooks displays the message seen in Figure 6-5, click No to prevent any changes in the generic donor record.

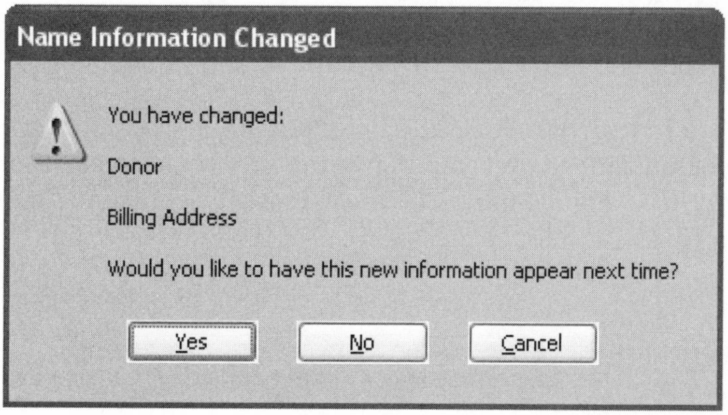

Name Information Changed

You have changed:

Donor

Billing Address

Would you like to have this new information appear next time?

Yes   No   Cancel

Figure 6-5: Don't change the generic customer record.

Incidentally, when you view the pledge later (by opening it from a report or by using the Previous button to move back through the pledges you entered), the name and address you entered on any individual form remains on the form.

TIP: *If you use a generic customer for pledges, you don't have to enter each pledge individually; if you received twenty pledges on a given day; enter the total amount in the pledge transaction window to record the total A/R. Track the names and addresses in other software.*

Invoicing for Reimbursable Expenses

Some expenses may be reimbursable under the terms of a contract or a grant, and you can mark those expenses when you're entering them as vendor bills or checks. Once marked as reimbursable, you can automatically add them to an invoice. (Chapter 7 has instructions for entering reimbursable expenses on a vendor's bill, and charging them to a specific customer or job.)

When you save the vendor bill, or the check, the reimbursable amounts you linked to a customer are saved in the customer or job file. When you create an invoice for the customer or job, you can add the reimbursable expenses to the invoice, or you can create an invoice specifically for those expenses.

In the Create Invoice window, after you enter the customer or job name, QuickBooks notifies you that reimbursable expenses are recorded for that customer (see Figure 6-6). The alert message contains an option to stop showing this reminder when you're creating invoices, but this feature is too handy to turn off.

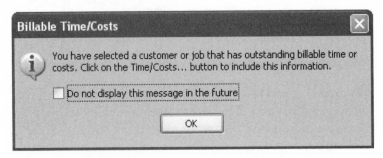

Figure 6-6: QuickBooks tracks reimbursable expenses, and reminds you to add them to the invoice.

Adding Reimbursable Expenses to an Invoice

To add the reimbursable expenses to the invoice, complete the header and enter any line items that are separate from the reimbursable expenses (often the invoice only contains the reimbursable expenses). Then follow these steps:

1. Click the Time/Costs icon at the top of the Create Invoices window to open the Choose Billable Time And Costs window.
2. Move to the Expenses tab, which displays the reimbursable amounts you posted for this customer when you entered vendor bills.
3. Click the Use column to place a check mark next to the expenses you want to include on the invoice you're currently creating (see Figure 6-7).
4. Click OK to move the item(s) to the invoice, to join any other items included in this invoice.

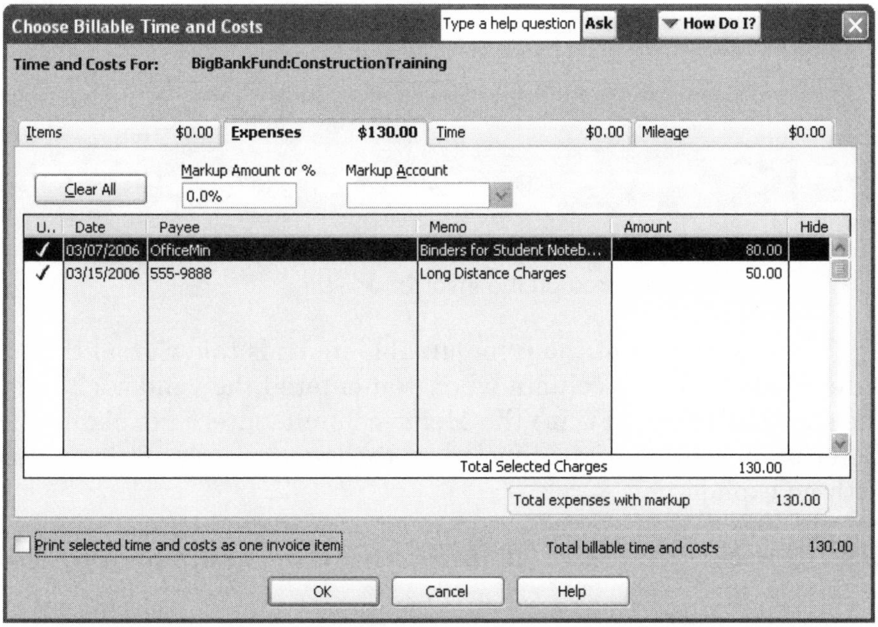

Figure 6-7: Select the expense(s) to add to the customer invoice
you're currently preparing.

If you select multiple reimbursable costs, QuickBooks enters an invoice line item called Reimb Group, lists the individual items, and enters the total for the reimbursable items (see Figure 6-8).

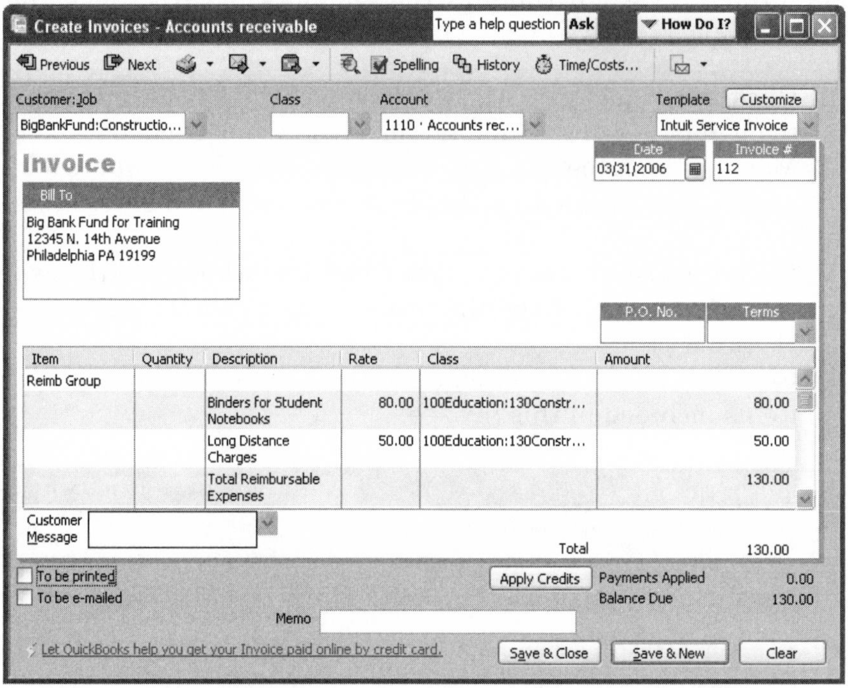

Figure 6-8: The reimbursable costs you selected are automatically entered on the invoice.

The description of the reimbursable items is taken from the text you entered in the Memo column when you entered the vendor's bill, or wrote the check. If you didn't use the Memo column, enter text manually in the Description column of the invoice, or the customer sees only an amount with no explanation.

Using a Single Item for Multiple Reimbursable Items

If you selected multiple reimbursable items, you can combine all of them into a single line item on the invoice. In the Choose Billable Time And Costs dialog, select the option Print Selected Time And Costs As One Invoice Item.

When you click OK and return to the invoice window, you still see each individual item (as shown in Figure 6-8). However, only the on-screen version of the invoice continues to display the individual items.

The printed invoice (even if it's a PDF file that's e-mailed), displays a single line item, named Total Reimbursable Expenses, with the total in the Amount column. If the customer has a question about the details, you can view the invoice and see the original detailed items.

TIP: *To see what the printed invoice will look like, click the arrow next to the Print icon on the invoice window, and choose Preview.*

Excluding a Reimbursable Expense

If you want to exclude a reimbursable expense from the current invoice, merely avoid putting a check mark in the Use column. The item remains in the system, attached to this customer or job, and shows up on the Choose Billable Time And Costs window the next time you invoice this customer.

Removing a Reimbursable Expense from the List

Sometimes a reimbursable expense was charged in error during input of a vendor bill (usually because the user who created the vendor bill didn't realize your contract doesn't permit reimbursement for this type of expense).

If you don't ever want to invoice the customer for this expense, the first thing you notice is that the Choose Billable Time And Costs window has no Delete button, and appears to have no method of deleting an item. You can deselect the check mark in the Use column, but every time you invoice the customer and open the Choose Billable Time And Costs window, the item is still there.

The solution lies in the Hide column. If you place a check mark in the Hide column, the item is effectively deleted from the list of reimbursable expenses you see when you're preparing invoices. However, the details are still in your system, which provides two advantages:

- You won't accidentally invoice the customer for the item
- The expense continues to appear in reports about this customer's activity, so you have an effective means of job costing).

Changing the Amount of a Reimbursable Expense

You're free to change the amount of a reimbursable expense. To accomplish this, select (highlight) the amount in the Amount column of the Billable Time And Costs window, and enter the new figure.

If you reduce the amount, QuickBooks does not consider the remaining amount as an amount still due. It won't ever appear in the Billable Time And Costs window. QuickBooks makes the assumption you're not planning to pass the remaining amount to your customer in the future.

You can increase the amount (perhaps to cover overhead), but if you're increasing all the charges, it's easier to apply a markup (covered next) than to change each individual item.

Marking Up Reimbursable Expenses

You can mark up any reimbursable expenses you're invoicing, which many for-profit companies do to cover any additional costs such as handling, time, or general aggravation. Nonprofits don't usually mark up items, unless there's a contractual provision permitting it.

To apply a markup, select the items you want to mark up by placing a check mark in the Use column in the Choose Billable Time And Costs window. Then enter a markup in the Markup Amount or % field in either of the following ways:

- Enter an amount.
- Enter a percentage (a number followed by the percent sign).

Enter the account to which you're posting markups. You can create an account specifically for markups (a good idea, because it helps you analyze the source of all income) or use an existing income account.

The item amounts and the total of the selected charges don't change when you apply the markup; the change is only reflected in the amounts on the invoice. When you click OK to transfer the reimbursable expenses to the customer's invoice, you'll see the reimbursable expenses and the markup as separate items. The markup is clearly indicated—it has its own line item.

If you don't want the invoice to display the markup amounts as a discrete item, select the Print Selected Time And Costs As One Invoice Item option. You'll see the breakdown on the screen version of the invoice, but the printed invoice will contain only the grand total.

The difference between using the markup function, and just changing the amount of the reimbursable expense in the Amount column is the way the amounts are posted to your general ledger.

If you use the markup function, the difference between the actual expense and the charge to your customer is posted to the markup account. If you change the amount of the expense, the entire amount is posted to the income account you linked to the reimbursable expense account.

Giving Credits to Customers

Sometimes you have to return money to a customer. This isn't likely to occur with customers who provide grants or contracts, but sometimes have to issue credits to customers who pay for goods and services you provide.

For example, if you hold a series of classes for a fee, and a participant drops out, you may have to issue a credit. The same is true if a customer purchases an item you sell, and then returns it.

When you issue a credit to a customer, you can apply that credit in any of the following ways:

- Credit the amount against a current amount due (existing invoices for this customer).
- Credit the amount against a future transaction (sometimes called a *floating credit*).
- Give the customer a refund check.

Regardless of the method you want to use to apply the credit amount, QuickBooks performs the appropriate task automatically.

Creating a Credit Memo

To create a credit memo, follow these steps:

1. Choose Customers → Create Credit Memos/Refunds from the menu bar to open a blank Credit Memo template.
2. Select a customer or job.
3. Move to the line item section and enter the item, the quantity, and the rate for the items in this credit memo. Don't use a minus sign—QuickBooks knows what a credit is and posts the amounts appropriately.
4. Remember to insert all the special items you need to give credit for, such as shipping if you're crediting a product you sold and shipped.
5. Print the credit memo if you want to send it to the customer.
6. Click Save & Close to save the credit memo.

When you save the credit memo QuickBooks displays a message asking how you want to apply the amount (see Figure 6-9).

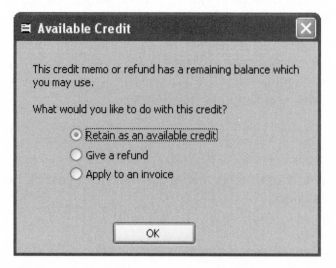

Figure 6-9: Choose the way you want to apply this credit.

NOTE: *Versions of QuickBooks prior to 2005 do not offer the option dialog for selecting the application method. You can automatically create a refund check (using the Refund button on the transaction window), but you must apply credits against invoices manually (see the section "Applying a Credit").*

If the customer has existing invoices, and you want to apply this credit against the open balance, select Apply To An Invoice. QuickBooks opens the Apply Credit to Invoices dialog, which lists the customer's open invoices. The oldest invoice is selected, and the credit you just created is applied against the total (see Figure 6-10).

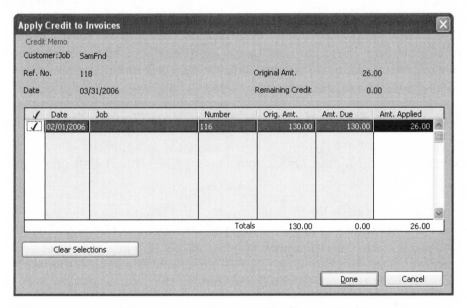

Figure 6-10: QuickBooks automatically applies the credit against an invoice.

If the credit is larger than a single invoice, the excess amount is applied to another invoice. If no other invoices exist, or if the amount of the credit is larger than the total of open invoices, QuickBooks holds the remaining credit amount against future invoices (see "Applying a Credit"), or you can send a refund check.

If no open invoice exists for the customer, you can select the option to reserve the credit against future invoices, or create a refund check.

If the customer receiving the credit isn't in your system, because you're not tracking individual donors, members, or retail customers, you must create a refund check. Customers that aren't in the system don't have invoices for you to apply credits.

Creating a Refund Check

You can create a refund check to cover a customer credit at the time you create the credit, or later. The "later" usually means you were planning to apply the credit against future invoices, but you've decided the customer will probably not receive any invoices in the future (or the customer called and asked for a refund check instead of a credit against a future invoice). If you applied the original credit to an existing invoice, but the credit was larger than the invoice, it's common to send a refund check for the credit balance.

Creating a Refund Check When You Create the Credit

If you selected Give A Refund in the dialog that appeared when you saved the credit memo, QuickBooks opens the Issue A Refund dialog seen in Figure 6-11.

If the option To Be Printed is selected, the check will be waiting for you the next time you choose File → Print Forms → Checks. If that option isn't selected, the check is entered in the register of the bank account selected in the dialog. Write the check and open the account register to insert the correct check number.

Creating a Refund Check Later

You can create the refund check later, if you'd originally applied the refund against open invoices, but there is still a remaining credit balance, or if you told QuickBooks to hold the credit memo and now you want to refund the money.

Open the original credit memo transaction and click the arrow to the right of the button labeled Use Credit To (at the top of the transaction window). Select the option Give Refund to open the Issue A Refund dialog discussed in the previous section.

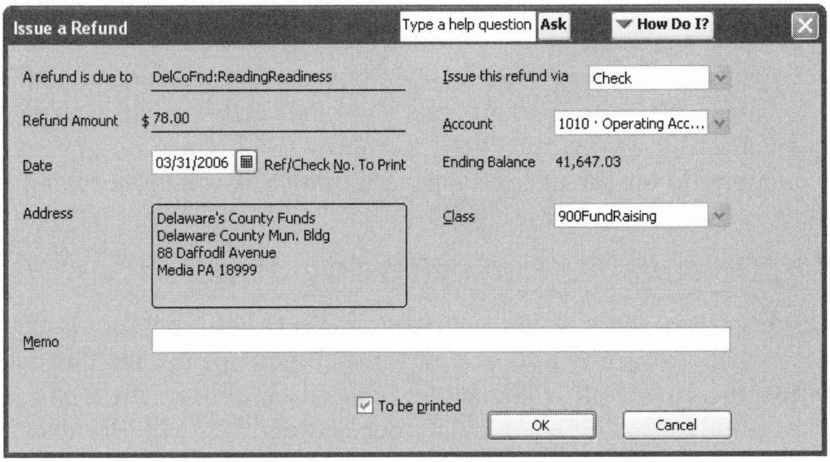

Figure 6-11: Create a refund check automatically.

Receiving Revenue

You can receive revenue in either of two ways:

- You receive a check you expected, and for which you created an invoice to track the A/R. QuickBooks calls this a *customer payment.*
- You receive income without a linked invoice in the system. QuickBooks calls this a *sales receipt.*

Each time you receive revenue, you must enter the transaction in QuickBooks with the appropriate transaction window.

Receiving Payments on Invoices

When you create invoices, you can assume that money will eventually arrive to pay off those invoices. This is true even if you merely enter invoices to track expected grants, donations, and contracts, and you don't actually send the invoices. In accounting, there are two ways to apply payments to invoices:

- Balance forward. This method considers the total of all the out-standing invoices as the amount due from the customer, and you apply payments against that total. It doesn't matter which partic-ular invoice is being paid, because it's a running total of payments against a running total of invoices.
- Open item. This method applies payments received to specific invoices. Most of the time, the customer either sends a copy of the invoice along with the check, or notes the invoice number that is being paid on the check stub, to make sure your records agree with the customer's records.

Setting Defaults for Receiving Payments

QuickBooks offers some default settings for receiving payments from cus-tomers, and choosing the options that match your preferred methods can save you some keystrokes. The settings are available in the Company Preferences tab of the Sales & Customers category in the Preferences dialog. The following options affect receipt of payments:

- Automatically apply payments
- Automatically calculate payments

Automatically Apply Payments

This option tells QuickBooks to apply payments to invoices automatical-ly. If the payment matches the amount of an invoice, it is automatically applied to that invoice. If the payment doesn't match the amount of an invoice, the payment is automatically applied to the oldest invoice.

This option is enabled by default, and if you use balance forward accounts receivable, it saves you some steps. If you want to apply pay-ments against invoices, and most of the time your customers pay off the oldest invoice, this option is quite handy. If you disable this option, you must manually select the invoice(s) against which you're applying pay-ments.

Even if this option is selected, you can change the automated selec-tion of invoices when necessary. Merely deselect the invoice that QuickBooks selected, and select the invoice that the customer is really paying.

Automatically Calculate Payments

If you tell QuickBooks to calculate customer payments automatically, you can skip entering the amount of the payment in the Amount field at the top of the Receive Payments window, and head directly for the list of invoices.

As you select each invoice for payment, QuickBooks calculates the total and places it in the Amount field. If your customers' checks always match the amount of an open invoice, this saves you some data entry.

Because the option is automatically enabled, the first time you select an invoice before entering the payment amount in the Amount field, QuickBooks displays a message explaining the option, and asking if you'd like to disable it.

If you disable this option, when you select an invoice listing without entering the amount of the payment first, QuickBooks issues an error message and you have to enter the amount of the customer's check in the Amount field before you can begin applying payments to invoices.

Recording the Payment

When a check arrives for which an invoice is in the system, you have to record that payment, and apply it against the right invoice.

Choose Customers → Receive Payments from the menu bar to bring up a blank Receive Payments window. Click the arrow to the right of the Received From field to display a list of customers and select the customer or job that sent this payment.

In the A/R Account field, select the A/R account to which you posted the invoice(s) for this customer or job. If you don't have multiple A/R accounts, the A/R Account field doesn't appear in the Receive Payments window.

All the existing invoices for this customer or job appear in the lower part of the window. If no invoices appear, or if fewer invoices than expected appear, you may have posted invoices to the wrong A/R account when you created them. The only invoices that appear in the Receive

Payments window are those that were posted to the same A/R account you specified in this window.

> **TIP**: *If you inadvertently posted an invoice to the wrong A/R account, edit the original transaction to change the A/R account.*

Enter the amount of the payment in the Amount field, select the payment method in the Pmt. Method field, and enter the appropriate details (e.g. the check number) in the applicable field.

Applying the Payment

Now you have to apply the payment against an invoice or multiple invoices for this customer. Numerous scenarios are possible when receiving customer payments:

- The customer has one unpaid invoice, and the payment is for the same amount as that invoice.
- The customer has several unpaid invoices, and the payment is for the amount of one of those invoices.
- The customer has one or more unpaid invoices, and the payment is for an amount lower than any single invoice.
- The customer has several unpaid invoices, and the payment is for an amount greater than any one invoice but not large enough to cover two invoices.
- The customer has one or more unpaid invoices, and the payment is for a lesser amount than the current balance. However, the customer has a credit equal to the difference between the payment and the customer balance.

If the customer's intention isn't clear, call the customer and ask how the payment should be applied. You can manually enter the amount you're applying against any invoice in the Payment column. You must apply the entire amount of the payment, no matter how many invoices you have to select (even if an applied payment is only a partial payment against an invoice amount).

If the payment exactly matches the amount of an invoice, or if only one invoice appears in the Receive Payments window, QuickBooks automatically applies it correctly. Otherwise, QuickBooks applies the payment to the oldest invoice. If you are using the balance forward system, just let QuickBooks apply payments against the oldest invoices.

If the payment is smaller than any single invoice amount, apply the payment to the oldest invoice (unless the customer specified an invoice number for this payment).

If the payment is larger than any single invoice amount, but not large enough to cover two invoices, apply the payment amount to the oldest invoice, and then select one or more additional invoices to apply the remaining amount.

After you finish applying the payment, if there are insufficient funds to pay off an existing invoice, the Receive Payments window displays a message that asks whether you want to leave the underpaid amount as an underpayment, or write it off.

It's almost always best to retain the underpayment, which means the invoice you selected for partial payment remains as a receivable, with a new balance (the original balance less the payment you applied). When you save the payment QuickBooks makes the appropriate postings. If you send statements to customers, the unpaid balance appears on the statement.

Occasionally, you may want to write off the unpaid balance. If the customer made a mistake in the check amount, and it's off by pennies (or nickels or dimes), you may decide it's not worth calling the customer to arrange for another payment. On the other hand, you may have some reason to believe that an unpaid balance (more substantial than small change) will never be paid, and you might as well write it off.

When you select the option to write off the unpaid amount and save the transaction, QuickBooks opens the Write Off Amount dialog so you can choose the posting account, and, if applicable, apply a class to the transaction.

Discuss the account to use for a write off with your accountant. You can create an Income or Expense account for this purpose, depending on the way your accountant wants to track receivables you've decided to forgive. (Writing off a balance is not the same as managing bad debts, which are a whole 'nother category of accounting).

Applying a Credit

If the customer has a credit, the payment that arrives probably reflects that credit—the customer has withheld the credit amount from the payment.

To apply the credit, and therefore mark the invoice as paid, first enter the amount of the payment. Then click the button labeled Discounts and Credits, select the credit amount, and click Done.

When you return to the Receive Payments window, the credit has been applied to the invoice.

Receiving Payments from a Generic Customer

You may be keeping the names of your individual donors or members outside of QuickBooks, but still entering invoices (using a generic customer name) in order to track the amount of money you're expecting to receive for pledges and membership fees.

As money arrives, you have to record invoice payments in QuickBooks. Use the other software to note that a specific donor or member sent money in response to the pledge or invoice, and then record the payment in QuickBooks by selecting the generic customer name.

Understanding Customer Payment Postings

When you save the payment, QuickBooks posts the amount of payment to the general ledger, as follows:

- The Accounts Receivable account is credited for the amount received.
- If you chose to deposit the funds into a bank account, that bank account is debited for the amount received.

- If you chose to deposit the funds to the Undeposited Funds account, that account is debited for the amount received. When you make the deposit, the Undeposited Funds account is credited for the amount, and the bank account is debited.

See the section "Making Bank Deposits" to learn about the Undeposited Funds account.

Receiving Income with No Associated Invoice

QuickBooks provides a way to receive revenue when the receipt isn't connected to an invoice. QuickBooks calls this type of transaction a *sales receipt*.

Nonprofits frequently receive revenue for which no invoice exists in the system. Donations, and sales of services or goods, are all examples of revenue you often don't invoice.

In addition, if you don't create invoices for the grants and contracts you're expecting, you must use the sales receipt feature to record the income when it arrives.

TIP: QuickBooks uses the term sales receipt instead of cash sale (the common jargon). A sales receipt usually describes a piece of paper given to a customer after a cash sale.

Creating a Sales Receipt

To record a sales receipt, choose Customers → Enter Sales Receipts from the menu bar, to open the Enter Sales Receipt window seen in Figure 6-12.

Select the customer or job from the drop-down list in the Customer:Job field. Fill in the rest of the header (the class and the payment method information).

Enter the item, amount, and other data in each column (the Enter Sales Receipts window works the same as invoices—just fill in the information). Click Save & New to bring up a blank Sales Receipt window, or click Save & Close if you're finished.

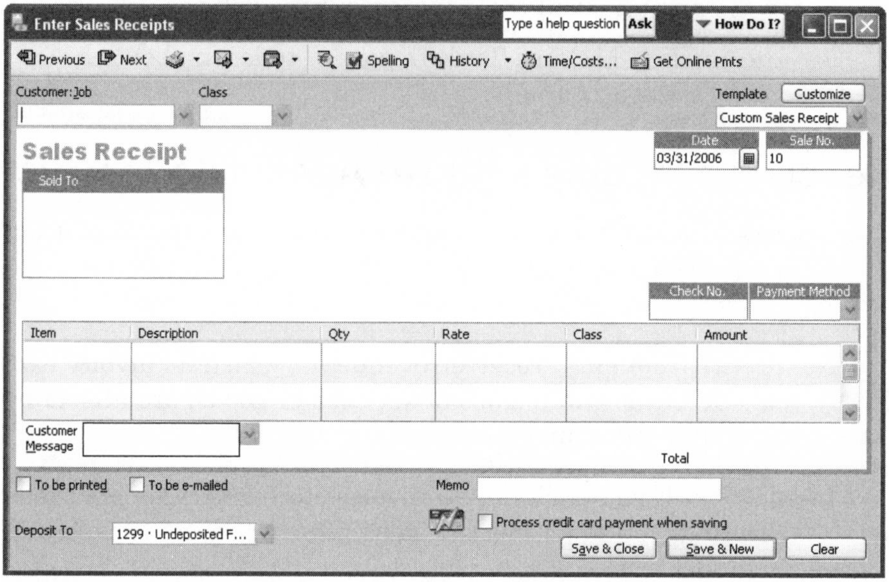

Figure 6-12: The Enter Sales Receipts form is similar to the invoice form.

First, Check for Invoices

When you select the customer or job in the Enter Sales Receipt window, if invoices exist for that customer or job QuickBooks doesn't warn you of that fact. As a result, you must be careful to avoid entering cash sales if they're really invoice payments.

To avoid recording income while an invoice remains unpaid in the customer's record, check the A/R for the customer or job to see if the check might be a payment.

To view a QuickBooks QuickReport on the customer's current balance, open the Customers & Job List, select the customer's listing, and press Ctrl-Q.

Recording a Donation

If the revenue is a donation from an individual, you should use a template designed for that purpose. QuickBooks Premier Nonprofit edition has a template named Standard Donation, which is better suited to this situation than the regular sales receipt template (which is named Custom Sales Receipt).

TIP: If you're running QuickBooks Pro, you can create a Donation template (see the section "Creating a Donation Receipt Template", later in this chapter).

The Donation template looks exactly like the Custom Sales Receipt template, except the word Donation appears at the top of the form, instead of the phrase Sales Receipt. If you print and mail the form to the donor, the title Donation is more appropriate.

You don't have to add each donor to your QuickBooks file. You can keep those names in another software application. Create a generic customer name (such as Donor), and post all donations to that customer.

If you want to print and mail the form to the donor as a receipt, see the discussion on using a generic customer for pledges earlier in this chapter.

Understanding Sales Receipt Postings

When you enter a sales receipt, QuickBooks makes the following postings to your general ledger:

- Credits the Income account(s) linked to the item(s) you entered in the transaction.
- If you chose to deposit the funds into a bank account, that bank account is debited for the amount received.
- If you chose to deposit the funds to the Undeposited Funds account, that account is debited for the amount received. When you make the deposit, the Undeposited Funds account is credited for the amount, and the bank account is debited.

Making Bank Deposits

If you haven't set the Undeposited Funds account as the default recipient of income received, QuickBooks offers two options for depositing your payment on the Receive Payments window and in the Enter Sales Receipts window:

- Group With Other Undeposited Funds
- Deposit To [*a specified existing bank account*]

In the following sections, I explain the choices, so you can decide how you want to handle deposits.

Defaulting to the Undeposited Funds Account

By default, QuickBooks sets an option to use the Undeposited Funds account when you're working in any payments window (Receive Payments or Enter Sales Receipts). If you leave this setting enabled, you won't see any options for depositing the funds in the payment transaction windows.

If you don't use the Undeposited Funds account, or if you want to choose whether to use it when you're filling out a payment window, you can disable this option. When you do, the payment windows display options for depositing payments to the Undeposited Funds account, or to a specific bank (which you select from a drop-down list if you have more than one bank account).

To change this setting, open the Preferences dialog and select the Sales & Customers category. In the Company Preferences tab, deselect the option Use Undeposited Funds As A Default Deposit Account.

Using the Undeposited Funds Account

When you set up your company file, QuickBooks establishes an account named Undeposited Funds automatically, with an account type of Other Current Asset. Selecting this account as the deposit account means that each payment you receive is individually posted to this account.

When you go to the bank to make your deposit, you move the total amount of the deposit you made from the Undeposited Funds account into the bank account. QuickBooks posts the total bank deposit to the bank (not the individual amounts for each payment). That total matches the amount on the bank statement that shows up next month, making it easier to reconcile the account.

It's clearly more efficient to use this approach, unless you never get more than one payment a day, and you always run to the bank to deposit the check, never letting checks pile up between deposits. (Or, unless you get some enjoyment from spending a lot of time and effort reconciling the bank statement)

After you return from your trip to the bank, you have to enter the deposit in QuickBooks. Choose Banking → Make Deposits to open the Payments to Deposit window seen in Figure 6-13.

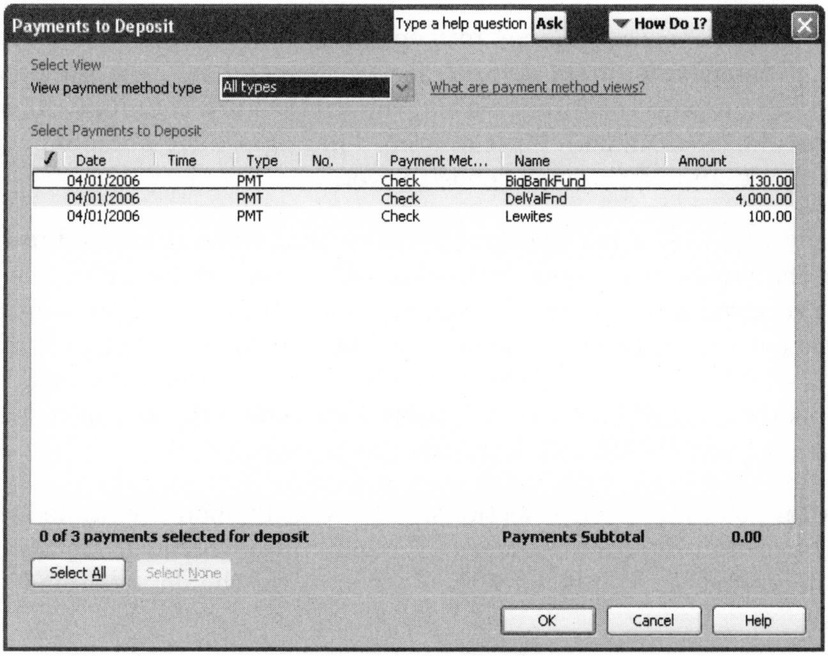

Figure 6-13: The funds you've accumulated since the last bank
deposit are waiting to be deposited.

If any of the funds were collected by credit card or by direct deposit, don't select them, because your bank probably lists those deposits separately on your statement.

To make it easier to exclude credit card and direct deposit amounts, select Cash and Check from the Payment Method Type drop-down list at the top of the window. Only cash and check payments appear in the list, and you can select all of them. When you know the credit card or direct deposits have been sent to your bank, you can return to this window and make those deposits.

If you're depositing money into bank subaccounts (using fund accounting), select all the cash receipts that should be posted to the restricted subaccount and click OK to open the Make Deposits window. Deposit the money to the right subaccount. After you create that deposit, return to this window and select the cash receipts going into the unrestricted subaccount, and click Next.

If you're depositing money into one bank account, click Select All to select all the payments for deposit. If you want to hold back the deposit of any item, deselect it by clicking in the check mark column (which removes the check mark). For example, you might have accepted a post-dated check, and you cannot deposit it yet.

You may have other deposits to make, that weren't entered into either the Payment window or the Sales Receipts window. Perhaps you've received a refund check from a vendor, or a check representing the proceeds of a loan. Enter those deposit items in the next transaction window (the Make Deposits window). The Payments to Deposit window only displays the cash receipts you've entered into QuickBooks through the Payments and Sales Receipts transaction windows.

After you make your selections, click Next to open the Make Deposits window seen in Figure 6-14. Select the bank into which these payments were deposited, and make sure the date matches the day you made the deposit.

Figure 6-14 shows additional line items to provide examples of the adjustments you can make to your bank deposit. For example, you can deposit checks that weren't in the original Make Deposit window, because they weren't a revenue receipt, such as a refund check for an expense.

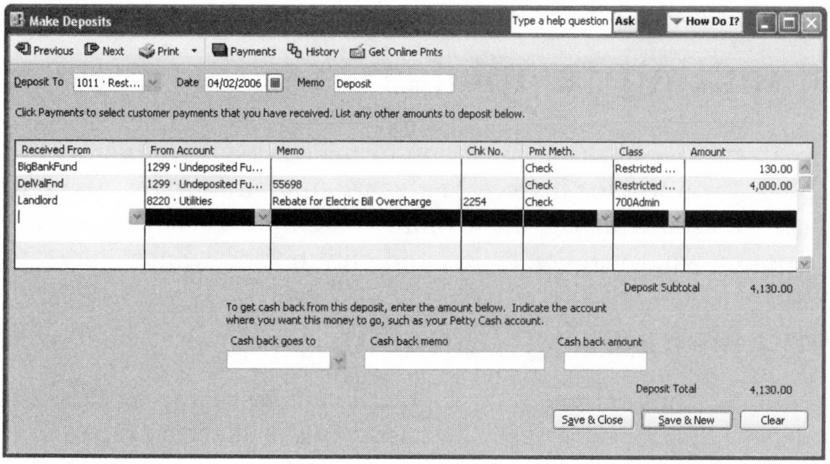

Figure 6-14: Make any necessary adjustments and record the deposit.

You can deduct the merchant card fee for a credit card sale, if your merchant bank deposits net amounts (don't forget the minus sign). You can also make adjustments to get cash back, although that's a rare occurrence.

Depositing to the Bank Account

Depositing each payment directly to the bank means you don't have to take the extra step involved in using the Make Deposits window. However, each payment you receive appears as a separate entry in QuickBooks when you reconcile your bank account.

For example, if you received six invoice payments and/or cash receipts, for a total of $6350.00, and took the checks to the bank that day, your bank statement shows $6350.00 as the amount of the deposit. When you reconcile the bank statement, you'll have to select each of the six payments individually (which may require some work with a calculator).

If you've separated the bank account into subaccounts (for fund accounting), be sure you select the right bank subaccount for the transaction. If this is income connected to restricted funds, use the Restricted account. If this is an individual donation or membership, deposit the amount into the Unrestricted account.

Customizing Templates

It's easy to customize the transaction forms (called *templates* in QuickBooks) you use for invoices, sales receipts, and so on. You can use an existing template as the basis of a new template, copying what you like, changing what you don't like, and eliminating what you don't need.

Editing an Existing Template

You can make minor changes to a QuickBooks template by choosing the Edit function. Open the transaction window (for instance, the Create Invoices window), and click the Customize button on top of the Templates drop-down list box. This opens the Customize Template dialog, which lists the available templates for this transaction type.

Select the template you want to change and click Edit. After a message appears telling you that this Edit process has limited features, the Customize Invoice dialog appears with the Edit mode options.

Use the Format tab to change the font for the various parts of your invoice form. Select the part of the invoice you want to spruce up and click the Change button. If your printer setup is configured for blank paper, the options to change the font you use to print the company name and address are available. You can change the font, the font style (bold, italic, etc.), the size, the color, and the special effects (such as underline).

You can also disable the printing of any status stamps, such as the Pending notification, that may appear on the printed invoice. The status stamp continues to appear on the screen when you display the invoice, but won't appear on the printed form.

Use the Company tab to change the elements that print on your invoices. If you're switching from blank paper to preprinted forms, deselect the check boxes that enable printing of company information. Don't forget to go through a new printer setup, including alignment, when you use this edited template. When you're finished making your changes, click OK.

Designing a New Template

If you want to add, remove, or reposition elements in your transaction form, you have to design a new template. This is also the way to put any custom fields you may have created on the template.

Click the Customize button above the Template drop-down list box and select the template you want to use as the basis of your new template. Click New to open the Customize Invoice dialog.

Unlike the dialog you see when you merely edit a template, QuickBooks doesn't enter the name of the template you're using as a model in the Template Name box. That's because the changes you can make here are major, so you must give the template a new name to create a new form (you cannot use your new design to replace an existing, built-in, QuickBooks template).

Enter a name for your new template, and then move through the tabs to make changes. You can add, remove, or rename fields for the printed version of the template, for the screen version of the template, or for both.

Any custom fields you created are displayed and are available to add to the printed form, the on-screen display, or both. Go through all the tabs, making changes as needed.

NOTE: *Custom fields you created for the Names lists are available in the Fields tab, and custom fields you created for the Items list are available in the Columns tab.*

When you're finished making changes, click OK to save the new template. Its name appears in the drop-down list of templates so you can select it when you need it.

TIP: *You can also use the layout designer to change the position of the elements in the template, which is necessary if you add fields without removing existing fields to make room. You might want to play around with the designer feature, which seems complicated, but the logic becomes apparent after you've used it for a few moments. Use a newly created template, not a template you need, as a test template when you're learning how to use the layout designer.*

Creating a Pledge Template

If you're using QuickBooks Pro, you should create a template for pledges (QuickBooks Premier Nonprofit edition comes with a Pledge template). I'll describe the basic changes you should make, but you're free to create your own design.

Open a blank invoice form and click the Customize button. In the Customize Template dialog, select the template you want to use as the basis of your Pledge template (the Intuit Professional Invoice is the easiest to convert to a pledge). Click New to open the Customize Invoice dialog seen in Figure 6-15. The Header tab is in the foreground.

Enter a name for this template in the Template Name field at the top of the dialog. You can call it Pledge, or you can call it Pledge-1 if you plan to create multiple Pledge templates (the name you use doesn't appear in the template).

Customizing Header Information for Pledges

Make the following changes to the Title fields in the Header tab:

- **Default Title**: Change the text to Pledge. Select both Screen and Print to have the title appear in both places.
- **Date**: Make no changes.
- **Invoice Number**: Change the text to Pledge # or Pledge No. Select both Screen and Print to have the title appear in both places.
- **Bill To**: Change the text to Donor or Contributor. Select both Screen and Print to have the title appear in both places.

- **Ship To**: Deselect both the Screen and Print options to have the field disappear (it isn't needed for a pledge). Since the field won't appear, you don't have to delete the existing text (but you can if you're compulsive about these things).

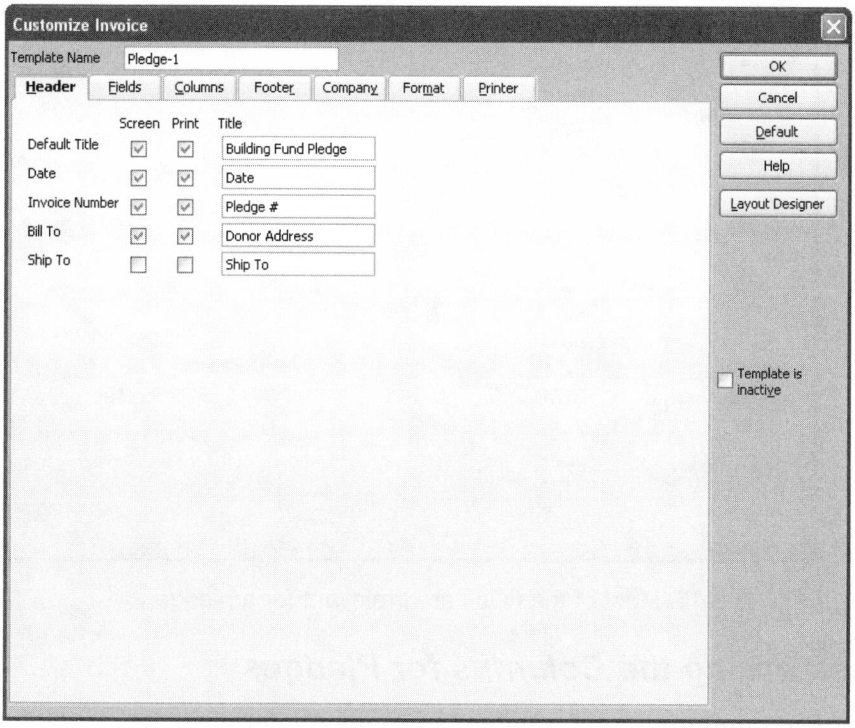

Figure 6-15: Make changes in the Header to create a form that looks like a pledge instead of an invoice.

Customizing the Fields for Pledges

Click the Fields tab, where all the possible fields for an invoice are listed. Any custom fields you created appear at the bottom of the list (see Figure 6-16).

Deselect both the Screen and Print options for the built-in fields you don't want to use, most the fields are unnecessary for a pledge form. If a custom field is relevant for a pledge, you can select it for the screen, the printed document, or both.

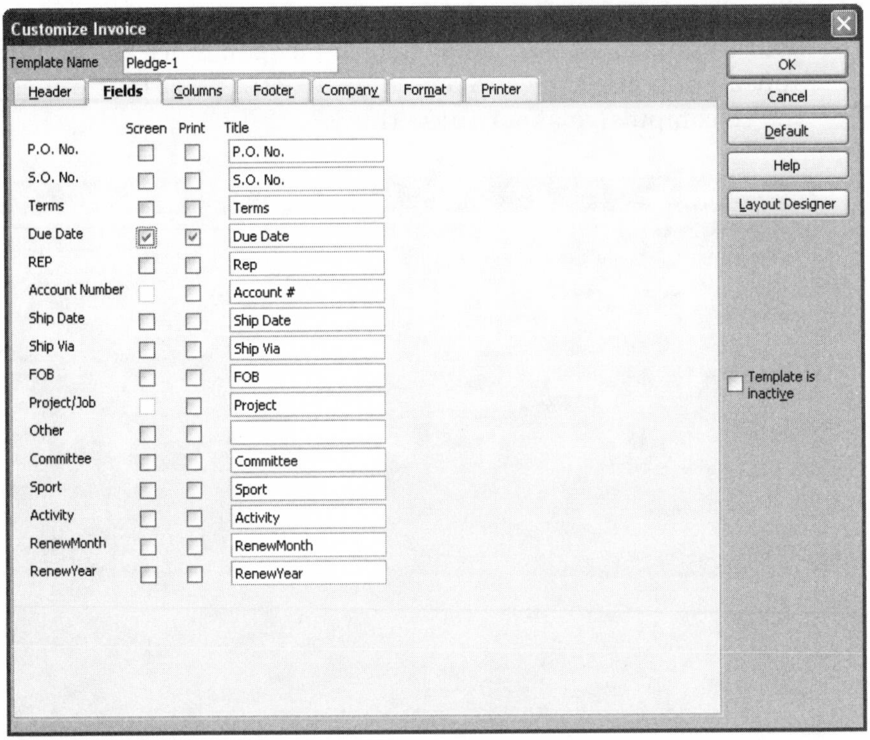

Figure 6-16: Most of the fields are irrelevant for a pledge.

Customizing the Columns for Pledges

Click the Columns tab and make the following changes:

- Deselect the Screen option for the Quantity column to remove the column from the template. The Order number assigned to that column changes to zero.
- Deselect the Screen option for Rate column to remove the column from the template. The Order number assigned to that column changes to zero.
- Change the Order number for the Class column to 3, which automatically changes the Order number for the Amount column to 4.

If you created any custom fields for items, they're listed in this tab. It's unlikely that any of your custom fields are needed for a pledge, but if so, select the field for inclusion on the template.

Customizing the Footer for Pledges

Click the Footer tab, and change the text for the Message field from Customer Message to Donor Message.

Click OK to save your new pledge template, which is now listed in the drop-down list when you open a blank invoice form.

Creating a Donation Receipt Template

QuickBooks Pro users lack a handy template that's included in Premier Nonprofit edition: a template you can use for recording donations. This template is used for recording income that arrives without an invoice (technically, it's a cash sale, which QuickBooks calls a *sales receipt*).

Most of the time, you enter donations as a total, without entering each donor's name and the amount of that donation. Tracking individual donors in QuickBooks is unworkable unless you only have a handful of donors.

You could use the standard Sales Receipt template (named Custom Sales Receipt), but that contains fields you don't really need for tracking donations. In addition, if a donor asks for a printed receipt, it's better to be able to print a form that doesn't look like a cash sale at a retail store.

To create a donation receipt template, choose Customers → Enter Sales Receipts. In the Enter Sales Receipts window, click the Customize button atop the Template field, to open the Customize Template dialog.

Select Custom Sales Receipt as the template, and click New to design a new Donation template. Then use the following steps to create your template:

1. In the Template Name field at the top of the dialog, enter a name for your template (e.g. Donation).
2. In the Header tab, make the following changes:
   • Change the text for the Default Title to Donation.
   • Change the text for the Sale Number to Donation No.
   • Change the text for Sold To to Donor.

3. In the Fields tab, deselect the Print option for Project/Job to remove the field. Only Check Number and Payment Method should be selected for Screen and Print options.

4. In the Columns tab, make the following changes:
   - Deselect both Screen and Print options from the Quantity column to remove the column.
   - Deselect both Screen and Print options from the Rate column to remove the column.
   - Select the Screen option for the Class column. Deselect the Print option if it's selected.
   - Change the number in the Order field for the Class column to 3, which automatically changes the number in the Order field for the Amount column to 4.
   - In the Footer tab, change the text in the Message field from Customer Message to Donor Message.

6. Click OK to save your new template.

This template is available in the Template drop-down list whenever you create a receipt for a donation.

Tracking Receivables

QuickBooks provides a multitude of tools to help you collect money due. The tools that exist give you the ability to set up and assess finance charges, send letters to customers who are overdue by a time period you select, and send statements.

I'm not going to cover all of those accounts receivable tools, because nonprofits don't usually need them. However, it's important to understand how to run reports to see the revenue that's overdue, or is due in the future. These reports are called *aging reports*. Your board of directors usually wants to see this information, and your staff needs it when planning budgets.

Aging reports are compiled from the invoices you enter into the system. That's why it's important to use invoices for grants and contracts, even though you're not mailing those invoices to the donors.

To see aging information, choose Reports → Customers & Receivables and then choose the report you want to view.

- The A/R Aging Summary report displays a quick, uncomplicated view of amounts you haven't yet received, sorted by customer.
- The A/R Aging Detail report displays the amounts due with individual listings of each invoice you sent to each customer.

By default, the report uses the current date, so you can see what's overdue, and by how many days. To see how much revenue is expected in the future, change the date range at the top of the report window to a date in the future.

Chapter 7

Managing Expenses

Accrual and cash expense tracking

Entering bills

Entering vendor credits

Paying bills

Creating direct disbursements

Tracking payroll expenses

Allocating expenses to programs

anaging expenses is more complicated for nonprofit organizations than it is for pro-profit businesses. Nonprofits must classify expenses by program, and often must allocate some expenses across multiple programs. Every expense must be reported to funding agencies, and, if the nonprofit organization files a 990 Tax Return, expense reporting follows strict rules.

In this chapter, I'll go over the tasks you face as you track expenditures appropriately for nonprofits.

Accrual Vs. Cash Expense Tracking

In accounting, we say that books are maintained on either an *accrual basis*, or a *cash basis*. The difference between the two is the way in which expenses are tracked.

Vendor bills get paid in either of two ways: you enter the bill in QuickBooks and then pay the bill later (hopefully, before it's overdue), or you just write a check to pay the bill, without entering the bill into the system (called a *direct disbursement*). Most for-profit business, and some nonprofit organizations actually use both methods.

In accrual based accounting, an expense is recognized as soon as it exists. When you get a vendor bill, that expense exists, and must be entered into your accounting software. (The same is true of revenue, because revenue is recognized when it exists, which means at the time enter an invoice, not at the time the invoice is paid.)

In cash based accounting, an expense is recognized when it is paid. Often, the expense exists well before it's paid, but in a cash based system, only the payment is tracked and reported on. (For revenue, a cash based system only recognizes revenue that is received—the point at which the customer's payment is in the bank.)

One of the important distinctions between accrual and cash accounting is the way you file tax returns. Most businesses, especially small businesses, file cash based tax returns. Businesses that have to manage inventory usually file accrual based tax returns. Businesses that want to change the basis of their tax returns have to get permission from the Internal Revenue Service.

Nonprofit organizations that file tax returns (Form 990) usually file accrual based returns. However, even for nonprofit organizations that don't file tax returns, accounting standards demand that nonprofit organizations track and report finances on an accrual basis.

The truth is, cash based accounting isn't a good system, because you never see an accurate state of your financial health. If you want to get a good picture of your financial position, it's useless to see reports on earnings without also seeing your upcoming expenses (as well as your future revenue). As a result, most businesses keep books on an accrual basis, and then adjust the accrued amounts (e.g. Accounts Payable and Accounts Receivable) to create their tax returns.

QuickBooks users have an advantage in the fact that all QuickBooks reports have an option to perform calculations on either an accrual or cash basis. Business owners run accrual based reports to keep an eye on their business health, and run cash based reports to prepare tax returns. (Not all accounting software applications have this ability to let users choose the basis of reports.)

In the discussions in this chapter, I'm assuming you're using accrual based accounting.

Entering Bills

When the mail arrives, after you open all the envelopes that contain checks from donors (it's more fun to do that first), you need to enter the bills that arrived. To do so, choose Vendors → Enter Bills from the menu bar to open the Enter Bills window seen in Figure 7-1.

The Enter Bills window has two sections:

- The header section contains information about the vendor and the bill.
- The details section contains the data related to your general ledger accounts.

The details section has two tabs:

- Expenses, for ordinary expenses.
- Items, for purchasing inventory items that you resell.

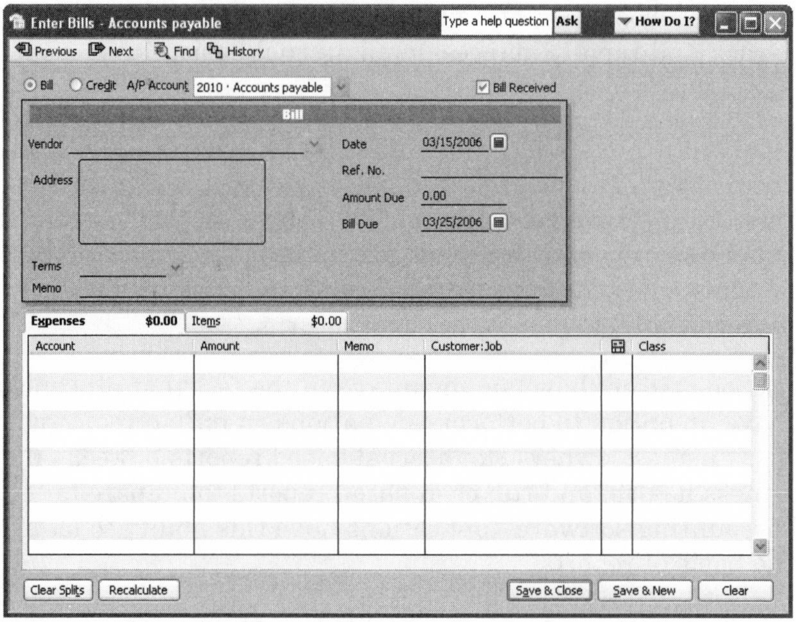

Figure 7-1: Use the Enter Bills fields to track details of each bill.

Entering Header Data

If you have multiple Accounts Payable accounts, an A/P Account field is at the top of the transaction window. Use it to enter the A/P account to which you want to post this bill. If you don't have multiple A/P accounts, the field isn't displayed.

NOTE: *It's usually not necessary to maintain multiple A/P accounts. However, some nonprofit organizations that give grants to other nonprofits create a specific A/P Account to track grants they've committed to other organizations, but haven't yet written the check.*

In the Vendor field, click the arrow to choose the vendor from the list that appears. If the vendor isn't on the list, choose <Add New> to add this vendor to your QuickBooks vendor list. The go through the fields as follows:

- Enter the Bill Date, which is earlier than the current date by the number of days it took the bill to travel through the mail.
- The Due Date fills in automatically, depending on the terms you have with this vendor. If you have no terms entered for this vendor, the due date is automatically filled out using the default number of days for paying bills. QuickBooks sets this at 10 days, but you can change the default in the Preferences dialog (in the Purchases & Vendors section.)
- Enter the Amount Due.
- Enter the vendor's invoice number in the Ref. No. field.

Entering the Details

Click in the Account column to display an arrow you can click to see your chart of accounts. Select the account to which you're posting this bill. QuickBooks automatically enters the Amount Due you entered in the header into the Amount column.

If the entire amount of this bill is posted to the same account, the same job (if you're posting bills to jobs for job costing), and to the same class, move through the rest of the columns and enter the data.

Depending on the bill, you may be able to assign the entire amount to one expense account, or you may have to split the bill among multiple expense accounts. For example, your utility bills are usually posted to Utilities, or to a specific utility account (electric, heat, and so on). However, credit card bills are often split among numerous expense accounts.

Even if the entire amount of the bill is posted to one expense account, you may have to split the posting to accommodate multiple classes, or grants. In fact, you may have to split the bill across multiple accounts and multiple classes (and even multiple grants). I'll go over these scenarios in the following sections.

Posting to Multiple Expense Accounts

If the amount due has to be posted to multiple expense accounts, you need to enter the transaction over multiple line items.

After you select the first expense account in the Account column, QuickBooks automatically enters the total amount due in the Amount column. Change the data in the Amount column to the amount you're posting to the selected account. Fill out the remaining columns in the row for Customer:Job (if you're tracking that information for this bill), and for Class (nonprofits should consider the Class column a required entry).

Return to the Account column and enter the account to which the next amount you enter is posted. QuickBooks automatically changes the Amount column to reflect the descending balance of the bill. If necessary, change the amount in the Amount column to the amount you're posting to the next account. Continue to add lines until you've split this bill among the appropriate accounts.

Allocating to Multiple Programs

Even if the entire bill can be posted to one expense account, you may want to allocate the amount among programs or grants. In that case, you must create multiple lines, similar to splitting a bill over multiple accounts.

1. In the first line of the details section, enter the expense account to which you're posting this transaction.
2. In the Amount column, change the amount to reflect the amount you're assigning to one class (program).
3. In the Class column, select the program to which you're allocating this amount.
4. In the next line, enter the same expense account, the amount required for the next class, and enter the class.
5. Repeat these steps on the next line, and continue to fill out the lines until the entire amount has been allocated to classes.

When you finish entering the bill, click Save & New to enter another bill, or click Save & Close if you're finished entering bills.

Allocating to Grants and Contracts

You can also allocate expenses to grants and contracts, which lets you create detailed reports for the expenses involved in administering those entities. Many grants and contracts have clauses that specify covered expenses (both program-specific and overhead), and some have clauses that permit you to collect reimbursement for some expenses.

Use the previous instructions for allocating expenses to multiple programs, and select a donor and grant in the Customer:Job column (see Figure 7-2).

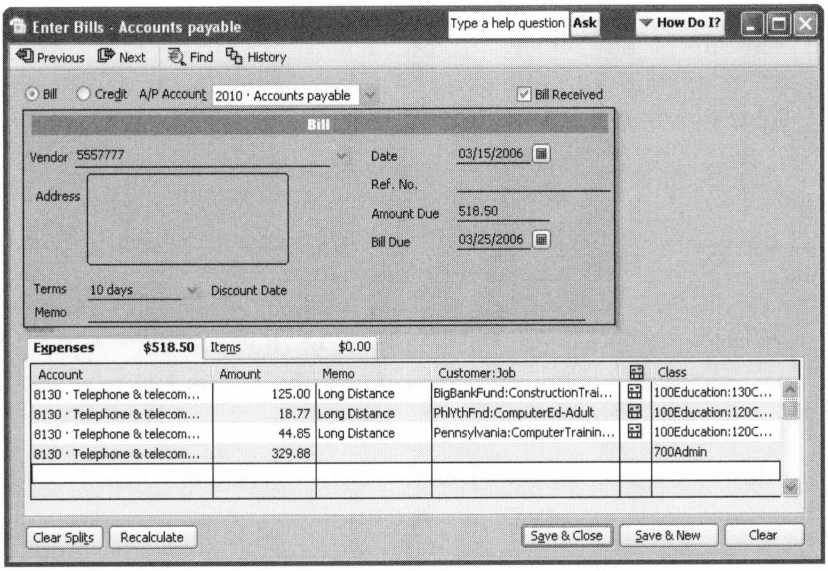

Figure 7-2: This telephone bill is allocated across grants and programs.

When you have data in the Customer:Job column, QuickBooks automatically puts an invoice icon in the column to the right of that column. That invoice icon signifies a reimbursable expense, and you must take one of the following actions.

- If you're merely tracking expenses against a grant or contract, click the invoice icon to superimpose a red X on the icon.

QuickBooks will not automatically create an invoice to charge this donor for reimbursement.

- If the terms of the grant or contract include a provision to send an invoice to the donor for reimbursement of this expense type, don't nullify the icon. QuickBooks stores the expense data so you can invoice the donor. Read Chapter 6 to learn how to create invoices for reimbursable expenses.

Accounts Payable Postings

When you enter vendor bills, QuickBooks posts amounts to your general ledger as follows:

- The A/P account is credited for the total amount of the vendor bill.
- Each account you selected in the detail section is debited for the total amount of its associated line item.

Although most vendor bills are posted to expense accounts, some transactions use an account type other than an expense account. For example, when you purchase equipment you post the transaction to a fixed assets account. If you send a deposit against a purchase, you post the transaction to a current asset account that tracks advance deposits. When you make a loan payment, the part of the total that represents principal is posted to the loan's liability account, and the interest is posted to the interest account (which is an expense account).

In addition, QuickBooks posts the data to the appropriate Customer:Job record, and the Class record.

Memorizing Bills

Some vendors don't send bills. For example, your landlord, your mortgage company, and a bank that holds a loan may expect you to pay automatically, or they may provide a coupon book instead of sending bills. In that case, many businesses and nonprofit organization just write a check, without entering a bill into their accounting system (cash-based account).

Nonprofits should not use this method of paying expenses; all bills should be entered as of the date they're recognized as existing, because nonprofits should be using accrual based accounting.

For vendors who do not send bills, you should create bills. This way, you can see an accurate picture of your organization's financial position, including future months.

It's too much work to create a bill for your rent every month, but you can have QuickBooks perform this task for you with the memorized transaction feature.

Creating a Memorized Bill

Create the vendor bill in the Enter Bills transaction window, as described previously in this chapter. Split the bill among accounts, classes, and jobs if warranted. Use the upcoming due date for this vendor when you create the bill. Then, before you save the bill, press Ctrl-M to open the Memorize Transaction dialog. Figure 7-3 shows the bill entry, as well as the Memorize Transaction dialog for that bill.

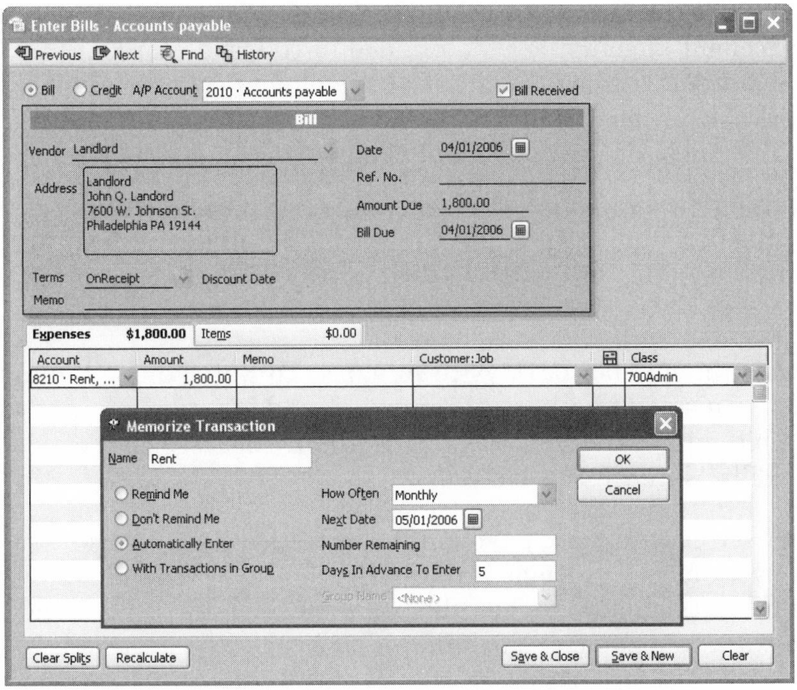

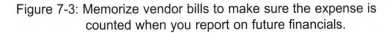

Figure 7-3: Memorize vendor bills to make sure the expense is
counted when you report on future financials.

Use the Name field to enter a name for the transaction. QuickBooks automatically enters the vendor name, but you can change it. Choose a name that describes the transaction so you don't have to rely on your memory to connect the vendor name to the transaction.

Select the interval for this bill from the drop-down list in the How Often field. Then, enter the next due date for this bill in the Next Date field.

Choose a reminder option from the following choices:

- Select Remind Me (the default) to tell QuickBooks to issue a reminder that this bill must be put into the system to be paid. Reminders only appear if you're using reminders in QuickBooks. Choose Edit → Preferences and click the Reminders category icon to view or change reminders options.
- Select Don't Remind Me if you don't want a reminder, and prefer to enter the bill in the Bills to Pay List yourself. (This requires an excellent memory, or a note taped to your monitor.)
- Select Automatically Enter to have QuickBooks enter this bill as a payable automatically, without reminders. (Most organizations find this is the most efficient choice.)

If this bill is finite instead of perpetual, such as a loan that has a specific number of payments, use the Number Remaining field to specify how many times this bill must be paid, after which the memorized bill is no longer active.

Specify the number of Days In Advance To Enter this bill into the system. If you selected automatic entry instead of a reminder, at that time the bill appears in the Select Bills To Pay list (see the section "Paying Bills", later in this chapter).

Don't select automatic payment for bills that don't have the same amount every month (such as utility bills). Use the Remind Me option so you can fill in the amount when the bill comes. On the other hand, you may not want to memorize the bill.

Click OK in the Memorize Transaction window to save it, and then save the bill. The memorized bill appears in the Memorized Transaction List (on the Lists menu).

TIP: *If you created the original bill only for the purpose of creating a memorized transaction and you don't want to enter the bill into the system for payment at this time, after you save the memorized transaction, close the Enter Bills window and respond No when QuickBooks asks if you want to save the transaction.*

Using the Memorized Transaction List

The memorized transaction list contains all the transactions you've memorized, which could include bills, invoices, or other transactions (see Figure 7-4). You can use this list to manipulate your memorized transactions. To open the Memorized Transaction list, take one of these actions:

- Press Ctrl-T
- Choose Lists → Memorized Transaction List from the menu bar

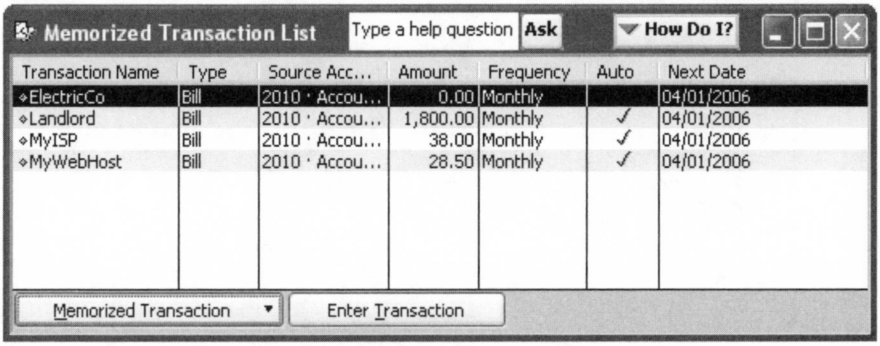

Transaction Name	Type	Source Acc...	Amount	Frequency	Auto	Next Date
◈ElectricCo	Bill	2010 · Accou...	0.00	Monthly		04/01/2006
◈Landlord	Bill	2010 · Accou...	1,800.00	Monthly	✓	04/01/2006
◈MyISP	Bill	2010 · Accou...	38.00	Monthly	✓	04/01/2006
◈MyWebHost	Bill	2010 · Accou...	28.50	Monthly	✓	04/01/2006

Figure 7-4: All your memorized transactions are stored in one convenient list.

Modifying or Deleting Memorized Transactions

Use the Memorized Transactions list to modify or delete a transaction. Select the transaction's listing, and use one of the following actions:

- Press Ctrl-E to edit the memorized transaction. The original Memorize Transaction dialog opens so you can modify the data in any field, or change any options.
- Press Ctrl-D to delete the memorized transaction.

Changing the Display of the Memorized Transaction List

By default, the Memorized Transaction List displays basic information about each transaction. You can add or remove columns as needed. To change the display, click the Memorized Transactions button at the bottom of the list window, and choose Customize Columns. In the Customize Columns dialog (seen in Figure 7-5) remove, add, or change the order of, any column.

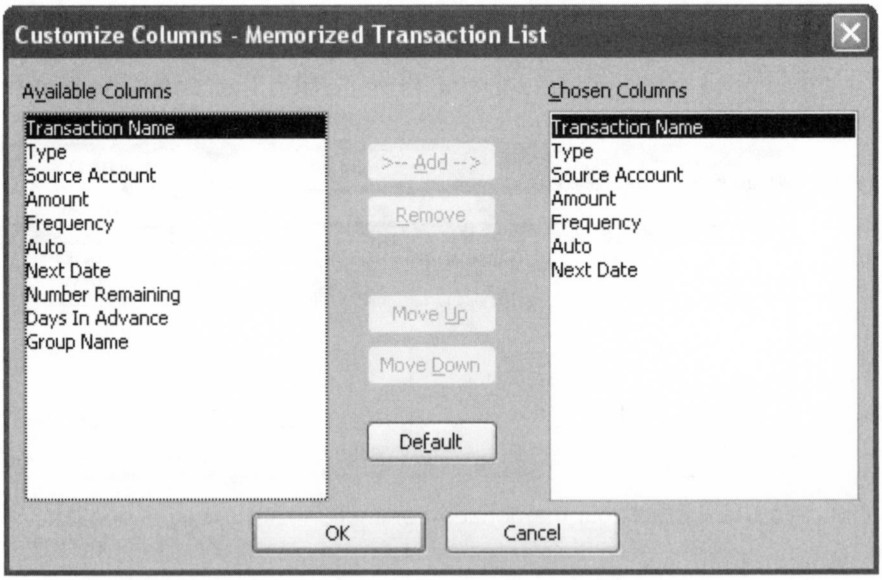

Figure 7-5: Change the data the memorized transactions list displays.

Marking a Memorized Bill for Payment

If you chose one of the "remind me" options when you created a memorized bill, you have to make the bill active. (If you told QuickBooks to enter the bill for payment automatically, you don't have to take this additional step.)

To include a memorized bill in the Pay Bills list, double-click the appropriate listing to open the bill in the usual Enter Bills window, with the next due date showing. Click Save & Close to save this bill so it becomes a current payable and is listed in the Pay Bills window you open when you write checks to pay bills.

Creating Memorized Transaction Groups

If you have many memorized transactions, you don't have to select them for payment one at a time. You can create a group and then invoke actions on the group (automatically invoking that action on every bill in the group). The steps to accomplish this are easy:

1. Press Ctrl-T to display the Memorized Transaction List.
2. Click the Memorized Transactions button at the bottom of the list window, and choose New Group. In the New Memorized Transaction Group window, give this group a name.
3. Fill out the fields to specify the way you want the bills in this group to be handled (see Figure 7-6).
4. Click OK to save this group.

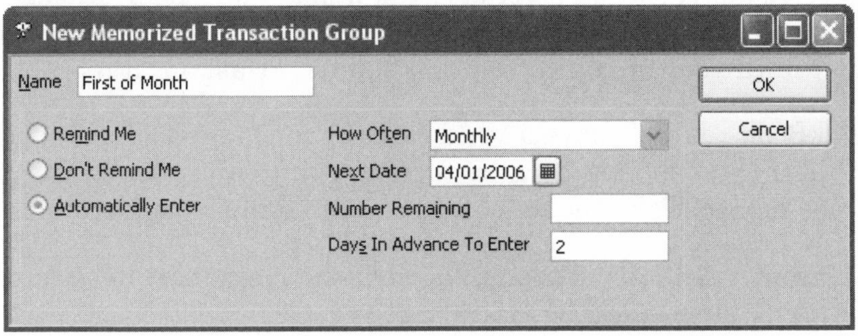

Figure 7-6: Create groups of memorized transactions to make it easier to manage them.

Adding Transactions to a Group

Now that you've created the group, you can add memorized transactions to it as follows:

1. In the Memorized Transaction List window, select the first memorized transaction you want to add to the group.
2. Press Ctrl-E to edit the memorized transaction.
3. When the Schedule Memorized Transaction window opens with this transaction displayed, select the option named With Transactions In Group. Then select the group from the drop-down list that appears when you click the arrow next to the Group Name field.
4. Click OK and repeat this process for each bill in the list.

Once you've created a group, every time you create a memorized transaction in the future the With Transactions In Group option is available in the dialog. That means you can add the transaction to a group when you create the memorized transaction, instead of using the Edit function after you memorize the transaction.

If you have other recurring bills with different criteria (perhaps they're due on a different day of the month, or they're due annually), create groups for them and add the individual transactions to the group.

Entering Vendor Credits

If you receive a credit from a vendor, you must record it in QuickBooks. Then, you can apply the credit against an existing bill from that vendor, let it float until your next bill from the vendor, or ask for a refund.

QuickBooks doesn't have a vendor credit form; instead, you use the vendor bill transaction window, by turning it into a vendor credit with a click of the mouse. Take the following steps to enter a vendor credit:

1. Choose Vendors → Enter Bills from the menu bar) to open the Enter Bills window.
2. Select the Credit check box at the top of the transaction window, which automatically deselects Bill and changes the fields in the form so they're appropriate for a credit (see Figure 7-7).

3. Choose the vendor from the drop-down list in the Vendor field.
4. Enter the date of the credit memo.
5. Enter the amount of the credit memo.
6. In the Ref. No. field, enter the vendor's credit memo number (if one exists).
7. In the line item section, assign an account for this credit (usually the account you used when making the original purchase). QuickBooks automatically fills in the amount to match the amount you entered in the top of the transaction window.
8. Click Save & Close to save the credit.

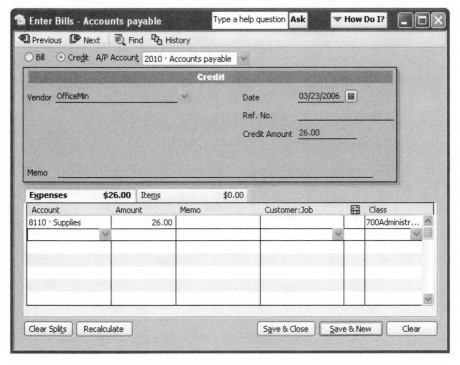

Figure 7-7: Select the Credit option to turn the Enter Bills transaction template into a Vendor Credit template.

Don't forget to assign the same class to the credited item you assigned when you originally entered the bill.

Paying Bills

At some point after you've entered the vendor bills into QuickBooks, you have to pay those bills. You don't have to pay every bill that's in the system, nor do you have to pay the entire amount due for each bill.

When you're ready to pay bills, choose Vendors → Pay Bills. The Pay Bills window seen in Figure 7-8 appears, and each field in the window influences the bills that are displayed.

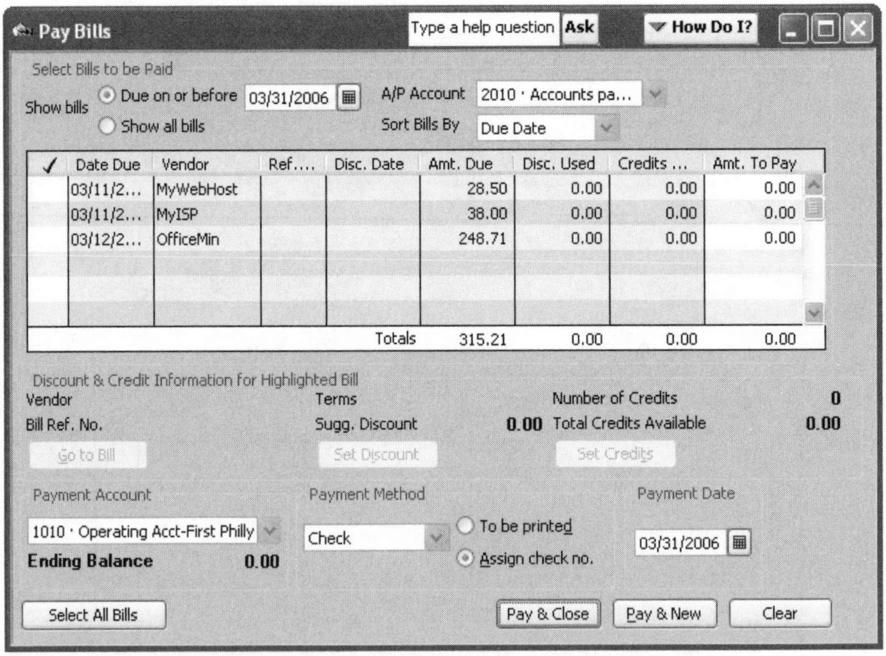

Figure 7-8: Set the options to match the bills you want to pay.

Working in the Pay Bills Window

The options in the Pay Bills window determine the list of bills you see. The Show Bills section of the window has two options: Due On Or Before, and Show All Bills

- Due On Or Before displays all the bills due within the next ten days by default, but you can change the date specification to display more or fewer bills.
- Show All Bills displays all the bills in your system, regardless of when they're due.

The A/P Account field is where you select the accounts payable account to which the bills you want to pay were originally posted. If you don't have multiple A/P accounts, this field doesn't appear in the window.

The option labeled Sort Bills By determines the way your bills are displayed in QuickBooks. The choices are:

- Due Date (the default)
- Discount Date (only important if you receive a discount from the vendor for timely payment—not a common scenario for nonprofits).
- Vendor
- Amount Due

At the bottom of the window, the Payment Account field is where you select the bank account you want to use for these payments.

In the Payment Method section, a drop-down list displays the available methods of payment: Check and Credit Card. Online Payment is also listed if you signed up for QuickBooks online payment services.

If you are paying by check and QuickBooks prints your checks, be sure the To Be Printed option is selected.

If you're writing the checks manually, select Assign Check No. When you finish configuring bill payments, QuickBooks opens the Assign Check Numbers dialog so you can specify the starting check number for this bill paying session.

In the Payment Date field, enter the date that you want to appear on your checks. By default, the current date appears in the field, but if you want to predate or postdate your checks, you can change that date.

If you select the bills today, and wait until tomorrow (or later) to print the checks, the payment date set here appears on the checks. You can tell QuickBooks to automatically enter a check date that matches the day you print the checks by changing the Checking Preferences in the Preferences dialog (see Chapter 4 for information about setting preferences).

Selecting the Bills to Pay

If you made changes to the selection fields (perhaps you changed the due date filter), the list of bills to be paid may change. When all the bills displayed are to be paid, either in full or in part, you're ready to move on.

Selecting a bill for payment is simple—just click the leftmost column to insert a check mark. If there are bills on the list that you're not going to pay, don't select them, and they'll return the next time you open the Pay Bills window.

If you want to pay all the listed bills in full, click the Select All Bills button. This selects all the bills for payment (and the Select All Bills button changes its name to Clear Selections, in case you want to reverse your action).

If you're using bank subaccounts to separate restricted from unrestricted funds, select only the bills that are to be paid from the first subaccount. Then select the other bank account and repeat the steps to the bills that are paid from the other subaccount.

Adjusting the Amounts to Pay

If you don't want to pay a bill in full, adjust the amount of the check by selecting the bill (click the left-most column to insert a check mark), and then change the amount in the Amt. To Pay column.

The next time you pay bills, or run an Accounts Payable report, the listing for this bill will display the balance due.

Applying Credits

If the list of bills includes vendors for whom you have credits, you can apply the credits to the bill. Select the bill, and if credits exist for the vendor, information about the credits appears on the Pay Bills window.

Click Set Credits to open the Discounts And Credits window. Select the credit, and click Done to return to the Pay Bills window. QuickBooks automatically changes the Amt. To Pay column to reflect the credit.

Preparing the Checks

When you've selected the bills to pay (and perhaps adjusted the amounts), take one of the following actions:

- Click Pay & New to repeat this process for bills that were posted to a different A/P account or are paid from a different bank account.
- Click Pay & Close if you're finished paying bills.

When you click Pay & Close, all the bills you paid are turned into checks (albeit unwritten checks) and you can see them if you open the bank account register.

If you selected the To Be Printed option in the Pay Bills window your bank account register displays To Print as the check number. (See the section "Printing Checks"),

If you selected the Assign Check No. option for manual checks, your bank account register uses the check number you specified in the Assign Check Numbers dialog. (See the following section, "Writing Manual Checks.")

Writing Manual Checks

If you're not printing checks, you must make sure the check numbers in the register match the checks you write. It's a good idea to print the bank account register so you can refer to it as you write the checks.

To print the register, open it and click the Print icon at the top of the register window. When the Print Register window opens, select the date range that encompasses the checks you need to write (they're probably all dated the same day), and click OK to print the report. Then write your checks, matching each check number to the register.

Printing Checks

Printing checks is easier and faster than writing manual checks. It's also more accurate, because the amount of the check is the same on the check and in your bank register (because QuickBooks enters the data automatically). I've found that most organizations that enter check data after they write manual checks have at least one month a year with bank reconciliation problems—the problem is always a typo because the check amount in the register doesn't match the amount on the check.

Before you can print checks in QuickBooks, you have to purchase computer checks, and then you must set up and configure the check-printing printer to match those checks.

Setting Up a Printer for Checks

Before you can print checks, you have to go through a setup routine. You must configure your printer for the type of check you're using, and you supply that information in the Printer Setup dialog. To set up your printer for checks, follow these steps:

1. Choose File → Printer Setup from the menu bar.
2. In the Printer Setup dialog, select Check/PayCheck from the drop-down list in the Form field.
3. In the Printer Name field, select the printer you want to use for printing checks
4. Select the check style of the checks you purchased. Three styles are available for QuickBooks checks, and a sample of each style appears in the window to show you what the style looks like.
   - **Standard checks** These are plain checks. They're the width of a regular business envelope (usually called a *#10 envelope*). If you have a laser or inkjet printer, there are three checks to a page. A dot matrix pin-feed printer just keeps rolling, since the checks are printed on a continuous sheet with perforations separating the checks.
   - **Voucher checks** These have a detachable section on the check form. QuickBooks prints voucher information if you have voucher checks, including the name of the payee, the date, and the individ-

ual amounts of the bills being paid by this check. The voucher is attached to the bottom of the check. The check is the same width as the standard check.

• **Wallet checks** These are narrower than the other two check styles (so they fit in your wallet). The paper size is the same as the other checks so the printer can handle them, but there's a perforation on the left edge of the check, which you tear off before sending the check.

5. Click the Align button and follow the instructions in the dialog to move the alignment, so that the text QuickBooks prints on your checks lands in the right places on the check form.

TIP You don't have to waste checks to test the alignment of the text, use a blank piece of paper and put it in front of the check, then hold both pieces of paper against a window or a light. Keep wasting plain paper until everything lines up properly.

Printing the Checks

To print your checks, choose File → Print Forms → Checks to open the Select Checks To Print dialog (see Figure 7-9).

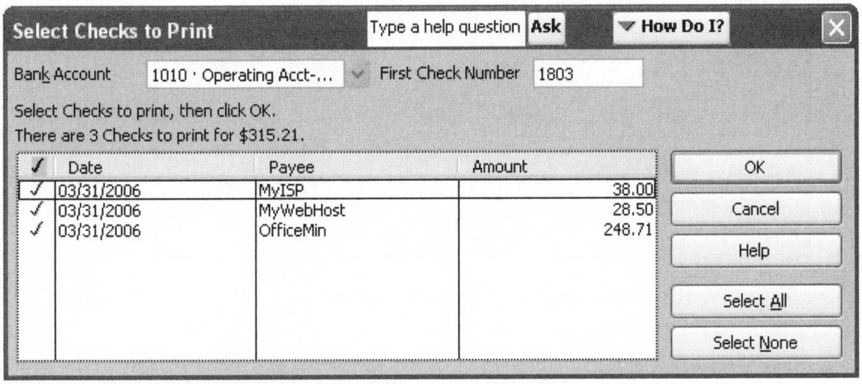

Figure 7-9: All the checks you specified in the Pay Bills window are selected for printing.

By default, all the unprinted checks in the bank register are selected for printing. The first time you print checks, check number 1 is displayed, so enter the real first check number. Hereafter, QuickBooks will track the check numbers and offer the next unused number when you print check. Click OK to open the Print Checks window.

If you're using laser/inkjet checks, QuickBooks asks how many checks are on the first page (in case you have a page with a check or two remaining). Fill in the number and place the page with leftover checks in the manual feed tray (QuickBooks prints those checks first). Then let the printer pull the remaining check pages from your standard letter tray. If you indicate there are three checks on the page, printing starts with the checks in the standard letter tray.

Reprinting When Problems Occur

Sometimes things go wrong during printing. The paper jams, you run out of toner, the cartridge ran out of ink, whatever. QuickBooks checks the print run for success or failure before finalizing the check writing process (see Figure 7-10).

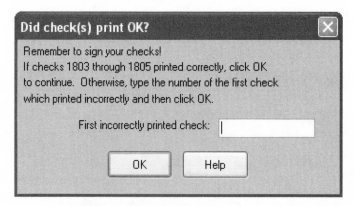

Figure 7-10: QuickBooks takes care of reprinting checks if a problem occurs.

If everything is fine, click OK. If anything went wrong, enter the number of the first check that had a problem. Put more checks into the printer (unless you're using a dot matrix printer with continuous check forms, in which case you don't have to do anything). Then click OK to have QuickBooks reprint all the checks that failed to print.

QuickBooks starts printing checks from the first bad one, and continues on to the end of the check run. Open the register for your bank account, and you'll see that the checks are numbered to match the print run.

Missing Check Numbers

If you have to restart the print run with the next available check number, QuickBooks does not track the number(s) of the checks that were misprinted. Those numbers are missing from your bank register, and that's sloppy bookkeeping.

Unfortunately, QuickBooks (unlike all other accounting software I've worked with) has no automatic, easy, method for voiding checks. In other accounting software, if you enter a check number with a zero amount, without filling out any other data, the software figures out what you're doing and displays a message asking if this is a void check. Clicking Yes records the check in the account register with a zero amount, and the text VOID is in the memo field (or some other field, depending on the accounting software).

This is useful for tracking check numbers for checks that aren't used, which means not only checks that failed to print, but checks you send as samples when you buy checks, checks you send as samples when you're setting up electronic fund transfers, checks that accidentally fell into the shredder, or checks your dog ate. (When you send sample checks, be sure to write the word VOID across the check.)

In QuickBooks, you must enter the check number, a payee, the amount (0.00) and post the transaction to some account. Then right-click the transaction line and choose Void, then choose Record.

This means you have to reconstruct the print run to enter the right payee or account, which is a pain. Of course, since the check is void, you could select any payee and any account to speed up the process of entering the check. However, the void check carries the payee and account information permanently, and it appears on reports for the payee and the account. Instead, invent a vendor and an account for voiding checks.

Check Purchase Reminders

When you finish printing checks, QuickBooks issues a message asking if you want to be reminded to purchase checks when your current supply gets low (see Figure 7-11). This message reappears every time you print checks until you say Yes and set up the reminder, or until you click the option Do Not Display This Message In The Future and then click No.

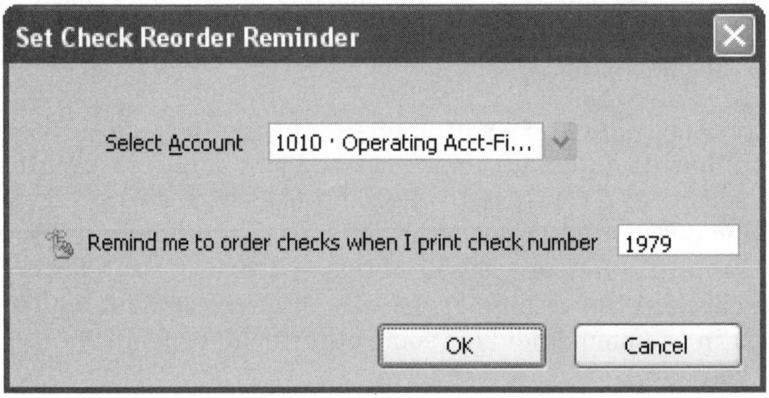

Figure 7-11: You can ask QuickBooks to remind you when it's time to reorder checks.

If you want the reminder, enter the check number that triggers the reminder. When that check number is included in a print run, QuickBooks will display a reminder that it's time to order more checks. The check number you enter depends on how many checks you print a week, and how fast your check printing company delivers.

Bill Payment Postings

Here's what happens in your general ledger when you make pay bills you'd previously entered in QuickBooks:

- Accounts Payable is debited for the total bill payments.
- The bank is credited for the total bill payments.

I've had clients ask why they don't see the expense accounts when they look at the postings for bill paying. The answer is that the expenses were posted to expense accounts when they entered the bills. That's a major difference between entering bills and then paying them, or writing checks without entering the bills into your QuickBooks system (called *direct disbursements*, which is covered in the next section).

Using Direct Disbursements

A direct disbursement is a disbursement of funds (usually by check) that is performed without matching the check to an existing bill.

Nonprofits shouldn't use direct disbursements, because before you write the check, the bill is due but you can't see it in your reports. However, sometimes you need to write a quick check and it's easier to bypass the bill entry process (for example, when a courier delivery person is standing in front of you waiting for a C.O.D. check).

Using Manual Direct Disbursement Checks

If you use manual checks, you can write your checks and enter the data in QuickBooks later. Or you can bring your checkbook to your computer and enter the checks in QuickBooks as you write them.

To enter checks in QuickBooks, you can work directly in the bank register, or you can use the Write Checks window. However, the bank register offers no field for assigning a class, and nonprofits should be posting every transaction to a class. In addition, you may be posting expenses to customers and jobs (for job costing, or for reimbursement), which is also not available in the check register.

Therefore, you should always use the Write Checks window (see Figure 7-12). To open it, press Ctrl-W, or choose Banking → Write Checks.

In the Bank Account field at the top of the window, select the bank account you're using for this check. The next available check number is already filled in unless the To Be Printed option box is checked (if it is, click it to toggle the check mark off and enter the check number).

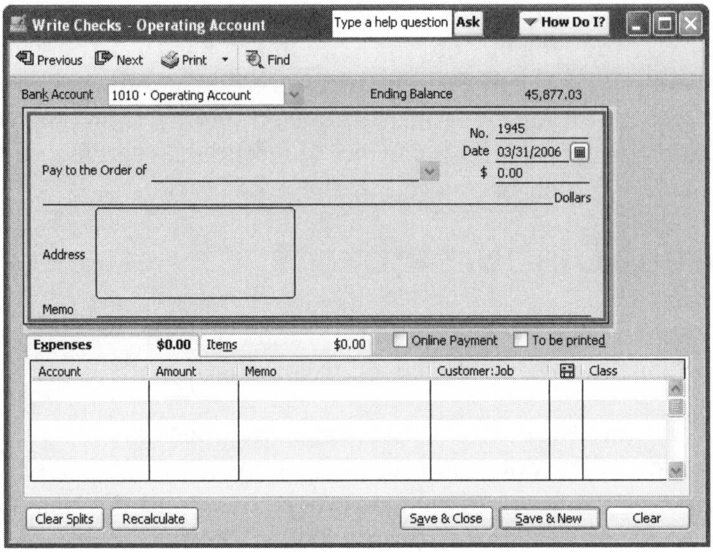

Figure 7-12: Fill out the fields to record the manual check you wrote.

Fill out the check, posting amounts to the appropriate accounts, customers, jobs, and classes. If necessary, split the postings among multiple classes and multiple grants as described earlier for entering bills.

When you finish, click Save & New to open a new blank check. When you're through writing checks, click Save & Close to close the Write Checks window. All the checks you wrote are recorded in the bank account register.

Printing Direct Disbursement Checks

You can print direct disbursement checks quite easily, whether you need one quick check, or you want to pay all your bills because you're not using the Pay Bills window to enter bills when they arrive.

Printing a Single Check Quickly

If you normally enter vendor bills and then print checks to pay those bills, you can print a check for a bill that isn't entered in your accounts payable system. This is handy for paying a C.O.D. charge, or for writing a quick petty cash check.

Click the Check button on the icon bar or press Ctrl-W to open the Write Checks window. Make sure the To Be Printed option is selected, and fill in the fields in the check. Click the Print icon at the top of the window when the check form is complete.

A small window opens to display the next available check number. Make sure that number agrees with the next number of the check in the printer (if it doesn't, change it), and then click OK. When the Print Checks window opens, follow the instructions for printing described earlier in this chapter. When you return to the Write Checks window, click Save & Close.

Printing Checks in Batches

If you're creating multiple direct disbursement checks, you can print them in a batch instead of one at a time. Fill out all the fields for the first check and click Save & New to open another blank Write Checks window. Repeat this step for every check you want to print. Click Save & Close when you are finished filling out all the checks.

Choose File → Print Forms → Checks and follow the instructions for printing checks described earlier in this chapter. Repeat these steps to print checks from another bank account.

Postings for Direct Disbursements

The postings for direct disbursements are quite simple:

- The bank account is credited for the total amount of checks written.
- Each posting account is debited for the amount posted to that account.

In addition, the data is recorded in the class (program) record, and in the record of any jobs (grants) involved in a transaction.

Tracking Payroll Expenses

In this section, I go over the steps you need to take to enter your payroll into QuickBooks if you're using a payroll service. Most small nonprofits use a payroll service, because it's more economical than hiring a book-keeper with payroll expertise, or having an accountant issue the payroll checks.

Payroll is always a complicated issue, but for nonprofit organizations, it's often more convoluted than it is for for-profit businesses. That's because personnel expenses are frequently covered (partially or in toto) by grants or contracts. Allocating payroll expenses across programs and grants is part of tracking payroll costs.

Some grantors require nonprofits to maintain detailed payroll records in the form of timesheets. QuickBooks contains a time tracking feature and you can create timesheets for each employee to track hours, grants, and programs. See the section "Tracking Time", later in this chapter. (You can also use a spreadsheet program for this purpose.)

If you use a payroll service you can enter the payroll data into QuickBooks in either of the following ways:

- Use a journal entry.
- Use fake payroll checks to record each individual paycheck (so you can reconcile your bank account).

TIP: If you offer direct deposit, and you've convinced all your employees to sign up for the service, you don't have to worry about reconciling checks.

Entering Payroll as a Journal Entry

Each time the payroll report arrives from the Payroll service company, make the following journal entries:

- A Journal Entry for the payroll
- A Journal Entry for the remittance of withholding amounts and employer payroll expenses.
- A Journal Entry for the allocation of payroll expenses to any grants and/or programs that permit that action.

> **NOTE**: *QuickBooks uses the term General Journal Entry (abbreviated GJE), instead of the more common term Journal Entry (abbreviated JE). I tend to use the familiar JE, but the terms are interchangeable.*

Some payroll services remit withholding and employer expenses for you at the same time they issue paychecks, and provide that information with the paycheck information. If so, you can enter those amounts in the same JE you use to record the payroll run.

> **TIP**: *Remind your payroll service that 501(c)(3) organizations aren't liable for FUTA (federal unemployment tax).*

If your payroll service doesn't remit withholding or employer expenses, don't use the second journal entry. The checks you write will take care of those postings. If you allocate payroll expenses, when you write the checks for employer expenses, you can use either of the following methods to allocate the expenses:

- Split the transaction lines in the Write Checks window to post the appropriate amounts to programs and grants.
- Post the total of each expense in the Write Checks window, and then create a journal entry to allocate those totals to programs and grants.

If your payroll service can manage your allocation algorithms, and report the payroll data broken down by grant and program, those reports provide the information you need to create the payroll journal entry with the appropriate allocations.

If your payroll service can't allocate payroll expenses, (or the price is prohibitive), you must allocate payroll manually. You can do this using either of the following methods:

- Enter the payroll data and the allocation information within the same journal entry.

- Enter the payroll data totals in one journal entry, and then create a second journal entry to allocate the amounts to programs or grants.

Most nonprofits find it easier, and more accurate, to use the second method (two journal entries). You can create the first JE immediately after each payday (from the payroll company report), and then create the second (allocation) JE at your convenience (but before any reports to grantors are due).

To use separate JEs, first create a journal entry to record the payroll totals from the payroll service report. You can post all expenses to the Administrative class.

Later, create a journal entry to allocate the payroll expenses by grant and program. You can calculate the allocations in Microsoft Excel and record the totals in this JE, or perform the calculations while you're creating the JE. Some organizations wait until the accountant or bookkeeper arrives to create the allocation entry, which may be at month or quarter end.

Creating the JE for the Payroll Run

To record the payroll JE in QuickBooks, open a General Journal Entry window by choosing Company → Make General Journal Entries. Enter the data from the payroll service report. For the payroll run, your JE should resemble Table 7-1. All entries are posted to the Administrative or Other Class.

In Table 7-1, the remittance of withholdings and employer payroll expenses are not included, because this is a payroll-run JE. The payroll liabilities are documented in a separate JE. Many organizations prefer to record those transactions in a separate journal entry (or as regular disbursement transactions when they write checks, if the payroll service doesn't remit these amounts).

Creating the JE for Payroll Liabilities

If your payroll service submits your payroll liabilities, you need to create a JE to enter those payments into QuickBooks. Follow these steps to accomplish the task:

1. Debit each withholding account that was credited in your payroll JE.
2. Debit the employer expenses to a payroll expense account (or individual expense accounts for each employer expense, if that's the way your accountant set up your chart of accounts).
3. Credit the bank account for the total remittance.

Account	Debit	Credit
Salaries & Wages - Officers	Total Gross Payroll	
Salaries & Wages -Other	Total Gross Payroll	
FWT		Total Federal Tax Withheld
FICA		Total FICA Withheld
Medicare		Total Medicare Withheld
State Income Tax		Total State Tax Wit hheld
Local Income Tax		Total Local Tax Withheld
State SDI		Total State SDI Withheld
State SUI		Total State SUI Withheld
Benefits Contrib		Total Benefits Contributions Withheld
Other Deductions (medical, pension, etc.)		Total Other Ded Withhe ld
Payroll Bank Account		Total Of Net Payroll

Table 7-1: Basic entries for a payroll journal entry.

TIP: *If you maintain a separate bank account for payroll, don't pay the payroll service from that account, because it's an operating expense, not a payroll expense. If the payroll service automatically takes its fee from the payroll account, transfer the amount from your operating account to the payroll account, posting the transaction to the expense account for the payroll service.*

Allocating Payroll

Your allocation journal entry splits the original totals among grants and/or programs. Credit the amount of the original expense that is available for allocation, and assign the line to the original administrative class (which "washes" the allocation to that class). Then, debit the expenses again, but this time divide the totals so they can be assigned to grants and programs as required.

Table 7-2 is a sample JE that allocates payroll to both grants and programs. You may be allocating payroll to grants only, or you may be allocating only some payroll expenses to both grants and classes.

Account	Debit	Credit	Memo	Customer:Job	Class
Salaries & Wages - Officers		3500.00			Administrative
Salaries & Wages - Officers	2000.00		Smith	Grant #1	Education
Salaries & Wages - Officers	1500.00		Jones	Grant#2	HealthServices
Salaries & Wages - Other		2000.00			Administrative
Salaries & Wages - Other	1000.00		Jackson	Grant#2	HealthServices
Salaries & Wages - Other	1000.00		Green	Grant#3	SeniorCitizen
CompanyMedicare		50.00			Administrative
CompanyMedicare	30.00		Smith	Grant#1	Education
CompanyMedicare	20.00		Green	Grant#3	SeniorCitizen
CompanyFICA		300.00			Administrative
CompanyFICA	180.00		Smith	Grant#1	Education
CompanyFICA	120.00		Green	Grant#3	SeniorCitizen

Table 7-2: Sample payroll allocation journal entry.

Only the portion of the original payroll expense that is available for allocation is journalized. Unallocated payroll expense is left in the Administrative class.

Notice that only expenses are allocated, not withholding (because that's not your expense, it's the employees money that's withheld).

Your payroll expenses may include additional categories, such as employer contributions to state unemployment, employer pension contributions, employer health benefit contributions, and so on.

The name of the employee in the memo field is optional, and your use of it depends on the level of detail you prefer to track.

If you don't have any grants that permit payroll postings, you should still allocate by program to produce accurate reports on each program. In that case, your payroll allocation journal entry uses only the Class field, omitting data in the Customer:Job field.

Memorizing Payroll Journal Entries

The best way to handle payroll journal entries is to create all the payroll and payroll liability journal entries without entering any financial data (every Debit and Credit column has a zero). Only enter the account names, the classes, and the customer or job (if appropriate).

After the accounts are filled in, press Ctrl-M to memorize the transaction. In the Memorize Transaction dialog, name the journal entry, select the option Don't Remind Me, and click OK. Name the memorized transaction appropriately, such as Payroll-Run, Payroll Liabilities, Payroll Allocation, and so on.

Close the GJE window, and when QuickBooks asks if you want to save the transaction, click No. You don't want to save a transaction with no real financial data, and you don't have to save a transaction to memorize it.

Thereafter, when it's time to enter the payroll information, press Ctrl-T or choose Lists → Memorized Transaction List, to open the Memorized Transaction List window. Double-click the appropriate listing to open the transaction window, enter the date, fill in the amounts, and save the transaction.

Entering Fake Checks for Easy Reconciliation

If your payroll service issues checks from your bank account, reconciling the account when the statement arrives is complicated if you haven't entered the checks. (You don't have to do this if you use direct deposit for payroll.)

The payroll journal entry took care of all the real postings, and you can create fake checks without affecting those numbers. You avoid changing the financial information by "washing" each transaction, posting it back to its source (the bank account).

You can either enter the real name for each check, or create a fake paycheck payee and use that name (entering the real name in the Memo field). If you want to use the real name, you can't use a name that's in your Employee list (because those names are only for real payroll transactions). Create an entry in the Other Name list for each employee. QuickBooks doesn't permit duplicate names, even from multiple lists, so you must create a slightly different name (such as a first initial and last name instead of a full name).

Use the report from the payroll service to enter the individual checks, using the following steps:

1. Open the account register for the bank account you use for payroll.
2. On the next available transaction line, enter the payroll check date.
3. Move to the Number field and enter the first check number on the payroll service report.
4. Enter the payee.
5. Enter the amount of the net paycheck.
6. In the Account field, choose the same bank account you're working in. QuickBooks displays a message warning you that you're posting the payment to the source account. Click OK. (In fact, click the check box that tells QuickBooks to omit this warning in the future.)
7. Click the Record button to save this check, and then enter the next check.
8. Repeat until all the checks are entered.

You can use the same technique to enter the checks the payroll service wrote to transmit your withholdings and employer payroll expenses.

As long as the real postings were entered in the journal entry you can post everything back to the bank account. You're "washing" every transaction, and you're not changing the balance of the bank account. Then, when you want to reconcile the payroll account, the individual checks are there. This procedure is quite easy, and you only have to do it on payday (or once a month if you want to wait until the bank statement comes in).

Allocating Expenses to Programs and Grants

At some point, you need to allocate all the administrative expenses that are eligible for allocation, to the appropriate jobs and classes. Most expenses are allocated at the time they're incurred, but other expenses, especially occupancy and other overhead costs, are allocated later using a journal entry.

The method is the same as explained earlier for allocating payroll expenses:

1. Credit the original expense using the Administrative class.
2. Debit the individual amounts for that expense and enter the appropriate class (and job, if you're also allocating by grant).

You have to allocate expenses before you print reports for grantors and your board. Some nonprofit organizations allocate on a regular basis—weekly, monthly, or quarterly, regardless of when they have to deliver reports.

I would love to be able to give you a step-by-step list of tasks for allocating expenses, but no such list exists. The terms and conditions built into your funding contracts, and the structure of your organization determine the way expenses are allocated.

For example, you may be able to allocate rent among all your programs, based on the amount of square footage used to support each program, or you may be able to split the square footage evenly among all programs. It's impossible to cover all the permutations and combinations

If you're going to create the allocation journal entries in-house, you should always work with your accountant to determine the formulas you need for allocation. Many nonprofit organizations, especially those that lack a financial professional on staff, let the accountant perform all the allocation tasks.

To determine the amounts you need for your expense allocation JE, follow these steps:

1. Choose Reports → Company & Financial → Profit & Loss Standard.
2. In the Dates field, select the appropriate time range. For example, if you're allocating last month's expenses, choose Last Month; if you perform this task quarterly, choose Last Fiscal Quarter.
3. Click the Modify Reports button.
4. Select the Filters tab.
5. In the Filter list, select Account.
6. In the Account field, select Expense And Other Expense Accounts from the drop-down list.
7. Click OK to return to the report, where all expense postings for the selected period are displayed.
8. Print the report, so you can use it to perform the calculations needed to create your journal entry.

The report includes payroll expenses, and if you've already allocated those expenses, ignore them when you use this report to allocate overhead expenses. Also ignore any expenses that aren't deemed "overhead".

Memorize the report so you don't have to customize it again. Click the Memorize button and use a name that reminds you of the contents of the report.

TIP: If you're comfortable working in Excel, you could export the report, use formulas to allocate the amounts, and print the spreadsheet. Then enter the allocated amounts in a JE.

Chapter 8

Managing Bank Accounts and Cash

Transferring funds between accounts

Handling bounced checks

Voiding disbursements

Reconciling bank accounts

Managing bank accounts with co-mingled funds

Tracking petty cash

Managing expense accounts

In addition to the day-to-day routine of entering revenue transactions and paying vendor bills, you occasionally have to perform some special chores to manage your accounts, and to track cash that's floating around.

You may have to move money from one bank account to another, checks you received might bounce, checks you wrote can get lost in the mail, you have to keep track of the petty cash you disburse, and you have to reconcile your bank account when the statement arrives. This chapter covers the processes involved with managing your bank accounts and your cash.

Transferring Funds Between Accounts

Moving money between bank accounts is a common procedure. Some organizations move funds from an operating account to a payroll account every payday. Some organizations have money market accounts and then transfer the necessary funds to an operating account when it's time to pay bills. Others do it the other way around, moving money not immediately needed from the operating account to a money market account.

The difference between a regular transaction and a transfer of funds between banks is that a transfer has no effect on your financial reports; it's neither a deposit nor a disbursement, and it has no effect on your net assets. Postings are made only to balance sheet accounts—bank accounts. However, if you don't handle a transfer properly in QuickBooks, you may inadvertently post amounts to income or expenses, which *does* affect your net assets.

The way you actually transfer money between accounts depends on your arrangement with your bank. There are three common ways to move funds between bank accounts.

- Using the telephone to notify a bank employee to transfer the funds, or use the buttons on the telephone to effect the transfer via an automated transfer system.
- Going to your bank's Internet website and clicking the appropriate links to transfer funds between accounts.

- Writing a check on the sending account and depositing the check to the receiving account. This is frequently the method used when the accounts are in separate banks, because checks are cheaper than the electronic transfer fee.

We can consider the first two options automatic, and the last option manual. However, to QuickBooks, it's still a transfer of funds and all postings are made to the appropriate balance sheet accounts.

Using the Transfer Funds Feature

If you use a form of automatic transfer, which means no check is involved in moving money from one account to the other, use the QuickBooks Transfer Funds feature. Choose Banking → Transfer Funds to open the Transfer Funds dialog seen in Figure 8-1.

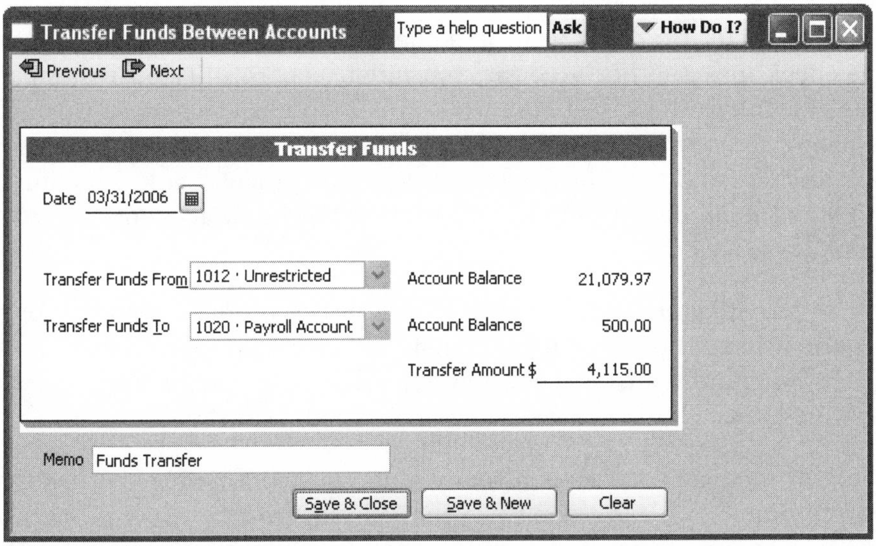

Figure 8-1: The Transfer Funds dialog is essentially a journal entry between bank accounts.

Then take the following steps:

1. In the Transfer Funds From field, select the bank account from which you're removing money.

2. In the Transfer Funds To field, select the bank account into which you're depositing the money.

3. In the Transfer Amount$ field, enter the amount being transferred.

4. In the Memo field, optionally enter an explanation for this transfer.

5. Click Save & New to enter another transfer; click Save & Close if you're finished.

QuickBooks posts the transaction to both banks, and if you open the bank registers you see the transactions are of the type TRANSFR. The sending bank is credited with the amount of the transfer, and the receiving bank is debited with the amount of the transfer. This means the total for current assets on your balance sheet remains exactly the same.

Writing a Check to Transfer Funds

If you transfer funds by writing a check on one account, and depositing the check into another account, you must be careful to post the transaction carefully. The safest way to do this is to pass the check through a transfer account in both directions. This means you have to create an account for fund transfers, with an account type of Bank. I usually use 1099 as the account number, and I name the bank account BankTransfers.

To create a check for transferring funds, you need a payee. In most organizations, the payee for a transfer is the organization, the bank, or Cash. For fund transfers, you have to create a payee as an Other Name, not a vendor.

If the payee you use is already a vendor (common if you use the bank's name, or Cash), don't use the existing vendor account, because you don't want transfers showing up as part of the activity report for a vendor. Instead, create a new Other Name payee.

If you have vendors named Cash and Bank (substitute your bank's name for Bank), either use your organization's name as the payee (which is probably not a vendor), or use a different version of the bank's name. For example, if your bank is a vendor with the name First

National Bank, create an Other Name of 1st National Bank, or First Natl Bank.

If you write checks manually, you can create the check in either the Write Checks window, or the bank register of the sending account (the latter is faster). If you print checks, use the Write Checks window (and be sure the To Be Printed option is selected). Post the transaction to the Transfers account you created.

After the deposit is made at the bank, enter the transaction in the receiving account, using the following steps:

1. Open the account's register by double-clicking its listing in the Chart of Accounts window.
2. Enter the date.
3. Use the Tab key to move to the Deposit column and fill in the amount.
4. In the Account field, enter the BankTransfers account.

When you open the Chart of Accounts window, QuickBooks displays the current balances for balance sheet accounts. As a result, you know at a glance whether the deposit has been entered. If the deposit hasn't been entered, the Transfer account has a balance. When the deposit is entered, it washes the transaction (equal debits and credits), so the Transfer account has a zero balance.

You could also post the transaction directly to the receiving bank. However, if you do, the receiving bank's register shows the transaction as a type CHK, and records the check number of the sending bank. For the receiving account, that check number may already be in use, or may be used in the future. You can delete the check number by selecting it and pressing the Delete key, but you can't change the transaction type from CHK to TRANSFR.

Here's the weird thing—if you work directly in the bank registers and you create the transaction in the receiving bank instead of the sending bank, posting the deposit to the sending bank creates a transaction type of TRANSFR in both banks. (You can't do this if you print checks, of course, because the Write Checks window has to be the first step in the transaction.) Omit the check number in the receiving bank, and then open the register of the sending bank, and add the check number to the transaction.

Handling Bounced Checks

Sometimes checks bounce. Most of the time, the checks that bounce are from donors or members, or people who bought products from your gift shop (it would be highly unusual for a check for a foundation grant or government contract to bounce). When checks bounce, you have to perform the following tasks to adjust your QuickBooks records (all these tasks are covered in this section):

- Deduct the amount of the bounced check from your checking account.
- Record any bank charges you incurred as a result of the bounced check.
- Remove the payment applied to the invoice or pledge (if either existed) so the amount is once again due.
- Recover the money from the customer.

In addition, you should collect a service charge from the customer (at least for the amount of any charges your own bank assessed).

Adjusting Account Balances

You must remove the amount of the check from your bank account, and also adjust the offset account that received the posting. Depending on the history of the bounced check, either you make the adjustment in the bank register, or you create a journal entry.

For the following scenarios, use the bank register to make the adjustment:

- The bounced check was a payment against an invoice or a pledge, and you deposited the check directly into a bank account instead of using the Undeposited Funds account. The offset posting was to an Accounts Receivable account.
- The bounced check was a Sales Receipt (it didn't arrive as the result of an invoice), and you deposited the check directly into a

bank account instead of using the Undeposited Funds account. The offset posting was to an Income account.

Use a journal entry to make the adjustment if the check's history matches these scenarios:

- The bounced check was a payment against an invoice or a pledge, and you deposited the check into the Undeposited Funds account (and then used the Make Deposits window to deposit all the checks in that account). The offset posting was to an Accounts Receivable account.
- The bounced check was a Sales Receipt, and you deposited the check into the Undeposited Funds account. The offset posting was to an income account.

Using the Bank Register

If you deposited the check directly into the bank instead of using the Undeposited Funds account, you can adjust the bank account and the offset account from the bank register.

If the deposit was a payment for an invoice or a pledge, its listing in the bank register has a type of PMT. You must delete the payment by pressing Ctrl-D, or by choosing Edit → Delete Payment from the menu bar. (Unfortunately, there's no Void option for payments.)

QuickBooks displays a message warning you that the payment was used to pay an invoice and that deleting it will result in unpaid balances (which is exactly what you want to happen). Click OK, and the invoice that was paid returns to its balance due before the payment.

The Accounts Receivable account is also adjusted (the amount is added back). The invoice will show up as unpaid if you send a statement to the customer. You should also invoice the customer for any bounced check charges you incurred (see "Invoicing Customers for Bounced Checks" later in this chapter.)

If the deposit was a sales receipt, its listing in the bank register has a type of RCPT. Right-click the listing and choose Void Sales Receipt. The amount of the transaction changes to 0.00, the bank balance is adjusted, the check is marked as cleared (so it won't show up in the next bank reconciliation as waiting to be cleared), and the Memo field displays VOID: in front of any text you entered in the field when you created the Sales Receipt. Click Record to save the changes.

Using a Journal Entry

If you used the Undeposited Funds account, create a journal entry to remove the amount of the bounced check from the bank. The alternative is to remove the original deposit from the Undeposited Funds account, which affects the Make Deposit transaction you created. If that deposit contained other payments, you have to re-create the entire deposit. Therefore, a journal entry is easier and less prone to mistakes.

To create a journal entry to adjust the amounts, choose Banking → Make General Journal Entries, which opens the Make General Journal Entries window. Then take the following steps:

1. Click the Account column, then click the arrow and select the bank into which you deposited the payment.
2. Move to the Credit column, and enter the amount of the bounced check.
3. Use the Memo column to write yourself a note (e.g., Jackson Ck #2345 bounced).
4. Click in the Name column and select the customer whose check bounced.
5. In the Class column, enter the class that was used in the original transaction.
6. On the next row, click in the Account column and choose one of the following accounts:
   • If the deposit was a payment of an invoice, select the Accounts Receivable account to which the invoice/pledge was posted.
   • If the deposit was a sales receipt, select the income account to which the sales receipt was posted.
7. QuickBooks automatically fills in the amount in the Debit column.
8. In the Class column, enter the class that was used in the original transaction.
9. Click Save & Close.

Don't forget to invoice the customer to collect the amount of the bounced check (see "Invoicing Customers for Bounced Checks" later in this section).

Recording Bank Charges for Bounced Checks

If your bank charged you for a returned check, you have to enter the bank charge. To do so, start by opening the register for your bank account. Then fill out the fields as follows:

1. Click the Date field in the blank line at the bottom of the register and enter the date that the bank charge was assessed.
2. Delete the check number that's automatically entered.
3. Tab over to the Payment field and enter the amount of the service charge for the returned check.
4. In the Account field, assign this transaction to the expense account you use for bank charges.
5. Click the Record button in the register window to save the transaction.

Your bank account balance is reduced by the amount of the service charge. You should charge the customer for this, and in the following sections, I'll cover the steps needed to accomplish that.

Invoicing Customers for Bounced Checks

If you have to re-invoice your customers after a check bounces, you don't submit an invoice for the same item (membership or donation) because you don't want to increase the activity for that item—this is a replacement for a previously entered transaction.

Instead, you have to create a specific item for bounced checks, and another item for service charges. Then use those items in the invoice. Those tasks are covered in the following sections.

Creating an Item for a Bounced Check Replacement

If you want to issue an invoice for the bounced check, you need an item for bounced checks. Open the Item List window, and press Ctrl-N to open

the New Item dialog. Then fill out the fields using the following guidelines:

- The item Type is Other Charge.
- The item Name is Returned Check (or another phrase of your
  choice).
- The Description is optional.
- The Amount is blank (you fill in the amount when you create the
  invoice).
- The item is not taxable.
- Link the item to an income account.

The income account can present a problem. The bounced check was
originally posted to an income account, and you probably have multiple
income accounts to track different types of revenue.

When you voided the check, you also removed the amount from the
income account, but when the customer pays the invoice for the bounced
check, the same income account has to be credited.

If you have multiple income accounts (such as all the income
accounts available in the UCOA), you have to create a bounced check
item for each income account. That's because QuickBooks, unlike most
accounting software applications, forces you to create a link between an
item and an account.

Most software lets you specify the income account in the transaction
window while you're creating the invoice. When you're creating an
invoice for a bounced check you merely select the income account that
was used in the original transaction.

However, you're using QuickBooks, so you have to make a decision
between the following choices:

- Create a subaccount named Returned Checks for each of the par-
  ent income accounts (Returned Checks-Contributed Support,
  Returned Checks-Earned Revenues, and so on).
- Create a new parent account named Collections.

If you create a new parent account named Collections, when the customer sends the payment, deposit the money and then create a journal entry as follows:

1. On the first line, select the Collections income account.
2. In the Debit column, enter the amount of the payment for the bounced check.
3. In the Memo column, enter an optional description to remind yourself of this transaction's use.
4. In the Name column, enter the customer or job name.
5. In the Class column, select the Administration Class (which you used to create the invoice, as explained later in this section).
6. On the second line, select the original income account you used for the transaction that resulted in the bounced check.
7. In the Credit column, QuickBooks has already entered the amount you entered in the Debit column of the previous line.
8. In the Class column, select the Class you used for the transaction that resulted in the bounced check.

Before making a decision on subaccounts vs. parent accounts, check with your accountant.

Creating an Item for Service Charges

To create an item for invoicing customers for the bank service charges you incur when their checks bounce, use the following guidelines:

- The item Type is Other Charge.
- The item Name is RetChkChg (or something similar).
- The Description is optional.
- The Amount is blank (you fill it in when you create the invoice).
- The item is not taxable.
- The Income Account is an account you create for this purpose (or use the Collections account you created for the bounced checks item).

Creating the Invoice

Send an invoice to the customer for the bounced check. You can use the invoice template you normally use, or create a new template for this type of invoice (see Chapter 5 to learn how to customize an invoice template). Then take the following steps to complete the invoice:

1. Assign the transaction to the class Administration.
2. Enter the name of the customer who gave you the bad check.
3. Enter the date on which the check bounced.
4. Click in the Item column and select the item you created for returned checks.
5. Enter the amount of the returned check.
6. If necessary, add another line item for the service charge you incurred for the bounced check, using the item you created for service charges.
7. Save the invoice.

Voiding Disbursements

Sometimes you have to void a check that you've written. You made a mistake in preparing the check, you decided not to send it for some reason, or you sent it but it never arrived. Whatever the reason, if a check isn't going to clear the bank, you must void it.

To void a check, open the register of the bank account you used for the check, and find the check's listing. If the check was written as payment for a vendor bill, its transaction type is BILLPMT. If the check was a direct disbursement, its transaction type is CHK.

Select the check's transaction line, right-click, and choose Void Bill Pmt-Check (for a bill payment) or Void Check (for a direct disbursement) from the shortcut menu. Then click Record.

If the check you're voiding was a bill payment, QuickBooks displays a warning that your action will change previous transactions. This means the vendor bill, which had been paid, will be changed to unpaid, and the Accounts Payable account will be incremented by the amount of this check. Since those are exactly the results you're looking for, click Yes to continue.

If the check you're voiding was a direct disbursement, QuickBooks merely voids the check. The expense account(s) to which you posted the check are credited with the appropriate amounts (the original posting was a debit).

The check amount is changed to 0.00, the check is marked as cleared so it doesn't show up as waiting to be cleared in your bank reconciliation, and the text VOID: appears in the Memo field in front of any existing text.

QuickBooks lets you delete a check instead of voiding it, which is a terrible idea. Deleting a check removes all history of the transaction, and the check number disappears into la-la land. This is not a good way to keep financial records. Voiding a check keeps the check number, but sets the amount to zero, which provides an audit trail of your checks.

(The ability to delete a check is a terrific feature for an embezzler who wants enough time to cash the check and run, before you learn about the check in your next bank statement.)

Reconciling Bank Accounts

Reconciling bank accounts is bookkeeping jargon for "I have to balance my checkbook". In this section I'll go over the steps required to reconcile your bank accounts in QuickBooks.

TIP: *If you're using subaccounts of bank accounts to track restricted and unrestricted funds separately, choose the parent account when it's time to reconcile. All transactions from all subaccounts appear in the Reconcile window. See the section "Managing Bank Accounts With Co-Mingled Funds", later in this chapter, to learn more about tracking funds with bank subaccounts.*

Preparing to Reconcile

If your bank sends your canceled checks in the envelope along with the statement (many banks don't include the physical checks), you can arrange the checks in numerical order before you start the reconciliation process.

However, instead of sorting and collating the physical checks, it's much easier to use the list of check numbers, which appear in numerical order on your statement. An asterisk or some other mark usually appears to indicate a missing number (usually a check that hasn't cleared yet, a check that cleared previously, or perhaps a voided check).

Open the register for the bank account you're about to reconcile by double-clicking the account's listing in the Chart Of Accounts window. If the bank statement shows deposits or checks (or both) that are absent from your bank register, add them to the register. If you miss any, don't worry, you can add transactions to the register while you're working in the Reconcile window, but it's usually quicker to get this task out of the way before you start the reconciliation process.

Interest payments and standard bank charges don't count as missing transactions, because the bank reconciliation process treats those transactions separately. You'll have a chance to enter those amounts during bank reconciliation.

Adding Missing Disbursements to the Register

The way you add missing disbursements to the register depends on whether the disbursements were checks or non-check withdrawals (such as electronic payments, or debit card withdrawals).

To enter a check, you can add the data directly to the register, or use the Write Checks window (press Ctrl-W), entering the check number, payee and amount.

To enter a disbursement that isn't a check, add the data directly to the register. QuickBooks automatically enters the next check number, which you should delete and replace with an appropriate code (such as

ET for Electronic Transfer, or ATM for a debit card withdrawal). You don't need to enter a payee for a debit card withdrawal.

Adding Missing Deposits to the Register

You may see deposits in the bank statement that don't appear in your check register. This almost always means you forgot to make the deposit in QuickBooks. Check the Undeposited Funds account to see if you entered the deposits when they arrived, but neglected to run the Make Deposits procedure.

Choose Banking → Make Deposits and see if the deposits are there (the odds are quite good that they are). Select the deposits that appear on your statement and deposit them into the appropriate bank.

If you have multiple undeposited collections listed, you can either deposit the funds in groups that match the transaction list on the statement, or group all the deposits and don't worry about matching the transaction list on the statement.

For example, your bank statement may show a deposit of $145.78 on one date, and a deposit for $3,233.99 on another date. Both deposits still appear in the Make Deposits window. Select one of the deposits, process it, and then repeat the procedure for the other deposit. When you reconcile the account, your transactions reflect the transactions in your bank statement.

On the other hand, you could select both deposits and process them in one transaction. When you reconcile the account, the joint deposit adds up correctly, so the reconciliation succeeds mathematically.

If a missing deposit isn't in the Undeposited Funds account, you have to create the deposit, which may have been a customer payment of an invoice, a cash sale, a transfer of funds between banks, a payment of a loan, or a deposit of capital.

For customer invoice payments, or cash sales, fill out the appropriate transaction window.

- If you deposit the proceeds to the Undeposited Funds account, don't forget to take the additional step to deposit the funds in the bank so the transaction appears in the reconciliation window.
- If you deposit the proceeds directly to the bank, the transaction appears in the reconciliation window automatically.

If you made deposits unconnected to customers and earned income, such as a refund check, or the proceeds of a loan, the fastest way to enter the transaction is to work directly in the bank account's register.

Enter the deposit amount and post the transaction to the appropriate account (you can skip the payee). If you're not sure which account to use for the offset posting, ask your accountant.

Using the Begin Reconciliation Window

Reconciling your bank account starts with the Begin Reconciliation window (see Figure 8-2, which you open by choosing Banking → Reconcile. If you have more than one bank account, select the bank account you want to reconcile from the drop-down list in the Account field.

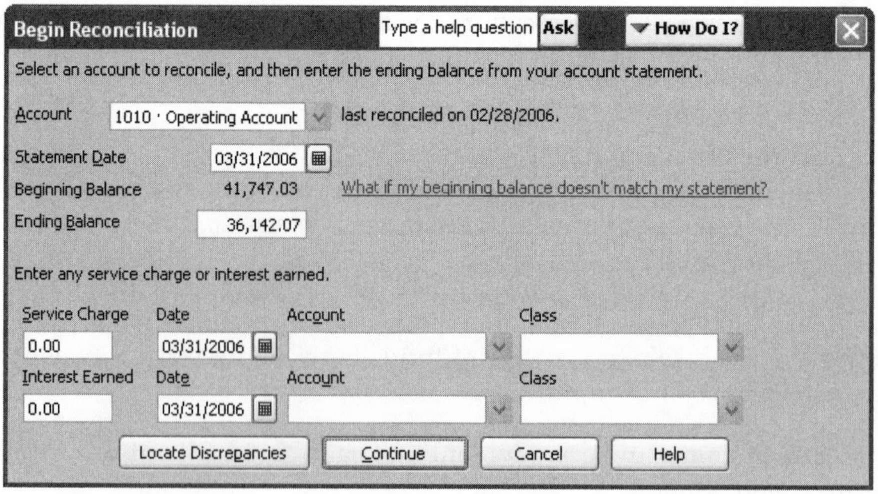

Figure 8-2: Bank Reconciliation starts in the Begin Reconciliation window.

Check the Beginning Balance field in the window against the beginning balance on the bank statement. (Your bank may call it the *starting balance.*) If the beginning balances don't match, see the section "Resolving Differences in the Beginning Balance".

If your beginning balances match, enter the ending balance from your statement in the Ending Balance field, and enter the statement date.

Entering Interest Income and Service Charges

Your statement shows any interest and bank service charges if either or both are applied to your account. Enter those numbers in the Begin Reconciliation window and choose the appropriate account for posting (usually Interest Earned, and Bank Charges).

TIP: If you have online banking, and the interest payments and bank charges have already been entered into your register as a result of downloading transactions, don't enter them again in the Begin Reconciliation window.

Bank charges refers to the standard charges banks assess, such as monthly charges that may be assessed for failure to maintain a minimum balance, monthly charges for including checks in your statement, or any other regularly assessed charge.

Bank charges do not include special charges for bounced checks (yours or your customers'), nor any purchases you made that are charged to your account (such as the purchase of checks or deposit slips). Those should be entered into the bank register as discrete transactions (using the Memo field to explain the transaction). This makes it easier to find the transactions in case you have to talk to the bank about your account.

Reconciling Transactions

After you've filled out the information in the Begin Reconciliation dialog, click Continue to open the Reconcile window, shown in Figure 8-3.

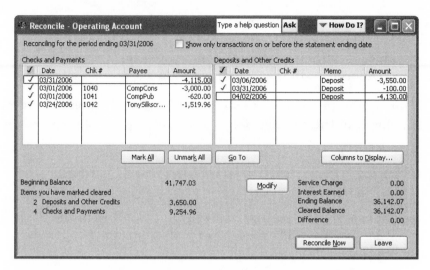

Figure 8-3: The Reconcile window displays all the uncleared transactions for this bank account.

Eliminating Future Transactions

If the transaction list in the Reconcile window has a great many entries, select the option Show Only Transactions On Or Before The Statement Ending Date. Enter the statement ending date in the dialog that appears, and the list gets smaller.

Theoretically, transactions that were created after the statement ending date couldn't have cleared the bank. Removing those listings from the window leaves only those transactions likely to have cleared.

If you select this option and your reconciliation doesn't balance, deselect the option so you can clear the transactions, in case you made a mistake when you entered the date of a transaction. You may have entered a wrong month, or even a wrong year, which resulted in moving the transaction date into the future.

Clearing Transactions

All the transactions that are printed on your bank statement are cleared transactions. If the transactions are not listed on the statement, they have not cleared.

In the Reconcile window, click each transaction that cleared. A check mark appears in the left-most column to indicate that the transaction has cleared the bank. If you clear a transaction in error, click again to remove the check mark—it's a toggle. Use the following shortcuts to speed your work:

- If all, or almost all, of the transactions have cleared, click Mark All. Then de-select the transactions that didn't clear.
- Mark multiple, contiguous transactions by dragging down the Cleared column.
- If the account you're reconciling is enabled for online access, click Matched to automatically mark all transactions that were matched when you downloaded data throughout the month. QuickBooks asks for the ending date on the statement, and clears each matched transaction up to that date.

As you check each cleared transaction, the Difference amount in the lower-right corner of the Reconcile window changes. Your goal is to get that figure to 0.00.

Viewing Transactions During Reconciliation

If you need to look at the original transaction window for any transaction in the reconcile window, double-click its listing (or select the listing and click the button labeled Go To).

Adding Transactions During Reconciliation

When you're working in the Reconcile window, if you find a transaction on the statement that you haven't entered into your QuickBooks software (probably one of those ATM transactions you forgot to enter), you don't have to shut down the reconciliation process to remedy the situation. You can just enter the transaction into your register.

Open the bank account register by right-clicking anywhere in the Reconcile window and choosing Use Register from the shortcut menu. When the bank register opens, record the transaction. Return to the Reconcile window, where that transaction is now listed (QuickBooks automatically updates the Reconcile window). Mark the transaction as cleared, because it was on the statement.

TIP: *You can switch between the Reconcile window and the account register all through the reconciliation process. I automatically open the register of the account I'm reconciling as soon as I start the reconciliation process, just in case.*

Deleting Transactions During Reconciliation

Sometimes you find that a transaction that was transferred from your account register to this Reconcile window shouldn't be there. This commonly occurs if you entered an ATM withdrawal twice. Or perhaps you forgot that you'd entered a bank charge, or even a deposit, and entered it again.

To delete a transaction from the account register, select the transaction and press Ctrl-D. (QuickBooks asks you to confirm the deletion). When you return to the Reconcile window, the transaction is gone.

Editing Transactions During Reconciliation

You may want to change some of the information in a transaction. For example, when you see the real check, you realize the amount you entered in QuickBooks is wrong. You might even have the wrong date on a check. (These things only happen, of course, if you write checks manually; they don't happen to QuickBooks users who let QuickBooks take care of creating and printing checks.)

Whatever the problem, you can correct it by editing the transaction. Double-click the transaction's listing in the Reconcile window to open the original transaction window. Enter the necessary changes, and close the window. Answer Yes when QuickBooks asks if you want to record the changes, and you're returned to the Reconcile window where the display has been updated to reflect the changes.

Resolving Missing Check Numbers

Most bank statements list your checks in order and indicate a missing number with an asterisk. For instance, you may see check number 1234, followed by check number *1236, or 1236*. When a check number is missing, it means one of three things:

- The check cleared in a previous reconciliation.
- The check is still outstanding.
- The check number is unused and may actually be missing.

If a missing check number on your bank statement is puzzling, you can check its status. To see if the check cleared previously, check the bank register, which shows a check mark in the Reconciled column if a check cleared.

To investigate further, right-click anywhere in the Reconcile window and choose Missing Checks Report from the shortcut menu. When the QuickBooks Missing Checks Report opens, select the appropriate account. You'll see asterisks indicating missing check numbers.

If the check number is listed in your Missing Checks Report, it's just uncleared, and will show up in a future bank statement (unless someone is framing your checks instead of cashing them).

If the check never shows up in a future statement, you probably deleted the check instead of voiding it (don't do that anymore).

Finishing the Reconciliation

After all the transactions that cleared are marked in the Reconciliation window, the Difference figure at the bottom of the Reconcile window should display 0.00 (if it doesn't read the following section). Click Reconcile Now and select a report to print (detail or summary), or click Cancel to skip a printed report.

Resolving Reconciliation Problems

If the Difference figure at the bottom of the Reconcile window isn't 0.00, try the following suggestions to locate the problem:

Count the number of transactions on the bank statement. Then look in the lower-left corner of the Reconcile window, where the number of items you have marked cleared is displayed. Mentally add another item to that number for each of the following:

- A service charge you entered in the Begin Reconciliation box
- An interest amount you entered in the Begin Reconciliation box

If the number of transactions now differs, the problem is in your QuickBooks records; there's a transaction you should have cleared but didn't, or a transaction you cleared that you shouldn't have. Find and correct the problem transaction.

Check the totals for deposits and withdrawals on the bank statement, and make sure they match the deposit and withdrawal totals in the Reconcile window. If they don't match, do the following:

- Check the amount of each transaction against the amount in the bank statement.
- Check your transactions and make sure a deposit wasn't inadvertently entered as a payment (or vice versa). A clue for this is a transaction that's half the difference. If the difference is $220.00, find a transaction that has an amount of $110.00 and make sure it's a deduction if it's supposed to be a deduction (or the other way around).
- Check for transposed figures. Perhaps you entered a figure incorrectly in the register, such as $549.00 when the bank cleared the transaction as $594.00. A clue that a transposed number is the problem is that the reconciliation difference can be divided by nine.

When (or if) you find the problem, correct it. When the Difference figure is 0.00, click Reconcile Now.

> *TIP*: Let somebody else check over the statement and the register, because sometimes you can't see your own mistakes.

Pausing the Reconciliation Process

If the account doesn't reconcile (the Difference figure isn't 0.00), and you don't have the time, or will, to track down the problem at the moment, you can stop the reconciliation process without losing all the transactions you cleared.

Click the Leave button in the Reconcile window and go about your business. When you're ready to work on the reconciliation again, restart the process, and everything will be exactly the way you left it.

Creating an Adjusting Entry

If you cannot find the problem, you can have QuickBooks make an adjusting entry to force the reconciliation to balance. The adjusting entry is placed in the bank account register, and is offset in the Beginning Bal Equity account. If you ever figure out what the problem was, you can make the proper adjustment transaction and delete the adjusting entry.

To force a reconciliation, click Reconcile Now, even though there's a difference. A message appears to offer the opportunity to make an adjusting entry. Click Enter Adjustment.

Resolving Differences in the Beginning Balance

The beginning balance that's displayed on the Begin Reconciliation window should match the beginning balance on the bank statement. That beginning balance is the ending balance from the last reconciliation, and nothing should ever change its amount.

If the beginning balance doesn't match the statement, you probably performed one of the following actions, all of which are major mistakes and should never happen:

- You changed the amount on a transaction that had previously cleared.
- You voided a transaction that had previously cleared.
- You deleted a transaction that had previously cleared.
- You removed the cleared check mark from a transaction that had previously cleared.

These are all things you must never do, but if you did, you have to figure out which one of those actions you took after you last reconciled the account. QuickBooks has a tool to help you. Click the Locate

Discrepancies button on the Begin Reconciliation window to open the
Locate Discrepancies dialog. Select the bank account you want to check.

Viewing the Previous Reconciliation Discrepancy Report

Click Discrepancy Report to open the Previous Reconciliation
Discrepancy Report. You can see any transactions that were cleared during a past reconciliation, and then were changed or deleted. This report
shows you the details of the transaction when it was cleared during a
previous reconciliation and the change in the transaction since that reconciliation.

If the reconciled amount is a positive number, the transaction was a
deposit; a negative number indicates a disbursement (usually a check).

The Type Of Change column provides a clue about the action you
must take to correct the unmatched beginning balances.

- Uncleared means you removed the check mark in the Cleared column of the register (even though QuickBooks issues a warning
  when you do this).
- Deleted means you deleted the transaction.
- Amount is the original amount, which means you changed the
  amount of the transaction. Check the Reconciled amount and the
  amount in the Effect Of Change amount; the difference is the
  amount of the change.

Unfortunately, QuickBooks doesn't offer a Type Of Change named
"Void," so a voided transaction is merely marked as changed. A transaction with a changed amount equal and opposite of the original amount
was probably voided.

Open the register and restore the affected transactions to their original state. This is safe because you shouldn't have made the change in the
first place. It's an absolute rule that a transaction that cleared should not
be changed, voided, deleted, or uncleared.

TIP: You don't have to open the Begin Reconciliation window to see a Discrepancy Report. You can view the contents at any time by choosing Reports → Banking → Reconciliation Discrepancy.

If you haven't found the problem that's causing the discrepancy in the beginning balances, and want to search for it manually, you can compare the reconciliation report and the account register. Any transaction that is listed in the reconciliation report should also be in the register.

- If a transaction is there, but marked VOID, re-enter it, using the data in the reconciliation report.
- If a transaction appears in the reconciliation report, but is not in the register, it was deleted. Re-enter it, using the data in the reconciliation report.

Also, open the last reconciliation report and check the amounts against the data in the register. If any amount was changed after the account was reconciled, restore the original amount.

Managing Bank Accounts With Co-mingled Funds

Nonprofits used to face accounting requirements that required them to report finances by tracking funds. A fund is a program, a specific activity center, and financial reports were program/fund oriented, reporting activity in the bank account that held the funds for each program, and also reporting income and expenses for that program. You could not mingle funds from one program with funds from another program.

The need to have multiple bank accounts was expensive (the cost of checks, service charges, etc.), and onerous (imagine how many times deposits or checks went through the wrong bank). In addition, when a program/grant ended, after a year or two, the bank account was empty, and had to be closed, or had to be switched to a new program/grant.

Today, both government agencies and accounting rules let nonprofits report on programs and grants without the need to maintain separate bank accounts (see Appendix A for more information about nonprofit accounting rules).

However, putting all your funds into one bank account (co-mingling restricted and unrestricted funds) poses some serious risks. The restricted funds can't be used until the terms removing the restrictions are met. Those restrictions, imposed by grants, are commonly time restrictions (you can begin using the funds on a certain date, for a certain period of time), or activity restrictions (you can use the funds only for activities specified in the grant). As you're writing checks, how do you know when you've used up your unrestricted funds, and are inappropriately spending your restricted funds?

Luckily, QuickBooks provides a nifty way to track both types of funds. In QuickBooks, when you create subaccounts for a bank account in your chart of accounts, QuickBooks manages the subaccounts separately, and together, all at the same time. I know that sounds impossible, but it's true. Even some of the expensive, more powerful, nonprofit accounting applications can't do this easily, if at all.

For any bank account that contains co-mingled funds, create two subaccounts; one for restricted funds, and another for unrestricted funds. For example:

- 1010 Operating Account
- 1011 Operating Account:Restricted
- 1012 Operating Account:Unrestricted

As you create transactions for receiving income or disbursing funds, post each transaction to the appropriate subaccount instead of the parent account.

When you view the chart of accounts, you'll see that the parent bank account displays the total deposited in the bank, and the two subaccounts display amounts that add up to the amount displayed for the parent account (see Figure 8-4).

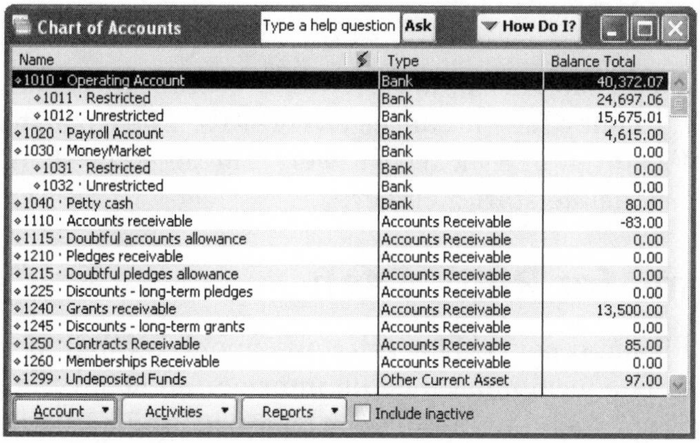

Figure 8-4: The Chart of Accounts window displays the total of the funds in each subaccount.

When you run balance sheet reports, QuickBooks provides specific totals for each subaccount, and assigns no funds to the parent account (see Figure 8-5).

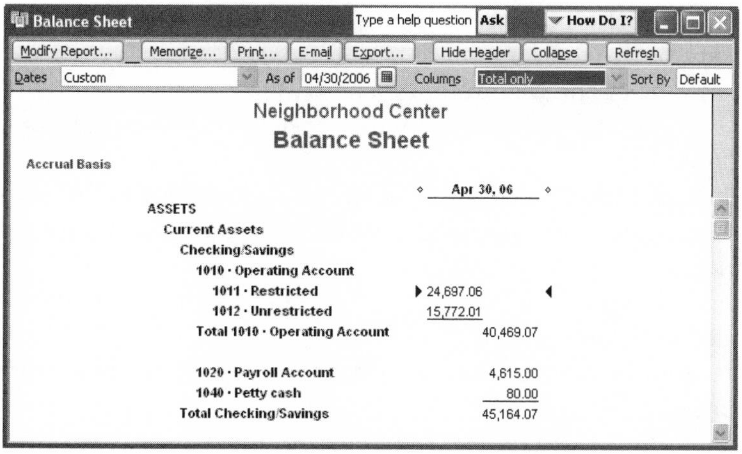

Figure 8-5: QuickBooks reports display the subaccount details for your bank accounts.

To reconcile the account, choose the parent account. All transactions from all subaccounts appear in the Reconcile window.

Tracking Petty Cash

Most organizations keep cash on hand to reimburse staff and volunteers who spend their own money for purchases or services. The cash should be in a locked box that's stored in a locked drawer, and the keys should be in the hands of a responsible staff member.

Creating Forms for Petty Cash

You need a set of rules and policies for reimbursement, as well as a form for people to fill out. The form must include information about the purchase, the program for which the purchase was made, and any other details needed to keep accurate records.

You can buy receipt forms at office supply stores (including forms that are already numbered), or you can create your own forms in a word processing program. Keep a bunch of forms near the cash box, and distribute forms around the office. The form you buy or create must hold the following information:

- The name of the person receiving the cash.
- The date of the disbursement.
- The amount of the disbursement.
- A code to indicate whether the disbursement is a reimbursement or an advance.
- The date of the expense (unless the disbursement is an advance).
- The item or service purchased (unless the disbursement is an advance).
- The class to which the disbursement should be assigned (which includes administration).
- A code to indicate whether the expense is reimbursable from a customer.
- A place to enter the date the disbursement was entered in QuickBooks (which prevents duplicate entry of the same receipt).

Creating a Petty Cash Bank Account

To track petty cash, your chart of accounts needs a petty cash bank account. This account parallels the activity in your cash box: you put money in it, then you account for the money that's spent, and periodically you put more money into the box to replenish the balance.

Whatever happens to your cash box must be reflected in your QuickBooks petty cash account. If you don't have a petty cash account in your chart of accounts, you need to create one.

Open the chart of accounts and press Ctrl-N to open a New Account window. Fill in the account information using the following guidelines:

- The Account Type is Bank.
- If you number your accounts, use a number that places your new petty cash account at the end of the other (real) bank accounts in your chart of accounts.
- Leave the opening balance at zero.

Now you can use this account to track the cash you disburse from your cash box, as explained in the following sections.

Putting Money into Petty Cash

You must decide how much money your cash box should hold. This is the amount you start with, and it's the target of each future check you write to replenish the cash supply.

For example, if you decide to target $150.00 for petty cash, when the cash box holds $50.00 in cash and $100.00 in receipts, you write a petty cash check for $100.00 to bring the cash amount back to the target.

The first thing you have to do is put money in the cash box by cashing a check. Use an Other Name as the payee, because you're not dealing with a vendor. Common payees for this transaction are the organization's name, the bank's name, or Cash.

Post the check to the petty cash account, not to an expense account. Assign the transaction to the Other class (you assign the real class at the time you record the disbursement).

Send someone to the bank to cash the check, and make sure that person asks for small bills, and at least $5.00 in coins.

Recording the Disbursements

The balance in the petty cash account should equal the amount of cash in the cash box. The definition of "the cash in the cash box" is the amount of cash plus the total amount of receipts for cash disbursed. For example, if your petty cash account has a balance of $200.00, and your cash box has $120.00 plus receipts that total $80.00, you're in balance.

You can record disbursements every time cash leaves the cash box, wait until you're so low on cash that it's time to replenish the box, or set a regular schedule for recording disbursements. To record petty cash disbursements, use a journal entry that follows the pattern seen in Figure 8-6.

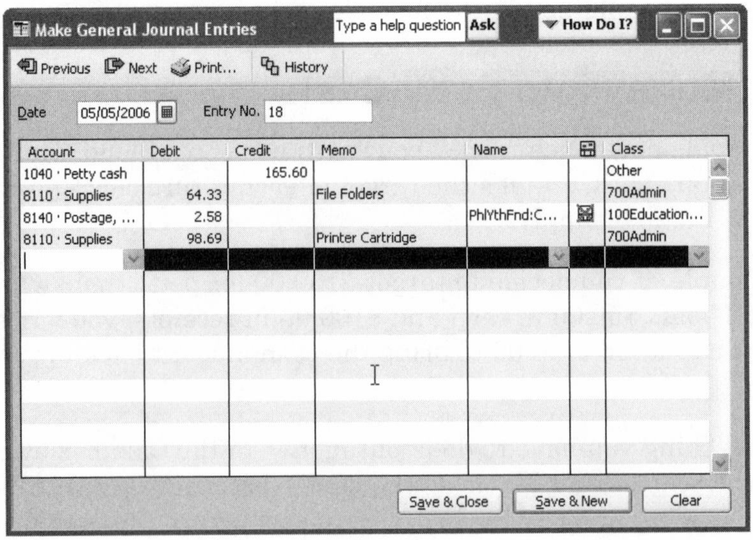

Figure 8-6: Use a journal entry to reconcile the petty cash bank
account to your cash box.

- Assign each disbursement to the appropriate class.
- If the expense was for a specific contract or grant, enter that job in the Name column.
- If a job-related expense is not reimbursable, click the invoice icon in the invoice column to place a red X atop. The customer isn't billed, but you're tracking the expense as part of job costing.

TIP: *If you're using QuickBooks Premier Nonprofit edition, be sure to deselect the option Autofill Memo, because in this case the memo fields are specific to each line in the journal entry. The Autofill Memo feature isn't available in QuickBooks Pro.*

Have a folder or large envelope available for storing receipts that have been entered in QuickBooks. The receipts that haven't been entered in QuickBooks usually stay in the petty cash box. Before you store the receipts, mark each receipt to note the fact that it was entered in QuickBooks. You can write "Q" or "QB" on the receipt (use a color pen or marker), and note the General Journal Entry number of the journal entry that has the transaction.

Handling Petty Cash Advances

If you decide on a policy that permits the disbursement of petty cash in advance of an expense, you must keep track of the people who are walking around with your organization's money in their pockets.

In addition, you should develop a policy that limits the amount of time an advance can be held. For example, many organizations have a 24-hour or 48-hour rule: "Spend it or return it".

Additionally, if you permit advances, you must create an account to log those advances in QuickBooks if the advances are not yet spent when you are ready to post the disbursements. (Covered previously in the section "Record the Disbursements".)

An advance is a receivable, and therefore an asset. If you're using the UCOA, an account named Employee & Trustee Receivables exists, which is appropriate for posting advances for petty cash. If you want to create a separate account for posting petty cash advances, or if you're not using the UCOA, create an account for this purpose (use the name Petty Cash Advances). The account type is Other Current Asset.

When an advance is spent, you must post the amount to the appropriate expense account and program. The steps required to accomplish this vary, depending on whether you've created a journal entry to post petty cash transactions between the time the advance was given out and the employee spent the money and delivered a receipt.

Expense is Less Than the Advance

If the amount of the expense is less than the amount of the advance, the recipient should hand in a receipt (for the actual expense) and cash (the difference between the expense and the advance).

If you haven't yet created the journal entry that included the original advance, mark the original receipt for the advance as being cancelled or satisfied, Keep the new receipt for the purchase (along with the returned cash, of course) in the cash box. Enter it in QuickBooks the next time you record petty cash disbursements in a JE.

Technically, there's no reason to keep the receipt for the advance, because it wasn't recorded. Therefore, even during an audit, there's no tieback required between the receipt and the general ledger. Check with your accountant to see if it's okay to throw away receipts for advances under these circumstances. (I always like to find a reason to avoid stuffing file cabinets with paper that isn't really needed.)

If you already recorded the journal entry that posted the advance, keep the new receipt and make the journal entry shown in Table 8-1.

Expense is More Than the Advance

If the amount of the expense is more than the amount of the advance, the recipient hands in a receipt for the expense, and wants more cash.

If you haven't yet posted the journal entry that covered the original advance, file or toss the original receipt for the advance. Give the recipient the additional cash, and keep the new receipt in the cash box. Record the expense the next time you create a petty cash journal entry.

Account	Debit	Credit	Class
PettyCash Advances		Amount Advanced	Other
Expense	Amt of Expense		Program Class
PettyCash Bank	Amt of Cash Returned		Other

Table 8-1: Enter the disbursement for a previously posted a petty cash advance.

If you already recorded the journal entry in which you posted the advance, keep the new receipt and make the journal entry shown in Table 8-2.

Account	Debit	Credit	Class
PettyCash Advances		Amount Advanced	Other
Expense	Amt of Expense		Program Class
PettyCash Bank Accnt		Difference between advance and exp	Other

Table 8-2: Record the new amounts for a previously posted petty cash advance.

Advance and Expense are Equal

If the amount spent is the same as the amount advanced, the recipient hands in a receipt for the expense.

If you haven't yet posted the journal entry that covered the original advance, file or throw away the original receipt for the advance, and keep the new receipt. Record the expense the next time you create a petty cash journal entry.

If you already recorded the journal entry that posted the advance to the asset account for petty cash advances, keep the new receipt and make the journal entry described in Table 8-3.

Account	Debit	Credit	Class
PettyCash Advances		Amount Advanced	Other
Expense	Amt of Expense		Program Class

Table 8-3: Swap the advance for the expense.

Replenishing the Cash Box

Periodically you must replace the money that was disbursed from the cash box, to make sure there's sufficient petty cash to operate. The process is the same as it was when you wrote the first petty cash check, but the amount differs.

Most of the time, the check is for the difference between the original check and the amount of cash that's been disbursed. For example, if you originally put $150.00 into the cash box, and you've disbursed $130.00, write a petty cash check in the amount of $130.00.

However, you may want to increase the amount of the check if the cash box ran out of money quickly. You have to find a balance between keeping a lot of cash on hand (which makes most of us nervous), and the number of times you have to go to the bank and stand in line to cash a check.

Managing Expense Accounts

Some organizations permit employees or board members (or others) to submit expenses in the form of expense account reports. This is useful if some people incur large expenses and you don't want to use up the cash in your cash box for one expense, or if some expenses are usually higher than the total you keep in the cash box. For example, the expenses incurred for travel (tickets and car rentals) are candidates for expense reports instead of petty cash reimbursements.

Expense Account Policies and Forms

Make sure you develop a policy that clearly states the types of expenses that qualify for submission on an expense account form, and the type of receipts you require.

You can purchase expense account forms or design them in a word processing or spreadsheet software application. The form should have fields for the following information.

- The name of the person submitting the expense account form.
- The ending date of the expense account period (you should have a policy of weekly or monthly submissions for submitting expense account forms).
- The date of each expense.
- The amount of each expense.
- The item or service purchased for each expense.
- The program (class) to which each expense should be assigned (which could be the administration class).
- A code to indicate whether the expense is reimbursable from a customer.
- A place to enter the date the expense check was created in QuickBooks and the check number (which prevents duplicate entry of the same expense report).

Creating Expense Account Checks

Expense account checks are made out to the person being reimbursed, and the payee should be an Other Name in QuickBooks. If the payee is an employee, and exists in the Employee list, you cannot use the employee name for the expense check (that would mess up your employee reports).

Create the same person in the Other Name list, which means you must change the way the name is entered to avoid a duplicate. For example, if the employee name has a middle initial, omit that initial in the Other Name list (or the other way around). Alternatively, use a nickname in the Other Name listing, so that the employee Deborah Ivens becomes an Other Name listing of Debbie Ivens.

The check is posted to the appropriate expense accounts, which usually means a split transaction, covering multiple expense accounts. Link the expense to the customer so you can track job costs and/or invoice the customer for reimbursement. (If the cost isn't reimbursable, click the invoice icon to put a red X on it). Don't forget to assign the appropriate class to each expense.

Managing the Organization's Credit Cards

Some organizations have credit cards, and certain people are authorized to use those credit cards for specific types of expenses. Usually, the allowable expenses are for travel, such as airline tickets, hotel rooms, and so on.

Expenses billed to your credit card aren't included in the expense check you write to the person who incurred the expense—you write a check to the credit card company. However, you must insist that the person who incurred the expenses hand in an expense account form so you can accurately post the expenses when you write the check. Make sure your expense account form has a section covering credit card purchases, or create a separate form for this situation.

Managing Expense Account Advances

If you have a policy of permitting advances against expenses that will ultimately be reported on expense accounts (instead of petty cash), the process for handling the transactions is similar to that of handling a petty cash advance.

Write a check to the payee (the person who requested the advance) and post the amount to the Other Current Asset account you're using to post advances of this type. Assign the class Other to the transaction.

When the expense report arrives, if the amount of the expense is the same as the amount of the advance, create a journal entry to move the amount of the advance from the asset account to the appropriate expense accounts, and to assign the appropriate classes. Table 8-4 displays a typical journal entry for this task.

Account	Debit	Credit	Class
Advances Account		Amount Advanced	Other
Expense #1	Amt of Expense		Program Class
Expense #2	Amt of Expense		Program Class

Table 8-4: Turn an advance into an expense.

If the amount of the expense is higher than the amount of the advance, either have the person submit the additional sum in his or her next regular expense report, or create another check for the additional amount, posting the amounts to the appropriate expense accounts and classes.

If the amount of the expense is lower than the amount of the advance, you should have a policy to cover the situation. You can leave the money in the Advances asset account and apply it against the next expense report. Or, you can ask for a check from the person to reimburse the organization for the unspent advance, and post the Sales Receipt to the Advances asset account.

If your policy is to let the unspent advance wait for the next expense report, you need to track the total in that asset account on a person-by-person basis. Choose one of the following protocols to accomplish this:

- Create subaccounts under the Advance account for each individual who might receive an advance against expenses.
- Keep those records in another software application, such as a spreadsheet program.

The first option is best. The advance checks and the journal entries you create are posted to the appropriate subaccount. When you open the Chart of Accounts window, you can tell at a glance who owes money to the organization, and who needs repayment for expended funds. In addition, the detailed data appears in QuickBooks reports.

Chapter 9

Budgets and Projections

Creating budgets

Reporting on budgets versus actual figures

Exporting and importing budgets

Projecting cash flow

Other planning and projection tools

Nonprofits rely on budgets and cash flow reports more than for-profit businesses do, because most nonprofits are required to present detailed reports about these financial matters.

QuickBooks provides several tools for projecting your finances. The tool that's probably most familiar to you is a budget, which lets you chronicle your expectations, and then check them against reality. In addition, QuickBooks provides a way to project cash flow. I'll cover these tools in this chapter.

QuickBooks' Rules for Budgets

Unfortunately, the budget feature in QuickBooks is rather limited. As a result, if you count on budgets, and use them extensively, you should plan to do a lot of your work outside of QuickBooks (using Microsoft Excel or a software application designed for budgeting).

However, there are some advantages to starting your budget efforts in QuickBooks, even though you may have to export those budgets to a spreadsheet application to apply formulas that are more powerful. First, you can design a budget that's based on a customer, a job, or a class, using data that exists in your QuickBooks file. In addition, you can start your budget by bringing last year's figures for each account into the budget window.

QuickBooks supports the following types of budgets:

- Budgets based on your Balance Sheet accounts
- P&L budgets based on your income and expense accounts
- P&L budgets based on income and expense accounts, and a specific customer or job
- P&L budgets based on income and expense accounts, and a specific class.

You can only create one of each type of budget, and once you do, whenever you select that type of budget in the Create New Budget Wizard the budget window opens with your previously entered figures. To get a blank budget window, you have to clear all the figures manually, and then enter new data. That replaces the budget you created, which is usually not the result you desired.

Alternatively, you can export the budget file to Excel, and then delete the budget (see the section "Deleting a Budget").

Here's how the "one of each budget type" rules work:

- If you create a P&L or Balance Sheet budget, you cannot create a second budget of that type.
- If you create a P&L Customer:Job budget, you can create additional P&L Customer:Job budgets using a different customer/job. This means you can have a separate budget for each grant.
- If you create a P&L Class budget, you can create additional P&L class budgets using a different class. This means you can have a separate budget for each program.

See the sections "Customer:Job Budgets" and "Class Budgets" for instructions on creating multiple budgets of those types.

About Balance Sheet Budgets

It's unusual to need a Balance Sheet budget, because you can't predict the amounts for most Balance Sheet accounts. Even if you want to keep an eye on the few accounts over which you have control (such as fixed assets and loans), there's rarely a reason to use a budget for that purpose.

As a result, I'm not going to spend time discussing Balance Sheet budgets in this chapter. If you feel you need to create one, when the Create New Budget Wizard opens, select the year for which you want to create the budget, and select the Balance Sheet option. Then click Next, and because the next window has no options, there's nothing to do except click Finish. The budget window opens displaying all your Balance Sheet accounts, and you can enter the budget figures. See the sections on creating P&L budgets for information on entering budget figures in the budget window.

Creating a P&L Budget

The most common budget for any organization, for-profit or nonprofit, is based on your income and expenses. After you've set up a good chart of accounts, creating a P&L budget is quite easy. To create a P&L budget choose Company → Planning & Budgeting → Set Up Budgets.

If this is the first budget you're creating, the Create New Budget Wizard opens automatically to walk you through the process (see Figure 9-1). If you've already created a budget, the Set Up Budgets window appears. To create a new budget, click Create New Budget, which opens the Create New Budget Wizard. Enter the year for which you're creating the budget, and select the P&L budget option.

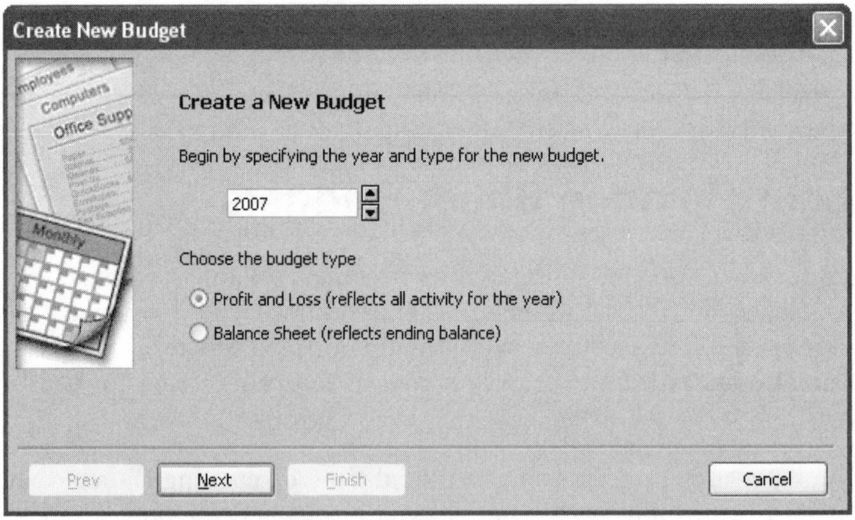

Figure 9-1: A wizard walks you through the configuration process for a new budget.

NOTE: *If you're not operating on a calendar year, the budget year field spans two calendar years, for instance 2006-2007, to accommodate your fiscal year.*

Click Next to select any additional criteria for this budget. You can include customers, customers and jobs, or classes in your budget. For this discussion, I cover regular P&L budgets, so select the option No Additional Criteria. Later in this chapter, I'll go over budgets for customers/jobs, and for classes.

Click Next, and choose between creating a budget from scratch, or by using figures from last year's activities. (Of course, if you weren't using QuickBooks last year, you have to start from scratch.)

Click Finish to open the budget window, where all your income and expense accounts are displayed (see Figure 9-2).

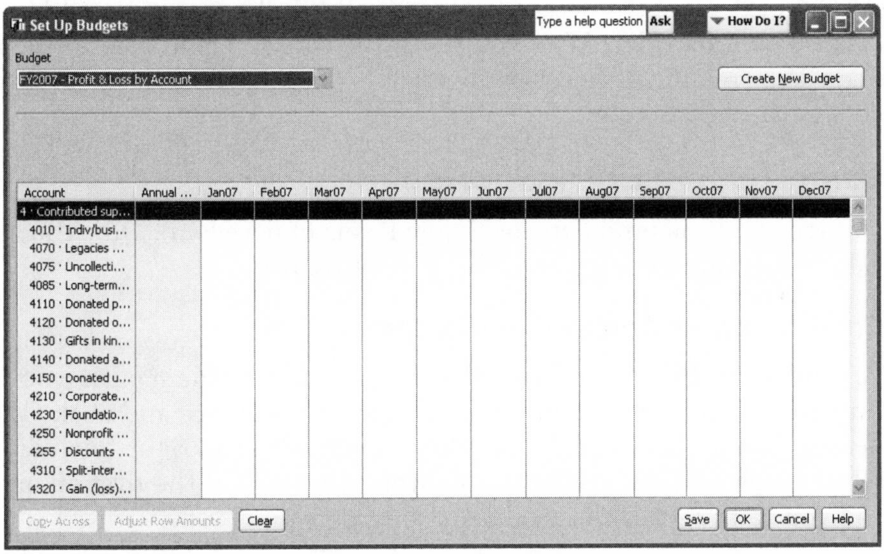

Figure 9-2: All your active income and expense accounts are available for your budget.

If you're creating a budget from scratch, the budget window opens with empty cells. If you're creating a budget from last year's activities, the budget window opens with last year's actual data displayed. For each account that had activity, the ending monthly balances are entered in the appropriate month.

Working in the Budget Window

If you've configured your computer's display resolution at 1024 x 768 (or higher), you can see all twelve months in the budget window. However, if your display resolution is lower, perhaps at 800 x 600, only six months of the budget can be seen in the window. In that case, QuickBooks adds buttons to the window to move the display to the next or previous six-month display.

If the buttons exist, when you enter the amount for the sixth month, you must click the Show Next 6 Months button to continue through the rest of the months. Pressing the Tab key in the 6th Month column moves your cursor to the first month of the next account, not to the 7th Month column of the current account row (which I find annoying, and I wish Intuit would fix this). After you fill in the last six-month figures, click Show Prev 6 Months to return to the first half of the year so you can budget the next account.

Using Budget Entry Shortcuts

To save you time (and extraordinary levels of boredom), QuickBooks provides some shortcuts for entering budget figures.

Copy Numbers Across the Months

To copy a monthly figure from the current month (the month where your cursor is) to all the following months, enter the figure and click Copy Across. The numbers are copied to all months to the right (including the 7th through 12th months if you're starting in one of the first six months and you can't see all the months).

You can perform this shortcut as soon as you enter an amount (but before you press the Tab key), or you can return to the month you want to designate the first month by clicking its column (useful if you've entered figures for several months and then want to use the same figure for the ensuing months).

This is handier than it seems. It's obvious that if you enter your rent in the first month, and choose Copy Across, you've saved a lot of manual data entry. However, if your rent is raised in June, you can increase the rent figure from June to December by selecting June and clicking Copy Across.

The Copy Across button is also the way to clear a row. Delete the figure in the first month and click Copy Across to make the entire row blank.

Automatically Increase or Decrease Monthly Figures

After you've entered figures into an account's row, you can raise or lower monthly figures automatically. For example, you may want to raise an income account by an amount or a percentage starting in a certain month, because you expect to receive a new service contract. On the other hand, you may want to raise an expense account because you're expecting to spend more on supplies, personnel, or occupancy costs as the year proceeds.

Select the first month that needs the adjustment and click Adjust Row Amounts to open the Adjust Row Amounts dialog seen in Figure 9-3.

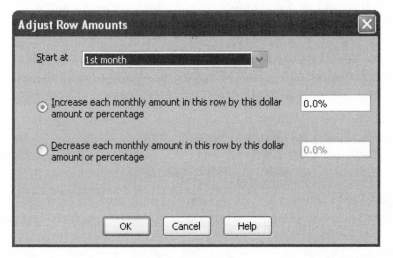

Figure 9-3: Automatically increase or decrease amounts across the months.

Choose 1st Month or Currently Selected Month as the starting point for the calculations. You can choose 1st Month no matter where your cur-

sor is on the account's row. You must click in the column for the appropriate month if you want to choose Currently Selected Month.

- To increase or decrease the selected month and all the months following by a specific amount, enter the amount.
- To increase or decrease the selected month and all columns to the
  right by a percentage, enter the percentage rate and the percentage sign.

Compounding Automatic Changes

If you select Currently Selected Month, the Adjust Row Amounts dialog
adds an additional option named Enable Compounding. When you enable
compounding, the calculations for each month are increased or decreased
based on a formula starting with the currently selected month and taking
into consideration the resulting change in the previous month.

---

*TIP: Although the Enable Compounding option appears only
when you select Currently Selected Month, if your cursor is in
the first month and you select the Currently Selected Month
option, you can use compounding for the entire year.*

For example, if you entered $1000.00 in the current month and indi-
cated a $100.00 increase, the results differ from amounts that are not
being compounded, as seen in Table 9-1.

Compounding Enabled?	Current Month Original Figure	Current Month New Figure	Next Month	Next Month	Next Month
Yes	1000.00	1000.00	1100.00	1200.00	1300.00
No	1000.00	1100.00	1100.00	1100.00	1100.00

Table 9-1: The pattern for compounded changes vs. non-compound-
ed changes.

Budget Window Buttons

The Set Up Budgets window has the following buttons:

- **Clear** Deletes all figures in the budget window—you cannot use this button to clear a row or column.
- **Save** Records the current figures and leaves the window open so you can continue to work.
- **OK** Records the current figures and closes the window.
- **Cancel** Closes the window without any offer to record the figures.
- **Create New Budget** Starts the budget process anew, opening the Create New Budget Wizard. If you've entered any data, QuickBooks asks if you want to record your budget before closing the window. If you record your data (or have previously recorded your data with the Save button), when you start anew, the budget window opens with the saved data.

Creating a Customer:Job Budget

You can create a P&L budget based on a customer or job, and then create budget vs. actual reports on that customer or job.

Select the year for your budget, and choose P&L as the type. In the next wizard window, select the option Customer:Job. In the last wizard window, choose whether to create the budget from scratch, or from last year's figures, and click Finish.

When the budget window opens, an additional field labeled Current Customer:Job appears so you can select the Customer:Job for this budget from the drop-down list (see Figure 9-4). Most of the time, you'll create a budget for a specific job (grant), but if it's for a customer (donor), all the postings for all the jobs attached to that customer are included in the budget vs. actual reports.

Select the accounts for which you want to budget this job. In most cases, you should only select expense accounts (for most grants, the anticipated income isn't a budget figure; it's a known amount). The expenses you include depend on the scope of the job, and the expenses you're expected to track.

You must enter data in every account in the budget that you're posting expenses to for this customer:job. If you skip an account, your actual vs. budget reports won't work properly. If there are accounts that you don't care about budgeting, enter 0.00 for every month; don't leave the account row blank.

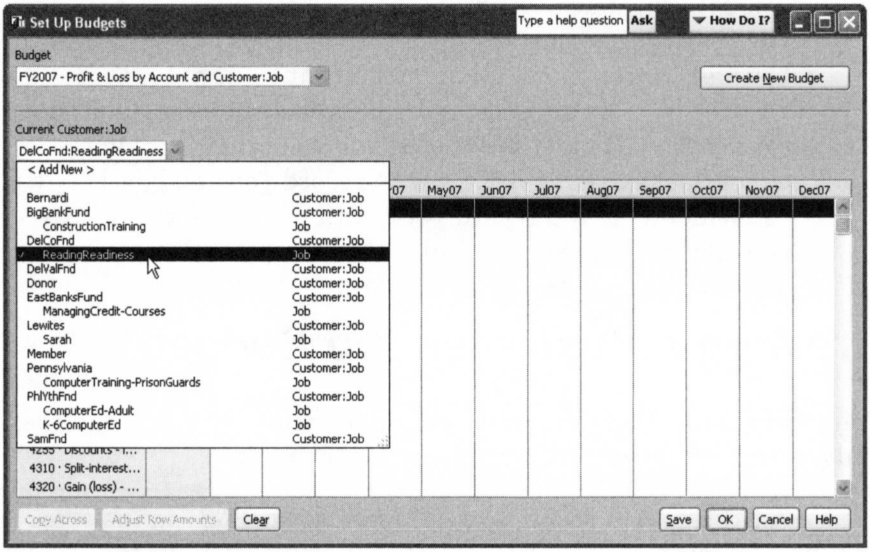

Figure 9-4: Select the job you want to budget.

You can enter a monthly budget figure, or enter a total budget figure in the first month. The latter option, called a *spend-down* format, lets you compare accumulated data for expenses against the total budgeted figure. When you create the report, change the date to reflect the current elapsed time for the project, and filter the report for this job.

Creating Additional Customer:Job Budgets

After you've created one budget based on a customer or job, creating a budget for a different customer or a different job for the same customer requires different steps.

To create a budget for another customer immediately (while the Customer:Job budget you just created is still in the budget window),

select another customer or job from the drop-down list. Then begin entering data. QuickBooks asks if you want to save the budget you'd been
working on before you changed the Customer:Job. Click Yes.

To create a budget for another customer or job later, choose the Set
Up Budgets command from the menu bar. The budget window opens with
the last budget you worked on loaded in the window.

- If the budget that appears is a Customer:Job budget, select a different customer or job from the Current Customer:Job drop-down
  list, and begin entering data.
- If the budget that appears is a different type of budget (P&L or
  Class), click the arrow to the right of the Budget field and select
  the budget type Profit And Loss By Account And Customer:Job.
  Then select a job from the Current Customer:Job drop-down list,
  and begin entering data.

Creating Class Budgets

You can create a budget for any class you've created—class budgets work
like customer:job budgets.

To create a class-based budget, use the steps described above to
start the Create New Budget wizard, and choose Class in the Additional
Profit and Loss Budget Criteria window. When the budget window
opens, a Current Class field appears. Select the class or subclass for
which you need a budget from the drop-down list. Then begin entering
data.

To create additional class budgets (for other classes, of course), use
the same approach discussed in the previous section on creating additional customer or job budgets.

Deleting a Budget

To delete a budget, open the budget you want to get rid of and choose Edit →
Delete Budget from the QuickBooks menu bar.

TIP: *If you want to create multiple budgets of the same type (some of us like to have backup plans), export the budget to a spreadsheet application, and then delete the original budget and start the process again. See the section "Exporting and Importing Budgets".*

Budget Reports

QuickBooks provides a number of budget reports you can view by choosing the appropriate command from the menu bar:

- In QuickBooks Premier Nonprofit Edition, choose Reports →
  Budgets & Forecasts
- In QuickBooks Pro, choose Reports → Budgets

Then select one of the following reports:

- Budget Overview
- Budget vs. Actual
- Profit & Loss Budget Performance
- Budget vs. Actual Graph

QuickBooks Premier Nonprofit Edition offers additional reports on the submenu. I'll cover those reports later in this chapter in the discussions on projecting cash flow.

Budget reports are created by the Budget Report wizard, which opens as soon as you select a report. In the first window, select the budget you want to work with (if you've created multiple budgets).

Click Next to move to the next window, the contents of which depend on the report you've selected from the Reports menu, and the type of budget you selected from the previous window. I'll go over the options as I discuss each type of report.

Budget Overview Report

This report shows a list of the accounts for which you entered a budget figure, and the amounts you budgeted for each month. Several choices are available in the Budget Report window that opens when you select Budget Overview from the submenu, and I'll go over them in the following section.

Profit & Loss Budget Overview

If you created a P&L budget, select Profit & Loss By Account in the first Budget Report window, and click Next. In the next window, the report layout labeled Account By Month is the only available report type.

Click Next, and then click Finish. The report opens and displays the P&L budget figures for each account, for each month.

If you assigned budget figures to subaccounts, click the Collapse button at the top of the budget window to see only the parent account totals. The button name changes to Expand, and clicking it re-displays the subaccount lines.

To condense the numbers, change the interval in the Columns field by selecting a different interval. The default is Month, but you can choose another interval, and QuickBooks will calculate the figures to fit. For example, if your budget has monthly figures (instead of a spend-down budget with the entire budget in the first month), you can select Quarter to see four columns of three-month subtotals.

If you want to tweak the budget, or play "what if" games by experimenting with different numbers, click the Export button to send the report to Microsoft Excel.

Balance Sheet Budget Overview

If you created a Balance Sheet budget, select Balance Sheet By Account in the first window, click Next, and then click Finish to see the report.

Customer:Job Budget Overview

If you created one or more budgets for a customer or a job, select Profit & Loss By Account And Customer:Job in the first window, and click Next. Select a report layout from the drop-down list (as you select each option from the list, QuickBooks displays a diagram of the layout). The following choices are available:

- **Account by Month** lists each account you used in the budget and displays the total budget amounts (for all the customer:job budgets you created) for each month that has data. No budget information for individual customers appears.
- **Account by Customer:Job** lists each account you used in the budget and displays the yearly total for that account for each customer or job (each in its own column).
- **Customer:Job by Month** displays a row for each customer or job that has a budget, and a column for each month. The budget totals for all accounts (individual accounts are not displayed) appear under each month. Under each customer is a row for every job that has a budget.

The name of each layout choice is a hint about the way it displays in the report. The first word represents the content of the rows, and the word after the word "by" represents the content of the columns.

Class Budget Overview

If you created a Class budget, select Profit & Loss By Account and Class in the first window, and click Next. Select a report layout from the drop-down list. You have the following choices:

- **Account by Month** lists each account you used in the budget and displays the total budget amounts (for all Class budgets you created) for each month that has data. No budget information for individual classes appears.
- **Account by Class** lists each account you used in the budget and displays the yearly total for that account for each class (each class has its own column).
- **Class by Month** displays a row for each class that has a budget and a column for each month. The total budget (not broken down by account) appears for each month.

Budget vs. Actual Report

This report's name says it all—you can see how your real numbers compare to your budget figures. For a plain P&L budget the report displays the following columns for each month, for each account:

- Amount posted
- Amount budgeted
- Difference in dollars
- Difference in percentage

The choices for the Budget vs. Actual Report are the same as the Budget Overview, so you can see account totals, customer totals, or class totals to match the budgets you've created.

The first thing you'll notice in the report is that all the accounts in your general ledger are listed, whether you included them in your budget or not. However, only the accounts you used in your budget show budget figures. You can change that by customizing the report to include only your budgeted accounts, using the following steps.

1. Click the Modify Report button at the top of the budget report window.
2. In the Modify Report window, click the Advanced button to open the Advanced Options window.
3. Click the option labeled Show Only Rows And Columns With Budgets.
4. Click OK to return to the Modify Report window
5. Click OK again to return to the Budget vs. Actual report window.

Now only the data for your budgeted accounts is displayed. You can also use the options in the Modify Report window to make other changes. For example, you can change the report dates, or change the calculations from Accrual to Cash. Choosing Cash means that unpaid invoices and bills are removed from the calculations, and only actual income and expenses are reported.

If you modify the report, you should memorize it so you don't have to make these modifications the next time you want to view a comparison report. Click the Memorize button at the top of the report window, and name the report. Only the formatting changes you make are memorized, not the data. Every time you open the report, it displays current data. To view the report after you memorize it, choose Reports → Memorized Reports, and select this report.

Profit & Loss Budget Performance Report

This report is similar to the Budget vs. Actual report, but it's based on the current month and the year to date, so you can see how you're doing so far. For that time period, the report displays your actual income and expenses compared to what you budgeted.

By default, the date range is the current month, but you can change it to see last month's figures, or the figures for any previous month.

Budget vs. Actual Graph

This report just opens; you don't have to make any choices about the display format in the wizard windows. All the choices are in the graph that displays, in the form of buttons across the top of the report window. Merely click the type of report you want to see.

Exporting and Importing Budgets

You can export your budgets so they can be viewed and manipulated in other software applications, and you can import budgets you've manipulated in that software.

Exporting Budgets

If you need to manipulate your budgets, export them to other software applications. However, you can't select specific budgets to export—it's all or nothing.

You can export all your budgets to any software program that supports documents that contain delimited fields. However, it's common to export budgets to a spreadsheet application, and for the rest of this section, I'll assume you exported your budgets to Microsoft Excel. Use the following steps to export your budgets:

1. Choose File → Export → Lists to IIF Files. When the Export dialog opens, it displays all the QuickBooks lists. Select the item named Budgets and click OK.

2. Another Export dialog opens (this one looks like the standard Save dialog). Select a folder in which to save this exported file.
3. Give the exported list a filename (for example, 2007Budgets). QuickBooks will automatically add the extension .iif to the filename.
4. Click Save. QuickBooks displays a message telling you that your data has been exported successfully.
5. Click OK.

Using Exported Budgets in Spreadsheet Software

You can view and manipulate your exported budgets in the software application that received the exported budgets. Here's how to import the .iif file into Excel:

1. Open Excel.
2. Choose File → Open, to see the Open dialog.
3. Move to the folder where you stored your .iif file.
4. In the Files Of Type field, change the specification to All Files (otherwise, you won't see your .iif file in the listings).
5. Double-click your exported .iif file to open it.
6. Excel recognizes that this file doesn't match its own default file type and begins the procedures for importing a text, tab-delimited, file.

When the import procedures are completed, your budget is displayed in the Excel window. You can use Excel features to manipulate the budget by changing the way the items are sorted, or by applying formulas to budget data.

This is a good way to play "what-if" games, so you can see what would happen if certain expenses increased. For example, suppose you wanted to hire another person for the office, or for a particular program or contract. Suppose the landlord raises your rent. Suppose someone comes up with a great idea for a fund raiser—what would the estimated advance costs do to your budget, and what's the best place to steal that money from?

If you want to change the budget dates so you can use the budgets next year in QuickBooks, move to the column labeled STARTDATE and update all the dates in the column to the following year.

If you're planning to import the budgets back into QuickBooks (covered next), be sure to save the file as a tab-delimited text document and give the file the extension .iif.

Importing Budgets Back into QuickBooks

The usual reason for importing budgets back into QuickBooks is to copy a budget to another year. (If you merely wanted to edit figures, you'd work in the QuickBooks budget window.)

If you changed the dates to next year, import the file so you can use the data in budget reports, or work with the data in the QuickBooks budget window. Use the following steps to import the budgets back into QuickBooks.

1. Choose File → Import → IIF Files.
2. When the Import dialog opens, locate and double-click the file you saved. QuickBooks displays a message to tell you the import was successful.
3. Click OK.

You can view the imported budgets in any budget report or in the budget window. QuickBooks checks the dates and changes the budget's name to reflect the dates. Budget names start with FY*xxxx*, where *xxxx* is the fiscal year.

When you select a budget report, or choose a budget to edit in the budget window, the available budgets include the budgets you created in QuickBooks and the budgets you imported after changing the date. Next year, you can delete the previous year's budgets.

Projecting Cash Flow

The Cash Flow Projector lets you project your cash flows for the next six weeks, using any criteria you want to use. The tool uses data in your company file, but you can remove accounts from the analysis, and you can also adjust the figures. These features make it easier to achieve the projection parameters and results you need. You can design very specific scenarios, which makes the tool useful in planning for either minor or major changes in your organization.

The Cash Flow Projector is a powerful tool for anyone who understands the accounting principles behind cash flows projections. Unless you have some expertise in this area, it's best to work with your accountant when you use the Cash Flow Projector.

It's beyond the scope of this book to provide a detailed explanation of all the ways to use this tool, so my discussion in the following sections is an overview.

Cash Flow Projector Vs. Cash Flows Reports

The Cash Flow Projector is not a report; it's a tool that helps you build a customized projection of cash flows. QuickBooks has two cash flows reports available:

* Statement of Cash Flows, which reports your cash flow activity over a period of time.
* Cash Flow Forecast, projects your cash flow for a specified period of time using existing information in your company file.

Like the Cash Flow reports, the projector uses information you've entered into QuickBooks, but then permits you to customize and tweak the data. You can change the data that was retrieved from your file, and you can also include additional data.

Starting the Cash Flow Projector

Before you open the Cash Flow Projector, make sure you've entered all transactions, including memorized transactions, into your company file. This assures the accuracy of your projection.

Open the Cash Flow Projector by choosing Company → Planning & Budgeting → Cash Flow Projector. The program operates as a wizard, and the opening window (see Figure 9-5) welcomes you and offers links to information you should read before you begin.

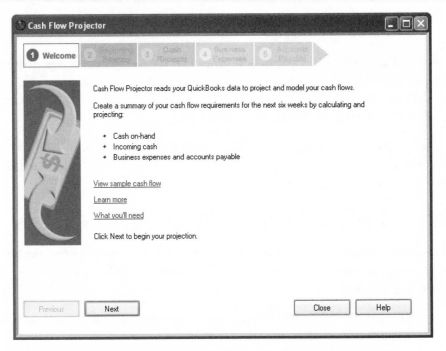

Figure 9-5: Start by going over the information the wizard presents.

Creating a Beginning Balance

Click Next to move to the Beginning Balance window, where you establish the beginning balance for your projection. The beginning balance is the total of the balances in the accounts you select to use in your projection, along with any adjustments you make.

Selecting Accounts for the Beginning Balance

The window displays all the accounts that contain cash (bank accounts), with each account's current balance (see Figure 9-6). Select the accounts you use for managing your cash. Include the accounts you use to receive income, pay loans, and pay expenses. Depending on your account setup, this could be one account, or multiple accounts.

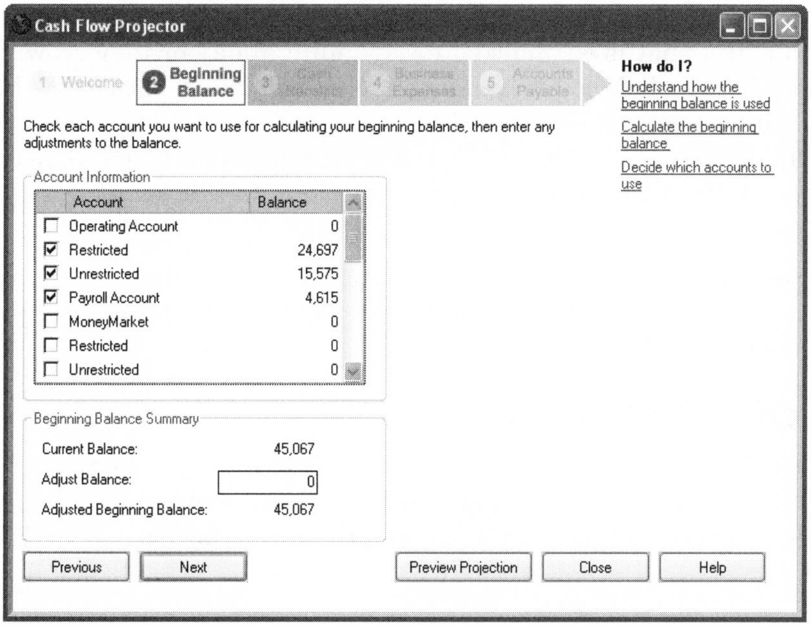

Figure 9-6: Choose the accounts to use for a beginning balance.

The Beginning Balance Summary section displays the balance based on the accounts you selected.

Adjusting the Beginning Balance

You can adjust your current balance in the Adjust Balance field. If you make an adjustment, the Cash Flow Projector remembers the adjustment and applies it whenever you use this tool. You can, of course, modify or delete the adjustment if it's not applicable to future projections.

If you haven't entered all your cash transactions into QuickBooks, you need to adjust the balance so it reflections those transactions (it's easier to make sure everything is entered before opening the Cash Flow Projector). In addition, you may need to make one or more of the following adjustments to the beginning balance:

• If you know you have additional revenue arriving today or tomorrow, and you want to include it, adjust the current cash balance to cover that amount.

- If the current balance of any selected account contains an amount that is earmarked for spending today or tomorrow, adjust the balance by removing that amount (don't forget the minus sign).
- If you have a "safety net" amount, a minimum cash balance you must keep on hand at all times, exclude that amount from your balance.

When you've made your adjustments, your beginning balance is set and you can move on with your projection. Click Next to move to projecting your cash receipts.

Projecting Cash Receipts

In the Cash Receipts window, project your cash receipts for the next six weeks. By default, the projection is made using a weighted average of the cash receipts for the last six weeks, and the totals for each week are displayed.

You can select another projection method from the drop-down list, and I'll present a brief overview of each method in the following sections. (If you don't understand the terminology in the list, discuss this step with your accountant.)

NOTE: *When you select a different method, the Cash Flow Projector displays a message warning you that all the existing figures in the window will be cleared, and asking if you want to continue. Click Yes.*

Manual Projection

Select I Want To Project Cash Receipts Manually if your accountant has some particular paradigm in mind, or if the methods offered don't match the way you want to project cash receipts.

The window changes so you can enter the date, description, and amount for each of the next six weeks (see Figure 9-7). The figures you enter are moved into the Cash Receipts Summary section.

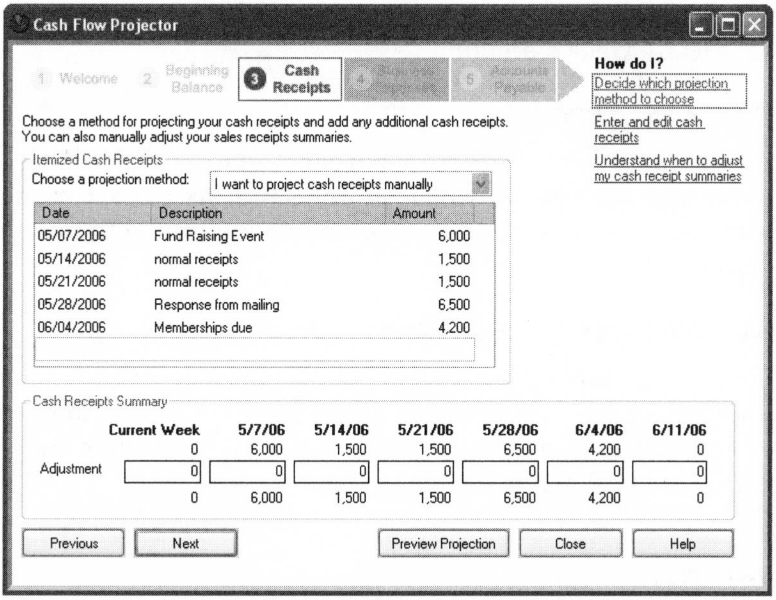

Figure 9-7: Manual entry lets you control descriptions and amounts.

Last Six Weeks

If you select Use Last 6 Weeks, the cash receipts amounts for the previous six weeks are duplicated, one week at a time, for the next six weeks. Use this method if your last six weeks are typical for the year. You can make adjustments to any week's amount if there's a reason to do so.

Average of Last Six Weeks

If you select Use An Average Of Last 6 Weeks, the total receipts for the previous six weeks are averaged, and that average amount is used for each of the upcoming six weeks. You can make adjustments to any week's amount.

Weighted Average of Last Six Weeks

If you select Use A Weighted Average Of Last 6 Weeks, the Cash Flow Projector uses the last six weeks of historical cash receipts entries, and then uses an algorithm that weights the most recent receipts as the most likely to occur in the future. The averaged amount calculated by this algorithm is duplicated for all of the next six weeks. You can make adjustments to any week's amount.

Same Period Last Year

If you select Same 6 Weeks Period Last Year, the Cash Flow Projector duplicates the cash receipts entries from the same six-week period one year ago into the next six weeks. You can make adjustments to any week's amount.

Average of Same Period Last Year

If you select Average Of Same 6 Week Period Last Year, the Cash Flow Projector takes the cash receipts from the same six-week period last year, and averages them. That averaged amount is used for each of the next six weeks. You can make adjustments to any week's amount.

Projecting Expenses

Click Next to move to the Business Expenses window, where you must enter your expected cash outlays. Do *not* include accounts payable expenses in this window. Instead, enter those expenses that aren't paid by paying a vendor's bill. Non A/P items include loan payments, payroll, rent, and so on. If you use memorized transactions to pay any of these expenses, you can use those amounts here.

Select an account from the drop-down list in the Expense column, or enter a category description of your own. Enter a date, a frequency for the expense, and an amount. As you enter data, the totals are displayed in the Business Expenses Summary section (see Figure 9-8). Note that the Cash Flow Projector does not read your data files to get the current amounts for accounts you select; you must enter your own figures.

For some categories, especially expenses tied to programs, you may want to list each type of expense as a discrete entry. For other categories, you can either use a parent account from the drop-down list, or enter a category description, and enter an inclusive figure. The amount of detail you use when entering data affects the amount of detail you'll see in the final projection.

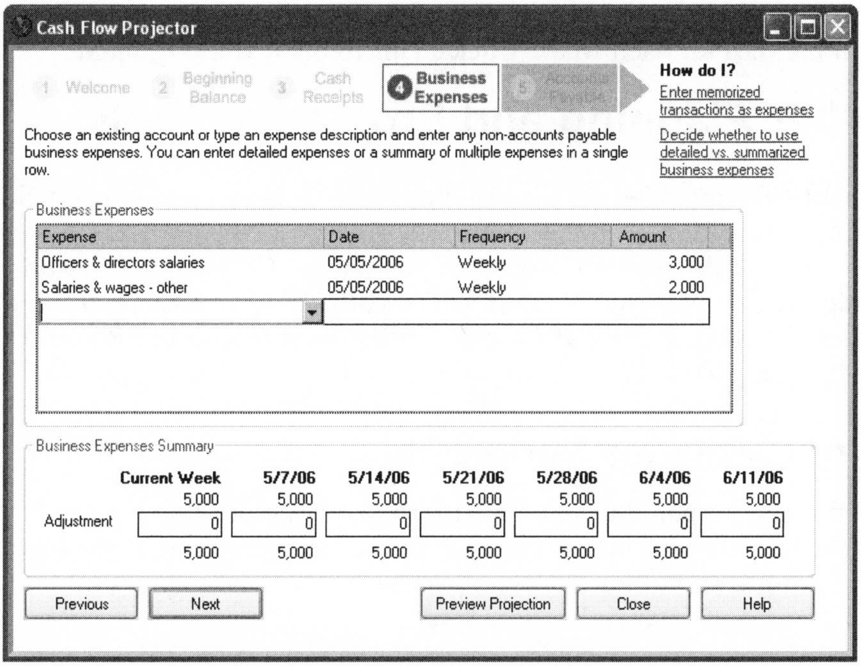

Figure 9-8: Enter your expected cash outlays for the next six weeks.

Projecting Accounts Payable

Click Next to move to the Account Payable window, where the Cash Flow Projector displays your current A/P amounts. In the Payment Date field, enter the date you plan to remit payment for each vendor, if the date differs from the date displayed (the Cash Flow Projector uses the bill's due date as the payment date).

The totals are transferred to the Accounts Payable Summary section, where you can make adjustments to the figures. For example, you should add any significant vendor bills you're expecting during the next six weeks.

Display and Print the Projection

Click Finish Projection to display the finished document, which projects your cash income and your expenses (as selected by you) for the current week and the next six weeks. The document also projects your ending cash balance for each week. Click Print to print the document.

Other Planning and Projection Tools

QuickBooks provides quite a few planning tools you can use to help guide your organization's management and growth. Investigate the tools available in the submenu you see when you choose Company → Planning & Budgeting → Decision Tools. If you're running QuickBooks Premier Nonprofit Edition, look at the Set Up Forecast tool in the Planning & Budgeting menu.

ProfitCents for Nonprofits

ProfitCents (a popular and favorite tool of accountants) and ProfitCents for Nonprofits are both web-based software programs that enable accountants and other financial professionals to provide an in-depth explanation of financial statements.

(The QuickBooks Premier editions have a free trial version of Expert Analysis, which is based on the ProfitCents application.)

The reports use ratio analysis, industry comparisons, and trend analysis to explain and analyze the financial health of an organization. These powerful tools produce plain-language, customizable reports that provide information that's invaluable.

Free Trial for ProfitCents for Nonprofits

CPA911 Publishing has made arrangements for anyone who buys this book to have a two-month free trial of ProfitCents for Nonprofits. You should give this information to your accountant, who is probably familiar with ProfitCents and might be interested in pursuing the free trial period of the nonprofit product (because your accountant can use the program for multiple clients).

Reserve a space for a ProfitCents webinar by calling 877-724-3967 (press Option 2 in the automated menu system) or send email to info@profitcents.com to ask for a reservation.

After you see the presentation, if you decide you're interested your Free Trial Code is NPO. Give that code to the representative who arranges your subscription, and you can use the software for two months without charge.

Chapter 10

Producing Reports

Customized reports for nonprofits

Standard financial reports

Accounts receivable reports

Accounts payable reports

One of the big advantages of using accounting software instead of keeping books manually is the ability to produce robust, detailed reports. QuickBooks provides a full complement of report types, and you can customize any report so it produces exactly the information you need.

You have to produce a variety of report types, because you have an assortment of entities that demand reports: foundations, government agencies, your board of directors, and any other group or person who requires information about your financial status.

Remember that QuickBooks is designed for regular, for-profit businesses, and some of the terminology you see in reports won't match the language usually employed by nonprofits. To overcome this deficiency, you can export any report to Excel, change the terminology, and print your reports from Excel.

Customized Reports for Nonprofits

QuickBooks Premier Nonprofit edition has a number of memorized reports designed for nonprofits. This section presents an overview of those built-in reports, which you can open by choosing Reports → Memorized Reports → Nonprofit, and selecting the report you want to see from the submenu. I'll go over these reports in this section.

If you're using QuickBooks Pro, you can modify the built-in standard reports to match these reports. I'll include instructions for customizing each report I cover in this section.

Biggest Donors/Grants Report

This report displays the customers from whom you've received revenue during the current fiscal year. The report is sorted by the income received from each customer. The sort order is descending, so the customer who has contributed the most is at the top of the list. For customers with jobs, each job and its associated revenue are displayed under the customer's name.

I'm not sure which entities would require this report, and I suspect you won't be generating it on a regular basis. However, I think it would be a nifty idea to put this report on the screen when a representative of any donor except the donor at the top of the list is visiting your office. Maybe this would spur the person's competitive nature, resulting in another grant or contract.

To create this report in QuickBooks Pro, choose Reports → Sales → Sales by Customer Summary. Then click the Modify Reports button and make the following changes on the Display tab.

- Change the Dates field to This Fiscal Year-to-date.
- Change the Sort By field to Total
- Click the Sort Order icon next to the Sort By field, and change the sort to Descending.

Click OK to save the changes. Then press Ctrl-M to memorize the report, and name it Biggest Donors/Grants Report.

Budget vs. Actual by Donors/Grants Report

This report is a standard budget vs. actual report, but it requires the existence of at least one budget of the customer:job type (covered in Chapter 9). The report is configured to display information by customer and job.

The left-most column of the Budget vs. Actual by Donors/Grants Report lists the income and expense accounts for which you budgeted amounts when you created your P & L Customer:Job budgets.

Data appears in the columns for those customers or jobs for which you specifically entered budgets. Each customer and job displays the following data across four columns:

- Amount posted this fiscal year to-date (the actuals)
- Amount budgeted
- $ over/under budget
- % of budget.

To create this report in QuickBooks Pro, choose Reports → Budgets → Budgets vs. Actual, and take the following steps:

1. In the first wizard window, select Profit & Loss by Account and Customer:Job.
2. Click Next.
3. In the next window, choose Account By Customer:Job as the layout.
4. Click Finish.
5. In the report window, change the date field to This Fiscal Year-to-date.
6. Memorize the report with the name Budget vs. Actual by Donor/Grants Report.

Budget vs. Actual by Program/Projects Report

This report is the same as the previous report, but the data is sorted by class instead of by job. If you created class-based budgets, you can see the actual amounts compared to the budgeted amounts for each class. Only those classes for which you created a budget have data displayed in the columns.

To create this report in QuickBooks Pro, choose Profit & Loss by Class as the report type, and use the same customizations described in the previous section. Memorize the report, and name it Budget vs. Actual by Program/Projects Report.

Donors/Grants Report

This report tracks the amount of money received for each job, and the expenses that posted against each job—essentially it's a Profit & Loss by Customer:Job report, tracing the entire financial history of your customers and jobs.

As you scroll through the report, you see a column for each job. To the right of those columns is a column totaling all jobs for that customer. You can see an example of a customer and the two jobs linked to that customer in Figure 10-1.

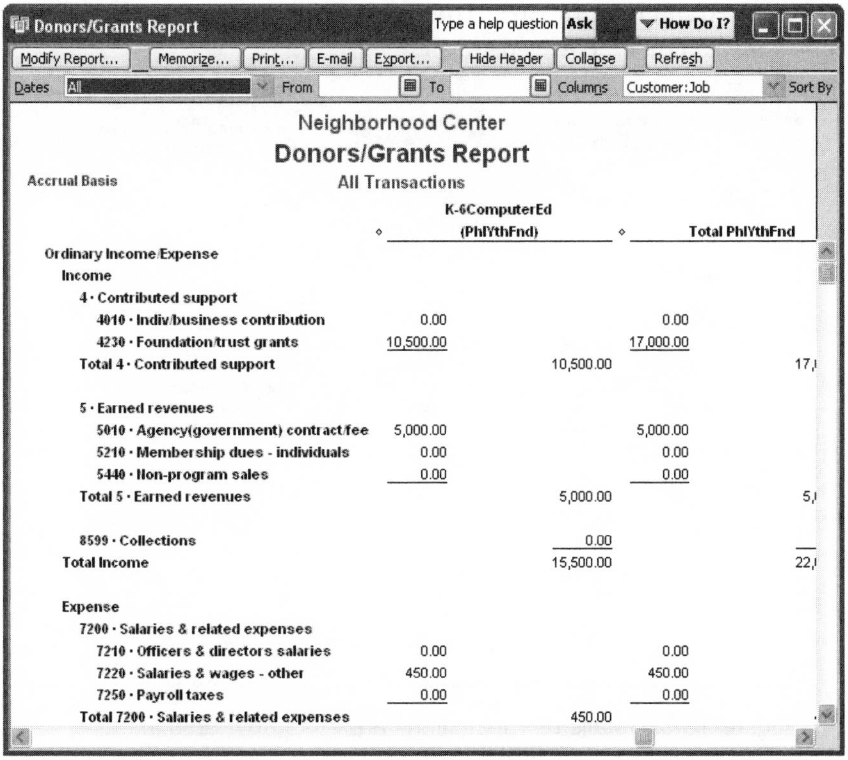

Neighborhood Center

Donors/Grants Report

Accrual Basis — All Transactions

	K-6ComputerEd (PhlYthFnd)		Total PhlYthFnd	
Ordinary Income/Expense				
Income				
4 · Contributed support				
4010 · Indiv/business contribution	0.00		0.00	
4230 · Foundation/trust grants	10,500.00		17,000.00	
Total 4 · Contributed support		10,500.00		17,
5 · Earned revenues				
5010 · Agency(government) contract/fee	5,000.00		5,000.00	
5210 · Membership dues - individuals	0.00		0.00	
5440 · Non-program sales	0.00		0.00	
Total 5 · Earned revenues		5,000.00		5,
8599 · Collections		0.00		
Total Income		15,500.00		22,
Expense				
7200 · Salaries & related expenses				
7210 · Officers & directors salaries	0.00		0.00	
7220 · Salaries & wages - other	450.00		450.00	
7250 · Payroll taxes	0.00		0.00	
Total 7200 · Salaries & related expenses		450.00		

Figure 10-1: Scroll through the report to see totals and net amounts for each job and customer.

To create this report in QuickBooks Pro, choose Reports → Company & Financial → Profit & Loss by Job. Change the date range to All, and memorize the report with the name Donors/Grants Report.

Programs/Projects Report

This is a detailed activity report for each class and subclass for the fiscal year to-date. As you can see in Figure 10-2, each class and subclass has a section, under which appear all the transactions for the class.

QuickBooks Pro has no report that matches this layout, but the information is the same as that available in a standard Profit & Loss by

Class report (which is, in turn, the same as the Statement of Financial Income and Expense, covered next).

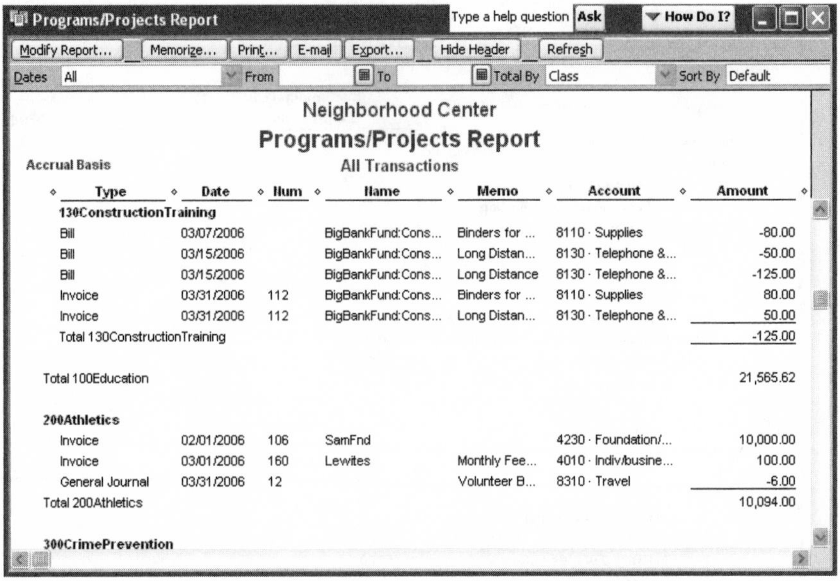

Type	Date	Num	Name	Memo	Account	Amount
130ConstructionTraining						
Bill	03/07/2006		BigBankFund:Cons...	Binders for ...	8110 · Supplies	-80.00
Bill	03/15/2006		BigBankFund:Cons...	Long Distan...	8130 · Telephone &...	-50.00
Bill	03/15/2006		BigBankFund:Cons...	Long Distance	8130 · Telephone &...	-125.00
Invoice	03/31/2006	112	BigBankFund:Cons...	Binders for ...	8110 · Supplies	80.00
Invoice	03/31/2006	112	BigBankFund:Cons...	Long Distan...	8130 · Telephone &...	50.00
Total 130ConstructionTraining						-125.00
Total 100Education						21,565.62
200Athletics						
Invoice	02/01/2006	106	SamFnd		4230 · Foundation/...	10,000.00
Invoice	03/01/2006	160	Lewites	Monthly Fee...	4010 · Indiv/busine...	100.00
General Journal	03/31/2006	12		Volunteer B...	8310 · Travel	-6.00
Total 200Athletics						10,094.00
300CrimePrevention						

Figure 10-2: Details of transactions are sorted by class in the Programs/Projects Report.

Statement of Financial Income and Expense

This is a Profit & Loss Report by Class, with a column for each class. It is identical to the Profit & Loss report you can open by selecting Reports → Company & Financial → Profit & Loss by Class.

Nonprofits don't produce reports with the word "profit" or "loss" in the title; instead, they produce statements of income and expense.

Statement of Financial Position

This report displays balance sheet account information for this year and last year, using the current date as the basis of comparison. In addition, the report shows the dollar difference and the percentage difference for each account.

If you didn't use QuickBooks last year, the report has no value. This report is identical to the Balance Sheet Previous Year Comparison report, which you can open by choosing Reports → Company & Financial → Balance Sheet Prev Year Comparison.

Statement of Functional Expenses (990)

This report displays the way you spent funds, sorting your expenses on a program-by-program basis (see Figure 10-3). Unlike other financial reports, this one isn't "bottom line" oriented; it doesn't look at your net assets (whether you're operating in the black or in the red).

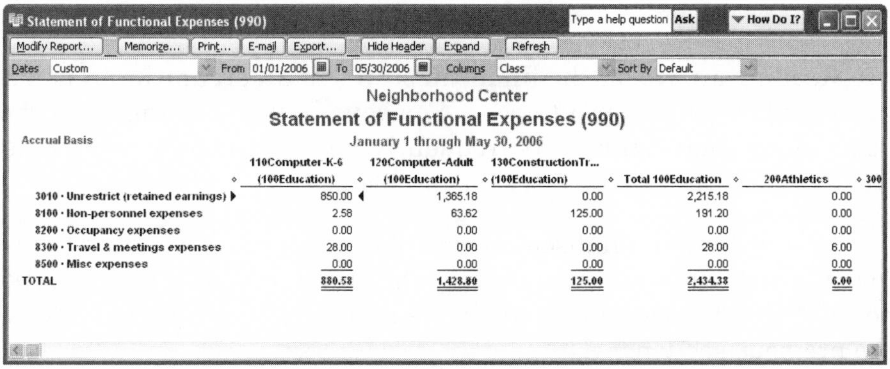

	110Computer-K-6 (100Education)	120Computer-Adult (100Education)	130ConstructionTr... (100Education)	Total 100Education	200Athletics	300
3010 · Unrestrict (retained earnings)	850.00	1,365.18	0.00	2,215.18	0.00	
8100 · Non-personnel expenses	2.58	63.62	125.00	191.20	0.00	
8200 · Occupancy expenses	0.00	0.00	0.00	0.00	0.00	
8300 · Travel & meetings expenses	28.00	0.00	0.00	28.00	6.00	
8500 · Misc expenses	0.00	0.00	0.00	0.00	0.00	
TOTAL	880.58	1,428.80	125.00	2,434.38	6.00	

Figure 10-3: This report gives you a quick view of the expenses assigned to each program.

The report shows how you've spent money in order to fulfill your mission. As a result, it could be considered one of the most important reports you produce. Unlike a for-profit business, a nonprofit organization isn't judged for success by the bottom line. Instead, the definition of success hinges on the way you approached your mandates and missions. The statement of functional expenses reflects your financial commitment to your programs.

The statement of functional expenses is designed to be transferred to Part II of IRS Form 990. However, even if you don't have to file a 990, the information in this report is important to donors, potential donors, and the community you impact.

More information about the statement of functional expenses, which is always produced as part of the year end package of reports, is in Chapter 11.

Standard Financial Reports

In the for-profit business world, bookkeepers and business owners constantly run reports, to keep an eye on the financial health of the business. The sales manager looks at the A/R aging report every day, and has the collections manager make calls to customers who are very late. The bookkeeper and business owner look at the Profit & Loss reports and the Balance Sheet reports on a daily basis, to stay abreast of changes in financial positions.

Keeping an eye on the financial status of an organization is just as important in the nonprofit arena. Someone in your organization should be checking financial reports frequently. This is the only way to see trends before they become serious problems.

In this section, I'll discuss some of the reports you should be reviewing on a regular basis. I'm omitting the standard Profit & Loss reports, because that information is available in most of the reports I covered in the previous section.

Balance Sheet Reports

A balance sheet is an indication of basic financial health. It displays the current totals of your balance sheet accounts: Assets, Liabilities, and Equity. Balance sheets balance because they work on a formula, which is **Assets = Liabilities + Equity**.

The equity amount is calculated when you generate the balance sheet, using the following algorithm:

1. All the income account balances are totaled.
2. All the expense account balances are totaled.
3. The expense total is subtracted from the income total.
4. The number generated in Step 3 is added to the existing totals in the equity accounts (previous year equity totals).

5. The total calculated in Step 4 becomes the figure for equity in a Balance Sheet.

QuickBooks offers several balance sheet reports, all of which are available by choosing Reports → Company & Financial, and choosing the balance sheet report you desire from the submenu. I'll provide an overview of each balance sheet report in the following sections.

Balance Sheet Standard Report

This report displays the balance of every Balance Sheet account that has a balance, and reports totals for each account type (asset, liability, and equity). By default, the date range is the current fiscal year-to-date.

Balance Sheet Detail Report

This report displays every transaction in every asset, liability, and equity account that had activity during the date range specified for the report. By default, the report covers a date range of the current month to date.

Even if it's early in the month, this report can be quite long. If you change the date range to cover a longer period (the current quarter or year), the report goes on and on and on. Unless you have some specific reason to examine every transaction, this is almost certainly more than you wanted to know about the activity in your balance sheet accounts.

Balance Sheet Summary Report

This report displays totals for each account type, making it a quick way to answer the question, "How are we doing?" Each balance sheet account type that has a balance is listed, as seen in Figure 10-4.

Balance Sheet Previous Year Comparison Report

Create this report to see what your financial situation is compared to a year ago. This is a quick way to see financial trends: Is your financial health as well as, better than, or worse than, last year?

By default, the date range is this fiscal year to-date, and the same date last year. The report displays the following four columns:

- The year-to-date amount for each balance sheet account for this fiscal year.
- The year-to-date amount for each Balance Sheet account for the last fiscal year.
- The change, in dollars, between last year and this year
- The percentage of change between last year and this year

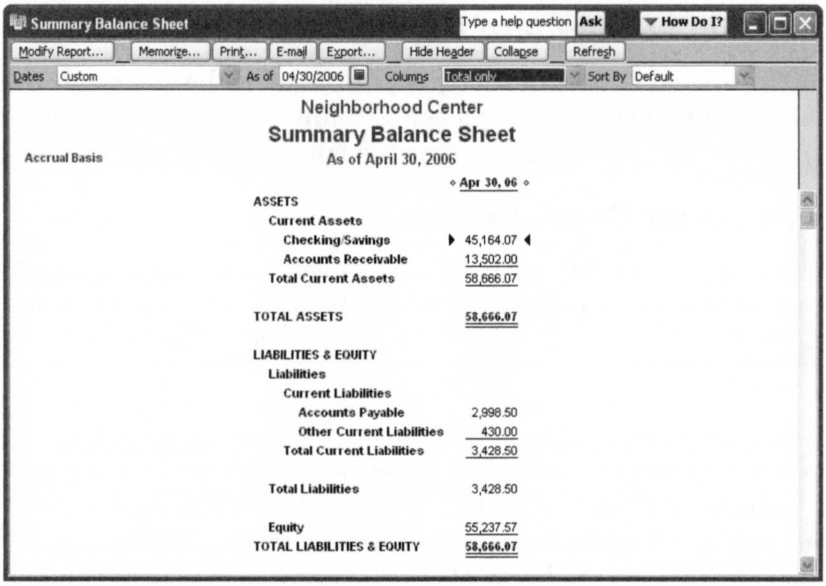

Figure 10-4: The Summary Balance Sheet provides a quick check on your financial health.

If you started using QuickBooks this year, this report isn't useful, but next year you'll be able to see how you're doing compared to this year.

Accounts Receivable Reports

Money that is owed to you (accounts receivable) is an asset, and therefore an important part of your organization's financial health. In for-profit businesses, the accounts receivable total is not just an asset; it's sometimes the basis of a line of credit (a lender assumes the money, or most of it, will be collected).

However, the fact that receivables are assets doesn't help your real (as opposed to theoretical) financial health. You can't write checks against the receivables balance, you need the cash. A high receivables total often means a poor cash position. To see the general state of your receivables, choose Reports → Customers & Receivables, and choose one of the A/R Aging Reports described in the following sections.

A/R Aging Summary Report

The A/R Aging Summary Report displays each customer and job with an A/R balance, and shows both the current balances, and the overdue balances. Overdue balances are sorted in columns by the amount of time the balance is overdue (1-30 days, 31-60 days, 61-90 days, and >90 days). This report is a good way to get a quick look at the amount of money "on the street" (the accounting jargon for uncollected receivables).

A/R Aging Detail Report

This report displays all the details about receivables, on a customer-by-customer basis. If you just want to get a handle on the size of your receivables, and the customers and jobs that owe you money, this report is more than you need. However, your board, your treasurer, or your development staff may find this report useful.

Customizing A/R Reports for Collections

One important reason to run reports on the state of your receivables is to collect money that's overdue. For nonprofit organizations, this means making collection efforts for receivables that aren't contractual obligations (such as grants or contracts).

You should make an effort to collect overdue pledges, receivables for sales of goods and services to customers, membership fees, program fees, and other customer receivables. In addition, if you send invoices for reimbursable expenses to your funding agencies, make an effort to collect the overdue amounts for those invoices as quickly as possible.

QuickBooks has a report called Collections, but it's merely an aging report. To collect money, you really need to see the customer's receivables along with contact information. Since no report with this information exists, you have to customize an existing report. Several of the QuickBooks reports are good starting places for a collection report, and all of them are available by choosing Reports → Customers & Receivables.

Customer Balance Detail Report

This report shows customer activity, including invoices and payments. The report has a lot of detail, but that's handy for having a conversation with the customer. You may have to confirm the receipt of a payment, or remind the customer of the details of an invoice. The report is missing contact information, and you can add that data by customizing the report, as follows.

Click Modify Report, and in the Columns list in the Display tab, make the following changes:

- Select Name Contact.
- Select Name Phone #.
- Deselect Account.
- Deselect Class.

If you've set up multiple A/R accounts to track different kinds of receivables, you should also modify the report to include only receivables that aren't connected to grants and contract. To do so, follow these steps:

1. On the Filters tab, select Accounts. By default, the selected accounts are All Accounts Receivable.
2. Click the arrow in the Account field, and scroll up to choose Selected Accounts.
3. In the Select Accounts dialog, choose the A/R accounts that aren't connected to grants or contracts. For example, choose Pledges Receivable, Memberships Receivable, Fees Receivable, and so on.
4. Click OK to return to the Filters tab.
5. Click OK again to return to the report.

You should memorize this report so you don't have to repeat these actions to get the report you need. Click the Memorize button at the top of the report window, and name the report appropriately (e.g. A/R Detail w/Contacts).

This report has enough information to print and give to someone who will make the calls. If the customer has a question about payment or invoice details, the data exists in the printout. This means that personnel who don't have permission to use QuickBooks (or don't have QuickBooks on their computers) can assist with collections.

Customer Balance Summary Report

This report displays only the current balance for each customer, omitting the invoice and payment details. If you're using the report for collections, you should telephone the customer from your computer, with the report loaded. That way, you can double-click a listing to see detailed information if the customer has questions.

To add the contact information to this report, customize it as described for the Customer Balance Detail report.

Collection Letters

QuickBooks works with Microsoft Word to provide Word's mail merge feature to send letters to customers, using criteria you specify. QuickBooks supplies several prewritten collection letters you can use, or you can design your own letter.

WARNING: If your customer records don't contain data for all the required fields (salutations, names, addresses, and ZIP codes), your mail merge won't work properly.

The letters are in the folder in which you installed QuickBooks, in a subfolder named QuickBooks Letter Templates. That subfolder has additional subfolders for each type of QuickBooks letters. If you want to look at the letters before you decide which collection letter to send, take the following steps:

1. Open Microsoft Word.
2. Click the Open icon on the Word toolbar (or choose File → Open).
3. In the Open dialog, use the Look In field to move to the folder that holds the QuickBooks letters.

4. Open the Collection Letters folder, and then open each letter to see which one you prefer to use.

Don't make changes in the letters while you're viewing them in Word. If you don't think any of the letters are suitable, you can customize one or more of them to match your needs (covered next).

Customizing Collection Letters

I don't think any of the existing collection letters are suitable for nonprofit organizations. Some of the letters are rather harsh, even threatening, which might work for a for-profit business, but doesn't inspire people to continue to support a nonprofit organization. Even the casual, friendly collection letter is inappropriate because it contains phrases such as "thank you for your business".

The important components of a mail merge letter are the fields. When you create the letter, Word inserts data from your QuickBooks file into each field. For example, the field <<AddrBlock>> becomes the mailing address of the customer, and the field <<OverdueInvTotal>> becomes the current overdue balance of the customer. When you customize an existing letter, be careful not to mess with the fields; instead, only make changes to the text in the body of the letter.

You can add, remove, or modify any of the text in a QuickBooks collection letter, and then save the new letter and use it for a collection letter. If you're comfortable with the Word mail merge feature, you can create a letter from scratch, inserting fields where needed.

Use the following steps to customize an existing QuickBooks collection letter (I'm using the Friendly Collection letter for this example):

1. Choose Customers → Customer Letters With Envelopes → Customize Letter Templates to open the Letters and Envelopes Wizard.
2. Select View Or Edit Existing Letter Templates, and click Next.
3. In the next wizard window, select Collection from the Types Of Letters List, and choose Friendly Collection from the list of letter templates. Then click Next to launch Microsoft Word with this letter open in the software window (see Figure 10-5).

4. Make changes to the text as desired. If you're comfortable with mail merge, you can add fields that link to text you add.
5. Choose File → Save As and give the letter a new name (for example, Friendly Nonprofit). Save the letter in the Collection Letters folder.
6. Close Word to return to QuickBooks.

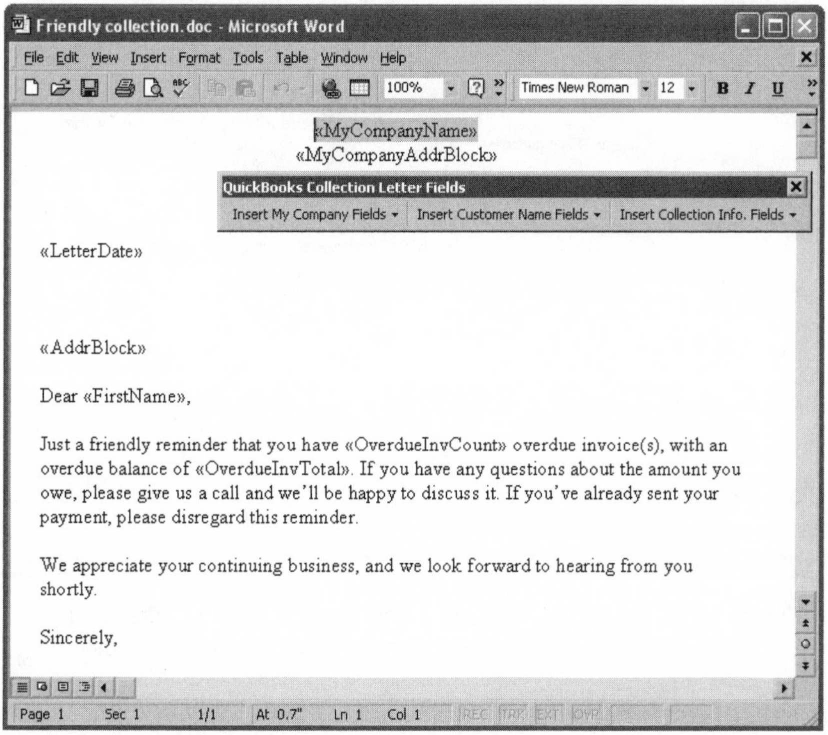

Figure 10-5: Edit the text, and use the toolbar to place fields within additional text.

___

NOTE: *As an example, you can change the last sentence of the letter to "These funds are important to our mission, and we appreciate your support. We look forward to hearing from you shortly." Or, use any phrase that will get the job done without losing the support of this customer.*

___

If you're ready to send the letters now, continue moving through the wizard, which assumes you want to use your new, customized letter (see Figure 10-6). Click Use Template and follow the prompts to move through the wizard. If you want to send the letters later, click Cancel and follow the instructions in the next section, "Sending Collection Letters".

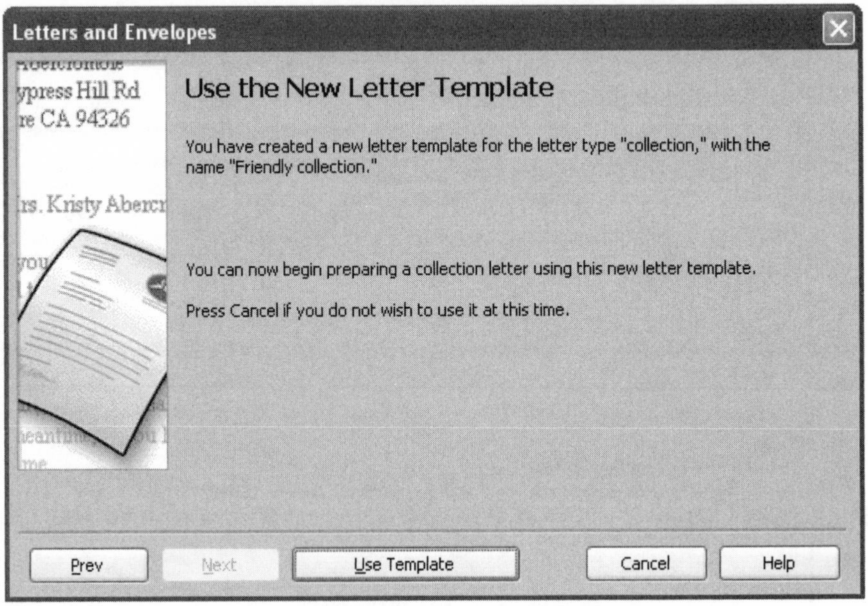

Figure 10-6: The wizard assumes you want to use the letter you just saved, and is ready to walk you through the steps.

Sending Collection Letters

Whether you're using an original QuickBooks letter, or a letter you customized, you use the Letters and Envelopes Wizard to send collection letters to overdue customers.

This feature is commonly used to collect overdue memberships, tuitions, fees for services and programs you offer, and other similar customer payments.

Before you begin, make sure you've applied payments (and credits, if they exist) to all customer invoices. (If any customers who meet your criteria have unapplied payments or credits, QuickBooks issues a warning message. You'll have to cancel the wizard, apply the payments, and start again.)

To launch the wizard, choose Customers → Customer Letters With Envelopes → Prepare Collection Letters. Then take the following steps:

1. Choose the criteria for selecting the customers who will receive your letter (see Figure 10-7).
2. Click Next to see the list of customers who match the criteria you used, along with their current A/R balance. Deselect any customer you want to omit from your recipients list.
3. Click Next to choose the collection letter you want to send. The names of customized letters you created appear in the list (because you saved them in the Collection Letters subfolder).
4. Click Next to enter the name and title of the person who is sending this letter.
5. Click Next to open your mail merge document in Word.

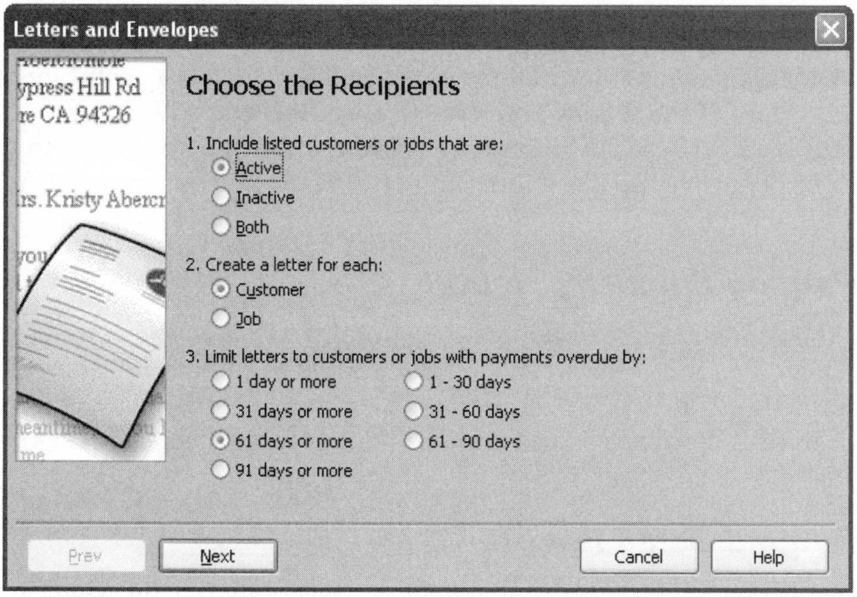

Figure 10-7: Specify the conditions for selecting customers for this letter.

All of your letters are displayed in a single document in the Word software window. A section break exists at the end of each letter. Print the letters, or save the document and print it later.

If you want to print envelopes, return to the QuickBooks wizard (click the QuickBooks button on your taskbar), and click Next. Select the specifications for the envelope, click OK, and follow the prompts to print the envelopes in Word.

If you aren't printing envelopes (perhaps you have labels for your customers, which is a much easier system than printing individual envelopes), close Word and click Cancel in the QuickBooks Letters And Envelopes Wizard window.

Accounts Payable Reports

You have to keep an eye on your payables to avoid problems with vendors, late charges, or fines. Your board probably wants to see the details of the current A/P balance at board meetings, as do your financial personnel and your accountant.

QuickBooks provides plenty of A/P Reports that are useful for tracking the state of the money you owe. Choose Reports → Vendors & Payables and choose the appropriate report from the submenu. In this section, I'll go over some of the commonly used (and very useful) A/P reports.

A/P Aging Summary Report

Use the Aging Summary Report to get a quick look at the state of your payables. The report lists each vendor for which unpaid bills exist, and sorts the totals by 30-day intervals. The report listings lack details, but you can drill down to see the original transactions by double-clicking the listings.

A/P Aging Detail Report

This report provides details about the transactions that make up your A/P totals. The presentation of data is different from the A/P Summary Report, because the rows are aging intervals instead of vendor names.

The vendor names appear in the Name column. You can double-click any listing to drill down to the original invoice.

Unpaid Bills Detail Report

This handy report is arranged by vendor, with subtotals for each vendor's current A/P total (see Figure 10-8). The listings are detailed, and you can double-click any listing to get to the original transaction window.

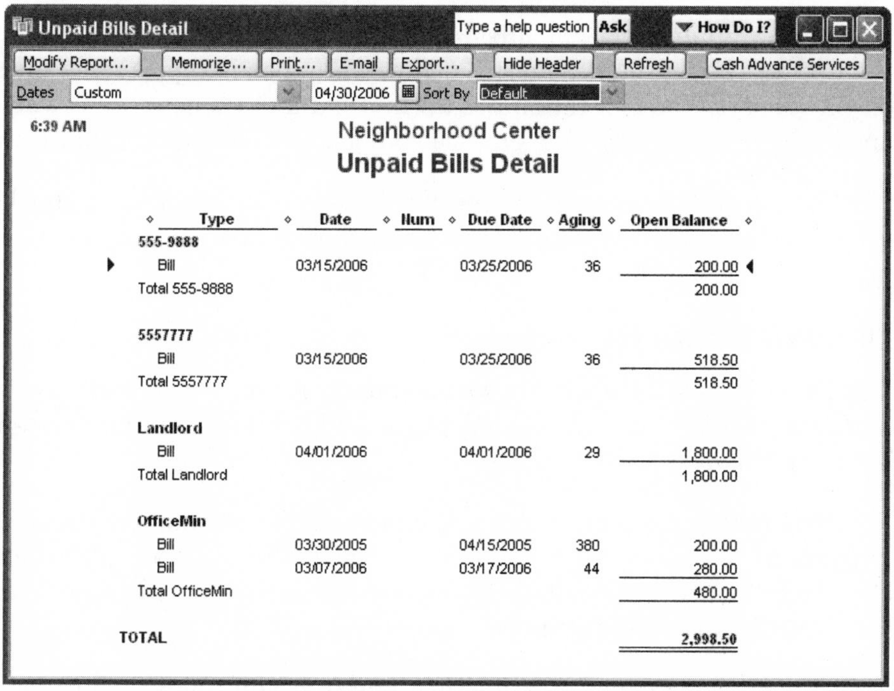

Type	Date	Num	Due Date	Aging	Open Balance
555-9888					
Bill	03/15/2006		03/25/2006	36	200.00
Total 555-9888					200.00
5557777					
Bill	03/15/2006		03/25/2006	36	518.50
Total 5557777					518.50
Landlord					
Bill	04/01/2006		04/01/2006	29	1,800.00
Total Landlord					1,800.00
OfficeMin					
Bill	03/30/2005		04/15/2005	380	200.00
Bill	03/07/2006		03/17/2006	44	280.00
Total OfficeMin					480.00
TOTAL					2,998.50

Figure 10-8: Use the Unpaid Bills Detail report to see your current A/P obligations for each vendor.

Banking Reports

QuickBooks has a number of reports available in the Banking submenu of the Reports menu. The reports that display information about deposits and checks don't have any connection to the current balance in your bank account, they just display the transactions you entered.

If you want to keep an eye on your bank accounts, sign up for online banking, which is a lot easier than telephoning the bank to get the current balance and find out which checks have cleared.

Missing Checks Report

One banking report I find useful is the Missing Checks report. If a check has gone missing, it's easier to use this report than to scroll through the bank register trying to figure out which check number isn't there.

Check numbers can be missing for a number of reasons, and most of them aren't sinister. However, if a check number is reported as missing on this report, and it later shows up in a bank statement when you reconcile the account, there's a chance somebody stole a check and used it.

Take security precautions for checks seriously. Lock your checks in a drawer, file cabinet, or safe. If you keep checks in a printer, locate that printer in a room that can be locked.

Deposit Detail Report

The Deposit Detail Report shows each deposit you made, including the bank account that received the deposit, and the individual receipts that made up the deposit (see Figure 10-9).

This report is handy when you can't find (or remember) the details of a payment you received. If you need to know when a particular donor's check was actually deposited (as opposed to received), this report provides the information you need.

This is also an easy way to learn whether you inadvertently deposited money into the wrong bank account. There's nothing more frustrating during bank reconciliation than having a deposit listed on the statement, and not seeing it in the reconciliation window. Run this report to see if you put the money in another account.

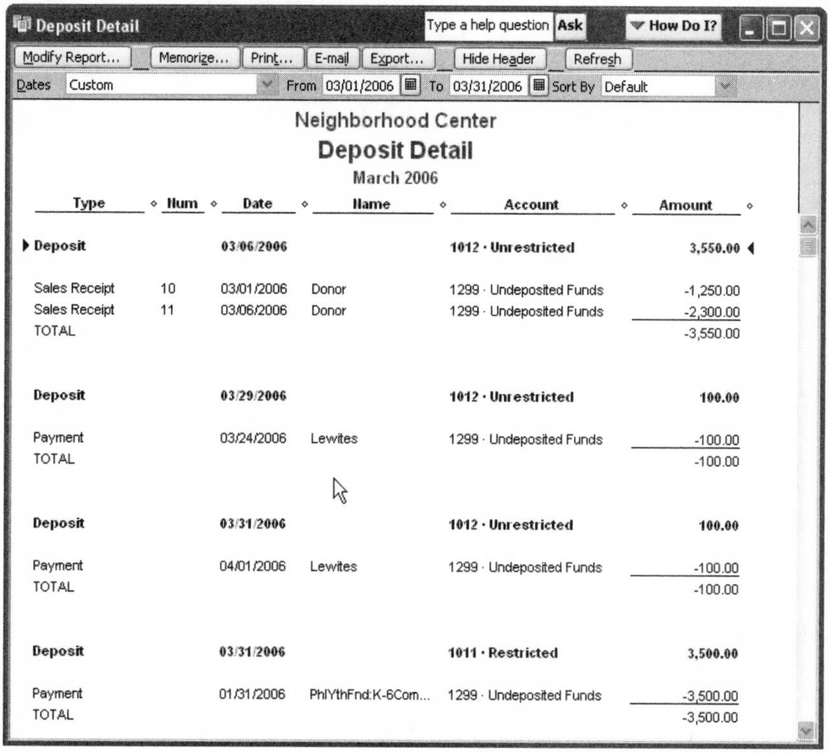

Figure 10-9: Use this report as a quick check-up on bank deposits.

Chapter 11

Year End Activities

Journal entries

Year end reports

Closing the year

Nonprofit organizations have to follow a great many rules for year-end financial activities. Many nonprofits have to file a federal tax return, and in order to do so they must make a number of adjustments to their accounting records.

In addition, the type of organization, the size of the organization (measured in dollars), and the state in which the organization operates, determine the reports that must be filed, as well as the form and content of those reports. Beyond the legal reporting requirements, nonprofits face reporting requirements from donor agencies, and from their own boards of directors.

This is complicated stuff, and the permutations and combinations are enormous. For example, voluntary health and welfare organiza-tions have different requirements than some other types of nonprofit organiza-tions. A nonprofit organization for a church, synagogue, or other house of worship also has a different set of requirements. As a result, I can't give you a specific list of tasks for your end-of-year procedures.

Your accountant is almost certainly involved in most, if not all, of your year-end financial tasks. Some accountants show up at your office, and other accounts ask for copies of your QuickBooks file. QuickBooks provides several methods for delivering financial data to your accountant, and I'll go over those in this chapter, along with a discussion of the common chores that nonprofit organizations face as part of the process of closing the year.

Year-end Journal Entries

The fewer details you include in your transactions, the more journal entries you or your accountant must make at the end of the fiscal year. This usually means that you're spending more money on accounting services than you need to.

If you're not using classes, all the transactions you've entered must be examined, subtotaled, and allocated to programs via journal entries. This can take a long time.

The most important journal entries are those that make adjustments so tax returns and government reports meet legal requirements. I give an overview of these journal entries in this chapter.

In addition, your own circumstances may require additional journal entries to meet reporting requirements for your funding agencies and board of directors. And, of course, there are always those year-end journal entries to correct postings to the wrong account, program, or grant.

Opening Balance Corrections

Many accountants tell me they frequently have to change the opening balances for accounts, because users have made changes to transactions that took place in the previous year. Accountants keep records of each year's closing balances, so they always know if you've changed the totals of the previous year by creating, deleting, or editing transactions.

These accountants report that regardless of the controls built in to prevent working in previous years, users override them. This is one of the things accountants have to accept because QuickBooks, unlike almost all other accounting software, doesn't have a real "close" feature that absolutely seals the books. That deficiency is exacerbated by an apparently unstoppable urge of users to mess around with transactions that are dated in the previous year.

Opening Bal Equity Account

One correction you must make to your opening balances is the removal of any balance in the Opening Bal Equity account that QuickBooks automatically creates in the chart of accounts. The Opening Bal Equity account you see in the chart of accounts is a QuickBooks invention. It doesn't have any connection to the phrase "opening balance" the way that term is usually applied in accounting.

QuickBooks uses the Opening Bal Equity account as the offset account when you enter opening balances during setup. Those opening balances might have been entered during the company setup, or when you manually created accounts, customers, vendors, or inventory items (those dialogs all contain a field for an opening balance).

In this book, during the discussions of setting up your company file, or creating accounts, customers, or vendor, I advised you to avoid filling in any opening balance data.

Instead, I suggested you create transactions that predate the QuickBooks start date to establish those balances (and post the amounts to the appropriate accounts). I advise accountants to take the same attitude when they work with QuickBooks users. If you followed my suggestion, your Opening Bal Equity account has a zero balance, which is the correct state of affairs.

If you opted to enter balances during setup, your Opening Bal Equity account has a balance, and your accountant will almost certainly create journal entries to reduce that balance to zero.

Even if the Opening Bal Equity account contains amounts that are linked to transactions dated before the QuickBooks start date, they may need to be journalized into the current year. Unless your QuickBooks start date was also the first day of your fiscal year, some or all of the balance in the Opening Bal Equity account may be current year numbers. It takes a long time for your accountant to figure out which accounts should receive postings as the Open Bal Equity account is emptied.

Even if you didn't enter opening balances when you created accounts, customers, vendors, or items, you may have funds in your Opening Bal Equity account. When your bank reconciliation procedure doesn't work (the difference between your bank register and the bank statement isn't zero), QuickBooks posts the difference to this account. When you find the bank reconciliation problem and fix it, you or your accountant should make the appropriate journal entry to move the funds out of the Opening Bal Equity account.

Depreciation

Depreciation is an accounting process in which you expense the purchase price of a fixed asset over the period of its useful life. When you purchase a fixed asset (equipment, furniture, vehicles, or other things that your accountant tells you are fixed assets instead of simple purchases, you post the purchase to a fixed asset account, instead of an expense account. Sounds simple, doesn't it? Forget it! It's not simple at all.

Government rules and regulations set forth the definition of the useful life of a fixed asset, and those rules are established on almost a product-by-product basis. This has made depreciation a complicated issue for both for-profit businesses and nonprofit organizations. Indeed, the rules for nonprofit organizations have additional levels of complexity that deal with contributed fixed assets and certain types of fixed assets (e.g. works of art).

You'll have to let your accountant determine the depreciation figures, but you should understand the process of entering depreciation and the effect on your financial reports.

NOTE: Some businesses depreciate fixed assets monthly or quarterly, but that's not common for nonprofit organizations. For this discussion, I'm assuming that your depreciation journal entries are part of the end-of-year procedure.

Fixed Asset Item List

QuickBooks offers a Fixed Asset Item List, which you can use to store information about fixed assets. This list is meant to track data about the assets you depreciate.

To add a fixed asset to the list, choose Lists → Fixed Asset Item List. Press Ctrl-N to open the New Item dialog where you can enter information about the fixed asset. As you can see in Figure 11-1, each asset's record includes detailed information and even has a field to track the sale of a depreciated asset.

This is merely a list, and it doesn't provide any method for calculating depreciation. It's designed to let you use QuickBooks to track your assets within QuickBooks, instead of a spreadsheet, a word processing document, a sheet of paper, or whatever other type of records you're keeping outside of QuickBooks for this purpose.

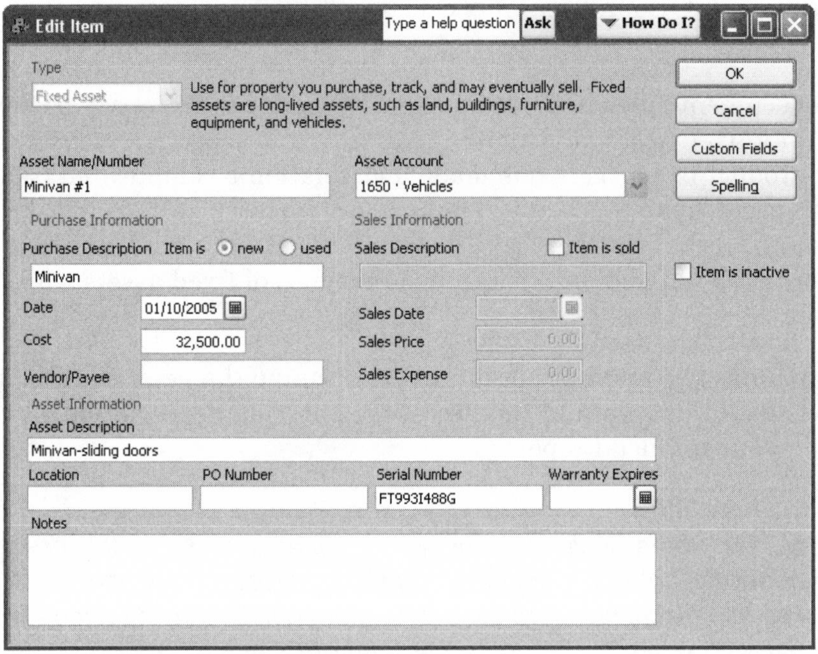

Figure 11-1: Track information about depreciable assets in the Fixed Asset Item List.

In a strange display of quirky logic, QuickBooks thinks of fixed assets as items (as in the items you use when preparing sales transactions). After you enter your fixed assets in the Fixed Asset Item list, they show up in your Items list.

Although it's a rather remote possibility that you'd ever want to put a fixed asset on an invoice or a sales receipt, when you click the Item drop-down list as you create a transaction, there they are! You have to scroll through them to get to the item you need.

Depreciate Your Assets Tool

QuickBooks provides a tool named Depreciate Your Assets, which is available by choosing Company → Planning & Budgeting → Decision

Tools → Depreciate Your Assets. You can use this tool to determine depreciation rates in QuickBooks, but it has some serious limitations.

The Depreciate Your Assets tool doesn't link to the Fixed Asset Item list. This means that when you use the tool you have to enter fixed asset information manually—the same information you entered in the Fixed Asset Item List.

If you want the Depreciate Your Assets tool to produce a depreciation schedule, you must have rather extensive knowledge about the depreciation rules. You have to select depreciation methods (Straight-Line, Sum of the Years' Digits, Double-Declining Balance, and so on). You have to select the basis of depreciation for each asset, and generally perform chores that require a high degree of expertise.

If you have the expertise to use the tool, after you calculate all your depreciation figures, the tool has no ability to interact with your QuickBooks file and produce the necessary journal entry. It merely gives you the figures, and then you have to depreciate your assets manually through a journal entry.

Creating a Depreciation Journal Entry

Depreciation is a journal entry that credits the fixed asset account, and debits the depreciation expense account that's created expressly for this purpose. If your chart of accounts doesn't have an expense account for depreciation, add one.

Here's the simple way to enter a depreciation journal entry (for this example, I'm using Equipment as the fixed asset):

- Credit the fixed asset account for Equipment.
- Debit the Depreciation expense account.

After the journal entry, the balance sheet shows the current value of the asset (which is its net value after depreciation). That's mathematically correct, but when you view your balance sheet the original price of the fixed asset, and the actual depreciation amounts you applied are lost.

A better method is to build that history into your balance sheet by using subaccounts for the transactions, which means the parent account shows the current (depreciated) value. That value is the net value of the subaccounts, which show the original cost and the accumulated depreciation. Create the following two subaccounts under each fixed asset account:

- Cost
- AccumDepr

When you purchase a fixed asset, post the amount to the Cost subaccount. If the cost is already posted to the parent account, use a journal entry to transfer it to the subaccount.

When you depreciate the fixed asset at the end of the year, post the credit side of the depreciation entry to the AccumDepr subaccount instead of to the parent account. The debit side is always posted to the depreciation expense account.

Applying this paradigm means that your general ledger and your balance sheet reports can provide a history of the fixed asset: its cost, and its depreciation.

You could also create a different subaccount for each year of depreciation, for instance Depr 2005, Depr 2006, and so on. Your balance sheet shows a complete year-by-year depreciation schedule, so you don't have to go back to a closed year to view a specific year's depreciation amount.

Moving Revenue

Using a complicated set of rules, your accountant may have to create a journal entry to move some restricted funds that are posted to revenue (income accounts) into a liability account that tracks the amount as if it were a refundable advance. Either of the following conditions can require this action:

- Restricted funds that are restricted for a period of time longer than your fiscal year.
- Restricted funds for which you have not shown expenses equal to the revenue by the end of your fiscal year.

The latter condition is the result of the rule that says you can only recognize money as revenue if you spent that money for the intended purpose; the rest of the money you received is a liability until you prove it is revenue by spending it. Once you spend it properly (according to the terms of the grant), you can keep it.

When it's appropriate (the purpose or the time period is met), a journal entry returns the money from the liability account to the appropriate income account. In some nonprofit organizations, the bookkeeper makes the journal entry as needed. Otherwise, the journal entry waits until the next visit from the accountant.

Managing Net Asset Accounts

QuickBooks automatically calculates the net difference between income and expenses, and displays it when you print any balance sheet report. The account in which the figure exists is an equity account named Retained Earnings. Nonprofit organizations do not post the difference between income and expenses to a single retained earnings account

On the first day of the next fiscal year, QuickBooks zeroes out the net difference between income and expenses from the previous year, and moves that amount to the retained earnings account. Nonprofit organizations do not carry retained earnings from year to year in a single retained earnings account.

Nonprofits are required to report restricted, temporarily restricted, and unrestricted net assets separately. The Retained Earnings account that QuickBooks provides, and uses exclusively, is the equivalent of an unrestricted net assets account.

As a result, you can rename the Retained Earnings account to Unrestricted Net Assets. In fact, in the UCOA, the account is named Unrestrict (retained earnings).

You or your accountant must create a journal entry to move the appropriate amounts out of the retained earnings account into the equity accounts you created for that purpose (creating the equity accounts is covered in Chapter 3).

Any income that has donor-imposed restrictions is originally posted as restricted revenue, and that posting increases the amount of restricted net assets. However, as the imposed restrictions are fulfilled, or the amount of time attached to the restriction elapses, the restricted amount is moved to unrestricted net assets.

When you print a balance sheet, you'll see the figures for net assets. If this is the first year you're using QuickBooks, and you didn't enter previous net asset balances, you only see the current net assets, because you have no retained net assets from previous years.

Year End Reports

Most nonprofits print a slew of reports as part of the end-of-year process. Many of the reports are customized for donors, and the board of directors. Other reports are printed (and sometimes customized) for internal viewing and discussion. There are four reports nonprofit organizations are expected to print as part of the year-end process:

- Statement of Financial Position
- Statement of Activities
- Statement of Cash Flows
- Statement of Functional Expenses

Statement of Financial Position

The statement of financial position is called a Balance Sheet in the for-profit world. It's a report on the organization's worth as of the date of the report. (The accounts included in the report are assets, liabilities, and equity.)

- If you're using QuickBooks Premier Nonprofit edition, the report is available in the Nonprofit section of the Memorized Reports menu. The report displays the previous year's totals, and shows the differences in dollars and percentages.
- If you're running QuickBooks Pro, use the Balance Sheet Prev Year Comparison report, which is available in the Company & Financial section of the Reports menu.

If you don't have previous year information in QuickBooks, or if your accountant wants only current year figures, choose the Balance Sheet Standard report from the Company & Financial section of the Reports menu.

Statement of Activities

This is essentially a Profit & Loss report, but we don't use those terms in nonprofit accounting. The report must provide information sorted and totaled by program.

- In QuickBooks Premier Nonprofit edition, the report is named Statement of Financial Income and Expense. You can find it on the Nonprofit submenu of the Memorized Reports menu.
- If you're using QuickBooks Pro, use the Profit & Loss by Class report on the Company & Financial menu.

If you haven't been posting transactions to classes, be prepared to spend a lot of money on accountant's services to create this report.

Statement of Cash Flows

A statement of cash flows presents an at-a-glance summary of the growth or decline of the organization's cash position. The report shows how much cash was earned or spent in the following areas:

- Operating activities, which means income and disbursements connected to providing services and meeting the organization's mission.
- Financing activities, which means cash that was provided by long term liabilities and equity (e.g. loans and retained net assets).
- Investing activities, which means the amount of cash that was invested in assets (e.g. equipment or furniture).

Choose Reports → Company & Financial → Statement of Cash Flows to display the report. The report displays the calculated net income figure, and then removes non-cash income or expenses, such as:

- Accounts Receivable
- Accounts Payable

• Other non-cash income or expense; for example, depreciation of fixed assets.

As you can see in Figure 11-2, the adjustments (non-cash totals) are displayed on the report. Your accountant may want to customize the report (or export it to Excel) to include additional non-cash transaction totals.

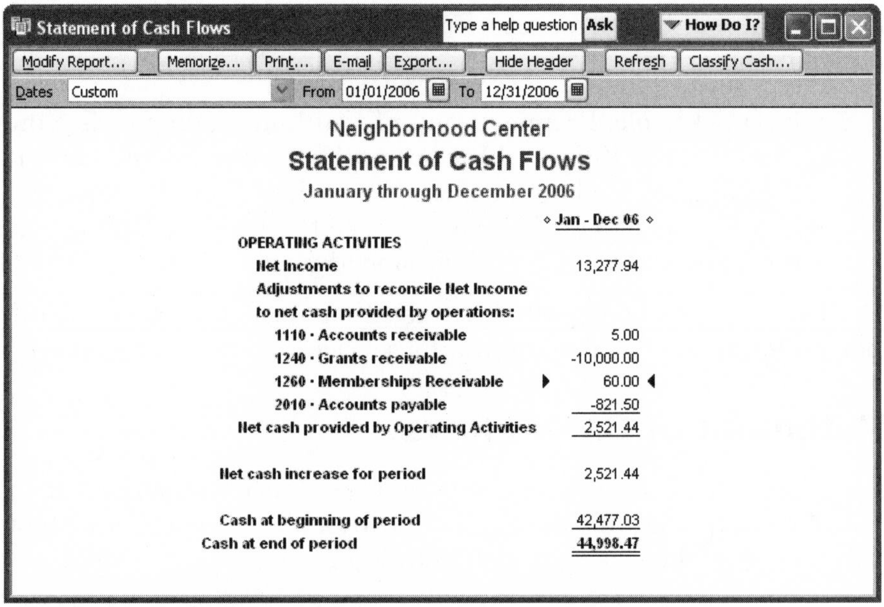

Figure 11-2: The Statement of Cash Flows displays the change in your cash position over the fiscal year.

Statement of Functional Expenses

This report displays information on expenses applied to each program (class). It's a way to see how much of your funding was actually spent on the programs and services that make up your organization's mission.

Two types of expenses are included in the report: Functional Expenses, and Natural Expenses. These terms are accounting jargon for the expenses applied directly to programs (functional expenses), and the expenses applied to supporting services such as rent, salaries, employee benefits, supplies, postage, and so on (natural expenses).

Many natural expenses are often connected to functional classifications. For example, an employee may spend time on program management, general office tasks, and fundraising (fundraising should be a class in your QuickBooks company file).

To report expenses by function properly, you must allocate the amounts in your natural expense classifications to program functions, to match the time or direct funds spent on each. For example, you should allocate employees' salaries, employer payroll costs, and even standard overhead expenses (telephone, supplies, and so on) according to the programs served.

The statement of functional expenses is based on Part II of IRS Form 990. In most nonprofit organizations, an accountant participates in the preparation of Form 990, and, in fact, many organizations give the accountant full responsibility for this chore.

Many accountants open this report, export it to Excel, and finish their preparation of the tax form in a worksheet (especially if the tax preparation software they use accepts imports from Excel).

If you aren't required to file IRS Form 990, you should still create this report. Funding agencies (both private and government), large donors, and the general public often base their support of your organization on the information in this report. There are standards of measurement applied to the amount of money you spend on administration vs. programs, and this report presents the data against which those standards are applied.

This report is built into QuickBooks Premier Nonprofit Edition. If you're using QuickBooks Pro, you can download the report template from www.cpa911publishing.com to create this report automatically.

Click on the Download link on the left side of the web page. On the Downloads page, click the link to download Statement of Functional Expenses (990). Save the file (do not choose the option to open it). Then take the following steps to import the report template:

1. Choose Reports → Memorized Reports → Memorized Reports List.
2. Right-click anywhere in the Memorized Reports List window and choose Import Template.
3. In the Select File To Import dialog, navigate to the folder where you saved the downloaded template.
4. Select Statement of Functional Expenses (990) and click Open.
5. In the Memorize Report dialog, click OK to add the report to your memorized report list.

NOTE: *If you've created memorized report groups, add the report to the appropriate group.*

To use the template, choose Reports → Memorized Reports and select this report from the submenu of memorized reports.

Additional Data for Nonprofit Financial Reports

Standard accounting rules and conventions require nonprofits to report certain specific data as part of their end-of-year reports. (These rules are specifically referenced in SFAS Section 117, which is discussed in Appendix A.)

Certain disclosures should be included in your financial reports, and must be included in the report created by your yearly audit, if you require an audit. (If you file Form 990, you are required to have an audit performed. See Chapter 12 to learn about preparing for an audit.) The following information should be disclosed in documents attached to your financial reports:

- The number and amount of unconditional pledges due in one year, one to five years, and more than five years.
- The details connected to conditional pledges.
- The details connected to temporarily restricted net assets.
- The details connected to permanently restricted net assets.
- The details of releases from restrictions of temporarily restricted net assets.

Giving Your File to Your Accountant

At various times your accountant might want to look at your books. He or she might want to make adjustments, allocate expenses, or perform some other task. Even if your accountant checks your books occasionally (or regularly) during the year, a year-end checkup is de rigueur.

Some accountants show up and work directly on your QuickBooks file. The downside of that action is that nobody can work on that computer while the account is there.

Accountants that run QuickBooks Premier Accountant Edition have a built-in tool that lets them access your QuickBooks file over the Internet. There's no direct connection between your computer and your accountant's computer; instead, you meet on a secure Internet web site (maintained by WebEx.com).

The feature is free (for you), and you can even continue to use the computer (although that might slow the accountant's work a bit). If you wish, you can watch what the accountant is doing, and ask or answer questions via a built-in Chat window.

Some accountants ask you to send them a copy of your QuickBooks file, either by copying the file to removable media, or by e-mailing the file. Some accountants ask for a backup file instead of the full file. Some accountants work with the Accountant's Review Copy that QuickBooks offers. In the following sections, I'll discuss the details for all of these scenarios.

NOTE: To work with your QuickBooks files, your accountant must have the same-year version of QuickBooks. Most accountants keep multiple yearly versions of QuickBooks on their computers. This is not necessary if the accountant is using Internet access via WebEx.com.

Sending Your Accountant Your Company File

You can send your accountant your entire QuickBooks file, either by copying the file to removable media, or creating a backup of the file to removable media. (You could also e-mail the file, but most QuickBooks company files are quite large and take a long time to download; in fact, some Internet Service Providers won't permit files that large to enter the e-mail system.)

> **WARNING**: If you've password-protected your QuickBooks data file, you must tell your accountant what the admin password is.

For removable media, you can use a CD (if you have a computer capable of "burning" a CD), or a USB detachable drive (one of the cleverest, most-needed, peripherals ever invented, in my view).

You can mail a CD, but a USB drive is more fragile, so send it in a padded envelope (it's better to use a courier service rather than the U.S. Postal Service), or deliver it in person.

Your accountant usually returns the modified file to you via the same media type; burning a new CD, or returning your USB drive with the updated file stored on it.

> **TIP**: If you have a web site with FTP storage space (or your accountant does), you can arrange for an FTP transfer, which is faster than transferring a file as an attachment to e-mail, and has no size limits. Ask your accountant if this feature is available. If you want to put your file in your own FTP folder, check the instructions from your web hosting company to learn how to let your accountant download the file.

While your accountant has a copy of your file, you cannot do any work in QuickBooks. Whatever you do will be overwritten when the accountant returns the file (the file the accountant used replaces the file you were using, because there is no way to merge the data in the two files). There are two ways to mitigate this problem:

- Make arrangements with your accountant that the file will be modified and returned within 48 hours (or some other time span during which it's okay for you to be locked out of using QuickBooks).
- If the accountant's work is mainly a matter of making year-end journal entries, tell the accountant to send you a document detailing the journal entries, so you can enter them in your copy of the file.

If you do the journal entries yourself, the accountant doesn't have to return the file. In fact, after using the file to prepare tax and other report forms, the accountant can delete the file. (After you enter the JEs, the files are identical.)

If you let the accountant modify the file, back up your current company file (in case something goes wrong during the transfer of the file from your accountant).

Then, copy the file you received from your accountant to the folder in which you save your company file. When you select the Paste command, Windows warns that you are replacing an existing file, and asks you to confirm your action. Click Yes to replace your copy with the accountant's copy.

Sending Your Accountant a Portable Company File

Starting with QuickBooks 2006, you can create a portable file, which is a copy of your QuickBooks file that has been condensed to save disk space (which also saves download time for e-mail attachments).

TIP: *You can also use a portable company file to move data between computers (such as your home computer, and your office). See Chapter 13 for information on managing QuickBooks company files in this manner.*

The smaller size is the only difference between a portable file and a regular company file. Well, there is one other difference—the file extension changes from .QBW to .QBM.

If you send a portable file to your accountant with the idea that the accountant will make changes, and return the file to you, you cannot work in your company file while the accountant has a copy. When the file is returned, it replaces your company file. Except for the smaller size, sending your accountant a portable company file works exactly the same as sending your full company file.

WARNING: *If you've password-protected your QuickBooks data file, you must tell your accountant what the admin password is.*

Creating a Portable Company File

To create a portable file, choose File → Portable Company File → Create File. QuickBooks displays a message tell you that your company file must be closed and then opened again to complete this task. Click OK.

When the file opens again, the Create Portable Company File dialog is on the screen. Select a name for the portable file. By default, QuickBooks uses the company file name (changing the extension to .QBM), and there's usually no reason to change it.

Select a location to house the file (by default, QuickBooks chooses the folder or subfolder in which you store the company file), and click Save. QuickBooks creates the file, which can take some time, depending on the size of your file.

After the file is created, send it to your accountant via e-mail, or on a CD. As with the transfer of a full company file, you cannot work in your QuickBooks file unless you've agreed that your accountant will send you a list of the changes, letting you enter those modifications in your company file.

Installing the Returned Portable Company File

If your accountant returns a modified file, you must replace your existing file with the portable company file. Bringing a portable company file into QuickBooks is a three-step process:

1. The file is opened (loaded into memory).
2. The file is uncompressed.
3. The uncompressed file is saved with the standard QuickBooks .QBW extension.

Do not bring the portable company file into your system until you've backed up your company file. I do not say this merely as a suggestion; consider it a demand (I'll bet you can guess why).

Choose File → Portable Company File → Open File. (When the accountant receives the file, he or she loads it using these same steps, and then uses the Create File submenu item to save the portable file that's returned to you.)

In the top section of the Import From Portable Company File dialog, select the filename and location of the portable company file you received from your accountant (it has a .QBM extension). Click the Browse button to locate the folder in which the file is stored (its location depends on where and how you received it from the accountant).

In the bottom section of the dialog, enter the filename and location of the regular QuickBooks company file you want to create. You should replace your existing company file with this returned portable company file. That way, you have all the accountant's changes. Because you didn't use the file while the accountant was working, you don't lose any work.

QuickBooks issues a warning that you are about to overwrite an existing file. Click Yes to confirm the replacement. Then, QuickBooks issues another warning, telling you that you're going to delete the existing file. Type "yes", and click OK, to confirm that you want to replace the existing file with the contents of the portable company file you received.

After the portable company file is uncompressed, and loaded, QuickBooks issues a dialog suggesting that you back up this file immediately. When you click OK, QuickBooks opens the Back Up dialog.

It never hurts to do a backup, but you'll be replacing the last backup you made, before you sent the file to the accountant. Therefore, if something goes wrong with this replacement file, you won't have a backup of the original, pre-accountant's-changes file. Click Cancel on the Back Up dialog, and make sure the file is working properly. Then, you can back it up normally.

Creating an Accountant's Review Copy

If you want to keep working in QuickBooks while your accountant works on your company file, QuickBooks offers a method called *Accountant's Review Copy*.

When you give your accountant an Accountant's Review Copy, you can continue to work in QuickBooks while your accountant works on the file. When the file comes back to you, it contains any changes the accountant made, and QuickBooks merges the changes into your copy of the company file.

Unlike sending your accountant a copy of your file, or a portable company file, this method provides a way to merge changes, instead of overwriting one file with another. However, there are limits to the types of tasks you and your accountant can perform when you use this method (the limits are described in the next section).

You can create the accountant's review copy on a CD, or save it to a file and send it to your accountant via e-mail.

From the menu bar, choose File → Accountant's Review → Create Accountant's Copy.

QuickBooks displays a message telling you it has to close all open QuickBooks windows to create an accountant's copy. Click OK.

The Save Accountant's Copy To dialog opens, where you can select a location and filename for the accountant's copy. By default, QuickBooks uses the company filename with the extension .QBX, and saves it in the same folder where your company file resides. There's rarely a good reason to change the default. Click Save to create the accountant's copy. QuickBooks notifies you when the process is complete.

Send the file to your accountant via e-mail, or copy it to a CD and mail it. If you've recently started using QuickBooks, and your company file isn't very large, you can probably fit the file on a floppy. However, check with your accountant to make sure there's a floppy drive available at the accountant's office (newer computers don't have a floppy drive unless the customer places a special order for one).

WARNING: If you've password-protected your QuickBooks data file, you must tell your accountant what the admin password is.

To remind you that an accountant's copy is outstanding, the title bar of your QuickBooks software window adds the text "(Accountant's Copy Exists)".

Working During the Accountant's Review

Both you and your accountant have some restrictions while the accountant's review copy is in use. QuickBooks locks certain parts of your company file to make sure you can't make changes that would affect the information the accountant is working on. The accountant also works with restrictions that are designed to make sure the records for customers, vendors, and other lists that you continue to use remain intact.

What You Can Do

You can continue to perform the following tasks while the accountant's review copy exists:

- Create transactions
- Edit transactions
- Delete transactions
- Add new items to lists

- Edit items in lists (except you cannot change an item's name)

What You Cannot Do

You cannot perform the following tasks while the accountant's review copy exists:

- Delete an entry in a list
- Rename an item or an account
- Change an account to a subaccount
- Change a subaccount to an account

What Your Accountant Can Do

Your accountant can perform the following tasks while working in your file:

- Create journal entries
- Edit account names
- Change account numbers
- Edit tax information for accounts
- Adjust inventory quantities and values
- Print 1099 forms
- Print 941 forms
- Print 940 forms
- Print W-2 forms

What Your Accountant Cannot Do

Your accountant cannot perform any of the following tasks in the review copy:

- Delete list entries
- Make list entries inactive
- Create transactions other than journal entries

Merging the Accountant's Changes

When your accountant returns your file, the changes he or she made must be merged into your QuickBooks files. It's faster to merge the files if you copy the file you receive to the folder that holds your QuickBooks company file.

Open your company file in QuickBooks and choose File →
Accountant's Review → Import Accountant's Changes. QuickBooks immediately insists on making a backup of your current file before importing
(an excellent idea, just in case something goes wrong with the import
process). Click OK and proceed with the backup.

When the backup is complete, QuickBooks automatically opens the
Import Changes From Accountant's Copy dialog. Make sure the Look In
field at the top of the dialog matches the location of the file your accountant sent. Choose the import file, which has an extension of .AIF, and
click Open (or double-click on the .aif file).

QuickBooks issues a message dialog to tell you the data has been
imported. Your QuickBooks data now contains the changes your accountant made, and you can work with your files normally. The title bar of the
QuickBooks software window changes to eliminate the text
"(Accountant's Copy Exists)".

---

*TIP: Make sure your accountant sends you a note or calls to
tell you about the changes. QuickBooks does not indicate
what has changed after your merge the files, and you should
know what specific alterations were made to your financial
records.*

Unlocking Your Accountant Copy without Merging Data

If you make an accountant's review copy in error, or if your accountant
tells you there are no changes to be made, you can unlock your file. This
puts everything back as if you'd never created an accountant's review
copy.

To accomplish this, choose File → Accountant's Review → Cancel
Accountant's Changes. When QuickBooks asks you to confirm your decision, click OK. You can now work normally; there are no restrictions on
the work you can perform.

Closing the Year

After all the year-end reports have been run, all needed journal entries have been entered, and your taxes have been filed, it's time to go through the exercise of closing the books. This usually occurs some time after the end of the fiscal year, within the first couple of months of the next fiscal year.

Understanding Closing in QuickBooks

QuickBooks doesn't use the traditional closing procedures that you find in most accounting software applications. In those applications, closing the year is mandatory (after a certain number of weeks or months following the fiscal year end), and once the books are closed you cannot post transactions to any date in the closed year, nor can you manipulate any existing transactions in the closed year.

Closing the books in QuickBooks does not really lock the information. Transactions can be added, deleted, or changed in the closed year. QuickBooks does not require you to close the books in order to keep working in the software. You can work forever, for years, without performing a closing process.

However, many QuickBooks users prefer to lock the transactions at the end of a fiscal year, to prevent any changes to the data. The QuickBooks closing (locking) procedure is tied in with the users and passwords features that are part of the software. Closing the books locks out some users, but permits an administrator (and other selected users) to make changes. If a restricted user attempts to change (or delete) a transaction in the closed period, an error message appears telling the user he or she is denied access.

Configuring the Closing Date

In QuickBooks, you close the year by entering a closing date. This action does nothing more than let you lock certain users out of the previous year's transactions. Use the following steps to enter a closing date:

1. Choose Edit → Preferences to open the Preferences dialog.
2. Click the Accounting icon in the left pane.
3. In the Company Preferences tab enter the closing date, which is the last date of your previous fiscal year.

Preventing Access to Closed Books

To prevent users from changing transactions in the closed year (or to permit certain users to), assign a password for manipulating closed data. Click the Set Password button below the closing date field. In the Set Closing Date Password dialog, enter the password, then press the Tab key and enter the password again in the Confirm Password field.

The characters you type are displayed on the screen as bullets (in case somebody is peeking over your shoulder). If you don't enter exactly the same characters in both fields, QuickBooks asks you to repeat the process. If that happens, you may have chosen a password so complicated that it invites typos, which could mean you'll have a problem using the password when you need it.

TIP: It's not necessary to have set up password-protected usernames on your QuickBooks system to enable this closing date protection. However, if you have enabled users and passwords, only the QuickBooks Administrator can set the closing date and password.

Make a written note of the password, and put the note in a secure place (your wallet, a locked desk drawer, etc.). Even if you're sure you'll remember the password when you need it, don't fail to take this step. History has already proven you wrong (and you can confirm this by querying any QuickBooks consultant or any Intuit support technician, who had to pass along the bad news that the file had to be sent to Intuit for unlocking—for a fee).

To make any changes that would affect balances within the accounting period you closed, you need to enter the password. If you know the password you can add, edit, or delete transactions entered on or before the closing date.

Making changes to a closed year is not a good idea. Remember, you don't have to close your books on the last day of your fiscal year—you can wait until everything is entered, even if it takes weeks or months. However, once the transactions are all in the system, there's no reason to change anything.

Creating a Year-End Backup

After all the numbers are checked, all the journal entries are made, and the books have been closed by entering a closing date as described in the previous section, do a separate backup.

Don't put this backup on one of the Zip disks or CDs you've been using for your normal backups. Use fresh media for this backup. Label the disk "Year-End Backup XX", where XX is the year (e.g. 2006, or 2006-2007 if you're on a non-calendar fiscal year)."

If you usually back up to a network computer, when you create this backup, change the filename of the backup file (e.g. add YE, for Year End, to the filename). Then burn that file to a CD.

NOTE: See Chapter 13 for information on backing up your company file.

Chapter 12

Audits

Preparing for an audit

Audit reports

Board responsibilities

Many nonprofit organizations are audited as part of the year-end procedure. An accountant performs the audit, and follows a routine that depends on the particular circumstances of your organization.

If your organization receives federal grants or contracts, the audit procedures are mandated by laws and rules. States, counties, and cities also have audit regulations. The audit is a tool that's used to make sure a nonprofit association's resources are used as agreed to in grants and contracts.

Auditors follow generally accepted auditing standards, to reduce the risk of failing to detect a material misstatement in your financial statements. Should any significant misstatements be encountered, they must be reported to the board of directors.

It's impossible to take you step-by-step through an audit, because no two are exactly alike. The auditor follows his or her own agenda for the order of audit tasks, and the level of detail varies from organization to organization.

Preparing for an Audit

The auditor needs information to perform his or her tasks, and it's the responsibility of the nonprofit association to make the information available. Technically, it's the responsibility of the association's board of directors, but it's usually the staff that gathers the information.

The nature of your funding (federal or state government funds, private funds, etc.) determines the specifics of the audit, and therefore has an impact on the information you need to provide the auditor. The following sections are intended as a guideline for preparing documents for the audit—your auditor may ask for more or fewer documents.

Board Minutes

Make available the minutes of the board of directors, and of any board committees that affect finances. You can either provide the auditor with copies, or make the official minutes book available for examination.

If this is a new organization, in its first year of operation, you should make the articles of incorporation and the by-laws available. In subsequent years, you should make any changes in the by-laws available.

Contracts

List any significant contracts entered into during the year, such as office and equipment leases, loans, or mortgages. Also, have the contracts available so the auditor can go over the terms and other details.

Receivables

Create a detailed list of receivables as of the audit date, including grants, contributions, employee advances, etc., and identify any that are of doubtful collection.

To create the list, choose Reports → Customers & Receivables → Customer Balance Detail. This report contains the comprehensive information required for the audit.

Payables

Create a detailed list of accounts payable as of the audit date, including the expense accounts to which bills were posted. Paid bills that are filed should be available for inspection.

None of the A/P reports provide the detail you need. If you create an A/P Aging Detail Report, it lacks information about the accounts to which the transactions were posted.

If you modify the report to show the posting account, the display shows you the A/P account, not the expense account. You can further modify that customization to show the split, but you end up with a report in which each transaction is listed twice; once for the A/P posting and once for the expense posting. If the bill was split among three accounts, each transaction is listed three times, and so on.

The best way to get the information you need for this report is to choose Reports → Accountant & Taxes → Transaction Detail By Account. This is an enormous report, covering far more than you need, but it can be customized to create a report of manageable size that displays only the information the auditor requires. You can download a customized report (see the next section), or build it yourself using the following steps:

1. Click Modify Report, and move to the Filters tab.
2. Select Account in the Filter list.
3. In the Account field, select All Accounts Payable from the drop-down list.
4. In the Include Split Detail section, select Yes.
5. Select Transaction Type in the Filter list.
6. In the Transaction Type field, select Bill from the drop-down list.
7. Select Paid Status in the Filter list.
8. In the Paid Status options that appear choose Open.
9. Move to the Display tab, and in the Columns list, find the following column names that have a check mark, and click them to remove the check mark:
   - Clr
   - Balance
10. Click OK.

Memorize the report immediately—you do not want to go through this customization again. Name the memorized report AP for Audit (or something similar).

> **NOTE**: You can also remove Class from the Columns list in the Display tab, if the auditor doesn't want to see program information in this report.

Once properly configured, the report displays all the accounts involved in the open payable transactions. The accounts are listed in numerical order, with a total for each account.

The postings to A/P accounts are negative because these are credit-side postings. The total of the A/P accounts (negative numbers) and the total of all the other accounts (positive numbers) equal zero.

Download This Report Template

If you don't want to go through the work of customizing this report, you can download a template and import the report to your Memorized Reports list. To download the file, go to www.cpa911publishing.com. Click the Downloads navigation button on the left side of the web page. On the Downloads page click the link to download the file named AP Report For Audit.

To import the file, follow these steps:

1. Choose Reports → Memorized Reports → Memorized Report List.
2. Click the Memorized Report button at the bottom of the list, and choose Import Template.
3. In the Select File To Import dialog, navigate to the folder where you saved the template, and select APReportFor Audit.QBR.
4. Select the default name, or change it to a name of your own choice.

To use the report, open it from the Memorized Report list, and adjust the date range.

Payroll

Make available all payroll documentation for the audit period, including 941, UC, W-2, W-3, state and local forms. If there are balances for payroll taxes or withholdings at your audit period end-date, they were probably paid at a later date. Document those payments, indicating the dates and amounts. Also, provide details of any accrued payroll, accrued vacation, and sick pay.

Nonprofit payroll records differ from for-profit payroll records because of the way nonprofit spending is tracked and audited. Nonprofits must track the monies disbursed in various facets of their operations, including administration, program services, and fundraising. Payroll and the associated employer costs of payroll are included in these break-downs.

This mandate means that nonprofits must have timesheets for all employees. Someone in a supervisory position must "sign off" on the accuracy of the time sheets for the auditor (and the auditor may take additional steps to "prove" the accuracy of the timesheets).

For the audit, you must show the percentage of time each employee spent on the following, making sure the total percentage equals 100% for each employee:

- Program Services
- Management and General Administration
- Fundraising

Of course, without timesheets, you can't provide this information with any confidence about accuracy.

Auditor Permissions

If you configured QuickBooks for user logins, and permission levels, give the auditor the administrator's password. If you're uneasy about giving out the password, create a user with full administrative permissions. Provide the login name and password to the auditor.

If you closed your previous year, and password-protected the closed transactions, give the auditor the password. This gives the auditor a chance to view earlier transactions if the closing balance from last year doesn't match the starting balance for this year.

Audit Activities and Tasks

In this section, I'll go over some of the activities that are commonly performed during an audit, to give you an idea of what to expect. To do so, I audited an audit (groan... awkward pun) as described by an auditor who audits many nonprofit organizations that use QuickBooks.

The following descriptions represent some of the common tasks involved in an audit, but are not necessarily all the tasks, nor are they in any particular order. The following "auditor's task list" is a very brief summary of a very complex and involved process.

Read the minutes of the board of directors to get a feel for what is going on.

Print a trial balance (from the Accountant & Taxes section of the Reports menu). A trial balance is a list of every account and its current balance, so it's a good starting point for an audit.

Compare the trial balance to the prior year. If there are substantial changes, have the staff provide explanations.

Review the system of internal controls and protocols by performing a "walk-through" of transactions. This means tracing a transaction from the beginning to the end. For example, the auditor will take vendors bills, and walk them through the appropriate processes:

- Check to see whether the bills were marked "approved for payment" by the director or another staff member with sufficient authority.
- Make sure the checks were created, the invoices were marked paid, and the invoices were filed. Also, the bank statements are checked to see that the checks were cashed.
- Make sure the appropriate person signed the checks.
- Check the general ledger to make sure the transactions were recorded properly.

Determine tolerable misstatement, which is the amount by which the financial statements can be wrong without changing the reader's opinion of the condition of the company. (Reader refers to the person reading the audit report.)

Audit each balance sheet account by tracing it back to supporting documentation. For example, trace cash balances to the bank account, test A/R by comparing subsequent cash receipts. All balances that exceed 1/3 of the tolerable misstatement are fully tested.

Test the expenses and tie large P & L accounts to tax returns. For example, test payroll by tracing transactions through to the payroll tax returns. Balance sheet accounts that affect the P & L are also tied back (e.g. depreciation is tested against the fixed assets). Generally, about 75% of the expenses are tested.

After the expenses are tested, the audit moves on to test revenue. Most of the revenue in a nonprofit organization is tightly linked to expenses, because so much of the funding is from grants. The auditor reads the grants to determine if the expenses charged to the contract are proper, and to make sure the expenses meet any purpose or time restrictions in the grant. (If you don't track classes and grants, you'll have to spend a lot of money on bookkeeping and accounting services to get ready for the audit.)

Other Auditor Responsibilities

In addition to the accounting and financial tasks that are designed to check the accuracy of the bookkeeping, auditors of nonprofit organizations have additional responsibilities.

An auditor looks at the processes and internal controls to make sure those systems contribute to accurate accounting. Part of the definition of processes and controls is the training and expertise level of the people who enter transactions into the accounting system. One auditor told me, "Part of our responsibility as auditors is to make sure the client is sophisticated enough to understand the accounting processes."

If the client lacks bookkeeping/accounting sophistication on staff, the organization should have periodic services of an experienced bookkeeper and/or an accountant to make sure the data entry meets legal and accounting standards, and to ensure that the books can be audited.

When an auditor finds problems with the processes or internal controls, the board must be notified (see the section "Management Letter to the Board", later in this chapter).

Auditors must ask for in-depth supporting documentation for all important transactions, for randomly selected "test" transactions, and for any transactions that don't make sense. If supporting documentation isn't available, the auditor may determine that the organization's records are unauditable. In that case, an auditor may "disengage", which is jargon for "I can't audit your books, goodbye". No nonprofit can afford the fallout if its books cannot be audited.

Audit Report

After the audit, the auditor reports the findings to the organization's board of directors. The format of the report varies, but generally contains the following data:

- A covering letter explaining the circumstances and protocols of the audit procedure, and an overview of the tasks performed.
- A Statement of Financial Position
- A Statement of Activities
- A Statement of Cash Flows
- A Statement of Functional Expenses
- Notes, frequently quite detailed, about the financial statements

Auditors sometimes create correcting adjustments arising from their verification work, and the financial statements generated after the audit are therefore more accurate than they would have been without an audit.

SFAS 117 (explained in Appendix A) also requires the following information as part of your audited financial reports:

- Amount of unconditional pledges due in one year, one to five years, and more than five years.
- Details about conditional pledges.
- Details about temporarily restricted net assets.
- Details about permanently restricted net assets.
- Details about releases from restrictions of temporarily restricted net assets.

Management Letter to the Board

The audit report doesn't address the organization's systems and procedures, even though those procedures created the figures that were audited.

In addition to the materials included in the audit report, the auditor often prepares what is called a management letter or report to the board of directors. This report cites areas in the organization's internal accounting control system that the auditor evaluates as weak, flawed, or an area of serious potential problems.

Board Responsibilities

The board of a nonprofit organization, not the staff, hires the auditor, although the staff is expected to prepare the information the auditor needs. The auditor works for, and reports to, the board.

An engagement letter, sent by the auditor to the board, sets forth the tasks the auditor will perform, the responsibilities of the staff, the fee for the audit, and the terms of payment. Both the board and the auditor sign the engagement letter, which has the effect of a contract.

Most of the time, the engagement letter is very specific about telling the board how to instruct the staff. For example, the engagement letter may specify that staff responses to questions from the auditor must be in writing, and may set forth a time period for access to the books (and the premises).

The federal government (especially the United States Senate) and many state governments have begun tightening the audit noose, proposing that all nonprofits that file 990s be audited, not just those receiving government funds or those with 990 returns that are questionable.

In the wake of the recent corporate accounting scandals, some states are proposing audits, or at least reviews, of all nonprofit books, and it's probably safe to bet that even small nonprofits will be undergoing mandatory reviews or audits, and nonprofit boards will have to meet new standards.

Board Audit Committees

One of the mandates being considered in legislation affecting nonprofit organizations is to insist on the formation of an audit committee of the board. Some states have already passed legislation requiring all nonprofit boards to create an audit committee.

If a nonprofit is subject to audits, the board should establish a direct relationship with the auditor through the creation of a separate audit committee.

Even if a nonprofit is not subject to audit now, it's imperative to plan for auditing by creating an audit committee (required audits for most nonprofits seems almost certain to become law in the future).

Roles of an Audit Committee

An audit committee is the link between the board and the independent auditor. The audit committee makes recommendations to the board regarding selection of the audit firm and serves as the liaison with the auditor, discussing the auditor's findings in a meeting at which staff are not present.

In addition, the audit committee plays an important role in helping the board fulfill its fiduciary duty to oversee the organization's finances.

The audit committee must include at least one board member, and should include at least one individual who is knowledgeable about nonprofit accounting (who may also be a board member).

For many small nonprofits, the finance committee can serve as the audit committee. If your finance committee also acts as your audit committee, be sure that staff members who work with the committee (executive director, fiscal manager, bookkeeper, etc.) do not vote on the selection of the audit firm and are not present when the audit report is first presented to the board.

Internal Audits

The finance committee or audit committee of the board should periodically conduct an internal audit, which is a review of policies and procedures that affect the way the organization does business and manages financial affairs. The audit can be performed by the organization's accountant, or by a member of the committee with expertise in nonprofit accounting. The purpose of an internal audit is to ensure the following:

- The organization uses generally accepted accounting methods.
- The organization complies with laws and regulations by filing government documents in a timely fashion (including remittance of payroll reports, withholdings, and employer taxes).

- The organization provides reliable financial information to board members and potential and current grantors.
- The organization is operating efficiently by keeping overhead costs at a reasonable percentage of revenue.

An obvious benefit of internal audits, and the repair of flaws discovered during those audits, is that an external audit will be less expensive and easier to "pass".

A less obvious benefit is one that applies to the members of the board, in that board members have an inherent fiduciary responsibility for the organization. The board members are entrusted by the public to use the finances of the organization properly, and for the purposes that match the organization's mission. This is more than a moral obligation; it can be (and has been) interpreted as a legal obligation and board members who don't exercise their responsibilities can be challenged by legal actions.

Creating Board Directives

Led by the auditing committee, the board should issue directives to the staff about the processes involved in accounting tasks. The directives should match the standards applied by an auditor.

The following sections offer some suggestions for directives. Some of the suggestions won't work if the organization has a very small staff, but every effort should be made to meet as many of these suggestions as possible.

Disbursements Controls

The following controls over the disbursement of funds should be implemented by a directive from the board:

- The board authorizes all check signers.
- Checks should not be prepared by anyone who approves the payment of vendor invoices.
- Check preparers should have the original vendor invoices (marked approved, with a signature), with any supporting documents attached (purchase orders, receiving reports, timesheets, etc.).

- An officer of the organization or the executive director should receive the unopened bank statement, and open, examine, and sign it before turning it over to the person who performs bank reconciliation.
- The person who performs the bank reconciliation should not be the same person who handles the disbursement of funds.
- A printed copy of the bank reconciliation report from the software should be given to an officer of the organization or the executive director, who should sign it before it is filed.

Cash Receipt Controls

The following controls over receipt of money and handling of petty cash should be implemented by a directive from the board:

- Incoming mail should be opened and checks received should be listed by someone other than the person who enters receipts and accounts receivable records in the software.
- Checks should be stamped "For Deposit Only" by the person opening the mail, before turning the checks over to the person who enters transactions in the software.
- The person handling petty cash should not be the person entering cash transactions in the software.
- A person with no access to petty cash should compare the petty cash receipts records and check them against software reports on the petty cash account.
- People who handle cash should be bonded.

Budget Controls

The audit committee should make sure the annual budgeting process is efficient and has a meaningful relationship to the organization's mission and grants. The committee should approve the formats of budgets, and of budget-to-actual comparison reports.

The board should issue a directive that directs the staff to produce budget-to-actual comparison reports in a timely manner. This ensures that the board has adequate information about the financial status of every grant and contract in time to investigate (and, if needed, fix) problems.

Educating Board Members About Accounting

It's difficult to tell the members of a board that they're morally and legally responsible for the organization's books, and the report of an auditor (either for an internal or external audit) if they don't understand what they're reading.

Board members of large nonprofit organizations are routinely given periodic lessons in reading accounting documents and audit reports. Experts in accounting (who also have expertise in explaining these arcane issues in lay terms) are frequently brought to board meetings to hold classes and go over financial reports and audit reports. The board members of small nonprofits should follow the same paradigm.

Chapter 13

Managing QuickBooks Files

Backing up

Restoring backup files

Archiving and condensing data

Updating QuickBooks

In addition to bookkeeping chores in QuickBooks, you have some computer housekeeping chores. It's important to keep your data safe, and to make sure your software is up-to-date. QuickBooks provides tools to help you with these responsibilities.

Backing Up

Backing up your QuickBooks data is terribly important and must be done on a daily basis. Your QuickBooks files backup plan should be part of a complete disaster recovery plan for your computer, or for your network.

Designing a Disaster Recovery Plan

Hard discs, system boards (sometimes called *motherboards*), and computers die. Sometimes computers or discs get sick before they die, and their illness may affect your files. A hard disc that's dying doesn't always notify you that something's amiss, so while it's dying it can corrupt files when saving data.

A disaster recovery plan involves backup plans and restore plans for everything on your computer: the operating system, the registry, the software, and the data. However, for this discussion, I'm taking a narrow view, and I'll talk about planning for disaster only as it applies to your QuickBooks data.

The most important rule to remember when you're creating a disaster recovery plan is that the purpose of the plan is to make restoring files as quick and easy as possible. While that sounds like a "given", it's a fact that many people design their plans to make backing up easy. They believe that if backing up is time consuming, or onerous, the backup won't be made.

In truth, that's not an imagined fear, the evidence is overwhelming that users frequently skip backing up until they "get religion" after a disaster. The real disaster is discovering that the last backup is weeks or months old, and every transaction since the last backup has to be reconstructed. After that, they back up regularly for a while, but too frequently, they fall back to old, lazy, habits.

If you back up your computer every night, and the backup includes your QuickBooks files, you should still back up your QuickBooks files separately. Not all file restore operations are initiated because of a disaster; sometimes you just need to return to a previous point in time (often caused by a totally erroneous series of transaction entries, following which you decide it would be easier to restore your QuickBooks file as it existed last night). Most computer backup software creates a single file for all the folders and files being backed up, and restoring one folder, or one file, is a difficult, time-consuming process. It's easier and faster to restore a specific, discrete QuickBooks company file.

Backup Media Options

You have several choices for the media you use to hold your backup files (the jargon for the receiving media is *target media*). In the following sections I'll go over the choices, along with the pros and cons of each choice.

The hard drive of the computer that holds your QuickBooks company file is not an option for backup media. The whole point of backing up is to have your data available when the hard drive dies.

Backing Up to Removable Media

Removable media is any device that holds files that can be inserted into a physical device on your computer. Removable media includes floppy disks, Zip disks, CDs, and USB stick drives.

When you use removable media, you must avoid backing up over the last backup. If something goes wrong during the backup, you don't want to face a scenario in which you've destroyed your last good backup.

Additionally, it's a good idea to make a separate backup, on separate media, after you've completed a major task. For example, if you decide to spend a day or two revamping your chart of accounts, make a backup as soon as you complete the chore. If you archive data, or close the year, make an immediate backup, and label the backup media appropriately.

In fact, you can change the filename of the backup file to reflect its contents, such as newcoa.qbb or yearend2006.qbb.

Floppy Disk Backups

At one time, everybody used floppy disks as the target media for backups, but today that's not a very common choice. Floppy disks are not trustworthy (the files on the disks become corrupted easily), and they hold so little data that it takes multiple disks to create a backup of a single QuickBooks company file.

If you have to sit in front of the computer throughout the backup process, in order to change disks periodically, backing up becomes onerous. When backing up is burdensome, you're more likely to skip the process.

If one of the floppy disks has a problem with a file, the entire backup is lost; you can't restore a backup unless all the disks restore their contents properly. If you're currently using floppy disks for backup, choose another media option as quickly as possible, to avoid the risk of losing data.

Zip Disk Backups

Zip disks have a much larger capacity than a floppy disk, but require you to purchase the drive, along with the disks. If you're using a Zip drive, you should have a separate disk for each day. That means if you work on your QuickBooks files seven days a week, you should have seven disks. Label each disk with the day of the week.

If you don't want to spend the money it takes to have a disk for each day, use three disks and rotate them in an even-odd pattern. Label one disk Even, one disk Odd, and one disk EOM (for End Of Month). The disk labeled EOM is for the 31st day of the month, so on the first day of the month you don't back up over the file you made on the 31st (Use that disk on February 29).

Because Zip disks can occasionally have problems, and corrupt data, it's important to back up to CD occasionally (weekly is best) and take the CD off site for safe storage.

USB Stick Drive Backups

USB stick drives, also called USB memory sticks, or USB keychain drives (because they usually come with keychain necklaces) are becoming less expensive, and they are a great choice for backup media.

You don't have to buy a separate drive for each day, but you must still avoid backing up over the last backup. Create three folders on the drive—Even, Odd, and EOM (End of Month, for months that end in an odd number).

To avoid the possibility of losing your backups if the drive develops a problem, be sure to copy a backup to CD every week (or more often) and take the CD off site for safe storage.

CD Backups

CDs are the safest backups because they're much less likely to suffer harm, or corrupt their files, than any other form of removable media. If you're running Windows XP, you can back up to a CD from within QuickBooks (see the section "Backing Up to CD in Windows XP").

If you're running an earlier version of Windows, you can back up to a CD outside of QuickBooks, by copying your QuickBooks file to the CD. A CD is also a good media choice for a weekly or monthly backup that is taken off-site. Of course, I'm assuming you have a CD-R or CD-RW drive.

Backing Up to Remote Drives

You can use the hard drive on another computer as your target media, and the computer can be on your own network, or on the Internet. In addition, you can use a standalone hard drive that's connected to your computer's USB port, or connected to your network hub or switch.

If you use any remote hard drive target except an Internet server, you should still burn a CD at least once a week, to keep the data safe (preferably taking the CD off site). A serious disaster that affects a computer on a network could affect the entire network, so an off site copy of your QuickBooks file is an important safety measure.

To use another computer on your network, you should create a shared folder on the remote computer to hold your company files. Then, map a drive to that folder, so you can access the folder easily (see the section "Mapping Drives to Network Folders", later in this chapter).

If you want to use a computer on the Internet, be sure that computer is backed up by the company that maintains the computer. Most web hosts and ISPs that provide storage space back up those computers every day.

There are numerous companies that offer backup storage services on their Internet servers. and they back up those computers several times a day. In addition, they provide security so that nobody but you (or your designated representative) can access your backup file. Most online backup services are reasonably priced, and offer automated backups.

TIP: *QuickBooks has an Internet-based backup service (see Backup in the help file index).*

Backing Up to CD in Windows XP

In Windows XP, which has built-in CD writing features, QuickBooks supports backups to CD-ROM. Use the following steps to back up to a CD:

1. Choose File → Back Up.
2. In the Location field of the QuickBooks Backup dialog, enter the drive letter of your CD-R/CD-RW drive.
3. When QuickBooks displays a message warning you that backing up to your hard drive isn't a good idea and asking if you're sure if you want to back up to your hard drive, click Yes. (The message appears because the way Windows XP writes to your CD is to write the file to the hard drive before burning the CD.)
4. When the backup file has been written to the hard drive, QuickBooks displays a message telling you your data has been backed up successfully. A balloon appears over the notification area of your taskbar, telling you that files are waiting to be written to the CD.

5. Click the balloon to open the folder for the CD drive, displaying a listing for your backup file. Select the file.
6. Select the command Write These Files To CD.
7. Follow the prompts in the Windows XP CD Burning Wizard to transfer the file to the CD.

The next time you select the backup command, the location for the backup file is automatically set to the folder that Windows XP uses to store files that are going to be transferred to a CD, to wit:

C:\Documents and Settings*YourUserName*\Local Settings\Application Data\Microsoft\CD Burning\

You could have entered that location in the Backup dialog the first time, but why type all those characters? Windows XP understood what you were doing and adapted the procedure appropriately, which is nifty.

In addition, the next time you perform this task, you won't see the warning about backing up to your hard drive, because by then, both QuickBooks and Windows XP will have figured out what you're doing.

If you're not using Windows XP, periodically use your CD-burning software to copy your QuickBooks company file backups (all of them, if you're running multiple companies).

If you're using Windows XP there's a trick to bypassing the need to copy the file to a CD from the hard drive. Instead, you can back up directly to a CD. See the next section, "Bypassing the Windows XP CD Writing Wizard".

Bypassing the Windows XP CD Writing Wizard

QuickBooks provides a way to back up to CD without using the Windows XP CD wizard and the built-in CD burning features of Windows XP. Instead, you can write your backup file to the CD immediately, omitting the step of moving the file from your hard drive to the CD.

This means you can write your backup file to a CD during an automated, unattended QuickBooks backup. You must remember to have a new blank CD in the CD drive. This is not a rewriteable task. This is a one time CD writing task. Rewriteable CD sessions require you to respond to prompts, and that doesn't work for an unattended backup.

In order to accomplish this you must have packet writing software, such as Roxio's DirectCD, or Nero's InCD (not Nero's Burning ROM) installed on your Windows XP computer, and the software must be configured to launch during Windows startup, so it's always available. (Launch during startup is usually the default configuration for packet writing software.)

If you have the necessary software installed, and you've configured it to start when Windows starts, you merely have to configure QuickBooks to bypass the Windows XP wizard. Use the following steps to accomplish this:

1. Choose File → Back Up to open the QuickBooks Backup dialog.
2. Click the Set Defaults button.
3. In the Set Defaults dialog, deselect the option Use Windows CD Writing Wizard.
4. Click OK twice.

QuickBooks bypasses the Windows XP wizard and uses your packet writing software to write the backup file directly to the CD.

Using QuickBooks Backup

You can back up manually, and you can also automate the QuickBooks backup process, which makes backing up easier. To create a backup of the currently loaded company, choose File → Back Up to open the QuickBooks Backup dialog seen in Figure 13-1.

Choosing a Location

Choose a location for the backup file. QuickBooks names the backup file for you, using your company filename, with the extension .QBB.

When you use a disk that's already received a backup file, QuickBooks will ask if you want to replace the existing file with the new one. Click Yes, because the old file is at least two days old, and perhaps a week old, depending on the way you're rotating media.

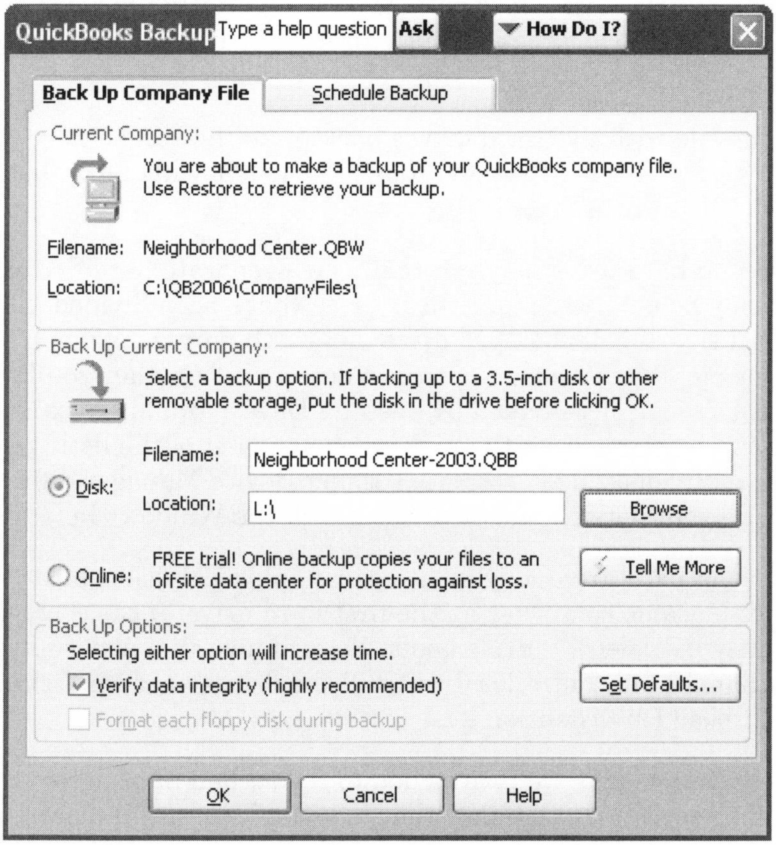

Figure 13-1: Back up your QuickBooks files every single day

If you're on a network, you can back up to a shared folder on another computer by clicking Browse, selecting Network Neighborhood or My Network Places (depending on your version of Windows), and choosing the shared folder that's been set up for your backups. It's better and faster, however, to map a drive to the remote backup location and enter the mapped drive letter in the Backup dialog. (See "Mapping Drives to Network Folders", later in this section.)

Never back up onto your local hard drive (unless you're temporarily storing the file on the hard drive and you will immediately transfer the file to a CD). Use removable media, such as a floppy disk or a Zip drive, or use a network drive (if you're on a network), because the point of backing up is to be able to get back to work after a hard drive or computer failure.

Many people with two hard drives back up to the second hard drive. Before you decide on that strategy, consider the following facts (listed in the order of "disaster probability").

The second hard drive may not really be a separate hard drive, instead it may be a partition of a large drive that's been divided into Drive C: and Drive D. If the hard drive dies, both partitions die. If you have two (or more) drive letters, you can determine whether you have one drive that's logically divided by opening Device Manager, expanding the Disk Drives listing (click the plus sign to the left of the listing), and seeing how many disks are listed. (Accessing Device Manager differs, depending on your version of Windows—check the Windows help files)

The second hard drive may be a separate physical drive, but attached to the same controller as the first hard drive. If the controller dies (and they *do*!), neither drive boots. You can install a new controller and hope that the old controller didn't kill the drives as it went through its death-throes (don't count on it).

If the second hard drive is attached to the second hard drive controller, and the system board dies, there's a small chance the hard drives on the system were damaged. However, if the hard drives aren't damaged, it's not difficult to move them to a new system board (or, a new computer, which is easier and faster).

Mapping Drives to Network Folders

If you're backing up across a network, selecting a target location is faster if you map a drive to the share on the remote computer that holds your backup. Mapping a drive is the process of assigning a drive letter to a shared folder on a remote computer. When a drive is mapped, it's easy to access because it appears in My Computer and Windows Explorer, along with your local drives.

To create a mapped drive you must first create a folder on the remote computer and share it. In fact, it's a good idea to create three folders and share them, so you don't perform a backup over the last good backup. For example, name the folders QBOdd (for odd dates), QBEven (for even dates), and QBSpecial for backups after a major event such as closing the year. You can also use the QBSpecial folder for the 31st day of the month, and for February 29th.

To map a drive to a shared folder, open Network Neighborhood or My Network Places and double-click or expand the computer that holds the shared folder. When you open a computer's icon, all of that computer's shared resources such as drives, folders, and printers are automatically displayed.

NOTE: The steps you take to expand the network and its computers vary, depending on the version of Windows you're running, and whether your network is peer-to-peer (a Windows workgroup) or client/server (a Windows domain).

Right-click the shared folder you want to map, and choose Map Network Drive from the shortcut menu. In the Map Network Drive dialog, accept the drive letter that's displayed, or choose a different drive letter from the drop-down list. Be sure the option to reconnect the mapped drive at logon is selected.

NOTE: Windows XP starts mapping at Z: and works back through the alphabet as you continue to map drives. All other versions of Windows start at the first unused drive letter on the computer and work forward.

Choosing Backup Options

The Backup dialog offers two options for the backup process:

- Verify Data Integrity
- Format Each Floppy Disk During Backup (available only if you select the floppy drive as the backup target)

Verifying data is a process that QuickBooks runs against the current data file (your company file) to make sure its structure is valid. Data verification features can detect corrupt files, or corrupt portions of files.

If you choose the option to verify the data during the backup procedure, the time it takes to back up your file is substantially longer. The Verify Data command is also available on the QuickBooks menu system (choose File → Utilities → Verify Data), so you can check your data files periodically if you don't want to select the option for backups.

> *TIP: Starting with QuickBooks 2006, the Verify Data Integrity option is selected by default, so you have to remember to deselect it before beginning the backup.*

I'm not going to explain any options involving floppy disks because you should not be using floppy disks for backups (and I'll bet QuickBooks eliminates the option some day soon). It's impossible to back up even a small company file on less than a handful of disks, and users who have to sit in front of the computer, inserting disks one after another, just stop doing backups.

Setting Default Backup Options

Click the Set Defaults button to open a dialog in which you can establish default settings for your backups (see Figure 13-2).

If you're performing manual backups, select the option for reminders, and enter the frequency specification for the reminder. The frequency is linked to the number of times you close your QuickBooks company file; it's not a specification for elapsed days.

If you open and close your QuickBooks files numerous times during the day, and you specify a small number, you'll see the reminder at least once every day (not a bad thing).

Select a default location, which can be an external drive, such as a floppy drive or a Zip drive, or a mapped drive to a shared folder on another computer on your network.

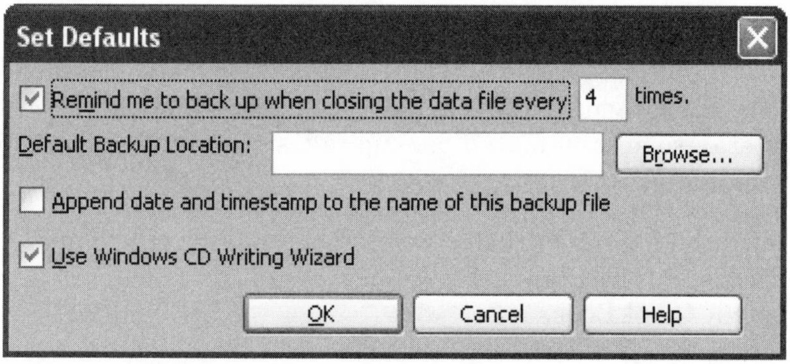

Figure 13-2: By default, QuickBooks reminds you about backing up every fourth time you close a company file.

If you select the option to append a date/time stamp to the filename, the backup filename contains the date and time information for the backup. This means you won't be overwriting the previous backup file—instead you'll be adding another file to the target media. This only works if you have a lot of space on the target media. Periodically, delete all the files except the two latest files.

> **NOTE**: If you select the date/time stamp option with a Zip drive, eventually your QuickBooks file will be too large to fit more than two backups on the disk (in fact, some QuickBooks files grow so large that it's possible to fit only one backup file on the disk).

The option to use the Windows CD Writing Wizard only appears if you're using QuickBooks on a computer running Windows XP. See the discussion about backing up to CD on Windows XP earlier in this chapter.

Automating Backups

You can schedule automatic backups of your company file, which is the preferred method for backing up—no excuses, no waiting around the office after hours. To configure the feature, click the Schedule A Backup tab on the Backup dialog (see Figure 13-3).

Automated Backup when Closing Files

The Automatic Backup section of the Backup dialog displays an option to back up your company data file whenever you close that file. The word "close" is literal, so an automated backup takes place under either of the following conditions:

- While working in QuickBooks, you open a different company file or choose File → Close
- You exit QuickBooks

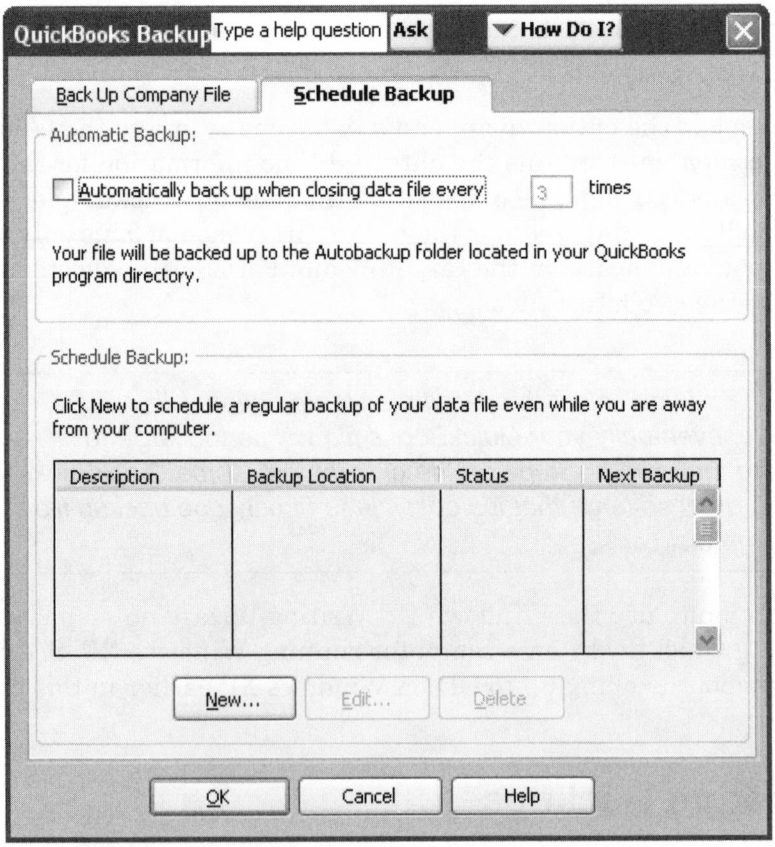

Figure 13-3: Automate your backups to make sure they're kept current.

The backup runs, and the backup file is located in the subfolder named Autobackup under the folder in which you installed QuickBooks. QuickBooks maintains three discrete automated backup files:

- The first time the automated backup runs, the filename is ABU_0_<CompanyFilename><TimeStamp>.QBB.
- The second time the automated backup runs, the file that starts with ABU_0 is copied to a file named ABU_1_<CompanyFilename><TimeStamp>.QBB, and the latest backup is named ABU_0_<CompanyFilename><TimeStamp>.QBB.
- During subsequent backups, the pattern continues. Previous files are copied to the next higher number and the most recent backup file starts with ABU_0.

If you have some reason to think your current file is corrupt, you can go back to a previous backup instead of restoring the latest backup (which may be a backup of corrupted data). However, you'll have to reenter all the transactions that aren't in the last-saved backup (which is a good reason to back up every day—you don't want to have to reconstruct more than one day's transactions).

The problem with this system is that the backup files are on the same hard disk as the QuickBooks data file, which means the backup files won't be available if the disk dies.

On a daily basis, copy the files to a Zip drive, another computer on the network, or a CD. Alternatively, e-mail the latest file to another person (or yourself at your home), or upload the files to your organization's web site.

Automatic Unattended Backups

You can configure QuickBooks to perform a backup of your company files automatically, at any time. This is a nifty feature, but it doesn't work unless you remember to leave your computer running when you leave the office. Before you leave, make sure the QuickBooks software is closed (open files can't be backed up).

To set up an unattended backup, in the Schedule A Backup tab of the QuickBooks Backup dialog, click New. The Schedule A Backup dialog opens (see Figure 13-4).

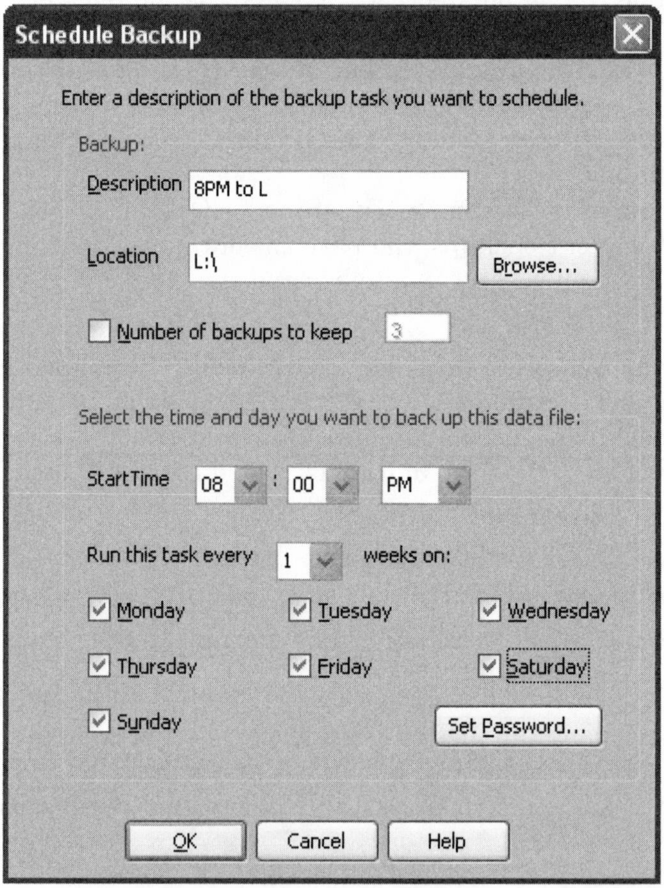

Schedule Backup

Enter a description of the backup task you want to schedule.

Backup:

Description   8PM to L

Location   L:\   Browse...

☐ Number of backups to keep   3

Select the time and day you want to back up this data file:

StartTime   08 ▾ : 00 ▾   PM ▾

Run this task every   1 ▾   weeks on:

☑ Monday   ☑ Tuesday   ☑ Wednesday

☑ Thursday   ☑ Friday   ☑ Saturday

☑ Sunday   Set Password...

OK   Cancel   Help

Figure 13-4: Configure the settings for an automatic backup.

You can give the backup a descriptive name (it's optional), but if you're going to create multiple unattended backup configurations, it's a good idea to identify each backup configuration by name.

Enter a location for the backup file. In Figure 13-4, the location is a mapped network drive. You can also use a Zip drive or a USB stick drive.

You can't use the floppy drive, because this backup is unattended, and you won't be there to see the message "please insert the next disk."

Be sure the target drive is available—insert the removable disk before leaving the computer. If the target drive is on a network computer, be sure that computer isn't turned off at night.

If you don't want to overwrite the last backup file every time a new backup file is created, select the option Number Of Backups To Keep, and specify the number. QuickBooks saves as many discrete backup files as you specify, each time replacing the first file with the most recent backup, and renaming older files as described earlier in this section.

Create a schedule for this unattended backup by selecting a time and a frequency.

The Set Password button is not related to your QuickBooks user and password configuration; it's for your operating system, and it's quite possible you don't have to use this function.

The username and password you enter into the dialog are for a Windows logon name and password, and it's needed only if you're running Windows with permissions and rights configured under NTFS (the secure file system available in Windows NT/2000/XP/2003). If you're using Windows 2000/XP/2003 and you're familiar with the RunAs feature, this Set Password dialog works similarly.

You can create multiple unattended backup schemes and configure them for special circumstances. For instance, in addition to a nightly backup, you may want to configure a backup every four weeks on a Friday to create a backup on a removable drive that is earmarked for off-site storage. Be sure to bring the backup media to the office on that day, and take it back to the off-site location later.

Offsite Storage of Backups

At least once a month (preferably once a week), you should make an additional backup and take the backup media offsite. Bring the media back the next time you're making an offsite backup. (This is also something you should do for your regular computer system backup).

Offsite backups are your insurance against disasters beyond dead hard drives or computers. Fire, flood, or burglaries can rob you of your computer, your network, and your locally stored backup media. I've had clients with offices in buildings that were unexpectedly closed due to a disaster, an electrical outage that took days to repair, and even an extended building shutdown because exterminators had to rid the building of pests and the air was unhealthy for a period of a week. In every case, because I insisted that my clients regularly took a backup offsite, the company was able to borrow, rent, or buy a computer, install QuickBooks, restore the file, and continue to run their organizations.

I've set up some clients with what I consider a nifty solution to offsite backups, and the solution can be used for nightly backups. Each user sends the QuickBooks backup file as an e-mail attachment to an e-mail sent to the user's personal (home) e-mail address. Of course, once your QuickBooks files get large, this becomes less efficient if you're operating with a telephone modem.

However, offsite backups are important enough to warrant paying for high-speed Internet access for at least one user. Don't do this unless your QuickBooks company files are protected with user passwords, because security at the home computer is generally weaker than the security systems in offices.

If your organization has a web site with sufficient storage space, set aside a folder for holding backups. Use FTP software to upload the files (your web hosting company has instructions for completing this task on its support pages).

If you don't have media large enough for an offsite backup, investigate the QuickBooks Online Backup Service. This service lets you use your Internet connection to transfer your files to the QuickBooks servers, which are secure and safe. To learn about the QuickBooks backup service and sign up for it (it's not free), choose Company → Company Services → Back Up Your Data Online. Alternatively, click the Tell Me More button on the backup dialog that appears when you choose File → Back Up.

Restoring Backup Files

If you need to restore a company file, you must have your last backup at hand. If you're restoring your company file to a new computer, or new hard drive, install QuickBooks, and download the latest update.

If you backed up to removable media, put the disk that contains your last backup into its drive. If you backed up to a network share, be sure the remote computer is running. If you used an online backup service, be sure you're connected to the Internet.

When everything is ready, open QuickBooks, and choose File → Restore, to open the Restore Company Backup dialog seen in Figure 13-5. Fill out the dialog as follows:

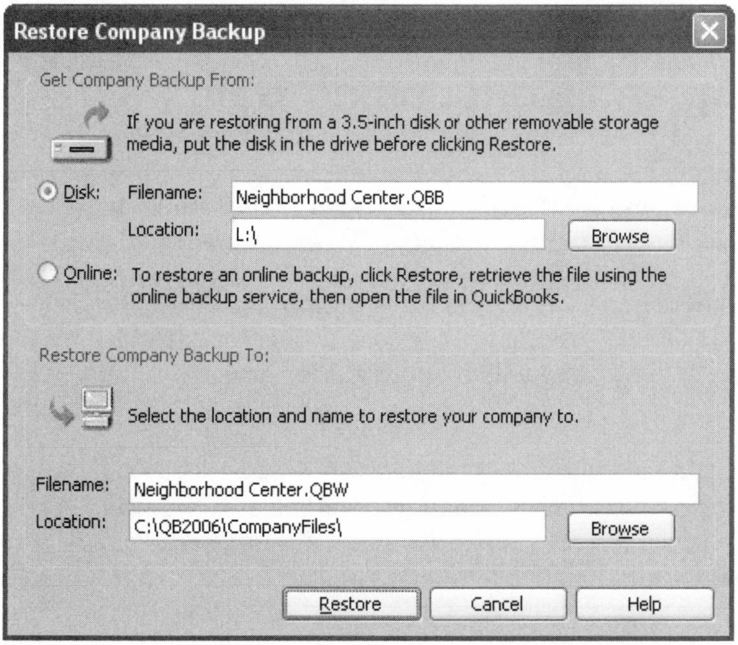

Figure 13-5: To restore a backup, select the backup file and the company filename for the restored file.

1. Enter the location and filename of the backup file. You can use the Browse button to navigate to the location, and select the file.

2. Enter the location and filename of the company file you're restoring (usually the same name as the backup file, but the extension changes from .QBB to .QBW).

3. Click Restore.

4. If you're restoring to an existing company filename (perhaps the problem was a corrupt data file), you receive a warning that you're about to overwrite the existing file. That's fine, because it's what you need to do.

5. When the process finishes, QuickBooks displays a message that your data files have been restored successfully.

TIP: *If this backup wasn't created yesterday (or after the last time you used your company file), you must re-create every transaction you made between the time of this backup and the last time you used QuickBooks.*

Archiving and Condensing Data

QuickBooks provides a feature that enables you to condense your company file to make it smaller. Smaller files open faster, make backing up faster, and use less space on your hard drive.

While condensing a file seems to be a handy feature, it carries some significant side effects, because you'll lose details about older transactions. Therefore, don't take this step until the size of your file has become cumbersome.

TIP: *To see the current size of your data file, along with information about the file's contents, press F2 while working in QuickBooks.*

Understanding the Condense Feature

Before I explain how to condense data, I'll go over some of the conventions that determine the result, so you have some guidelines for making the appropriate selections.

The Condensing Date

When you condense your data, QuickBooks asks you for the date you want to use as the cutoff date. Everything you no longer need before that date is condensed.

No open transactions are ever condensed; only those data items that are completed, finished, and safe to condense are targeted. In addition, any transactions before the condensing date that affect current transactions are skipped, and their details are maintained.

Summary Transactions

The transactions that fall before the condensing date, and are eligible for condensing, are deleted and replaced with summary transactions. Summary transactions are nothing but journal entry transactions that show the totals for the transactions, one for each month that is condensed.

You can recognize the summary transactions in the account registers because they're marked as general journal entry transactions (the transaction type is GENJRNL). Because the summary transactions maintain totals, account balances are not changed by condensing data.

Of course, because nothing remains of the transactions but the balances that posted to accounts, you can't run detail reports for dates that fall before the condensing date. Lacking detail reports, you can't look up details for a customer or a vendor.

Condensing Your File

When you condense your QuickBooks file, a wizard walks you through the process. To launch the wizard, take one of the following actions:

- In QuickBooks 2006 and later, choose File → Utilities → Clean Up Company Data.
- In QuickBooks 2005 and earlier, choose File → Archive & Condense Data.

If you've created any budgets, QuickBooks displays a message warning you that budget data may be removed, and asks if you want to continue. To make sure you don't lose your budget data, click No and export your budgets to Excel. Chapter 9 has information on exporting and importing budgets. Then return to this feature.

The first wizard window, seen in Figure 13-6, offers two choices for proceeding:

- Condense Transactions as of a Specific Date
- Remove All Transactions

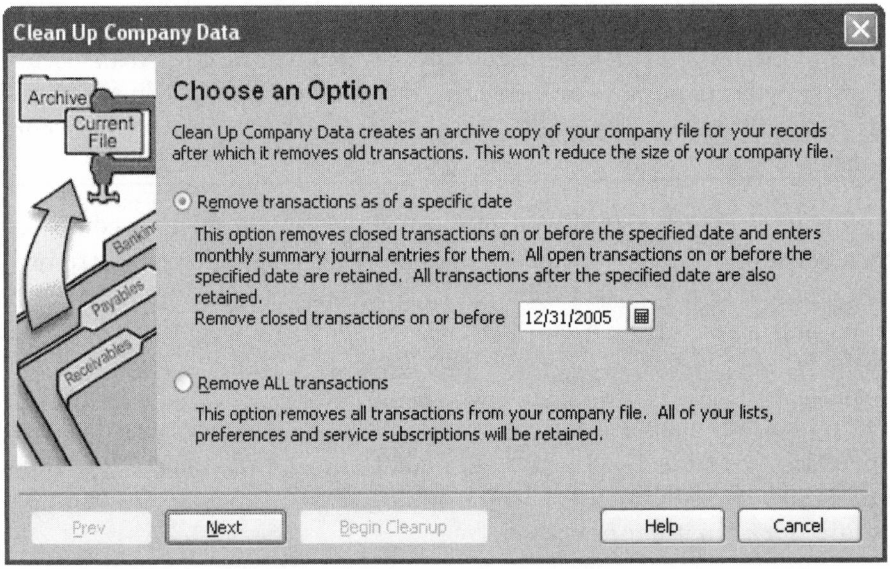

Figure 13-6: Select the action to perform on your company file.

Removing All Transactions

The option to remove all transactions does exactly what it says it does, so it's quite dangerous unless you're doing this for some purpose that matches this decision.

If you select this option, QuickBooks empties the file of all transactions. However, all the preferences and list entries are maintained. This means you can start all over, using the same company file. There are some scenarios in which you might consider this option, such as:

- Your current company file has become so large it takes forever to load, and it operates so slowly you're losing your mind.
- You have reached, or are about to reach, the size limitation for one or more lists (see Chapter 5 for detailed information about list limits).

If you want to use this option, be sure to complete the following tasks before proceeding:

- Copy your company file to another folder and rename it, using a naming convention such as *Filename-to Date* (substitute the name of your company file for *Filename,* and the date of the last use for *Date*).
- Make a backup of your current company file, in case you change your mind.
- Copy the backup file to another folder, and rename it.

Condensing Transactions

QuickBooks automatically displays the last day of the previous fiscal year as the condensing date. You can use this date, but if you've been using QuickBooks for a while choose an earlier date (try to use a date long past, because there's less chance you'll care about those old transaction details).

TIP: Choose the last day of a month or a quarter, because condensing should always be performed with reporting periods in mind.

Click Next to see a list of the transaction types that are excluded from the process by default (see Figure 13-7). You can select any of them to include them in the "to be condensed" list.

Because any transactions that fall in these categories are at least a year old (depending on the cutoff date you selected), it's not necessarily dangerous to select all the categories. For example, if a transaction has been waiting for printing for more than a year, it probably doesn't really need to be printed.

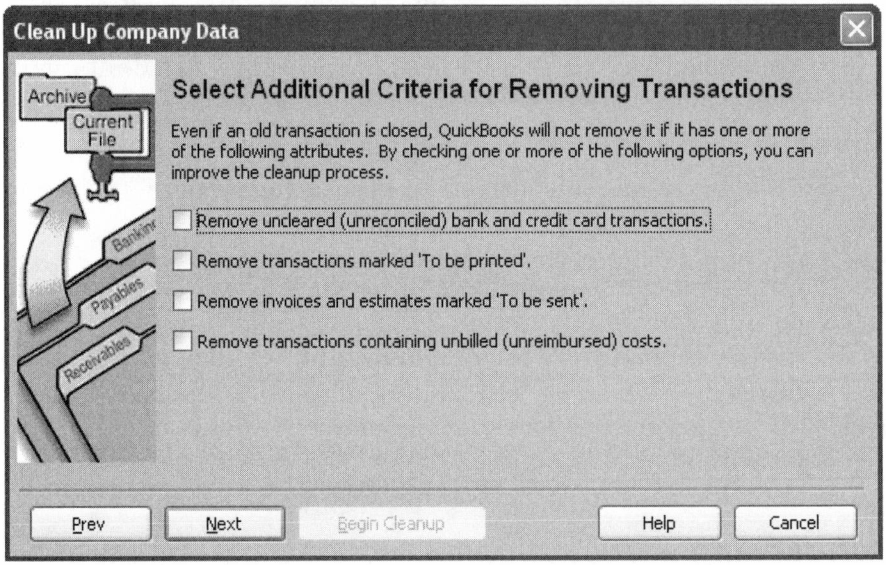

Figure 13-7: You can tell QuickBooks to remove transactions types that wouldn't be removed by default.

Click Next and select the lists (accounts, customers, vendors, items, etc.) you want QuickBooks to check for unused entries that should be removed. Then, click Next to see an informational window in which the condense process is explained.

Click Begin Condense to start the process. QuickBooks displays a message to tell you that your data file will be backed up before the file is condensed. This is not an everyday backup; it's the last backup of a full data file before information is removed. Therefore, use new disks for this backup (if you use removable media). Click OK to begin the backup.

As soon as QuickBooks finishes backing up, it starts condensing data. You'll see progress bars on your screen as each step is completed. If QuickBooks encounters an error during the condensing process, it automatically restores all your data, and does not create an archive file.

When the job is complete, you're given the name of the archive copy of your data file. The archive file, which contains the detailed transactions that were condensed in the company file, is actually just a QuickBooks company file. You can open this file the same way you open any QuickBooks file. Of course, you should never enter transactions in this file, but you can view information, and print reports.

TIP: *If you track inventory, condensing a file probably won't make much difference in the size of the file. Inventory transactions are kept in detail, because QuickBooks needs that information to track average costing.*

Updating QuickBooks

QuickBooks provides an automatic update service you use to make sure your QuickBooks software is up-to-date and trouble-free. This service provides you with any maintenance releases of QuickBooks that have been created since you purchased and installed your copy of the software.

An update (maintenance release) is distributed when a problem is discovered and fixed. This is sometimes necessary, because it's almost impossible to distribute a program that is totally bug-free (although my experience has been that QuickBooks generally releases without any major bugs, since Intuit does a thorough job of testing its software before it's released).

The Update QuickBooks service also provides enhancements to features, along with notes from Intuit that help you keep up with new features and information about QuickBooks.

NOTE: *This service does not provide upgrades to a new version; it just provides updates to your current version.*

The Update QuickBooks service is an online service, so you must have set up online access in QuickBooks. To check for updates, and to configure update options, use one of the following actions to open the Update QuickBooks dialog:

- In QuickBooks 2006 and later, choose Help → Update QuickBooks
- In QuickBooks 2005 and earlier, choose File → Update QuickBooks

Configuring the Update Service

Click the Options tab to configure the Update feature. As you can see in Figure 13-8, you have several methods of updating your software components. You can change these options at any time.

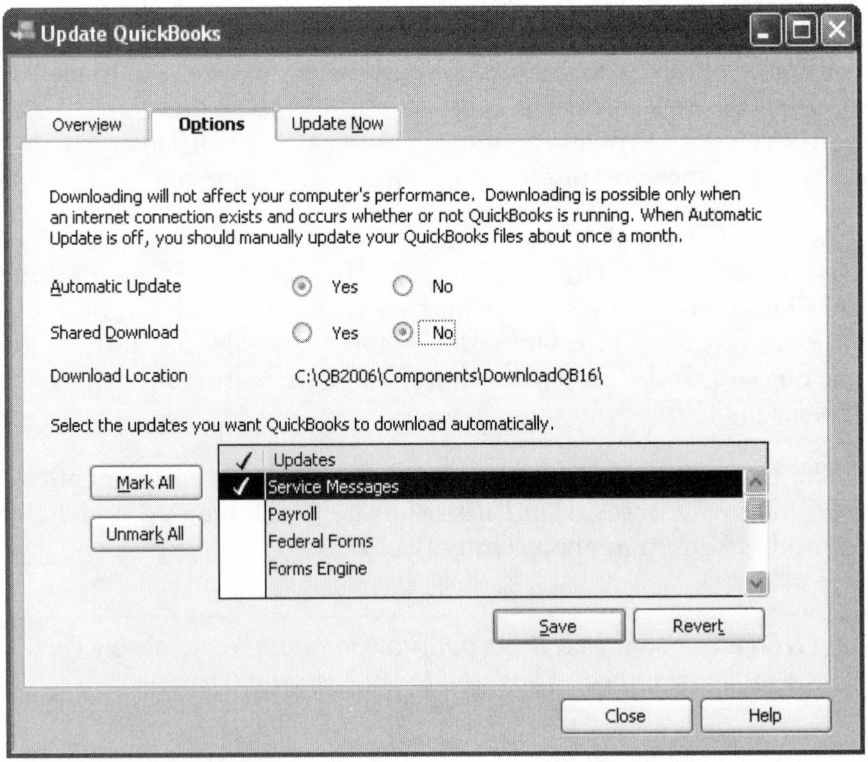

Figure 13-8: Configure the QuickBooks Update services.

Automatic Updates

Select Automatic Updates if you want to allow QuickBooks to check the QuickBooks update site on the Internet periodically while you're connected to the Internet. QuickBooks doesn't have to be open for this function to occur.

If new information is found, it's downloaded to your hard drive automatically, without any notification. If you happen to disconnect from the Internet while updates are being downloaded, the next time you connect to the Internet, QuickBooks will pick up where it left off.

If you don't like the idea of a software application downloading files without notifying you, select No to turn off the automatic option. However, you must periodically open the Update QuickBooks dialog and click Update Now to check for updates and install them.

TIP: *If you have any online services, such as Payroll or Online Banking, when you use those services QuickBooks checks for updates. This occurs even if you've turned off automatic updates.*

Shared Downloads

If you're using the multi-user version of QuickBooks, you must configure the Update QuickBooks service to share downloaded files with other users. The files are downloaded to the computer that holds the shared QuickBooks data files, and the location is noted on this dialog. Every user on the network must open his or her copy of QuickBooks and configure the Update options for Shared Download, pointing to the location on the computer that holds the shared data files.

Selecting Update Types

Select the types of files you want QuickBooks to update during automatic downloading. The most important selection is Updates (Maintenance Releases), which fix problems and add features. Select the other update types if you're using those features.

Checking the Status of Updates

Click the Update Now tab to view information about the current status of the update service, including the last date that QuickBooks checked for updates and the names of any files that were downloaded.

Click the check boxes next to each specific type of update to select/deselect those file types. Then click Get Updates to tell QuickBooks to check the Internet immediately and bring back any files. After files are downloaded, click the listing to see more information about that download.

Most of the time, the files are automatically integrated into your system. However, sometimes an information message appears to tell you that the files will be installed the next time you start QuickBooks.

Chapter 14

Managing Users and Security

Creating an administrator

Creating users

Setting permissions

If more than one person uses your QuickBooks company file, you should set up user logins. This forces people to enter a name and password to gain access to the files. You can also assign permissions to each name, limiting access to QuickBooks features on a person-by-person basis.

Managing users isn't an issue that's limited to the network version of QuickBooks. You should set up users and permissions if you have a single-user copy of QuickBooks that's used by more than one person. Sharing the work of entering transactions in QuickBooks on a single computer is a common scenario.

Even if QuickBooks is installed on only one computer, and only one person ever uses the software, setting up a login name and password keeps everyone else in the world out of your QuickBooks data.

Users and Company Files

QuickBooks manages users, passwords, and permissions on a company file basis. If you have multiple company files in your QuickBooks system, you must set up users separately for each file.

This means that all the steps described in this chapter must be repeated for each and every company file in your system. Don't let any company file remain unprotected.

Creating the Administrator

The notion of giving permissions implies the need for a person who's in charge of everyone and everything. In QuickBooks, that person is the administrator—the person with supreme power. QuickBooks uses the name Admin for the administrator.

You can set up other users with permission to access all areas of QuickBooks, which essentially makes them administrators. However, no user except Admin has absolute power. Only Admin can perform the following tasks:

- Change user permissions

- Import and export data
- Change the company setup information
- Change company preferences

Choosing the Administrator

To become the administrator, all you have to do is grab the title; the person who initiates the process of setting up users is de-facto the administrator. While it's preferable that the administrator is a QuickBooks expert and has some training in bookkeeping or accounting, QuickBooks presents no quiz and lets anyone become the administrator.

From a practical point of view, the only criterion is availability—an administrator should be someone who is in the office regularly so that administrative tasks can be performed when necessary. Usually, this means a staff person, preferably a full-time staff person. That person doesn't have to be a QuickBooks expert; in fact, the person doesn't have to be someone who uses QuickBooks regularly, or at all.

Creating the Administrator

To set up the administrator, choose Company → Set Up Users. The Set Up QuickBooks Administrator dialog opens, as seen in Figure 14-1.

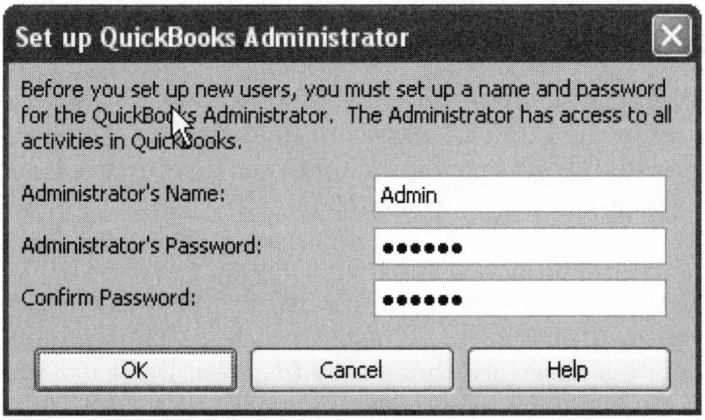

Figure 14-1: You must set up the administrator before you can set up other users.

NOTE: *In QuickBooks 2006 and later, if you created your company file with the EasyStep Interview, instead of manually, you may not see the dialog shown in Figure 13-1. This is true even if you didn't enter a password for the administrator during the interview. Instead, you'll see the User List dialog discussed later in this chapter in the section "Adding a User Name".*

QuickBooks lets you replace the name Admin to any name you choose, and some people change Admin to the name of the person who is the administrator. If you change the name, you need to understand that your action has the following effects:

- The new name becomes an alias, a second identity, for the name Admin; the new name doesn't replace Admin.
- If you forget the name you created to replace Admin, you can still log in as Admin by entering **Admin** in the User Name field of the Login dialog.
- The password you attached to the new name is also attached to the user named Admin.
- If you forget the administrator's password, you're out of luck. The QuickBooks support team will fix the problem, but there's a fee to do so.

Setting the Administrator Password

Enter a password in the Administrator's Password field, and then enter the same password in the Confirm Password field. You won't see the text you're typing; instead, the system shows bullets as a security measure (in case someone is watching over your shoulder).

Passwords are important, and the more thought you give to creating passwords, the better. Passwords are case sensitive, and an effective password mixes cases. In addition, no user, including the user named Admin, should create a password that's easy to guess. Don't use your dog's name, your child's name, your license plate number, or anything else that someone trying to break in could guess.

Passwords are optional, but there's no point in setting up a security system if you're not going to use passwords. If you click OK without entering text in the password fields, QuickBooks issues the admonishing message seen in Figure 14-2.

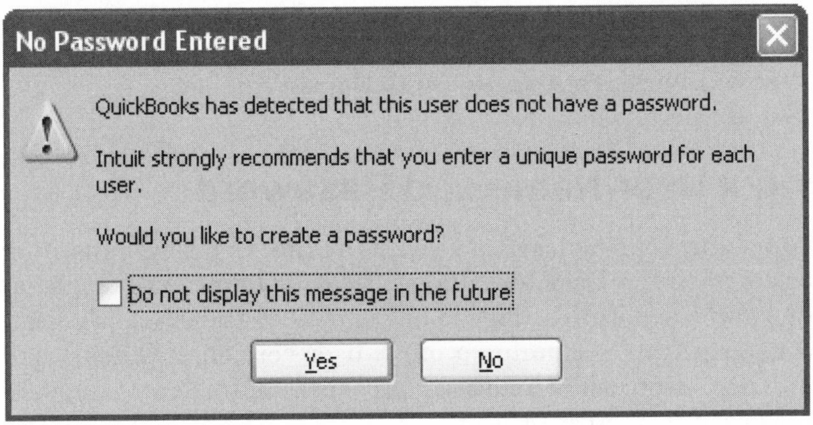

No Password Entered

QuickBooks has detected that this user does not have a password.

Intuit strongly recommends that you enter a unique password for each user.

Would you like to create a password?

☐ Do not display this message in the future

Yes   No

Figure 14-2: If you don't enter a password, QuickBooks tries to convince you to change your mind.

If you're creating an administrator account for the purpose of keeping the rest of the world out, and you don't plan to add more users, you must use a password. If the administrator is the only user account, and no password is attached to the account, no Login dialog appears when you open the company file. You might as well not bother setting up the administrator.

Either of the following scenarios is necessary to force a Login dialog to appear when you open a company file:

- There are multiple users set up for the company file (at least one user in addition to the administrator). It doesn't matter whether you set up any passwords; the existence of multiple user accounts triggers the Login dialog.
- Only the administrator exists as a user account, and it has a password.

Creating Users

Creating users is a multi-step process that can only be performed by the administrator. You have to complete the following tasks to create a user:

- Create a user name.
- Optionally assign a password to the user name.
- Set the permissions for the user.

Adding a User Name and Password

To add a user to your QuickBooks company file, choose Company → Set Up Users to open the User List dialog. All user names are displayed in the dialog and the notation (logged on) is next to the currently logged on user (or users, if you're running a multi-user version of QuickBooks). If this is the first user you're creating, only the administrator appears in the list, as seen in Figure 14-3.

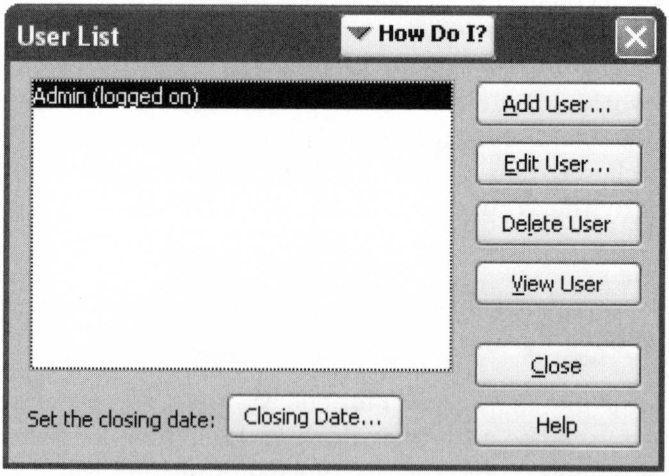

Figure 14-3: All user setup tasks start with the User List dialog.

To add a new user to the list, click Add User. A wizard appears to help you set up the new user. In the first wizard window, enter the user name, which is the name this user must type to log in to QuickBooks.

To establish a password for this user, enter and confirm the password. You can ask the user to give you a password, or invent one yourself and pass it along to the user. (Users can change their own passwords at any time. See the section "Changing Your Own Password" later in this chapter.)

Setting User Permissions

When you click Next, the wizard asks whether you want to let this user have access to selected areas of QuickBooks, or to all areas of QuickBooks. (Regardless of the choice you make, you can always return to this dialog and change the settings.)

If you choose the option All Areas Of QuickBooks, when you click Next, QuickBooks displays a message asking you to confirm that fact. Click Yes and then click Finish.

When you give blanket permissions to a new user, you're creating a virtual administrator. This person can do everything the administrator can do, except those tasks reserved specifically for the real administrator (enumerated earlier in this chapter).

If you choose the option Selected areas, when you click Next the wizard continues in order to let you specify the permissions for this user. Each of the ensuing wizard windows is dedicated to a specific QuickBooks component (see Figure 14-4). You can establish permissions for this user for each component.

For each QuickBooks component, select one of the following permission options:

- **No Access**. The user is denied permission to open any windows in that component of QuickBooks.
- **Full Access**. The user can open all windows and perform all tasks in that component of QuickBooks, except editing or deleting existing transactions (see the section "Changing or Deleting Transactions" later in this chapter).
- **Selective Access**. The user is permitted to view data and perform tasks as you specify.

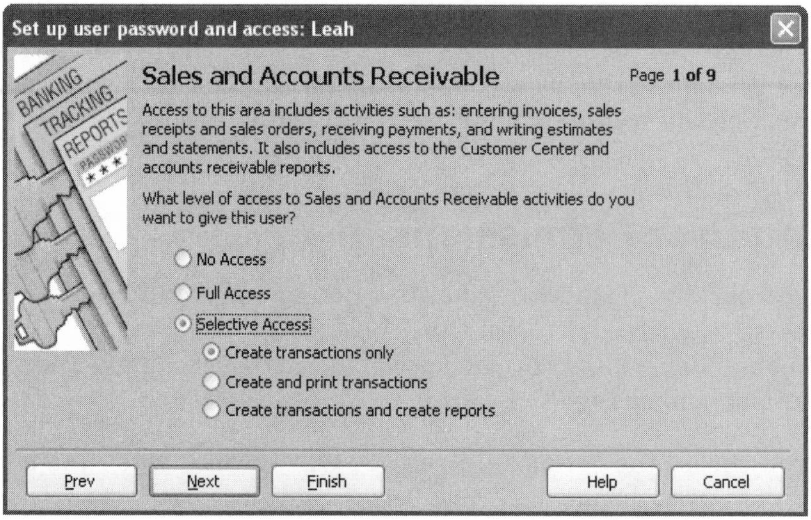

Figure 14-4: Each component of QuickBooks has its own window
where you can set permissions for this user.

If you choose Selective Access, you're asked to specify the rights this user should have. Those rights vary from component to component, but generally, you're asked to choose one of these permission levels:

- Create transactions
- Create and print transactions
- Create transactions and create reports

When you're configuring selective access, you can choose only one of the three levels. If you need to give the user rights to more than one of these choices, you can't custom-design a mix-and-match set of permissions. Instead, you must select Full Access for that component.

Notice that the list of permissions for selective access doesn't include any permissions for changing transactions or deleting transactions. The wizard handles those tasks separately (see the section "Changing or Deleting Transactions" later in this chapter).

As you move through the wizard windows, you can click Finish at any time. The components you skip are automatically set for No Access for this user. This means when you're setting up a user who should only be able to access Purchases and Accounts Payable tasks, after you make your selections for that component, you can click Finish instead of moving through the remaining wizard windows.

Setting Permissions for Special Areas of QuickBooks

Two of the wizard windows display permission settings that are not directly related to any specific component of the software: Sensitive Accounting Activities, and Sensitive Accounting Reports.

Sensitive Accounting Activities

Sensitive accounting activities are those tasks that aren't directly related to specific QuickBooks components or transactions. They include tasks such as the following:

- Making changes to the chart of accounts
- Manipulating the register for any balance sheet account
- Using online banking
- Transferring funds between banks
- Reconciling bank accounts
- Creating journal entries
- Preparing an accountant's review
- Condensing data
- Working with budgets

The configuration window presents the same three permission levels as the windows for the other components. If you choose Selective Access as the permission level, the three access choices are the same as those for the other components.

Sensitive Accounting Reports

Sensitive financial reports are those reports that reveal important financial information about your company, such as:

- Profit & Loss reports
- Balance Sheet reports
- Budget reports
- Cash flow reports
- Income tax reports

- Trial balance reports
- Audit trail reports

The configuration window for Sensitive Accounting Reports presents the same three permission levels as the windows for the other components. If you choose Selective Access as the permission level, the following choices are offered:

- Create Sensitive Reports Only
- Create And Print Sensitive Reports

I assume the difference between the permissions has to do with the user's ability to walk out of the office with sensitive reports.

Changing or Deleting Transactions

If a user has permissions for certain components, you can limit his or her ability to manipulate existing transactions within those areas. Figure 14-5 shows the wizard window that manages these permissions.

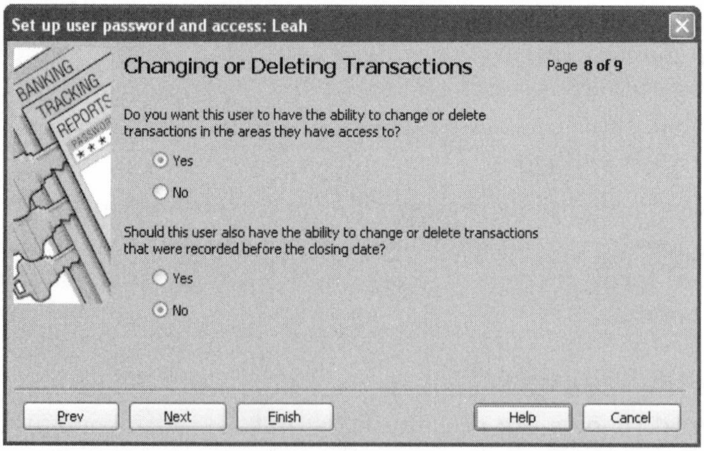

Figure 14-5: Set permissions for manipulating existing transactions.

If you choose Yes, the user can edit and delete transactions in any area where the user has been given access permissions.

If you choose No, the user can only edit and delete transactions that he or she created in the current QuickBooks session. Transactions created by other users, and transactions created by this user in the past or in the future cannot be edited or deleted.

Closed Period Permissions

The Changing or Deleting Transactions window also covers transactions that are in a closed period (which means you've taken the steps described in Chapter 11 to enter a closing date, and create a password for access to transactions dated on or before that closing date).

If you choose Yes, the user can edit and delete transactions entered on or before the closing date, as long as the user knows the password needed to access those transactions.

If you choose No, the user cannot access transactions in the closed period, even if he or she knows the password.

Permissions Summary

When you have finished configuring user permissions for components and sensitive areas, the last wizard window displays a list of the permissions you've granted and refused (see Figure 14-6). If everything is correct, click Finish. If there's something you want to change, use the Prev button to back up to the appropriate window.

Set up user password and access

Access for user: Leah   Page **9 of 9**

You have finished setting this user's access rights and password. Below is a summary of this user's access rights. Click the Finish button to complete this task.

Area	Create	Print	Rep...
Sales and Accounts Receivable	Y	N	N
Purchases and Accounts Payable	Y	Y	Y
Checking and Credit Cards	Y	N	n/a
Time Tracking	Y	N	N
Payroll and Employees	Y	N	N
Sensitive Accounting Activities	Y	N	N
Sensitive Financial Reports	Y	N	n/a
Changing or Deleting Transactions	Y	n/a	n/a
Changing Closed Transactions	Y	n/a	n/a

| Prev | Next | Finish | | Help | Cancel |

Figure 14-6: Check your work before saving the settings.

Changing User Settings

In addition to adding users, the administrator can remove users, change user passwords, and modify user permissions at any time. All user modifications are made in the User List dialog, which has the following functions available for the user name you select:

- **Edit User**. Opens the Change User Password and Access wizard, which is the same as the Add User wizard, so you can re-do the settings.
- **Delete User**. Removes the user from the User List.
- **View User**. Displays the summary page of the Set Up User Password And Access wizard, which shows all permissions (refer back to Figure 14-6).

Changing Your Own Password

Only the administrator can open the User List dialog, but QuickBooks provides a way for all users (including the administrator) to change their own passwords. To change your password, choose Company → Change Your Password.

The Change Password dialog opens with the currently logged-in user's name in the User Name field (see Figure 14-7). You cannot change the user name. Enter the current password in the Enter Old Password field, then type a new password and enter it again to confirm it.

If you want to login without a password (called a *null password*), enter the current password in the Enter Old Password field and click OK. Don't move through the New Password fields (to avoid entry of an inadvertent character or space).

If you previously logged on with a user name, but no password, and you're creating a password with the Change Password dialog, the dialog doesn't include the Enter Old Password field. Enter the new password, and enter it again to confirm it.

Figure 14-7: You must know the current password to create a new one.

Logging In

When you launch QuickBooks, the last-used company file is loaded and the QuickBooks Login dialog appears (see Figure 14-8). The name of the user who was logged in appears in the User Name field, and your cursor is in the Password field, waiting for you to enter a password.

Figure 14-8: Enter your own login name and then enter your password.

Move to the User Name field, remove the previous user's name, and enter your own login name. Press the Tab key to move to the Password field and enter your password.

Logging In to a Running Session

If QuickBooks is running, and a different user has to log in to the same company file, you don't have to shut down QuickBooks and restart it. Choose File → Open Company/Login. In the Open A Company dialog, the current company file is selected, so just click Open. The Login dialog appears, and the logging in user can enter his or her name and password.

Failed Logins

If you mistype either the login name or the password, QuickBooks issues the error message seen in Figure 14-9. Notice that QuickBooks does not indicate whether the problem is with the name or the password (a standard security paradigm). Click OK to return to the QuickBooks Login dialog and try again.

Figure 14-9: An error in either the User Name or Password field prevents you from logging in to this company file.

If the next attempt fails, check the following to try to resolve the problem:

- Are you opening the right company file? If more than one company file exists, you may have a different login name or password (or both) for this company file.

- Is your QuickBooks login name the same as your Windows logon name (for logging on to the computer)? If so, did you enter your Windows password instead of your QuickBooks password?
- Is the Caps Lock key on? Passwords are case sensitive.
- Are there numbers in your password? If so, did you use the number keypad without turning on Num Lock?
- Did you inadvertently press the space bar in front of (or at the end of) your password when you entered it originally, or when you changed it? If so, the space is part of the password so you must enter it.

If you can't resolve the problem, and you're not the administrator, give up and ask the administrator to log in and change your password by selecting your user name and clicking Edit.

Forgotten Admin Passwords

If you're the administrator and you forget your password, you have a serious problem. Nobody else can log in to QuickBooks and change your password. It's going to cost you money to have QuickBooks recover your password. Before going into panic mode, see if any of the following scenarios (that have solutions) match your circumstances.

Is this a new company file and you can't remember the password you entered during the EasyStep Interview? If so, start a new company file. Click Cancel on the login dialog to have QuickBooks close the company file and display the No Company Open dialog.

Click Create a New Company and set up a new company file. You can use the same name for the company you used previously, and when you save the file QuickBooks will ask you if you're sure you want to overwrite the old file.

Did you change your password the last time you used QuickBooks, and now you can't remember the new password? If so, and the following circumstances exist, there's an easy fix:

- There is another user with administrator permissions who can log in and open the company file.

- You have a backup that's two days old, made before you changed the password and backed up the file with the new password.

If both these circumstances exist, follow these steps:

1. Close QuickBooks.
2. Open My Computer and copy the current company file (named *CompanyName*.QBW) to another folder on your hard drive. Rename the copied file by adding "-2" to the filename (e.g. MyCompany-2.QBW).
3. Restore the backup you made two days ago (before yesterday, when you changed the password and backed up the file with the new password).
4. After you confirm the fact that you can log in as Admin in the restored file, close the file.
5. Have the user who didn't forget her password open the copy of the company file you stored with the new name (changing the location in the Open A Company dialog to find the file).
6. Create reports to recover information about the transactions created in the last two days.
7. Close the old, renamed file.
8. Open the restored file and enter the transactions.

If no user with administrative rights exists, but you have a backup that pre-dates the backup in which you saved your new password, restore the older backup and re-create the transactions made after that date. (It may take a while to catch up, but eventually the bank statement, delivery of purchase orders, etc. will help you reconstruct the missing transactions).

Chapter 13 explains the urgency of avoiding backups over the last good backup, and presents several methods for ensuring your ability to go back at least two backups when you need to restore a file. If you don't use these methods, you can't return to the older backup and log in with your old password.

QuickBooks Lost Password Support

QuickBooks has a service that will remove the administrator's password from the company file. When the password is removed you can log in as

Admin with no password. Then create a new password (and this time, make a note of it and put the note in a secure private place).

There's a fee for the service, and it involves several steps (designed for security reasons). After you make the request and QuickBooks confirms your request, you upload your file. QuickBooks support personnel remove the Admin password and return the file.

You can make the request by telephone or by filling in a form on the QuickBooks Support web site. To get the current telephone number, or open the online form, go to www.quickbooks.com and click the Support link. Select Password Removal Services from the Useful Links list on the left side of the page, and follow the prompts to arrange for the service.

Chapter 15

QuickBooks Fundraising Tools

Understanding file size limits

Managing members

Tracking donations

Creating fundraising mailings

Managing volunteers

Tracking fundraising events

Q uickBooks contains tools and features that can help you raise
money, especially from donors and members. These constituents
are the primary sources of income for many small nonprofit organizations. In addition, you need to track all your fundraising efforts in
QuickBooks transactions.

It's possible to track individual members and donors in QuickBooks,
but you need to be careful about keeping the number of entries within
the size limits imposed by the QuickBooks structure (see the next section
to learn about file size limits).

The more information you keep about members and donors, the easier it is to create targeted fund raising campaigns. Sending a fund raising
letter, or creating a fundraising event, and targeting people who have a
known interest in some specific angle of the fund raising topic can substantially increase the amount of money you raise.

In this chapter I'll show you how to track information about members and donors in ways that are useful for fund raising, and for tracking participation in activities. I'll also explain the configuration settings you need for tracking the income and expenses involved with
fundraising.

QuickBooks File Limitations

If you want to track members and individual donors in QuickBooks, you
have to be aware of the limits QuickBooks imposes on the number of
entries you can have in the QuickBooks names lists, which include the
following lists:

- Customer:Job
- Vendor
- Other Names
- Employee

There are actually two limitations—one for the combined total of all
names lists, and another for any one list.

- The combined total of entries in all the names lists cannot exceed
14,500.

- No individual names list can exceed 10,000 entries.

Once you have reached 10,000 names in a single list, you cannot create any new entries in that list. Once you have reached 14,500 names in your combined lists, you can no longer create any new names in any names list.

When QuickBooks locks a names list it's a permanent decision. Deleting names doesn't free up space for new names. It's too late.

NOTE: *QuickBooks also has limitations on other components, including the number of transactions. All of these limits are described in Chapter 5.*

If you think the limitations will get in the way of tracking members, or individual donors (or both), you can track member and donor information outside of QuickBooks.

Create a database, or spreadsheets, to track information about members and individual donors. You can post the financial transactions (dues and donations) in QuickBooks in batches, without linking the amounts to discrete names. Chapter 6 has information on recording donations and memberships in batches.

Managing Members

If you have a manageable number of members, you can track their names and activities in QuickBooks. QuickBooks offers features to help you manage all aspects of membership.

Creating Member Records

If you've decided to track your member list, enter each member as a customer in the Customer:Job list. Use a naming protocol that's consistent, such as last name-first initial or last name-first name (use hyphens or spaces, not both).

Using the Customer Fields Creatively

The fields in the Customer dialog aren't designed for membership records, but you can use them to match your information needs. For example, here are some of the uses I've applied at client sites:

- Ship To is the work address.
- Company Name holds the parents' names if the membership list is made up of children (perhaps you run sports teams or after school activities).
- On the Payment Info tab, the Account No. field holds membership numbers (if you use membership numbers).

You can use this list to jump-start your own imagination to match fields with the information you want to track.

TIP: *To make it easier to build reports and track renewals, make your membership renewal dates either the first of the month or the last of the month, regardless of the date you received the first payment.*

Using Custom Fields to Track Members

Custom Fields are extremely useful for tracking members (see the instructions for creating custom fields in Chapter 5). For members, you can track membership information, and the activities the members participate in, by creating the right custom fields.

For example, I have clients who use custom fields to track committee membership. The fields are named Committee1, Committee2, and so on (using real committee names). To indicate membership in a committee, data is entered in the appropriate custom field—usually an X. Filtering a report for an X in the appropriate field provides all the committee member names.

If you have more than a few committees, create a single custom field (in this case, named Committee), and enter the appropriate committee name in each customer's record.

You can use either of these methods to track any type of membership information, such as teams (for sports), volunteer days (e.g. Thursday), and so on.

Custom fields don't have a drop-down list, so you must be sure to type entries exactly the same way each time you add the entry to a customer record. For example, if you're tracking team membership for a team named Tigers, you won't be able to find the team members for whom you entered "Tiger", as the data.

> *TIP*: *The most efficient way to enter data in custom fields is to create a list of acceptable entries and make sure everyone who enters data in QuickBooks has a copy of that list.*

You can also create custom fields to track membership dues renewal information. For example, you can have two custom fields:

RenewalMonth, and RenewalYear.

Those fields even work for grantors, and donor agencies to track contract renewal dates, in addition to helping you track membership renewals and "in memoriam" donations.

Some organizations create a custom field for the renewal month, and use that data to generate letters or telephone calls every year, to remind members that their dues are payable. The problem they encounter is that when a member sends a payment for two years, the yearly reminders are annoying. The solution is to make sure you have a field for the renewal year.

> *TIP: If you're tracking renewal months, use numbers for the month instead of names. It's easier to create a report if you're looking for "9" instead of guessing the way users might have entered the name (Sep, Sept, September).*

Making the decision about whether to create a custom field for each discrete category (such as creating a field for each committee), or create a generic field that requires you to enter specific data (the committee name) depends on how many custom fields you need for this and other purposes. See the next section on custom fields limitations.

Custom Fields Limitations

When you open the Define Fields dialog, you see fifteen custom fields on the list. The same dialog, with the same defined fields, appears whether you open the dialog from a customer, vendor, or employee record. Enter the name of the field, and specify the list, or multiple lists, that should contain this field.

You can use all fifteen custom fields, but you cannot assign more than seven custom fields to any individual names list (Customer:Job, Vendor, or Employee).

If you assign one custom field to all three names lists, then each names list can contain another six custom fields (whether those fields are shared among lists or assigned to one list).

Using Customer Type to Track Members

The built-in Customer Type list is a convenient tool for tracking members. You can use subtypes for levels of membership. For example, Figure 15-1 shows a Customer Type List that's extremely useful for many types of nonprofit organizations.

Membership levels (subtypes) are handy if you have a variety of dues levels to differentiate among membership fees. You can produce reports filtered by subtype to generate fund raising letters or telephone calls that are designed to be of interest to each subtype.

Tracking Family Memberships

Some organizations that offer family memberships track individual family names. This gives them a way to track activities on a person-by-person basis. For example, the parents may be members of committees, and the children might participate in programs the organization offers. Tracking individual activities for the members of a family provides a couple of excellent benefits:

- You can easily create reports on the members who participate in a particular activity or program.
- You can create customized fund raising letters that are targeted to members who participate in certain activities.

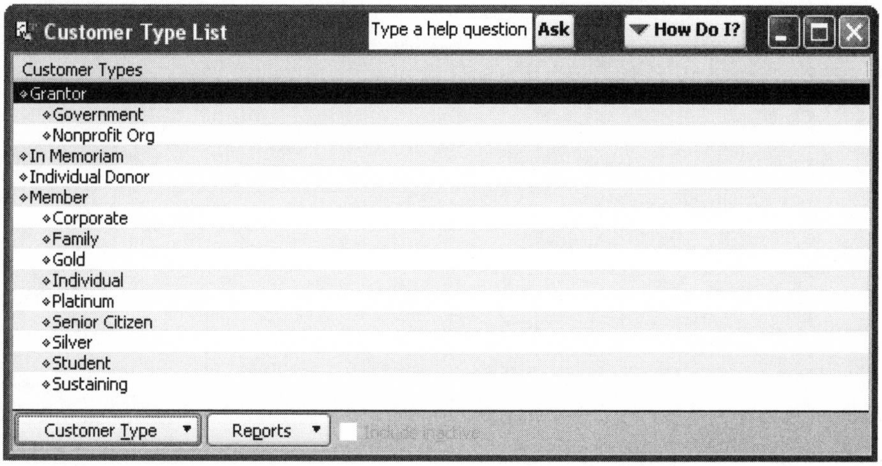

Figure 15-1: This list makes it easy to generate reports about who gives what, and why.

If you charge membership dues for each member of the family, even if you have different rates for different age groups, you should track each dues-paying family member as a customer.

If you have a family membership rate, create the family as a customer, and then create a job for each family member. When you create the job, you can enter the custom field data (such as activities, if that's what you track) that's specific to each family member. As an example, Figure 15-2 shows the Additional Info tab for a family member (a job).

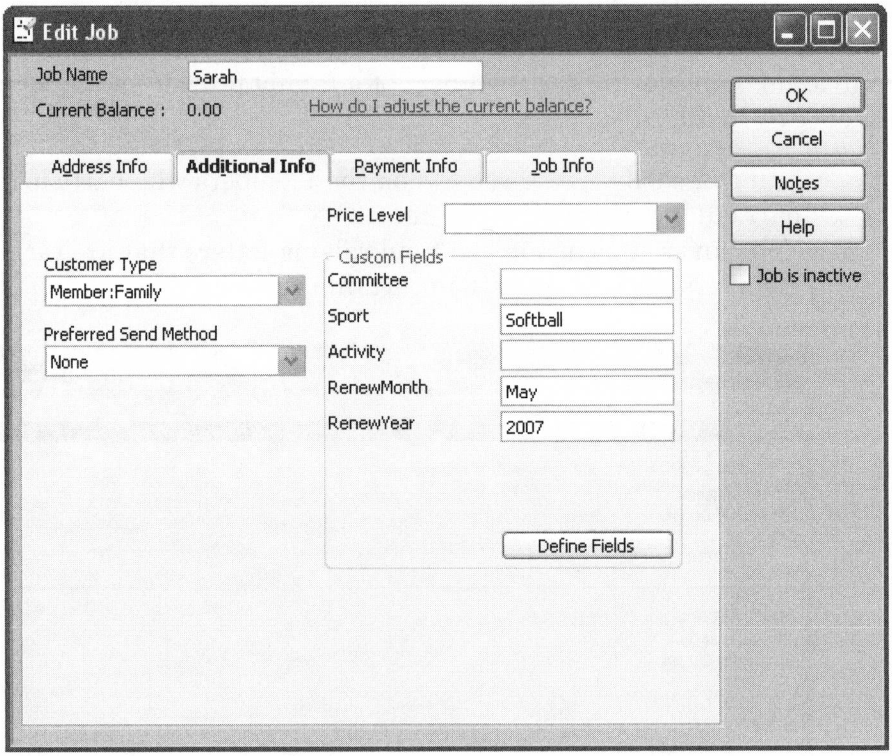

Figure 15-2: This family member has her own data, tracked as a job.

Creating Items for Memberships

The item, or multiple items, you create to track membership dues should reflect the way you charge for memberships. If you have different types of memberships, create a parent item named Membership, and then create subitems for different types of membership (Family, Individual, Corporate, and so on). Enter the rate for each subitem.

TIP: If you use subitems, don't attach a rate to the parent item—only the subitems have rates.

Make your membership items Service items, and link the items to the appropriate income account. If you're using the UCOA, use the account named Membership Dues-Individual, which is a subaccount of the Earned Revenues account. If you're not using the UCOA, create an account for membership dues if you don't have one. (Chapter 5 contains complete instructions for creating items.)

Invoicing for Membership Dues

You should send an invoice for dues at least 60 days before the dues expire. To determine who gets invoices, create a report that filters for the appropriate renewal date. If you have sliding scale membership fees that are linked to the Customer Type, be sure to include the Customer Type in the report. Use the report to create your invoices. (See the section "Generating Custom Reports on Members".)

TIP: To automate the process of sending an invoice for membership dues, be sure your customers who are members are configured for terms that match the number of days in advance you send the invoice.

Creating a Dues Template

Your invoice looks much more professional if it's a Dues template instead of a standard invoice template. The easiest way to create a Dues template is to use the Pledge template as the basis. If you're using QuickBooks Premier Nonprofit Edition, the software has a Pledge template built in. If you're using QuickBooks Pro, Chapter 6 has instructions for creating a Pledge template. Use the following steps to create a Dues template from the Pledge template:

1. Open a blank invoice form by pressing Ctrl-I.
2. Click the Customize button above the Template field to open the Customize Template dialog.
3. Select the Pledge template, and click New.
4. Name the new template Membership or Membership Dues.

Now you can begin customizing the template using the guidelines and suggestions in the following paragraphs.

Customizing the Dues Template Header

On the Header tab (see Figure 15-3), change the title of the template (Membership, Membership Dues, Dues, whatever). Then make other changes as desired.

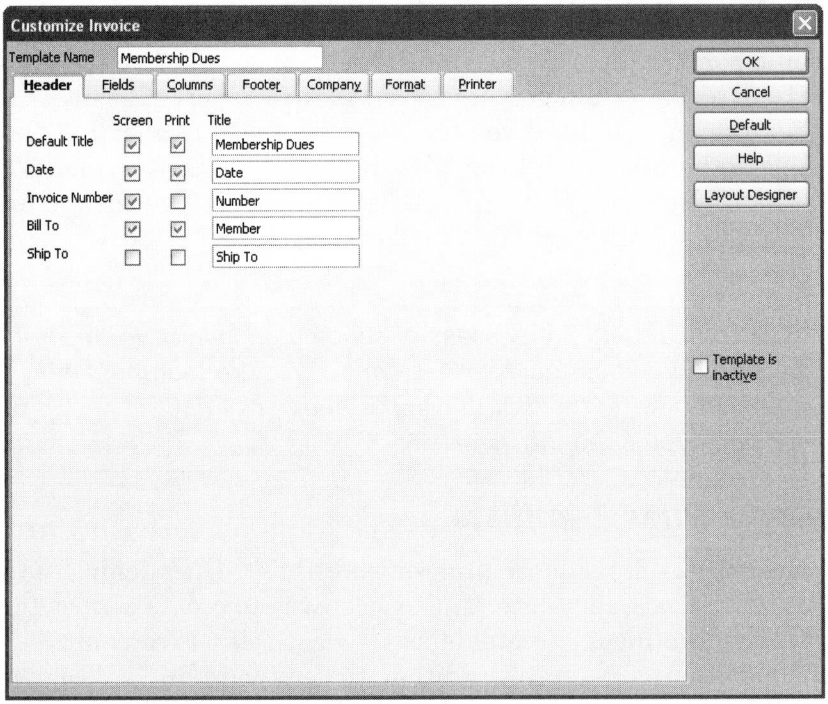

Figure 15-3: Change the text that appears on the template to reflect the new purpose.

For this template, I changed the Invoice Number text to Number (I didn't want the word "invoice" to appear), and removed the field from the printed copy. I keep the number on the screen copy for reference. (QuickBooks automatically assigns the next invoice number for the A/R account to which you post this transaction.)

I changed the title of the Bill To box (which has the Customer Name and Address data) to Member, and I eliminated the Ship To box from both the screen and printed versions.

Customizing the Dues Template Fields

On the Fields tab, most of the built-in fields are deselected, except the due date, which appears on both the screen and printed versions. If you assign membership numbers, select that field (it only appears on the printed document). You can opt to display any fields you need on either the screen, the printed document, or both.

This QuickBooks company file has customized fields for renewal month and year (see Figure 15-4), and those fields display on the screen, but not on the printed version.

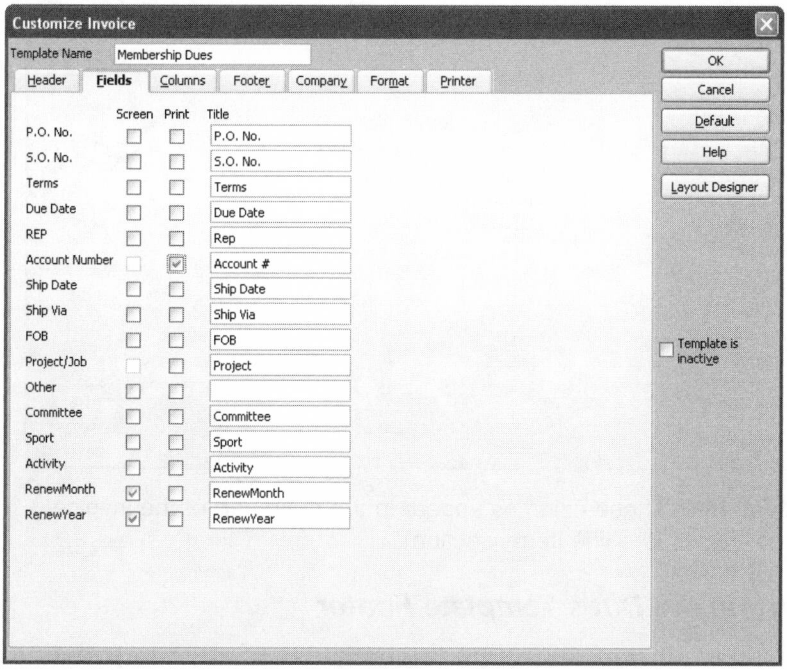

Figure 15-4: Deselect any fields that aren't needed for a membership dues invoice.

The renewal month data gives the person doing data entry a check-point for the due date that should appear on the invoice. The renewal year data ensures the data entry person won't accidentally send an invoice for a member who has paid an extra year's dues in advance.

Customizing the Dues Template Columns

On the Columns tab, seen in Figure 15-5, the needed columns appear on both the screen and printed version, except the Class column (which is for internal use only, and therefore is only on the screen version).

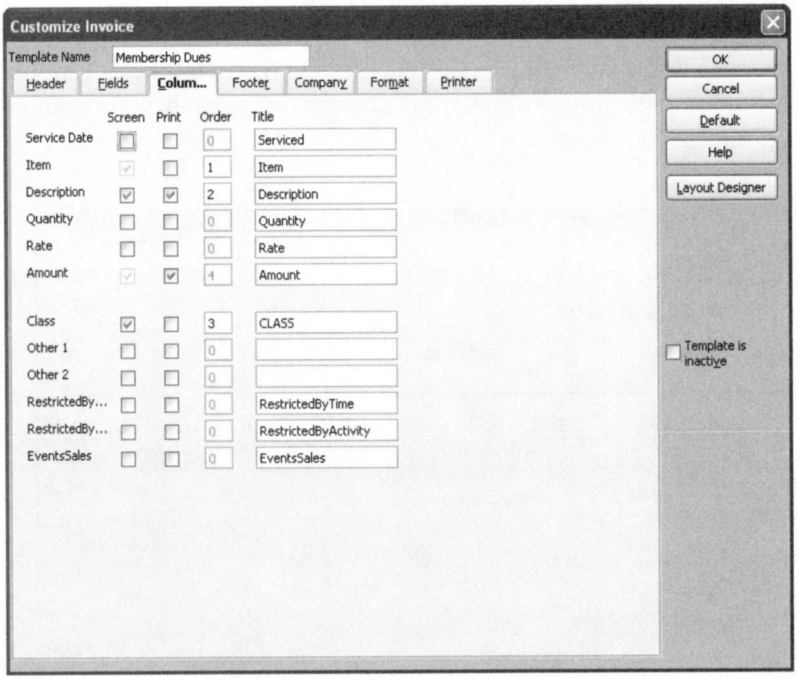

Figure 15-5: These columns appear in the main part of the invoice (the line items section).

Customizing the Dues Template Footer

On the Footer tab, you can refine the language of any component that appears on the template. For example, you might want to change the label for Customer Message to Member Message.

Using the Dues Template

When you're ready to send out invoices for membership dues, open the Create Invoices window and select your Dues template. If you've created an A/R account for dues, select that account from the drop-down list in the Account field. You can either enter the Class information in the Class field at the top of the form, or in the Class column in the line item section.

Select the first customer whose dues are due in 60 days (substitute your own interval if you don't work on a 60-days-in-advance schedule). If you've entered data for customers to match your customized fields, terms, and so on, all the data required for the header section of the invoice is filled in automatically. If not, you have to enter data that's missing, or wrong.

Enter the membership item that's appropriate in the line item section of the invoice. Unfortunately, if you have a sliding-scale membership structure, based on membership type, you can't include the Customer Type information on a template. However, that information should be on the report you generated for sending invoices. The resulting invoice should look like the invoice in Figure 15-6.

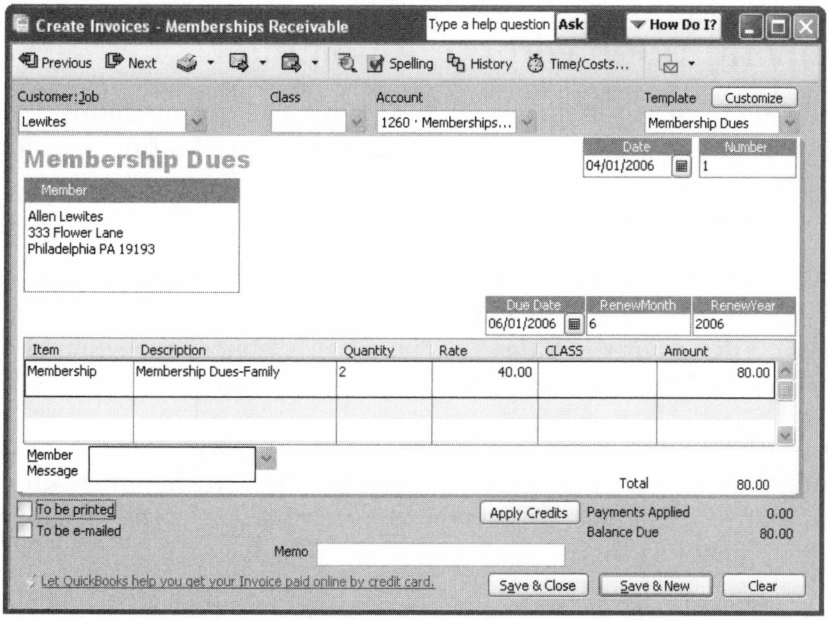

Figure 15-6: The Dues template has everything you need to send an invoice for membership dues.

Adjusting Member Records after Payment

If you're tracking membership renewal dates in custom fields, after you process the payment for the invoice, you must open the customer record and change the data to reflect the new renewal dates.

If you've created separate custom fields for the month and the year, you only have to change the data in the year field if the customer pays on time. If the customer is late, you can change the month field to reflect the month in which you received the payment (depending on the your policies for this situation).

WARNING: When you select the customer in the Receive Payments window, if no invoices appear check the account in the A/R Account field at the top of the window. You must select the A/R Account to which you posted the membership dues invoice.

Receiving Dues without Invoicing

It's common to collect membership dues without sending an invoice first. Membership dues are frequently paid as the result of a fund raisers (events or letters), when people show up to enroll in a program, or in any number of other ways.

When you receive money that isn't an invoice payment, you process it in QuickBooks as a sales receipt (choose Customers → Enter Sales Receipts). Filling out the Sales Receipt form is almost the same as filling out an invoice. You must enter the customer and the item.

As with membership dues, it's a good idea to have a special template for Dues that are received as sales receipts. You can customize an existing template for this purpose, using the instructions in the previous section about customizing invoices.

If you're using QuickBooks Premier Nonprofit Edition, use the Intuit Standard Donation template as the basis of your new Dues template.

If you're using QuickBooks Pro, you can create a Donation template or a Dues Template (or both). Instructions for creating a Donation template to match the one in Premier Nonprofit Edition are in Chapter 6.

Generating Custom Reports on Members

After you've determined the type of information you want to track about your membership, and you've entered information in the fields (including custom fields), you can create customized reports that match the information you need. Customizing a report involves two tasks:

- Selecting the information you want
- Sorting the information to match your needs

For example, the following section describes a method of building a report on committee members for a specific committee, which you can give to the committee chair. I'm using this example because it involves custom fields, and is therefore a bit more complicated. The process described is the same for any customization you want to perform.

In this example, I'm building a report of the membership in the Finance Committee. The Customer:Job list includes a custom field named Committee. As members joined committees, the appropriate committee name was placed in their customer records.

Choose Reports → List → Customer Contact List, which is a report that provides an excellent starting place for customized reports on customers. When the report window opens, click Modify Report. A modify dialog opens with the Display tab in the foreground, as seen in Figure 15-7.

In the Columns list, deselect and select the fields to match the information you need. For this report, you probably only need the Phone and Bill To columns (the Bill To data includes first and last names, and the address).

Move to the Filters tab, and select the field in the Filter list that holds the data you need for this report (in this case, Committee). Enter the text you need to match in the text box (in this case Finance), and press the Tab key to move the selection to the Current Filter Choices list (see Figure 15-8).

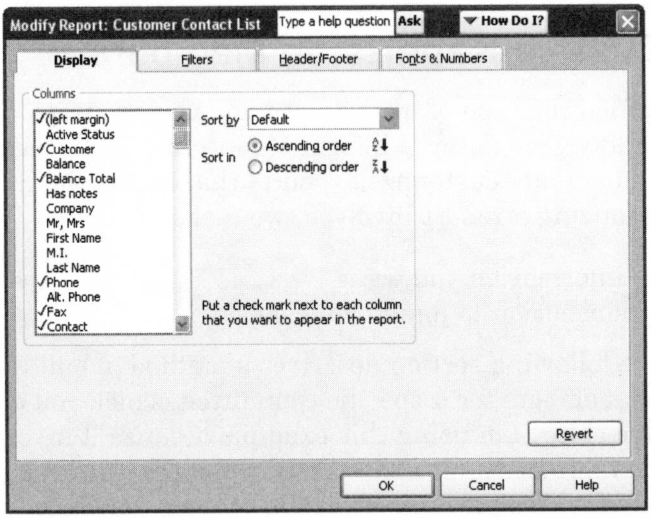

Figure 15-7: Begin customizing a report by selecting the data to display.

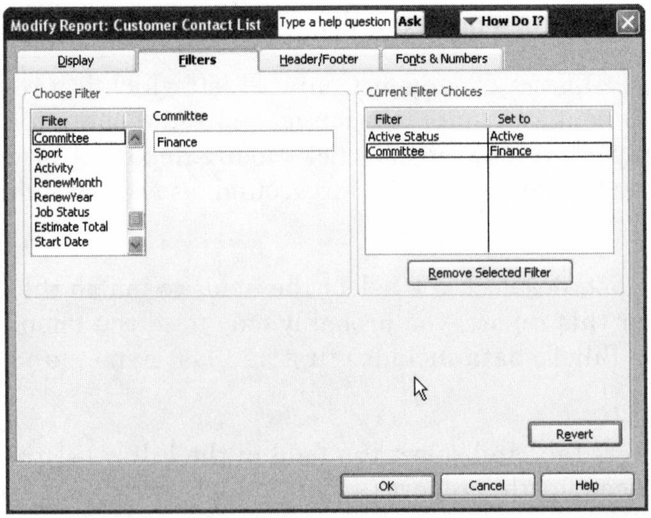

Figure 15-8: Specify the selection criteria for the report.

By default, QuickBooks sets the status to Active, but you can remove that if you're tracking inactive members and want to include them in your report.

In the Header/Footer tab, change the report title to create an appropriate title (see Figure 15-9). You can also deselect any fields that don't have to appear on the report.

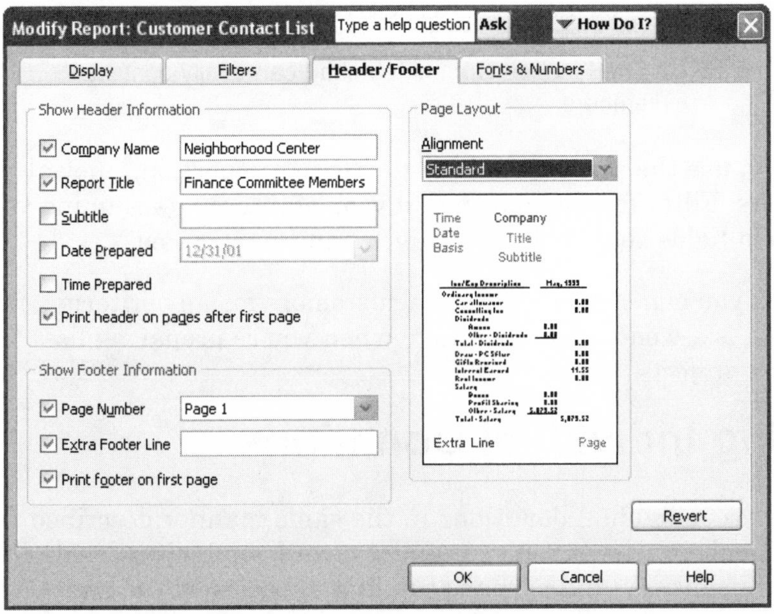

Figure 15-9: Title the report to indicate its contents.

Click OK when you've finished setting the criteria. All the records that match your criteria are displayed in the window (see Figure 15-10). You can print the report and give it to the appropriate person.

Click the Memorize button and give the report an appropriate name. QuickBooks uses the report title you entered as the default report name, and that's usually a good choice.

Remember that the data that's displayed isn't memorized; only the settings are. The report is generated with current data every time you select it from the Memorized Reports menu.

Figure 15-10: The Finance Committee chair can easily contact members.

You can use the same technique to create a report on renewal dates for members. Filter for the month and year of interest (assuming you have custom fields such as RenewMonth and RenewYear).

In fact, you can create reports on customers for any criteria you need, which is a wonderful advantage when you're preparing lists for fundraising projects.

Tracking Individual Donations

You can track individual donations in the same manner described for tracking memberships. If you're keeping records on both individual donors and members (and perhaps funding agencies, government agencies, and other entities from which you receive funds), dedicate the use of the Type field to distinguish these entities.

Refer to the discussion about using fields creatively in the previous section to establish a way to track individual donations. For example, you may want to use a field to track donations by categories, such as memorials, special occasions, or any other category. For memorials or other date-driven categories, use a custom field to record the date of the special occasion, so you can send fund raising letters on the anniversary of the occasion.

When you receive a donation for which no invoice exists, it's the equivalent of a cash sale in the for-profit world. To record the donation, choose Customers → Enter Sales Receipts to open the Sales Receipt window.

- In QuickBooks Premier Nonprofit edition, select the Donation template.
- In QuickBooks Pro, choose the Donation template if you created one. Otherwise, use the standard Sales Receipt template. (Chapter 5 has instructions for creating a Donation template.)

You should print and send a receipt to the donor, who may need it to take a tax deduction. Use the Customer Message field to add a note of thanks, a reminder that the donation is tax-deductible, or both.

Creating Fundraising Mailings

QuickBooks has a built-in feature that lets you send letters to customers. You can send a letter that's been supplied by QuickBooks, modify an existing QuickBooks letter, or create your own letter. The mail merge feature in Microsoft Word (which must be installed on your computer) takes care of creating the individual letters.

Unfortunately, the QuickBooks mail merge feature doesn't work well for many nonprofits. You can't select customers by any criteria except Active, Inactive, or Both. If your customer list includes foundations, government agencies, members, individual donors, and other assorted types of customers, your fundraising letters may not be suitable for all of those customer types.

However, if your customer list has only a handful of foundations and other grant-giving entities, you can deselect those names when you create fundraising mailings that are targeted to individual donors and members.

For sending fundraising mailings to a specialized list, you can create a QuickBooks report that filters for your criteria, and then create the mailing outside of QuickBooks. (See the section "Creating a Mailing Outside of QuickBooks".)

Using QuickBooks to Create a Mailing

QuickBooks provides a wizard to help you create letters for customers (and for other lists, too). The wizard uses built-in letter templates that are in the folder that holds your QuickBooks software.

Using a QuickBooks Letter Template

If you're running QuickBooks Premier Nonprofit Edition, the template list includes a nonprofit fundraising letter. (If you're running QuickBooks Pro, you can create a fundraising letter.) The built-in nonprofit fundraising letter is unlikely to be suitable, so even if you're running QuickBooks Premier Nonprofit Edition, you'll want to create your own document.

In the following sections, I'll go over the steps for creating a fundraising letter out of a QuickBooks template. Then, after your own letter is added to the list of predesigned QuickBooks letters, I'll explain how to use the wizard to create your fundraising mailing.

Editing a QuickBooks Letter Template

You can edit any of the QuickBooks letter templates to create your fundraising letter, or you can create one from scratch. Creating a mail merge letter from scratch requires some expertise with creating field codes and designing mail merge documents. If you use a QuickBooks template, the fields and codes are available in the document.

To edit a template, choose Customers → Customer Letters With Envelopes → Customize Letter Templates. In the first wizard window, select View Or Edit Existing Letter Templates. Then click Next and choose Blank Customer Letter.

If you're running QuickBooks Premier Nonprofit Edition, you could choose Nonprofit Fundraising Letter, but I'm so sure you'd replace almost all of the text that I'm suggesting you use the blank letter template. However, you should try the fundraising letter, in case you think it's partially suitable, and therefore easier than composing a new document.

When you click Next, Word opens and loads the Blank Customer Letter template (see Figure 15-11). The QuickBooks fields toolbar is in the window, and you can use it to add fields to the letter if you're comfortable with mail merge features. However, the fields required for a letter to customers are already in the document, so you probably don't have to add more.

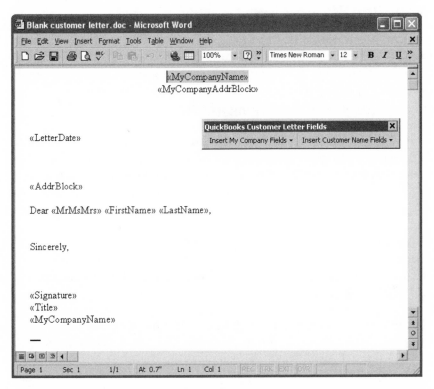

Figure 15-11: The needed codes are preloaded in the document, so all you have to do is write the text.

Place your cursor after the line that has the salutation codes, and create your fundraising letter. When you finish composing the letter, choose File → Save As and save the letter with an appropriate filename. An efficient file naming scheme is to use the format *Filename-Date*, such as Fundraiser-March2005. By default, Word saves the letter in the Customer Letters subfolder of the QuickBooks letter template folder, which is where you want it to be so its listing is available when you use the wizard to create your mailing.

Close Word to return to the Letters and Envelopes Wizard, which is asking if you want to use your new letter now (click Template), or wait until later (click Cancel). I'm assuming you're ready to use your new letter, so I'll go over the tasks in the following section.

Creating the Mailing

Click Template to move to the next wizard window, which asks you to specify the criteria for displaying customer names. You can select Active, Inactive, or Both. Also specify whether you want to select customer names or job names (in case the letter is going to the contacts for specific grants or contracts you're tracking as jobs).

Select the names you want to include in the mailing. By default, QuickBooks selects all the entries in your list. If the number of recipients you want to exclude isn't too great, scroll through the list and deselect them. On the other hand, if you're sending the letter to a small group, click Unmark All, and then click the names of the recipients you need.

Click Next to move to the next wizard window, which asks you to select the letter you want to use for this mailing. Select the letter you created, and click Next.

Enter the name and title of the person whose signature appears on the letters for this mailing. Then click Next to open Word with the mail merge document loaded in the software window.

If your customer records don't contain data for all the fields in the letter, (salutations, names, addresses, ZIP codes, and so on), a dialog appears, informing you of that fact. You can either cancel the letter printing and check all your customers to fill in missing information, or, if you're only printing a few letters, fill in the information manually on each letter in the document. However, if you don't go back to the customer records, the next time you write letters you'll face the same problem.

All of your letters are displayed in a single document in the Word software window. Here are some guidelines for using this mail merge document:

- There's a page break at the end of each individual letter.
- If you want to make a change in the text, you must change each individual letter.
- Changes you make to the text are not saved back to the original QuickBooks letter.

When everything is the way you want it you can either print the letters, or save the document and print it later. Return to QuickBooks, where you can move to the next step, which is to set up envelopes. Select the specifications for the envelope, and click OK.

If you already have labels for your customers, you can cancel the envelope printing. In fact, if you have a printer that requires you to hand-feed envelopes, and you have a substantial number of letters, envelopes are a pain.

If you click OK on the Envelope Options dialog, you're returned to Word to set up the envelope printing. Print the envelopes, close Word and return to QuickBooks. Click Cancel on the last wizard window to finish your work.

Creating Mailing Labels

You can create mailing labels within QuickBooks, by choosing File → Print Forms → Mailing Labels to open the Select Mailing Labels To Print dialog. Use the following guidelines to prepare the mailing labels.

- If your mailing is going to all the customers in your customer list, select All Customers/Jobs from the drop-down list in the Name field. A separate label is created for each job, in addition to a label for each customer.
- If your mailing is going to selected customers, choose Selected Names from the drop-down list in the Name field. All names from all lists (customers, vendors, and other names) are displayed without any indication of the list they came from, so you have to know the names you need, and select them.
- If you used the Customer Type list to specify different types of customers, and a customer type matches the target recipients of the mailing, choose Selected Customer Type from the drop-down

list in the Customer Type field. Then choose the customer type(s) for this mailing.

- If you want to send the mailing to only certain zip codes, enter as much of the zip code as you need to filter the zip codes. For example, to send a mailing only to those customers who live in Philadelphia, enter 191. To send a mailing to customers in the Philadelphia area, including suburbs, enter 19. To include any suburban areas with zip codes that start with 18, you must create a separate run of mailing labels.
- If you're doing a large mailing, and you're not using the labels to send personalized mail-merge letters, select the option to sort by zip code (otherwise, the labels are sorted by name).

- If these labels are for a mail-merge mailing, the names are on each letter and must be matched to the label, so you have to sort by name to save your sanity.

Click OK to open the Print dialog and select the printer that has the mailing labels. Also indicate the mailing labels you're using, such as Avery 5160.

Creating a Mailing Outside of QuickBooks

The problem with creating a mailing within QuickBooks is that you can't filter recipients by any criteria. For example, you can't select donors who have total contributions in excess of a certain amount, or donors who have failed to send donations within the past six months.

However, you can select names by customizing a QuickBooks report that reflects the criteria you need. Then send the report to Excel, and create the mail merge document in Excel and Word.

> **TIP**: When you customize the report, make sure you select all the fields connected to customer names— the honorific, the names, and the addresses.

It's beyond the scope of this book to go over the steps for creating mail merge documents in Microsoft Office. However, the basic steps are to create your list in Excel or Word. Then use Word to create and insert the codes, and create the letters.

Managing Volunteers

Volunteers are always helpful, but most nonprofit organizations count on volunteers the most when they're planning a fundraising event. Whether your fundraising event is a mailing, a bake sale, or a major fete, volunteers can help plan, organize, and run the event.

WARNING: If a volunteer provides a required service that you'd ordinarily pay for (such as a volunteer lawyer, accountant, computer consultant, etc.) you must track the volunteer's time as an in-kind service. See Chapter 16 to learn about the rules and methods for in-kind contributions.

You can track your volunteers in QuickBooks (if the number of volunteers, combined with the number of other names, doesn't endanger your file by coming too close to the QuickBooks limits).

It's best to use the Other Names list for tracking volunteers, because it keeps them separate from customers and vendors. However, the Other Names list isn't very configurable (you can't create types or custom fields), so it may not work well if you want to keep detailed information about your volunteers. In that case, use the Customer List, and make Volunteer a customer type.

Another problem arises when you want to track a volunteer who is also a member or a donor. All names in QuickBooks must be unique—you cannot use the same name for both a Customer and an Other Name. You can get around this by changing the name slightly when you create your donor/volunteer in the Other Names List. For example, if the Customer name is Ivens-Kathy, you can use Ivens-K or Kathy Ivens for the Other Names List.

Tracking Volunteers as Other Names

To create entries in the Other Names List, choose Lists → Other Names List to open the Other Names List window. Then press Ctrl-N to open a blank New Name record, as seen in Figure 15-12.

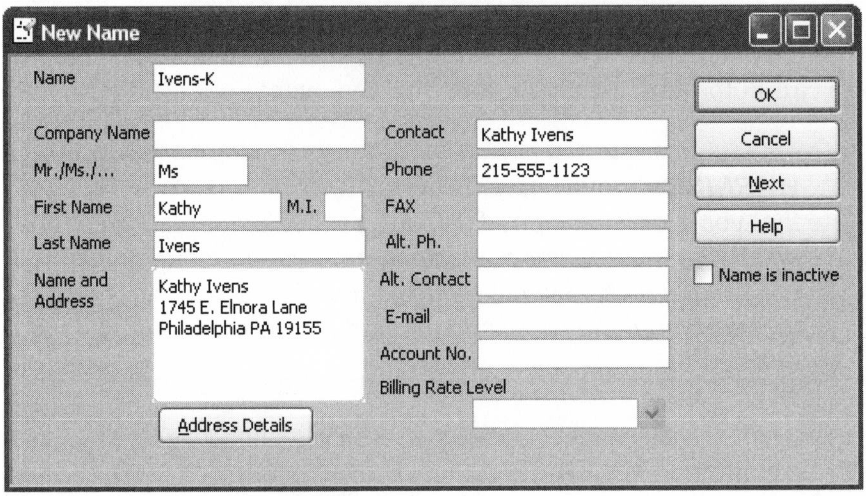

Figure 15-12: The Other Names dialog is less complicated than the Customer dialog.

The basic information you need about a volunteer is usually limited to the name, address, and telephone number. However, you may want to track the type of work a volunteer does, or the days the volunteer does the work.

Because you can't add custom fields to the Other Names records, you're limited to the few existing fields, as long as you're not using them for their intended purpose. For example, you have a choice between using the FAX field for a fax number or for some criterion you want to track.

Most of the time, I use the Contact and Alt. Contact fields, which are intended to track names in a company. Since volunteers are individuals instead of companies, you don't need the company-related fields for company information.

For example, you can use the Contact field to enter a description of the volunteer's work. Some of the descriptions I've used include Repairs, Cleaning, Docent, Guide, GiftShop, Coach, and Parking. Your own use of volunteers and the type of volunteer work that goes on in your organization determines the descriptions you use. Remember to be consistent about entering text so you can produce accurate reports.

You can use the Alt.Contact field to track the frequency of the volunteer's work, such as Weekly or Monthly. If you need to track more information about the schedule, use additional fields for that data.

For example, you can use the FAX field for Weekly volunteers to track the weekdays worked, as long as you use a consistent formula. I've found the following formula to be the most effective:

XXXXXXX, where the first X is Monday and each following X is the rest of the week. Each of the volunteer's days replaces one of the seven X's. For example, for a volunteer who works every Monday, enter Mxxxxxx. For a volunteer who works Mondays and Thursdays, enter MxxTxxx.

For Monthly volunteers who show up on the same date each month, use another field (such as Alt.Phone) to track the date. Just enter the appropriate number such as 1 or 15. For monthly volunteers who show up on a specific day of the week, use a different field (such as Account No) and enter FirstMonday, or ThirdThursday. Remember to be consistent about the data entry (for example, in this case spaces are always omitted).

As with customers, when you edit an Other Names listing, a Notes button appears on the dialog. You can use the notes field for comments, or dated reminders.

Tracking Volunteers as Customers

If your Customer:Job list is rather small and uncomplicated, and you're not tracking a lot of data categories, you can use the list to track volunteers. This lets you include volunteers when you send fundraising letters.

Create a Customer Type for volunteers, and use custom fields to track other information you want to catalog. If you have an existing customer (a donor or a member) who is also a volunteer, create two listings for that person. In that case, I've found it effective to put special characters in front of the data in the Name field for volunteer listings, such as a number, and then make the rest of the information the same as that of the customer listing.

For example, volunteer names could all start with 01*name*. This means the donor/member named Ivens-K becomes 01Ivens-K. All other basic information (address, telephone, etc.) remains the same, but the fields you use to track details, such as the Type field, differ. This paradigm makes it easy to create reports about customers, and customize the reports to exclude volunteers (or, include only volunteers).

Tracking Fundraising Activities

You have to keep accurate records on your fundraising activities, and the more detailed the record keeping, the more information you gain about what works well and what doesn't. To track fundraising activities properly you need a class, income account(s), and items.

Fundraising Class

You must have a fundraising class, which you use for expenses, and allocation transactions for time or money spent on fundraising activities.

When you spend money on fundraising activities (printing, purchase of items for resale, supplies, food, caterers, facilities rental, etc.) link the expense to the fund raising class.

Fundraising Income Accounts

Essentially, all the income accounts in your chart of accounts are fundraising accounts. Grants, contracts, membership dues, tuition, fees for programs, and all the other types of income could be considered fundraising.

You should, however, have specific income accounts that match your fundraising activities. For example, you might need an income account named Special Events. You can create that account as a parent account, or as a subaccount under the parent account named Earned Revenues.

Your definition of special events could include real events (such as dinners or fairs), as well as other specific fundraising activities such as an annual mailing for contributions.

In addition, if you sell products to raise funds, create a Product Sales account (or subaccount). In addition to an income account, product sales require the following additional configuration items (all discussed in the following sections):

- Items for products.
- A cost of goods account.
- Sales tax items (depending on the products you sell and the state in which you operate).

Fundraising Items

In order to create an income transaction (either an invoice or a sales receipt), you must have an item to enter in the line item section of the transaction window.

Your fundraising items should reflect your fundraising activities, and you can use item reports to see detailed information about the success of a fund raising activity.

You probably have items for grants, contracts, individual contributions, etc. and each is attached to an income account that matches that type of income. However, you need items for other types of fundraising you engage in. Here are some guidelines for creating other fundraising items:

- Special Events items. These should be of the type Service, and linked to an income account for special events.
- Advertising items (for publications or dinner programs). These should be of the type Service, and linked to an income account for advertising.

- Product items. This should be of the type Non-inventory Part and linked to an income account for sales of products.

If you sell products, you can create an item for each product, or create an item named Product Sales and create subitems for each specific product. If you don't have products for fundraising, you should consider this revenue stream. Some nonprofits sell products at a sales counter in the organization's office, and other nonprofits sell products at community fairs or other special events.

Many nonprofits sell T-shirts, publications, sports equipment, food (including running a lunch counter, or selling boxed lunches), and other products. I've seen publications for sale such as restaurant guides (with reviews, recipes, and even ads from restaurants that produce additional revenue).

Sales Tax Items

If you sell products, your state tax laws may require you to collect sales tax from the buyer and remit it to the state. Sales tax can be complicated, because some states have multiple sales tax rates, one for the state in which your organization resides, and an additional tax for the city or county in which the sale is made.

You need to apply to your state for a license to collect sales tax, and then set up QuickBooks to track taxable sales and remit the collected tax to the appropriate tax agencies.

All the permutations and combinations for creating sales tax items are beyond the scope of this book, but a good discussion of sales tax issues is available at www.cpa911.com. Click the link QuickBooks Tips on the left side of the home page and select the article titled Understanding Sales Tax in QuickBooks.

Fund Raising Expenses

You need to track the money you spend on fund raising activities. This means that all disbursements for fund raising should be posted to appropriate expense accounts, and linked to the Fundraising class.

You can create a parent account for fundraising expenses and create subaccounts for specific expense types. If you sell products, your expenses are the cost of the goods you sell, and you can either create a cost of goods account for this expense, or use an expense account (check with your accountant).

Job Costing for Fund Raising Events

If you can create a report that shows the amount a specific fund raising activity generated, along with its attendant costs, it's easy to analyze the fund raising events that work best. Then, you can plan your fund raising for the most profitable types of activities.

An easy way to accomplish this is to set up a customer for fundraising activities, and then create a job for each fundraising event. Post each transaction to the appropriate job, and link transactions to your fund raising class. The transactions include receipt of income, expenses, and allocations made in journal entries.

To gain more insight, create Job Type categories (dinners, mailings, raffles, flea markets, etc.) so you can also analyze your fund raising by category. After a while, you'll see patterns of fundraising success, which gives you a more efficient way to plan events.

Reporting on Fundraising Activities

Periodically, run a report on your fundraising activities so you can see what's working well and what isn't.

Reporting Fundraising Activity by Class

The easiest way to get an overall view is to open the Class List, select the fundraising class, and press Ctrl-Q to get a Class QuickReport (see Figure 15-13).

If you have multiple fundraising classes, you can customize a standard Profit & Loss report to show all your fundraising classes. Use the following steps to accomplish this:

1. Choose Reports → Company & Financial → Profit & Loss By Class.
2. Click Modify Report and move to the Filters tab.
3. Select Class in the Filter list, and then choose Multiple Classes in the drop-down list (it's near the top of the list).
4. In the Select Class dialog, put a check mark next to each fundraising class.
5. Click OK to return to the Modify Report dialog, and click OK again to view the modified report.

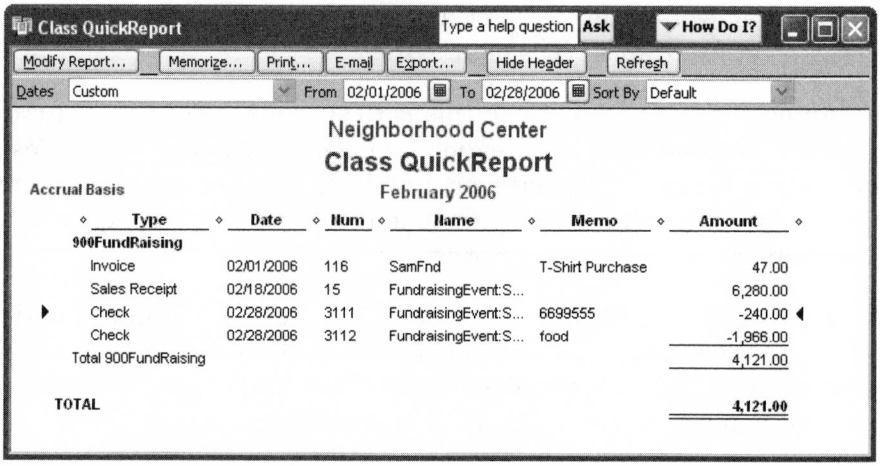

Figure 15-13: A fundraising class QuickReport shows you the activity for the selected period.

The report displays total income per class, and all expenses linked to each class including disbursements and allocations. Memorize the report so you don't have to create it from scratch each time you want to see this information.

Reporting Fundraising Activity by Customer & Job

If you've set up a fundraising customer and jobs for each event, you can create a report on the event by following these steps:

1. Choose Reports → Jobs, Time & Mileage → Profit & Loss By Job.
2. Click Modify Report and move to the Filters tab.

3. Select Name in the Filters list, and then select the job.
4. Click OK.

The report displays all the transactions connected to the job, and calculates the net (see Figure 15-14).

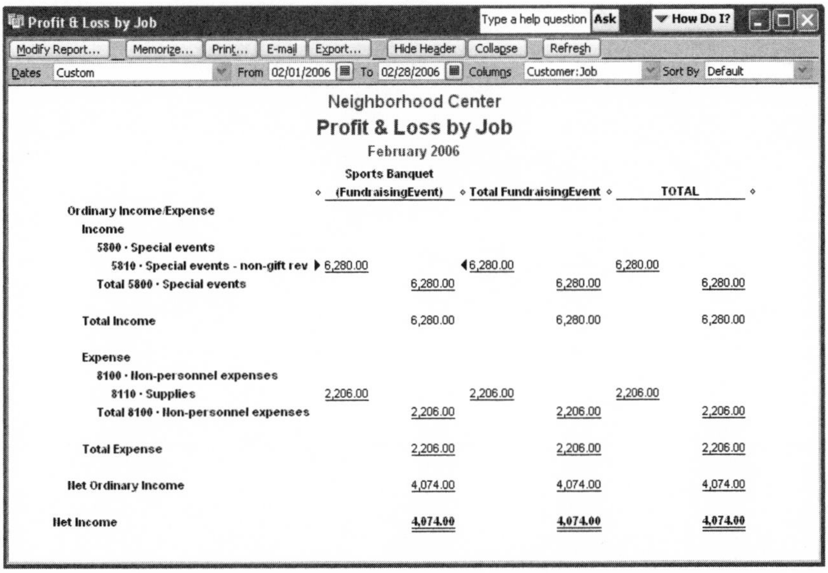

Figure 15-14: This report shows the net received income from the annual sports banquet.

If you want to see a report on all events, in the Filters tab select the customer name instead of the cob name.

If you used job types to categorize your fundraising events, in the Filters tab select Job Type in the Filters list, and then select the job type for the report.

As you can see, the more details you configure when you set up your QuickBooks company file, the more precisely you can track fundraising activities.

Chapter 16

In-Kind (Non-Cash) Revenue

Tracking in-kind transactions

Most nonprofits receive in-kind donations in one form or another. When an in-kind donation is accepted you have to enter it in QuickBooks, and acknowledge the donation to the donor.

Neither of these tasks is as straightforward or simple as it may appear, and there are a lot of rabbit holes you can fall through in the process. This chapter offers some general guidelines for managing in-kind donations, but you must check with your accountant before you do anything about an in-kind donation.

Types of In-Kind Donations

In-kind donations come in a variety of "flavors", and they're useful because they provide a way to receive contributions from donors that might not be able to (or want to) write a check. The following types of donations are frequently received by small nonprofits:

- Donated goods for the nonprofit's own use (such as furniture, computers, vehicles, office supplies, etc.).
- Donated goods that the nonprofit can sell.
- Donated professional services that save the nonprofit the cost of hiring a professional to perform the services (such as accounting, legal, or consulting services).
- Donated facilities that save the nonprofit the cost of renting the facilities.

Policies for In-Kind Donations

Every nonprofit organization should have a written policy for the way in-kind donations are managed. The policy is for internal use, although you can use it (or amend it) to inform donors of your standards. At minimum, the topics discussed in this section should be covered in the policy, and your accountant may want you to include additional topics.

Donor Responsibilities

Donors should ask before delivering goods. Nonprofits don't have to take anything that's offered, and you shouldn't take in-kind donations that you can't use and can't easily sell.

For most items (see the section "Cars, Boats and Planes for Resale" for exceptions), you should ask the donor to provide a written statement of the market value of the in-kind contribution. Your organization should not set a value on the donation. You may accept the donor's value for your own accounting purposes, or you may decide to assign a different value after you've done some research.

Donated professional services should only be accepted from a donor who is in business as a professional. For example, a schoolteacher who knows a lot about plumbing cannot donate services as a plumber.

Your organization should acknowledge the in-kind donation without getting involved in the tax ramifications (see the section, "Acknowledging In-Kind Donations").

Acknowledging In-Kind Donations

An acknowledgement is a thank you, it is not an official tax document for the donor, nor should your organization participate in assisting the donor's tax deduction efforts.

(The exception to this philosophy is when a donor provides a car, boat, or plane that you're expected to sell to gain the revenue. In that case you are required by law to assist the donor's tax deduction efforts. See the section "Cars, Boats, and Planes for Resale", later in this chapter.)

The value of the donated article and the tax consequences of a donation to a nonprofit organization are the donor's responsibility (and the donor's accountant's responsibility).

I've seen a number of creative ways in which nonprofit organizations send acknowledgements that are designed to keep them from becoming involved in donor-IRS disputes.

For inexpensive goods, some nonprofits send acknowledgements that mention the donation, but do not have any value mentioned in the acknowledgement note. The following acknowledgement text is an example of a warm thank you that doesn't mention value:

"Thank you for your gift of an answering machine to *<Name of Organization>*. This gift will help our staff be more productive. Please consult your tax advisor for any possible benefit to you for your contribution of the answering machine, which you delivered to us on *<Date of Delivery>*."

If the donor responds with a request for a value determination, the nonprofit returns a boilerplate document that explains that market value is determined by the donor, and the nonprofit is not in a position to set or confirm the market value that the donor declared. Some nonprofits attach the boilerplate document to the original acknowledgement note.

If the donation is for goods that you're going to sell or use in a fundraising event (except for cars, boats, and planes as discussed in the previous section), the text changes to reflect that fact, as follows:

"Thank you for your gift of a computer to *<Name of Organization>*. This gift will help make our upcoming auction fundraiser a great success. Please consult your tax advisor for any possible benefit to you for your contribution of the computer, which you delivered to us on *<Date of Delivery>*."

If your organization has a policy of mentioning the amount in the acknowledgement, be sure to indicate the fact that the amount was declared by the donor, and is not "certified" by your organization.

"Thank you for your gift of a computer to *<Name of Organization>*, which you stated has a value of $600.00. This gift will help our staff be more productive. Please consult your tax advisor for any possible benefit to you for your contribution of the computer, which you delivered to us on *<Date of Delivery>*."

If the gift is in-kind services, there shouldn't be any request for a valuation, because donated services aren't deductible (although out of pocket expenses involved in making the donation might be deductible, but they are usually considered ordinary business expenses by the IRS and don't need confirmation by the nonprofit organization).

Tracking In-Kind Transactions in QuickBooks

You should record all in-kind transactions in QuickBooks. The transaction is a journal entry, and the accounts you use depend on how your accountant wants you to differentiate between in-kind donations used by your organization and those sold for fundraising.

Setting Up Accounts for In-Kind Transactions

You need at least one income and one expense account for in-kind donations. The easiest way to set up QuickBooks accounts for in-kind transaction entry is to create the following accounts:

- An income account named In-Kind Goods and Services (or Non-cash Goods and Services).
- An expense account named Donated Goods and Services.

You can use the memo field in the journal entry to track details, such as whether the in-kind donation is goods or services.

Your accountant may want you to differentiate among the types of in-kind donations you receive. To separate income accounts by the type of in-kind donation, set up a discrete income account for each type, and a matching expense account for the offset posting.

If you're using the UCOA, a number of accounts exist for this purpose, but most nonprofit organizations use the following accounts (which you can create if you're not using the UCOA):

- **4110 Donated Pro Services** (Income account). Use this account for donated professional services (services donated by a professional in business to supply these services).
- **4130 Gifts In Kind-Goods** (Income account). Use this account for donated goods.
- **4150 Donated Facilities** (Income account). Use this account for donated facilities, such as a banquet hall or auditorium.

- **7580 Donated Pro Services** (Expense Account). Use this account as the offset account when receiving in-kind professional services.
- **8120 Donated Materials & Supplies** (Expense Account). Use this account as the offset account when receiving in-kind goods.
- **8280 Donated Facilities** (Expense Account). Use this account as the offset account when receiving in-kind donations of facilities.

Some accountants prefer to track certain types of in-kind goods (furniture, equipment, and vehicles) in asset accounts instead of expense accounts. If your accountant wants to use asset accounts, create the following accounts using the account type Other Current Asset.

- For goods that you accept for resale, create an account of the type Other Current Asset and name it Assets Held For Sale (or something similar).
- For goods that are kept for your organization's use, you can handle the transaction with the existing Fixed Asset accounts. For example, if you receive furniture, use the Furniture & Fixtures Fixed Asset account; if it's a computer use the Equipment Fixed Asset account; and if it's a vehicle use the Vehicle Fixed Asset account. (You can depreciate the fixed assets.)

Most accountants set a minimum value for in-kind goods that are posted to Fixed Asset accounts instead of expense accounts. The minimum value is usually $500, but your accountant may set a different threshold. Donated items with a value lower than the minimum are tracked with the Expense account(s) mentioned earlier in this section.

Creating In-Kind Transactions

It's common to use a journal entry to record in-kind donations. You could use a sales transaction (such as a sales receipt using a Donor Template), but that requires you to set up an item, or multiple items. A journal entry is easier.

In the following sections, I'm providing instructions for linking transaction lines in the JE to classes. These instructions represent common methods for linking the transactions to programs.

It's quite possible you should be using different classes than those mentioned here in your transactions, and you must check with your accountant before creating these journal entries.

In-Kind Goods Used by the Organization

If you received goods that you're going to use in your organization, the accounts you use in the journal entry depend on whether you're posting the goods to an asset account or an income account.

Before you can enter the transaction, you must determine the value of the in-kind donation of goods. You can use the value set by the donor, or set a different value (depending on the policies of your organization).

If your accountant hasn't instructed you to post goods that can be defined as fixed assets to an asset account, or if the item is below the minimum threshold set by your accountant, create the following journal entry:

- Credit the appropriate Income account.
- Debit the appropriate Expense account.
- Enter a note in the memo field of both lines to track the details (e.g. Scanner from Amy Jones).
- If the donor indicated a program as the beneficiary of the goods, link both lines to that program. If not, link the income account line to the Unrestricted Funds class and the expense account line to the Administration class.

If the goods can be defined as fixed assets, and your accountant wants you to post them to your fixed assets accounts, enter the following journal entry:

- Debit the appropriate Fixed Asset account.
- Credit the appropriate Income account.
- Enter a note in the memo field of both lines to track the details (e.g. computer from Ray Smith).
- If the donor indicated a program as the beneficiary of the goods, link the income line to that class. If not, link the income line to the Unrestricted Funds class.

Program/class tracking reports only use the data from income and expense accounts, so it's not mandatory to link a class to the asset account, because it's a balance sheet account.

In-Kind Goods for Resale

If you receive in-kind goods that you're going to sell, you have two journal entries. The first journal entry receives the goods, and the second journal entry disposes of them after you've sold or awarded them.

If your accountant has not recommended the use of an asset account for in-kind goods that are received for resale, make the following journal entry when you receive the goods:

- Credit the appropriate Income account and link that line to the Unrestricted Funds class.
- Debit the appropriate Expense account and link that line to the Fundraising class.

When you sell the goods, make the following journal entry:

- Debit the bank account for the amount of the proceeds of the sale. (The bank account is a balance sheet account, so it's not mandatory to assign a class to that transaction line.)
- Credit the amount of the proceeds of the sale to the same expense account you originally used when you received the goods. Link the line to the Administration class (unless the money you raised is earmarked for a specific program/class).

If the proceeds didn't match the original amount, the difference will show up in the income and expense postings. It's important that you use specific income and expense accounts (dedicated to in-kind donations) so your accountant can identify them. The proceeds of a sold donated item are reported separately on Form 990.

If you're using an asset account for in-kind goods that are received for resale, use the following entries.

When you receive the goods, make the following entries:

- Credit the appropriate Income account and link that line to the Unrestricted Funds class (unless the donor has named a specific program for this donation).
- Debit the Assets Held for Sale account.

When you sell the goods, make the following entry:

- Debit the bank account for the proceeds of the sale.
- Credit the Assets Held for Sale account for the original amount.

If the proceeds of the sale and the original amount are not the same, the JE doesn't balance. The instructions that follow represent the common method for balancing the transaction, but you should check with your accountant before creating the JE.

If the proceeds are greater than the original amount posted to the Assets Held for Sale account, post the difference to a regular income account, and link the line to the Administration class unless it was understood that the proceeds were to go to a specific program.

If the proceeds are less than the original amount posted to the Assets Held for Sale account, post the difference to the expense account you use for in-kind contributions. Link the line to the Fundraising class.

Cars, Boats and Planes for Resale

Beginning in 2005, the IRS changed the rules for donors who give you used motor vehicles, boats, or planes that the donors claim have a value greater than $500.

The donor's tax deduction is limited to the gross proceeds from the sale, so you must tell the donor what that amount is when you sell the donated item. Do not simply acknowledge the donation using the market value claimed by the donor.

The accounting transactions you use in QuickBooks when you receive and sell the item are the same as described earlier in this chapter for receiving and selling items using an asset account. You can use the same Assets Held for Resale account.

After the sale, you must send a letter to the donor to report the gross proceeds.

TIP: Most nonprofits find that cars, boats, and planes almost never reap the proceeds expected by the donor. Selling these items can be complicated and time consuming, so you may not always want to leap at the offer.

In-Kind Services

When a professional donates services to your organization, you must enter a transaction to record those services. Donated services to nonprofits are commonly professional services, such as legal, accounting, or consulting services.

The amount of the transaction should be the amount you would have paid if you'd hired someone to perform the services. The transaction should be a journal entry, as follows:

- Credit the income account for in-kind services and assign the Unrestricted Funds class.
- Debit the regular expense account for that service, and assign the Administration class unless the services were performed for a specific program/class.

Not all accountants advise debiting the regular expense account for a donated service (e.g. Legal & Accounting Fees); instead they recommend using an expense account set up for donated services. Check with your accountant to see the way he or she prefers you to record the transaction.

Volunteers

Strictly speaking, volunteers who perform jobs for which the organization would normally have to hire someone should have their time tracked and entered. This is often a gray area, and you should consult your accountant or attorney (or both) about the situations that arise in your organization.

For example, a volunteer who is not a plumber might offer to repair or replace the plumbing in the bathroom. Your accountant or attorney might ask if you'd planned to hire a plumber because the work is necessary, or is the work an enhancement to an otherwise serviceable bathroom? Some accountants and attorneys won't ask, and will just assume that if the work is done it must be tracked in software.

If you determine you should track this service, create a journal entry for the services rendered, as follows:

- Credit the Income account for in-kind services and assign the Unrestricted Funds class.
- Debit the regular Expense account for these services and assign the Administration class unless the service is performed for a specific program/class.

It's important to track the volunteer's time, and you should create a timesheet and have the volunteer sign in and out (and sign the timesheet).

Appendix A

Nonprofit Accounting Issues

Basic nonprofit accounting principles

Rules, regulations, and standards

In many ways, accounting is accounting, whether you're performing accounting tasks for a for-profit business or a nonprofit organization. However, two essential components create differences between the accounting methods used by nonprofits and those used by for-profit businesses:

- All nonprofit organizations are mission-driven, rather than existing to provide financial benefits for owners or shareholders
- Most nonprofits receive at least a portion of their income from contributions.

There are rules for accounting for contributions in nonprofits, and the rules are designed to ensure that donations are used as the donor intended. To meet the need to show that information in reports, there are accounting rules for tracking expenditures in nonprofits. Nonprofits must record disbursements in a way that produces reports showing *where* money was spent, not just *how much* money was spent.

All nonprofit boards should understand the basics of nonprofit accounting rules (ultimately, the board is responsible for the finances and the reports on finances), and make sure that the staff understands the rules and follows them.

Nonprofit Bookkeeping

The challenge for nonprofit bookkeepers is to enter transactions in a way that produces the reports that nonprofits need. To enter transactions properly, the person responsible for using accounting software must be aware of (or, even better, skilled in) nonprofit transaction entry requirements.

I've never seen a successful for-profit business that would let someone who lacked credentials work in the accounting system, but I've seen many small nonprofits that do just that.

This is a false economy, and will often hinder the ability to get grants and contracts because the bookkeeper (using the word loosely) can't have an intelligent conversation about the "whys and hows" of the transactions that went into the reports. Even more disastrous, the bookkeeper can't produce reports with the information required for nonprofits. Considering that nonprofit accounting reports are more complicated (and in some ways, more regulated) than those produced by the for-profit business community, this can be a dangerous cost-saving measure.

To prepare a proposal for a grant or contract, or to prepare a report for a donor agency that provided funds, a nonprofit that can't produce an appropriate report has to spend money on accountants to create that report. In addition, the nonprofit organization's books are not "auditor-friendly" and are sometimes not even "auditor-ready", so these organizations frequently have excessively large accounting and auditing expenses.

Nonprofit Transaction Entry

Entering transactions in accounting software starts the same way for the bookkeeper working in a for-profit business or a bookkeeper working in a nonprofit organization. Basically, the transaction is a receipt of income, a disbursement of funds, or a journal entry that moves funds from one component to another.

> **NOTE**: In these discussions, I'll use QuickBooks as the reference (because this book is about using QuickBooks in nonprofits), but the transaction-entry procedures are the same for all accounting applications.

The difference between for-profit and nonprofit transaction entry is the level of detail required for nonprofit transactions. In order to produce the reports that nonprofits are required to create, the transaction entries must include the data that is included in those reports.

Income Transactions

For contributed income, nonprofits must record contributions in one of the following categories: unrestricted, temporarily restricted, or permanently restricted.

In QuickBooks, this is accomplished by the use of classes. You must have a class for each of the three income categories, and every income transaction must be linked to one of those classes.

Unrestricted Funds

Unrestricted funds are donations that are given for general use. The donor has made a contribution without attaching a specific purpose or time period for the use of the funds.

Temporarily Restricted Funds

Temporarily restricted funds are donated for a specified purpose (usually a program), or are specified for use during a specific time period. Many grants specify both use and time period restrictions.

As you use the temporarily restricted funds for the specified purposes, or when the time restrictions expire, these funds can be released from restriction and become unrestricted funds (and can therefore be spent). Nonprofits are required to track the balances of temporarily restricted funds separately from unrestricted funds.

Permanently Restricted Funds

Permanently restricted contributions are almost always endowments. Nonprofits are required to track the balances of permanently restricted funds separately from unrestricted funds. Unlike temporarily restricted funds (which become unrestricted when the restrictions are met), permanently restricted funds are restricted forever.

Usually this means that organizations can invest the funds to generate income, but they are not allowed to spend the original contributions (the capital). The income generated by investing permanently restricted funds may be unrestricted or temporarily restricted, depending on the donor's instructions.

For example, the income generated by a scholarship endowment may be restricted to providing financial aid for books for student recipients. The income generated by an endowment made as an "in memoriam" gift may be restricted to capital repairs and additions. If no such restrictions exist, the nonprofit organization can transfer the generated income to unrestricted funds, and spend the funds for general use.

Disbursement Transactions

Disbursements are generated by bills from vendors, or by direct disbursements (writing a check without the need to receive a bill, such as rent payments or employer taxes). Most disbursements are expenses.

Nonprofits track expenses by expense type (using the expense accounts in the chart of accounts) just as for-profit businesses do. However, nonprofits also track expenses by functional categories (such as programs, administration, and fundraising).

Without tracking functional categories, you cannot report your expenses on a program-by-program basis. This means you can't produce reports needed by grantors, government agencies, or potential donors.

In QuickBooks, functional categories are tracked by classes. You must create a class for every program (or for every program type, and then use subclasses for the programs themselves). In addition to program classes, you must have a class for fundraising costs and for administrative costs (because these totals must be separated out in reports). Every disbursement for an expense must be linked to a class.

In addition to tracking functional categories, you must track the specific grant or contract in every expense transaction, or you won't be able to produce a report for the donor about that grant.

In QuickBooks, you track grants by entering the grant in the Customer:Job column of the transaction window. All donors are customers, and all grants and contracts are jobs attached to the appropriate customer.

Journal Transactions

Accountants and bookkeepers often use a journal entry (JE) to move funds from one category to another in the general ledger. This differs from transaction entries because a transaction entry always has a name attached (a donor or a vendor). Journal entries are commonly used in nonprofits for the following tasks:

- To move funds from temporarily restricted funds to unrestricted funds.
- To allocate administrative expenses to programs.
- To allocate expenses to specific grants.

The allocations you create in a JE are displayed in reports, letting you meet the requirements of nonprofit reporting.

For example, a staff member may perform services for multiple programs. Executive directors often spend time on both management matters (administration) and fundraising.

You must allocate the staff's time to reflect the amount of time they spent on each category (program, administration, and fundraising). This is impossible to do without timesheets, and all nonprofits should have timesheets for every employee.

NOTE: *Timesheets are usually part of report requests that auditors ask for.*

JE Source and Target: Solving the Mystery

One common JE is to allocate an administrative expense across programs, or across specific grants.

To allocate expenses, you debit the same expense account multiple times in order to select a class or grant for each applicable portion of the expense, and credit the original expense total.

After performing this task, however, it's a common complaint that the reports don't show the expenses that were allocated in the journal entry. In fact, for journal entries that move expenses from one donor or grant to another, often the wrong donor or grant receives the cost posting.

The problem is that all transactions in QuickBooks have a source and a target, and if you don't get them right, you end up with unexpected results.

The source is the account where the transaction originates, and the target is the account where it is completed. When you write a check to a vendor, the bank account is the source (it's where the money starts) and the expense account is the target (it's where the money ends up).

If you attach additional information to the check, it travels with its source or target counterpart. For example, assigning a grant to the line that contains an expense account (for job costing) links the grant information and the amount to the target (because the line in which it exists in the transaction window is the target).

For JEs that perform allocations there are two important facts to remember:

- QuickBooks assigns job costing or class assignments when they are part of the target, and ignores the data when it is part of the source.
- The first line of a JE is the source and all other lines are targets.

This means that if you're moving job costing information from one grant to another, you will almost certainly end up with one or more incorrect postings.

Creating JEs With No Source Accounts

I've learned that to play it safe, the best way to create a JE is to make every line in the transaction part of the target. Because the first line is the source, don't use the first line for anything "real".

In the first line of a JE, enter only a memo. Starting with the second line, enter real information. Because everything is a target, everything posts appropriately. After I learned to do this, I never had a problem with job costing reports.

If you've already encountered the problem, you don't have to void and re-enter all the journal entries that had a source/target mix up. Just edit the journal entry to change the source line, as follows:

1. Open the JE transaction and click anywhere in the first line to select that line.
2. Press Ctrl+ Ins (or Insert, depending on the label your keyboard uses) to insert a blank line above the current first line.
3. Enter text in the Memo field to create a source line.
4. Close the Make General Journal Entries transaction window.
5. QuickBooks displays a message that you've changed the transaction and asks if you want to save it.
6. Click Yes.

Everything posts correctly.

Financial Indicators in Reports

It's probably unfair to use financial reports as the way to judge whether a nonprofit organization is meeting its mission, but unfortunately, that's what happens. As a result, you must make sure your transactions and reports have the data necessary to produce a "high score" for your organization's mission.

Because there's no way to document an organization's effectiveness or success in simple formulas, donors, funders, government agencies, and charity watchdog organizations rely on financial indicators. Most of the financial indicators are based on examining expenses by functional classification (program, administration, and fundraising).

In addition, two commonly applied financial indicators that are of particular interest when judging a nonprofit's effectiveness are the following:

- Program-spending ratio, which is calculated by dividing total program expenses by total expenses. The more efficient you are at assigning program expenses to transactions, the better your ratio.
- Fundraising-efficiency ratio, which is calculated by dividing fundraising costs by total contributions.

Rules, Regulations, and Standards

Nonprofit organizations have a plethora of standards to meet in their accounting systems. The public and the agencies of government look carefully and critically at the financial reports of even the smallest nonprofit organizations, expecting standards of behavior that exceed their expectations for the for-profit world.

Recent corporate accounting scandals have turned the general public, and public agencies, into skeptics (if not cynics) about the way accounting standards can be used and abused to benefit individuals and to rip off investors. Effectively, a nonprofit has two sets of investors; its donors, and the community it serves.

The rules and regulations for nonprofit bookkeeping standards are set by a variety of organizations. You may find that your accountant, lawyer, and auditor (if you're audited) throw alphabet-soup jargon at you, and I think you should know what some of the important standard-setting groups are, and how they explicitly determine standards for nonprofits.

Financial Accounting Standards Board (FASB)

FASB is the regulator for proper accounting rules in the U.S., and describes its mission as establishing and improving standards of financial accounting and reporting for the guidance and education of the public.

FASB issues its rules in the form of documents called Statements of Financial Accounting Standard (SFAS), and the statements are numbered. Several FASB Statements apply specifically to nonprofits, and the most oft-quoted statement is SFAS 117, which sets the standards of reporting for health and welfare nonprofit organizations.

FASB and QuickBooks Data Entry

One of the most important clauses in SFAS 117 is the need for the Statement of Functional Expenses. This means that many nonprofits are required to track and report disbursements in a very specific manner.

The statement of functional expenses reports expenses by category (such as salaries, rent, postage, supplies, etc.) broken down by the purpose for which the expenses were incurred. The two primary functional classifications are:

- Program services, which means each expense category must be subtotaled on a program-by-program basis.
- Supporting services, which include administration and fundraising. Expense categories must be subtotaled for each supporting service.

The QuickBooks feature that lets you perform your bookkeeping tasks in concert with SFAS 117 is the Class List. Nonprofits using QuickBooks must create classes, and every transaction in QuickBooks must be linked to a class.

If your nonprofit isn't entering transactions with linked classes, your accounting costs (and audit costs) are almost certainly larger than they should be. Meeting the SFAS 117 rule is common for reports to grantors, the board of directors, and government agencies. To accomplish that in the absence of good transaction entry practices, accountants have to perform after-the-fact chores to create a report of functional expenses.

The money you'd save in after-the-fact accounting fees and audit fees would probably pay for the engagement of a competent nonprofit bookkeeper, or a training class for a bookkeeper who isn't tracking classes during data entry.

SFAS 117 and Religious Nonprofits

Within the accounting community (including accountants who provide audit services for nonprofits) quite a bit of debate takes place over the breadth of SFAS 117.

SFAS 117 specifically refers to "voluntary health and welfare organizations", and the debate centers on whether churches, synagogues, mosques, and other nonprofits established for a religious organization are included.

Some accountants and auditors don't look for or prepare a Statement of Functional Expenses for religious nonprofits, but among that group you'll find many professionals who think that it's appropriate to help religious nonprofits prepare for the day when this report is required.

Generally, in the presence of a debate, organizations such as FASB have to clear the fog by producing specific recommendations or rules. I've met very few accountants who believe that a future ruling will exclude religious nonprofits. In these days of regulations imposed as a result of accounting scandals, it's highly probable all nonprofits will be required to produce reports with more details than currently regulated. It's a matter of public trust as much as a matter of rigid accounting rules.

Religious nonprofits that use QuickBooks should begin customizing their company files for classes and link transactions to those classes. In that way, they'll be prepared for any change of rules; and, more important, the reports they provide their boards, members, and donors will inspire confidence.

Generally Accepted Accounting Principles (GAAP)

GAAP is an acronym frequently used by accountants and bookkeepers. It specifically refers to accounting standards set by the FASB for financial accounting in public companies.

However, in practice, it's applied much more generically than its original definition. When bookkeepers and accountants refer to GAAP, they mean a set of rules for entering financial transactions that meets both professional and ethical standards.

GAAP actually combines two sets of standards: Authoritative standards (set by policy boards such as FASB, SEC, etc.), and the generally accepted methods used for performing accounting tasks.

GAAP is international in scope, but in the United States, GAAP standards are extremely detailed, and they keep growing. This is largely a reflection of the litigious environment in the United States, which results in more and more detailed regulation.

Nonprofits that are not currently required to undergo audits, or file a Form 990, would be wise to pay attention to this "regulate everything" atmosphere and prepare for more regulation in the future.

It's not unheard of for businesses and nonprofits to use transaction entries that aren't GAAP-approved, or that aren't covered by GAAP. It's important, however, to perform such transaction entries in a way that identifies them as non-GAAP.

For example, the UCOA has accounts in the chart of accounts that are specifically marked non-GAAP (e.g. an income account named Donated Other Services-Non-GAAP).

Sarbanes-Oxley

The Sarbanes-Oxley Act of 2002 was passed in response to corporate scandals, and is almost entirely applied to for-profit corporations that are publicly traded, and registered with the Securities and Exchange Commission.

However, two Sarbanes-Oxley provisions apply to nonprofits: the whistle blower protection provision, and the retainage of documents and records provision.

Whistle Blower Protection

The whistle blower provision requires that nonprofits, just like for-profits, must avoid retaliation against anyone who brings ethical or legal issues into the open.

Nonprofit boards should create a clearly articulated process through which any employee, volunteer, or other person with knowledge of improper actions in the nonprofit may bring those concerns to the attention of the board outside the normal chain of command. The National Council of Nonprofit Associations has sample policies on the whistle blower issue on its web site (www.ncna.org).

Retainage of Documents and Records

Nonprofits as well as for-profits are forbidden from destroying records which could be of use in any investigation once the nonprofit becomes aware that an investigation is underway, contemplated, or likely to occur.

Records that are documents stored on computers should be periodically archived (use a CD) when you clean up your disks. Also, courts cases have held that records include e-mail, so you should have a system for archiving old e-mail messages instead of deleting them.

Board Responsibilities

The board has the primary fiduciary responsibility for a nonprofit organization, and the interpretation of fiduciary responsibility is becoming broader. The impact of the Sarbanes-Oxley Act is almost certain to hit nonprofits. Some states are already beginning to move for legislation that would apply provisions of Sarbanes-Oxley to nonprofits.

It's impossible to set out a list of absolute rules for board membership and board actions, because each state has (or will soon have) its own rules, and those rules often differ depending on the mission and scope of a nonprofit organization. However, there are some caveats that clearly apply to board members and board duties.

Duties and Constituencies

The members of the board of directors of nonprofit corporations, just like directors of for-profit corporations, owe specific duties to the organizations they serve. These duties are usually described as "duty of loyalty" and "duty of care."

The duty of loyalty means that directors must place the interests of the organization above their own; acting in what they reasonably believe is the best interest of the organization.

The duty of care means that directors take adequate steps to inform themselves before making decisions. The definition also includes the expectation that every board member acts as any prudent person would act in similar circumstances.

For example, the movement by many states to insist on an audit committee in nonprofit boards speaks directly to the duty of care. This is also an issue addressed by Sarbanes-Oxley that many states are beginning to apply to nonprofits. Sarbanes-Oxley requires not only an audit committee; the law also says that the audit committee should have at least one person who is familiar with GAAP and other accounting procedures.

A nonprofit organization with a Sarbanes-Oxley-compliant audit committee would be able to defend itself in the event of an accusation of financial mismanagement or fraud. The existence of the committee and a member who understands financial documents should satisfy the defense claim that the board exercised reasonable care in protecting the organization from harm.

The constituencies to whom directors are accountable are not at all similar when you compare directors of for-profit entities with directors of nonprofit organizations.

The board of a for-profit business owes its fiduciary duties and loyalties to corporate shareholders, and is accountable to the shareholders. Directors of nonprofits are frequently held accountable by multiple groups; the community served by the organization's mission, the donors, and in some ways, the community at large.

Unfortunately, the appearance of a conflict of interest in the membership of a nonprofit board incites more community outrage than the same complaint engenders when applied to a director of a for-profit entity. Most state agencies are either run by, or appointed by, politicians, who are quick to react (but necessarily fair) when a community is upset.

No member of a nonprofit organization's board of directors should reap any direct or indirect financial benefit from that membership. Some nonprofit boards unwittingly break this rule by including members that are obviously sympathetic to, and loyal to, the board's mission, even though they indirectly gain financial benefit. The most common scenario is a board member who has a vested interest (usually a staff position) in another nonprofit organization that receives funds from your nonprofit. For example, a community nonprofit that offers day care, or sports programs, and subcontracts the program to another nonprofit (by leasing facilities or staff) should not have a board member who is employed by the subcontractor.

Accounting Controls and Procedures

Sarbanes-Oxley requires that companies establish systems of controls and procedures to ensure that the company meets its financial reporting obligations. This is yet another Sarbanes-Oxley provision that is attracting the attention of state attorney generals and state legislatures.

Nonprofit boards are responsible for oversight for these issues, and in the face of possible strict legal controls, board members must begin to gather information about, and study, the way financial systems and controls are working.

It is imperative that accounting procedures adequately capture all relevant information, and enable that information to be recorded, processed, and reported.

In addition, for nonprofits that file Form 990, the board is ultimately responsible for the accuracy of the information on that form.

Index

year-end activities, 335–336, 340–342
rounding prices, 128

S
sales forms and price levels, 130–131
sales of in-kind donations, 456, 460–462
sales receipts
bounced checks, 250–252
for donations, 195, 205–206, 436–437
and income tracking, 193–195
for membership dues, 432–433
sales reps (contacts for donors), 111, 132–134
sales tax settings, 81–90, 112, 448
Sarbanes-Oakley Act (2002), 476–477, 478, 479
security issues. *See also* passwords
and Audit Trail option, 61
and Missing Check report, 330
and QuickBooks quirks, 257
user permissions, 409–410
service charges, 253, 255–256, 261
services and goods, donations of, 454–463
services provided. *See* items
SFAS (Statement of Financial Accounting Standards), 8, 37, 160
shared downloads and QuickBooks updating, 399
shipping, 106, 143
Show Lowest Subaccount Only option, 27, 28, 35, 60
sorting of accounts, 30–31

source/target mystery in QuickBooks journal entries, 470–472
spend-down format in budgets, 292
splitting classes, 101–103
spreadsheet program. *See* Excel, Microsoft
standard payment terms, 140–141
start date, setting up, 12–15
Statement of Activities, year-end, 343
Statement of Cash Flows, year-end, 343–344
Statement of Financial Accounting Standards (SFAS), 8, 37, 160
Statement of Financial Income and Expense, 316
Statement of Financial Position, 316–317, 342–343
Statement of Functional Expenses (990)
creating report, 317–318
and nonprofit accounting standards, 44, 473–474, 479
and year-end activities, 344–346
subaccounts
bill adjustments, 226
bounced check adjustments, 254–255
changing types of accounts, 40
creating, 34–37
and customizing UCOA, 53
deleting accounts, 40
depreciation uses, 339–340
and fund accounting workaround, 38–39
hiding accounts, 41, 48